Contemporary Latin American Revolutions

Contemporary Latin American Revolutions

Second Edition

Marc Becker

ROWMAN & LITTLEFIELD
Lanham • Boulder • New York • London

Published by Rowman & Littlefield
An imprint of The Rowman & Littlefield Publishing Group, Inc.
4501 Forbes Boulevard, Suite 200, Lanham, Maryland 20706
www.rowman.com

86-90 Paul Street, London EC2A 4NE

British Library Cataloguing in Publication Information Available

Library of Congress Cataloging-in-Publication Data

Names: Becker, Marc (Professor of history), author.
Title: Contemporary Latin American revolutions / Marc Becker.
Other titles: Twentieth-century Latin American revolutions
Description: Second edition. | Lanham : Rowman & Littlefield, [2021] | Series: Latin
    American perspectives in the classroom | Includes bibliographical references and index.
Identifiers: LCCN 2021045549 (print) | LCCN 2021045550 (ebook) | ISBN
    9781538163726 (cloth) | ISBN 9781538163733 (paperback) | ISBN 9781538163740
    (epub)
Subjects: LCSH: Revolutions—Latin America—History—20th century. | Revolutions—
    Latin America—Case studies. | Revolutionaries—Latin America—Biography. | Latin
    America—Politics and government—20th century.
Classification: LCC F1414 .B43 2022 (print) | LCC F1414 (ebook) | DDC 980.04—dc23
LC record available at https://lccn.loc.gov/2021045549
LC ebook record available at https://lccn.loc.gov/2021045550

Contents

Preface

This book presents a synthetic overview of revolutionary movements in Latin America during the twentieth and twenty-first centuries at a level appropriate for an undergraduate classroom or a general audience. Scholars will quibble over the selection of case studies, claiming that some were not sufficiently violent, transformative, or permanent to warrant that moniker. Events that appeared revolutionary at the time may not appear so in retrospect, and sometimes, looking back, it may surprise us how forward-looking our predecessors were. In short, no canon of Latin American revolutions exists, and the selections in this book are based on my years of study and analysis of transformative movements.

The book begins with a theoretical introduction that explores theories and assumptions that inform the concept of "revolution." This chapter provides a brief overview of the global **left** (bolded terms are defined in the glossary at the end of the book) in order to situate events in Latin America. It analyzes persistent and ongoing issues facing the Latin American left and examines factors necessary for a revolution. Each subsequent chapter presents an interpretive narrative of a single case study in chronological order, except for chapter 8, which explores the most significant **guerrilla** movements that failed to capture state power. The final chapter scrutinizes contemporary leftist governments in Latin America with an eye toward what they can teach us about past revolutionary movements.

Each chapter begins with a list of key dates that is designed to contextualize the discussion that follows. Interpretive explanations of each case study create a historical context for the appearance of each revolutionary movement and offer an understanding of its main goals and achievements, its shortcomings, and its legacies. Biographies of principal leaders provide an opportunity to explore the importance of charismatic and vanguard leadership. Given the gendered nature of revolutionary movements, these inevitably center on men, and often those from privileged backgrounds. The intent is not to reinforce a traditional historiographical approach but rather to critique the theme of vanguard leadership that runs throughout the book. Primary source documents illustrate the goals and tenets of each movement and connect to a broader theme of the importance of ideology in mobilizing support for a mass uprising.

In this second edition, these leadership narratives are supplemented with biographies and documents that introduce alternative and often marginalized voices of women, people of African descent, and **Indigenous** peoples who participated on a grassroots level in the movements. Also included are U.S. government documents. The purpose of these is not to critique U.S. policies—the heavy imperial hand of the U.S. government that undermines local democratic movements to the benefit of external economic interests should be immediately obvious to even the most casual observer of Latin America. Rather, a goal of all of these documents is to shed light on broader dynamics in these movements. Each chapter concludes with discussion questions to encourage deeper exploration of the key issues that each revolution raises. A short list of English-language books offers an entry point for further study, and a list of films summarizes visual representations of each revolution.

A brief note on capitalization: the *Chicago Manual of Style*, 17th edition (section 8.38), indicates that names of ethnic and national groups are to be capitalized, including adjectives associated with these names. Because "Indigenous" and "Black" refer to such groups of people, these terms are capitalized in this book. That convention is based on, and followed in respect for, the preference that the board of directors of the South and Meso American Indian Rights Center (SAIIC) specified as an affirmation of their ethnic identities.

This book was initially drafted while teaching the course Latin American Revolutions at Truman State University. I thank my students in that class for their suggestions and insights into conceptualizing this project and writing the text. Kevin Young, Patti Harms (particularly for suggestions on Ester de Urrutia and the AFG), Dan Saxon, Michelle Chase, Alan Knight, Linda Etchart, Steve Hirsch, Robert Austin Henry, Tanya Harmer, Matt Rothwell, Cheryl Musch, and others read the manuscript and/or provided suggestions for improvement. Once again, it has been a pleasure to work with Susan McEachern, Katelyn Turner, and their staff at Rowman & Littlefield.

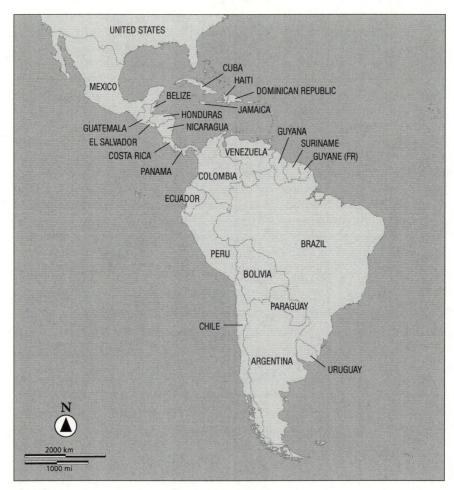

The Americas

1

Theories of Revolution

KEY DATES

1640   English Revolution
1789   French Revolution
1791   Haitian Revolution
1848   Karl Marx and Friedrich Engels publish *The Communist Manifesto*
1871   Paris Commune
1910   Mexican Revolution
1917   Bolshevik Revolution
1944   Guatemalan Spring
1949   Chinese Revolution
1952   Bolivian Nationalist Revolution
1959   Cuban Revolution
1970   Chilean Road to Socialism
1979   Nicaragua's Sandinista Revolution
1999   Venezuela's Bolivarian Revolution

LATIN AMERICA IN THE EYE OF THE HURRICANE

Historian E. Bradford Burns once aptly described Latin America as a place where "poor people inhabit rich lands." A common assumption is that Latin America is poor because of overpopulation or a lack of natural resources, but that is not the case. Today Bolivia is the least densely populated and poorest country in South America, but five hundred years ago, its Potosí silver mine made it the most valuable colony in the world. Sugar production on the Caribbean island of Hispaniola in the late

1

eighteenth century similarly made it the richest colony in the world, but today Haiti is the poorest country in the Americas. In comparison to the incredible wealth of Potosí and Hispaniola, North America had relatively few resources, but today the United States is the wealthiest country in the world.

Scholars refer to a "resource curse" that has impoverished Latin America to explain this dramatic change in economic standing, but such blanket statements gloss over intentional political and economic decisions that have underdeveloped the region. The Uruguayan journalist Eduardo Galeano condemned the imperialist powers that pillaged the continent in his book *Open Veins of Latin America*. Galeano observed that some areas of the world win and others lose, and that Latin America specialized in losing. "Our defeat was always implicit in the victory of others," he wrote. "Our wealth has always generated our poverty by nourishing the prosperity of others." Advanced industrialized countries in Europe and North America extracted wealth from Latin America in the form of labor and natural resources. Even more damaging to the region, those industrialized countries turned cheap, raw resources into expensive finished products that they imported back to Latin America, with most of the value of that production remaining in the industrialized countries. It was in their economic interest to maintain Latin America in a politically subservient status. As Burns, Galeano, and others came to realize, Latin America was not poor through any fault of its own but because of its location in a global **capitalist** system.

Poverty was not the only problem that Latin America faced. Extreme economic inequality further underdeveloped the region. In 1912, the Italian statistician Corrado Gini developed what has come to be known as the Gini coefficient as a measure of the distribution of wealth and resources. A Gini coefficient of zero represents perfect equality in which everyone shares equal access to the same quantity of assets, whereas a Gini coefficient of one represents maximum inequality where one person owns everything and leaves everyone else with nothing (see figure 1.1). A Lorenz curve (named after the economist Max O. Lorenz) graphically represents the unequal distribution of income or wealth in a society. By this measure, Latin America is the most unequal part of the world. While many people in Latin America suffer from deep poverty, the region is also home to immense wealth. The Mexican business tycoon Carlos Slim, for example, is one of the richest people in the world, even as almost half of the country's population lives in poverty.

The twin problems of poverty and inequality create a wide range of difficulties, including high crime rates, political instability, short life expectancies because of a lack of access to healthcare, and low productivity because of a lack of education. In this situation, the promises of a **socialist** revolution that would end poverty, eliminate inequality, and solve many of Latin America's economic, social, and political problems were very appealing. Revolutionaries identified their twin opponents as the U.S. imperialists who extracted their resources and the local capitalists who benefited from this extractive system to the detriment of the rest of society. Their goal was to free themselves from the control of the United States and to remove the wealthy ruling class from power, by any means necessary.

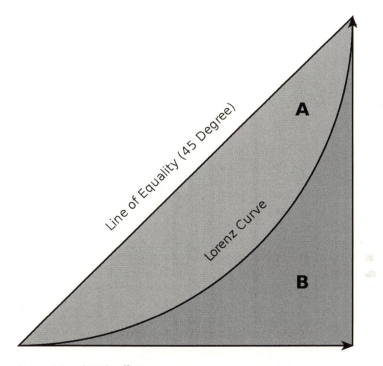

Figure 1.1. Gini Coefficient

Writing in a nineteenth-century European context, Karl Marx (1818–1883) contended that an urban **proletariat** with a developed awareness of its role in society would lead revolutionary changes. He considered Latin America, with its lack of an advanced industrial economy, not yet ready for a revolution. In the twentieth century, however, Latin America experienced more revolutions than did any other part of the world. Furthermore, rural **peasants** rather than industrial workers led many of them. Revolutionaries debated how quickly profound political and economic changes could be implemented and whether violence was necessary to achieve these changes. Did their movements need charismatic leaders to inspire people to action, or could everyone collaborate equally in the construction of a new society? Militant activists debated these and other compelling issues and, in the process, created a dynamic environment in which to study struggles for a more just and equal society.

* * *

This book includes seven case studies of revolutionary movements in Latin America during the twentieth century, one chapter on guerrilla movements that failed to take state power, and a concluding chapter on contemporary leftist governments at the dawn of the twenty-first century. The case studies begin with the 1910 Mexican

Revolution, which introduced a century of revolutionary activism and laid the groundwork for other revolutions that followed. In a sense, the Mexican Revolution can be understood as a standard-bearer through which subsequent revolutionary movements in Latin America can be interpreted—either as being inspired by the example it set or as attempts to achieve its unrealized promises. A series of leftist movements followed with varying degrees of success. The Guatemalan Spring (1944–1954) appeared to create an opening for a deep transformation of society, but both internal and external opposition collapsed the experiment. A short insurrection on April 9–11, 1952, brought the Revolutionary Nationalist Movement (MNR) to power in Bolivia and led to some of the most militant labor and peasant unions in Latin America before reversing course and collapsing in a military **coup**, or a direct attack on the existing government. The 1959 Cuban Revolution was the longest lasting, furthest reaching, and most successful of the twentieth-century revolutions. It fundamentally influenced subsequent leftist paths to power. The Cuban Revolution inspired a decade of guerrilla uprisings across Latin America, but the defeat of Ernesto Che Guevara in Bolivia in 1967 and the 1970 election of the Marxist Salvador Allende to the presidency in Chile swayed leftist sentiments toward searching for constitutional and institutional means to fundamental revolutionary changes in society. **Nationalization** of U.S.-owned copper mines contributed to U.S. support for Augusto Pinochet's brutal September 11, 1973, military coup that ended that experiment. The 1979 triumph of the Nicaraguan **Sandinistas** provides a second example of a successful armed struggle in Latin America. Unlike Cuba, however, their willingness to implement **neoliberal** reforms along with attacks by a U.S.-backed and funded counterrevolution (the "contras") eroded their domestic support and led to their electoral defeat in 1990. Similar attempts in Colombia, El Salvador, and Peru failed to take power through armed means, although their struggles led to highly politically aware societies. The election of Hugo Chávez in 1998 brought his uniquely styled Bolivarian Revolution (named after independence leader Simón Bolívar) to Venezuela and introduced a new wave of revolutionary movements in the twenty-first century. Chávez embodied many of the debates that swirled around revolutionary movements throughout the twentieth century. An examination of his administration and those of others that followed closes this book and provides an opportunity to reflect on lessons learned from twentieth-century revolutions.

Global events influenced political and ideological changes in Latin America, and these were reflected in shifts with alternations between a preference for armed struggle or institutional paths toward capturing power (see figure 1.2). The 1917 Bolshevik Revolution in Russia introduced a Marxist ideology of class struggle and a historical materialist interpretation of Latin American realities that had a notable influence on leftist insurgencies after the 1910 Mexican Revolution. Although the left came to power in both Guatemala and Bolivia through breaks in the established order, revolutionaries in both countries quickly established electoral systems that provided a mechanism to consolidate their reformist policies. In contrast, guerrilla

Figure 1.2. Timeline: Armed Struggle and Electoral Paths to Power

leaders in Cuba rejected electoral paths in favor of armed struggle to transform their country's political and economic structures. After a string of guerrilla defeats in the 1960s, the electoral victory of Allende in 1970 briefly shifted popular sentiments back toward an emphasis on electoral paths to power. A brutal military coup that deposed Allende only three years later strengthened the hand of those who argued that the Latin American left could only take and hold power through armed struggle that physically eliminated a right-wing opposition. The 1979 Sandinista victory in Nicaragua bolstered that position. The Sandinista electoral defeat in 1990, as well as the fall of the Berlin Wall and the collapse of the Soviet Union, reinforced **capitalism**'s hold over the entire world. The possibilities of the left gaining victory, whether in Latin America or elsewhere, through whatever means, appeared remote. Chávez's presidential win in Venezuela less than a decade later, however, firmly placed the left back on Latin America's political landscape and established the region in the vanguard of progressive changes around the globe. Chávez's victory also boosted the idea that elections were the preferred—if not the only—means for a socialist transformation of society.

Scholars debate which events can properly be characterized as revolutionary. Developments that at the time seemed to be truly transformative can in retrospect appear quite moderate or reformist. In contrast, previous policy proposals may now strike analysts as surprisingly progressive when compared to contemporary administrations. This is part of the terrain that this book enters. What was the intent of each movement? Did it seek to transform society in favor of previously dispossessed members or simply to reform or modernize society for the benefit of those who already held power? What do the movements look like from the perspective of those who had most to gain from their lofty promises? It is important to keep in mind that the goals, strategies, and ideologies of people and movements can and will change over time—particularly as the specifics of a situation change and evolve—and where a society or a movement starts out is not necessarily a predictor of where it may end up.

To be truly revolutionary, a movement needs to come from the bottom and the left to advance the interests of those whom the previous regime marginalized and excluded. In what is known as a "revolution within a revolution," this means favoring the concerns of women, people of African descent, and Indigenous peoples, both during and after a successful uprising. From that standard, all of these movements fell well short of the elusive goal of a fundamental transformation of society. Leaders were often men from privileged, European-descent backgrounds, and inevitably their perspectives and concerns dominated even as they were committed to imagining a new and better society. Even so, mass mobilizations reflected aspirations for a more equal and just world.

WHAT DOES "REVOLUTION" MEAN?

Although often studied, revolution is a relatively rare and only vaguely understood historical phenomenon. Contributing to this problem is the fact that sometimes language is a semantic minefield that can hide and distract more than it reveals or that can, alternatively, reflect underlying but unstated landscapes and political divisions. Proponents and opponents, for example, will respectively use the terms "protest" or "riot" to describe the same Black Lives Matter (BLM) actions, depending on whether they favor or oppose its objectives. As observers have long noted, one person's terrorist is another person's freedom fighter.

The word "revolution" comes from the physical world and refers to the rotation of an object. For example, the speed of a car's engine is measured in revolutions per minute, or rpm. In the political realm, a revolution happens when those in power are replaced with a previously dispossessed class of people. In this case, society has rotated, much like a crankshaft in a car's engine, so that those who were previously on the top are pushed to the bottom or out of power, and those on the bottom now have moved to the top and gained control over decision-making processes.

The term "revolution" is sometimes used so loosely to refer to any palace coup or change of government that it loses all meaning. Alternatively, some historians will restrict usage to highly exceptional events such as the 1640 English Revolution, the 1789 French Revolution, and the 1917 Bolshevik Revolution. Some scholars contend that even the structural changes accompanying these events were not profound or permanent enough to warrant use of the term. Others argue that the social changes that accompanied the Industrial Revolution were more significant than those in the political realm where the term is commonly applied. A true revolution in which society is completely flipped upside down is an exceedingly rare occurrence. Perhaps it has never happened, and if it were to happen, it would be so disruptive that it might be an undesirable development with unintended consequences.

A previous generation of scholars commonly applied the term "revolution" to late-eighteenth-century and early-nineteenth-century anticolonial revolts against European powers that resulted in independence for the Americas. Many scholars now view those as merely shifting control from one sector of the ruling class to another. While they led to political separation from Europe, they also entrenched preexisting and very unequal social, political, and economic structures. In Latin America, much as in the United States, a powerful land- and slaveholding class of men replaced the previous European overlords. Independence did not result in enslaved Africans gaining their freedom or advances in rights for women. Under the newly independent governments and without the paternalistic protection of distant European monarchs, many Indigenous communities lost access to their lands and were reduced to the status of serfs condemned to working on the estates of wealthy landowners. Those "revolutions" were not necessarily beneficial for the most dispossessed members of society.

A revolution, furthermore, is fundamentally different from a military coup, a civil war, or an armed revolt, even though participants will sometimes use those terms to describe their actions. At a most basic level, coups generally transfer power from one group to another within the same socioeconomic class. These competing groups seek to gain control over the reins of power to advance their own particular economic and political interests. Coups are rapid and typically involve a small number of people, often no more than a couple hundred, and leave the basic contours and structures of society essentially unaltered. In contrast, a true revolution mobilizes the masses for a fundamental transformation of society through a reversal of class relations as reflected in whose political and economic interests its structures serve. These changes require more time and effort than simply changing the faces of those in power, as is often the case with a coup.

In terms of competing interests, revolutions can assume the features of a civil war as they reflect a competition between two distinct classes or sometimes between different alliances, regions, or communities within a country. Revolutions require an ideology that imagines a different and better way of configuring society, and as such, not all civil wars rise to the level of embodying revolutionary aspirations. In fact, civil wars (and military coups) often reflect a desperate attempt to hold on to an unjust and oppressive system in the face of pressure for change. Furthermore, a socialist revolution challenges the logic of global capitalism and hence, as seen in the case studies in this book, typically draws in international actors. Although rooted in local realities and often exploiting nationalist rhetoric and sentiments, revolutions can quickly acquire transnational features and ramifications.

Because of these competing interests and the reality that those in control will never yield power peacefully, an assumption is that revolutions inevitably will be violent affairs. In this manner, revolutions can be similar to civil wars. But it is a mistake to equate conflict with revolution, even though some leaders will cling to the notion of the transformative power of the shedding of blood. Others, such as Allende in Chile, insisted that needed revolutionary changes could be made peacefully within the confines of existing institutional structures. Nevertheless, resistance to change provides a strong indicator that the proposed alterations to class relations are truly revolutionary.

Beyond understanding violence as a means rather than an end in itself, it can be a mistake to accept violence as an inevitable side effect of revolution. As with military coups, armed revolts are tempting because they provide a convenient shortcut to power rather than engaging in much longer and more complicated processes of political education and mobilization of the masses. A successful revolution requires organization of those whom the present system excludes, and this does not happen automatically. Armed struggle alone will not achieve that objective, and too often the violence hurts rather than helps those whose interests a revolution seeks to advance.

Some argue that revolutions follow a natural cycle, with a complete rotation from the collapse of an old regime to the radicalization of popular aspirations for a new society and finally to a **conservative** reaction against the excesses of the revolutionaries, which leads back to where everything started—a complete 360-degree turn. It is not uncommon to use this model to read the unfolding of the French Revolution onto other events. In France, workers stormed the Bastille fortress on July 14, 1789, which led to the collapse of the monarchy and the execution of Louis XVI. The Jacobins (so named because of the Dominican convent where they met) rose to power in that political vacuum as the most radical wing of the revolution, and their ruthlessness led to a 1793–1794 Reign of Terror. A conservative coup d'état in the month of Thermidor led to a restoration of the old order. Some scholars build a career out of looking for the inevitable moment of a conservative "Thermidor" reaction against radical revolutions. Such mechanical models, however, ignore the unpredictability of revolutionary developments and how they emerge at their own pace and with their own rhythms.

Revolutions are complicated and messy, and scholars have not reached consensus on which events to characterize as such. For some, a revolution is an inherently violent event that removes a previous government from power through force. Typically, the change must be rapid and profound. Participants in a revolution sometimes unify around a limited goal of overthrowing an entrenched and repressive **dictatorship** and, once that goal is achieved, will not necessarily support a more thorough transformation of society. Movements often draw on nationalist and anti-imperialist sentiments of resentment toward external powers (often the United States) that extract wealth from a country to the detriment of local economies and political control. For others, a political project needs to embrace an explicitly socialist ideology that challenges preexisting class relations to be categorized as a revolution. The case studies in this book vary significantly in terms of the strategies and ideologies that advocates employed to come to power. None of them began as an overtly socialist project, and often they did not entail significant violence. All of them, however, sought a rapid shift in wealth and power from the ruling class to an impoverished and dispossessed working class. From this perspective, a successful revolution requires an eventual adherence to an anticapitalist ideology that informs a coherent program that seeks to alter economic and political structures in favor of marginalized people. An ultimate goal is a more equal and just society that erases profound class divisions.

ANTICOLONIAL REVOLTS

Twentieth-century revolutionaries drew inspiration from previous generations of insurrections. Scholars debate the intent of these earlier movements, including whether they envisioned progressive political changes or sought to hold on to a quickly disappearing past. In either case, these prior mobilizations offer models for action as well as cautionary tales of what could go wrong when idealists seek to turn the world upside down.

Tupac Amaru

The 1780 Tupac Amaru revolt was one of the largest and most significant mass uprisings ever witnessed in the Americas. The movement is named after its leader, an Indigenous rights advocate named José Gabriel Condorcanqui, who traced his lineage to the last Inka emperor, Tupac Amaru. In 1572, the Spanish viceroy Francisco de Toledo executed the first Tupac Amaru after a failed revolt against the European invaders. Inka rule came to an end, but the memory of a society without colonial oppressors remained imprinted in the minds of the empire's descendants. Similar to his ancestor, Condorcanqui witnessed Spanish abuses of native communities and how these abuses contributed to growing discontent with colonial rule. He initially sought relief through legal means but realized little success in gaining the attention of colonial authorities. With institutional paths to change closed off, on November 4, 1780, Condorcanqui captured and executed a Spanish official. He took the name of Tupac Amaru (often designated the second to distinguish him from his predecessor) and called for the expulsion of the Spanish and for the establishment of an independent Inka Empire. As news of the uprising spread, supporters rushed to join the insurgent forces, and their ranks quickly grew to sixty thousand troops. They attacked Spanish estates, freed Indigenous prisoners, and removed colonial authorities from power.

Most studies center on Tupac Amaru's leadership and minimize the interests and motivations of a mass movement that wanted change and was prepared to fight, kill, and die for it. After suffering under centuries of Spanish colonial abuse, Indigenous peoples in the South American Andes were attracted to a vision of a society without economic exploitation and racial discrimination. Their hopes to regain control over their destinies spread like wildfire and rocked society. Without that pressure from below, the revolt never would have reached the dimensions it did. It is difficult to judge whether Tupac Amaru inspired others to follow him or if people were ready to act and only needed the opportunity that he had created. Inevitably, both a strong, charismatic vanguard leadership and a disgruntled mass of people created the necessary conditions for the spread of the revolt. Years of careful and painstaking organization probably also predated the insurrection, laying the groundwork for the movement.

Traditional treatments of revolts emphasize male leadership and ignore the important contributions that women made. Tupac Amaru's wife, Micaela Bastidas, played a key role. She served as the movement's chief propagandist and pushed Tupac Amaru to take more militant actions against colonial rule than he had initially proposed. When he was absent, she assumed command, but more importantly, she was a skilled strategist and ideologue in her own right. Her name has become a powerful **feminist** symbol of a capable woman playing a role equal to that of men in a movement for human liberation. On April 6, 1781, the Spanish captured the leadership of the revolt, and on May 18, they executed Tupac Amaru and his family members in the old Inka capital of Cuzco. In a patriarchal legal system that defined women (as well as Indigenous peoples and enslaved Africans) as incapable of rational thought and that thereby denied them political rights, the Spanish took the unusual action of executing Bastidas for her active participation in the revolt.

After the uprising, the Spanish engaged in a campaign of severe repression designed to destroy cultural elements of neo-Inka nationalism that the movement had inspired. Historians have subsequently debated whether the uprising was a messianic movement for ethnic rights, a class-based struggle against economic exploitation, or a failed anticolonial revolt that was a precursor to independence forty years later. Did it have an ideological underpinning, and did it articulate a vision for a new and better future? Or was it a mindless reaction against changes people did not understand and could not hope to influence? The answers to these questions are not simple or obvious. In any case, the name Tupac Amaru remains a potent symbol of resistance. Guerrilla movements in Uruguay in the 1970s and Peru in the 1980s took their names from the revolutionary leader, and the Black Panther activist Afeni Shakur gave the name to her son, the legendary rap superstar. More than two centuries later, Tupac Amaru still inspires people to action.

Haitian Revolution

An uprising in 1791 of enslaved peoples in the French colony of Saint-Domingue, on the Caribbean island of Hispaniola, that culminated in the independent country of Haiti in 1804 provides an example of what is perhaps the most thorough social revolution, in the sense that it completely inverted an established social order. Although not traditionally included in the pantheon of classic revolutionary movements, it is an example of one of the deepest and most profound revolutionary changes in the modern world. After ten years of sustained warfare, enslaved workers on plantations overthrew the planter class, destroyed the sugar-based export economic system, and created a new government under the leadership of formerly enslaved peoples. Unlike other anticolonial movements, the Haitian Revolution is the closest the world has come to a true revolution with extensive social, economic, and political changes.

In the eighteenth century, Saint-Domingue was the richest colony in the Caribbean and the supplier of half of the world's sugar and coffee. It also had the densest population of enslaved Africans in the Americas. The labor of overworked and underfed workers led to soaring profits for a small French planter class. On August 22, 1791, the enslaved workers revolted against their abusive masters. The revolt was long, bloody, and devastating, but unlike the Tupac Amaru uprising, it was ultimately successful in evicting the colonial power. The formerly enslaved Toussaint Louverture rose to a position of leadership in the movement. In 1802, the French ruler Napoléon Bonaparte captured Louverture and held him prisoner in France, where he died the following year. Louverture's lieutenant, Jean-Jacques Dessalines, continued the insurrection, finally defeating the French forces. On January 1, 1804, Dessalines declared independence for the colony. In a symbolic break from European control, the Black revolutionaries named the country Haiti, the original Taíno word for the island. Formerly enslaved workers were now in control, while the French planters were either dead or in exile.

Although the Haitian Revolution provides a successful example of exploited Blacks transforming social structures, the victory came at great cost. The war destroyed the island's infrastructure, and the new leaders lacked the technical or administrative skills necessary to run the government, which is a common problem for thoroughgoing social transformations. The government faced difficulties in growing the economy without laborers for the export-oriented plantation system. More significantly, both France and the United States were determined to undermine Haiti's model of independent development designed to benefit the working class. Both because of its alliance with France and because it did not want the example of a successful revolution to spread to enslaved peoples within its own borders, the United States refused to recognize the Haitian government. More importantly, France forced Haitians to pay reparations in exchange for international recognition, and those payments continued into the twentieth century. Haiti never recovered from that financial bankruptcy and today remains the poorest country in the Americas. The country's macroeconomic statistics would seem to indicate that the island was better off as a sugar plantation colony rooted in the labor of enslaved peoples, but that conclusion ignores extreme inequalities and the role imperial powers played in deliberately undermining an independent Black republic.

Some have taken the Haitian Revolution's level of brutal violence and the independent country's resulting impoverished condition as a caution against attempting revolutionary changes. Before venturing out on such an endeavor, protagonists must count the costs and weigh those against potential benefits. Others argue that such profound changes in social and economic structures cannot occur successfully in a single location but must happen simultaneously on a global level to be meaningful and sustainable. In the case of the Caribbean, surviving planters simply shifted their sugar production to the neighboring island of Cuba, where the system of slavery persisted until 1886, longer than anywhere else in the Americas except for Brazil. As long as wealthy capitalists remain in power anywhere in the world, they will continue to do battle against attempts at local endogenous development that seek to benefit the conditions in which marginalized peoples live.

Religious Movements

In Mexico at the dawn of the nineteenth century, Father Miguel Hidalgo rallied his rural parishioners in support of independence. Early on the morning of September 16, 1810, Hidalgo rang the church bells in his parish of Dolores. He appealed to the

Virgin of Guadalupe and called for death to the Spanish and their bad government policies. He marched on Guanajuato, picking up tens of thousands of unarmed but enthusiastic recruits along the way. He appeared to be heading a social revolution with promises of social programs, including land reform and a redistribution of goods. His campaign elicited a conservative reaction fueled by fears that Hidalgo had triggered a race war on behalf of impoverished Indigenous and African-descent peoples against wealthy European landholders. In an attempt to put an end to the revolt, the Spanish captured and executed Hidalgo. A decade later, Mexico gained its independence but did so under the control and direction of wealthy landowners. Hidalgo's uprising represented an inspired but ultimately futile effort to transform society.

During the nineteenth century, many millenarian movements emerged from marginalized communities. One of the most famous of these surfaced in the desperately poor zone of Canudos, in the semiarid backlands of Brazil. A local leader, Antônio Vicente Mendes Maciel, became known as Antônio Conselheiro (Counselor) because of the legal advice he dispensed to poor people. He worked as an itinerant mystic preacher, and his promises of a better world attracted thousands of followers. In 1893, he organized a religious commune at Canudos that quickly grew by leaps and bounds. The community functioned along utopian lines without money and with a common ownership of property. The commune alarmed the government, which in 1897 sent in troops and killed almost all of the thirty thousand residents. Conselheiro is alternatively remembered as a religious fanatic, saint, or messiah. Only recently, in 1888, had Brazil abolished slavery—the last country in the Americas to do so—and the following year, political leaders declared the country to be a republic. Opponents denounced Conselheiro as a monarchist who opposed the progress that the country was making and advocated for the return of the recently disposed emperor Pedro II. Others claimed that Canudos was a utopian community that expressed the aspirations of marginalized peoples who had lost their land and that racism and scorn for poor people had fueled the ferociousness of the government's attack.

Scholars debate whether these social aspirations were progressive or reactionary, whether protagonists imagined a new and better future or sought to hold on to a quickly disappearing past. Anticapitalist discourses can easily assume both aspects, but their underlying ideology and ultimate objectives are diametrically opposed. Some call these early movements prepolitical and contend that they lacked an ideology and clear demands for systemic and transformative change. Key questions to consider are whether the movements engaged the consciousness of a dispossessed class of people and addressed the structural issues that maintained these people in an impoverished situation, rather than simply raising the status of an individual leader or a small group of people. Some movements seek to return to an imagined and nonexistent past rather than moving society forward to a better future. As these early anticolonial revolts reveal, mass uprisings can have reactionary as well as progressive characteristics. Violence and the disruption of an established society alone do not make for a revolutionary situation.

BIOGRAPHY: JOSÉ CARLOS MARIÁTEGUI, 1894–1930

José Carlos Mariátegui was an innovative Peruvian thinker whom many revere as the founder of Latin American Marxist theory. His most famous book, *Seven Interpretive Essays on Peruvian Reality*, is a foundational work on Latin American Marxism that some scholars have cited as the one book to read to understand Latin American realities. Mariátegui presents a brilliant analysis of Peruvian, and by extension Latin American, problems from a Marxist point of view.

José Carlos Mariátegui
Source: Casa Museo José Carlos Mariátegui

In October 1919, the Peruvian dictator Augusto B. Leguía exiled Mariátegui to Europe. Mariátegui studied in France and Italy, which afforded him the opportunity to interact with many European socialists. His time in Europe strongly influenced the development and maturation of his thought, and it solidified his socialist tendencies. Upon returning to Peru in 1923, Mariátegui declared that he was "a convinced and declared Marxist."

Mariátegui interacted dynamically with European thought in order to develop new methods to analyze Latin American problems. He favored a nonsectarian, "open" Marxism in which Marxist thought should be revisable, not dogmatic, and adaptable to new situations. Rather than relying strictly on objective economic factors to foment a revolutionary situation, Mariátegui also examined subjective elements such as the need for the political education and organization of the proletariat, a strategy that he believed could move a society to revolutionary action.

In 1926, Mariátegui founded *Amauta*, a journal that he intended to be a vanguard voice for an intellectual and spiritual movement to create a new Peru. In 1928, he launched a biweekly periodical called *Labor* to inform, educate, and politicize the working class. Mariátegui published two books, *La escena contemporánea* (The contemporary scene) in 1925 and *7 ensayos de interpretación de la realidad peruana* (*Seven Interpretive Essays on Peruvian Reality*) in 1928, in addition to many articles in various Peruvian periodicals.

Unlike orthodox Marxists who denied the revolutionary potential of the peasantry, Mariátegui looked to the rural Indigenous masses in addition to an industrialized urban working class to lead a social revolution that he believed would sweep across Latin America. Mariátegui argued that once Indigenous peoples encountered **socialism**, they would cling to it fervently, since it coincided with their traditional communal forms of social organization. To be successful, modern socialism should fuse the legacy of "Inka communism" with modern Western technology.

Mariátegui's revolutionary activities did not remain only on a theoretical level. He was influential in the organization of **communist** cells all over Peru and served as the first secretary-general of the Partido Socialista Peruano (PSP, Peruvian Socialist Party), which he founded in 1928. In 1929, the PSP launched the Confederación General de Trabajadores del Perú (CGTP, General Confederation of Peruvian Workers), a Marxist-oriented trade union federation. Both the CGTP and the PSP were involved in an active internationalism, including participating in **Communist International**–sponsored meetings. Twice the Leguía dictatorship arrested and imprisoned Mariátegui for his political activities, but he was never convicted of any crime.

Although the political party and labor confederation that Mariátegui had helped launch flourished, his health foundered. In 1924, he lost his right leg and was confined to a wheelchair for the rest of his life. In spite of his failing health, Mariátegui increased the intensity of his efforts to organize a social revolution in Peru. Mariátegui was at the height of his intellectual and political contributions when he died on April 16, 1930, two months short of his thirty-sixth birthday.

DOCUMENT: JOSÉ CARLOS MARIÁTEGUI, "ON THE INDIGENOUS PROBLEM," 1928

Mariátegui reinterpreted Marxist thought for Latin American realities. In this essay that he wrote in 1928 at the request of the Tass News Agency in New York, Mariátegui dedicated attention to the need to address the economic exploitation that Indigenous peoples faced. He contended that their poverty was not a result of their ethnicity and dismissed the idea that education, social welfare, or religious conversion could overcome their marginalization. Rather than tackling these problems on an individual level, Mariátegui declared that they were structural in nature and could only be solved on that level. Furthermore, Indigenous peoples as an organized movement must be in charge of their own liberation. The essay complements and extends his discussion in his 1928 book Seven Interpretive Essays on Peruvian Reality.

According to conservative estimates, the population of the Inka Empire numbered at least ten million. Some place it at twelve million to fifteen million. More than anything, the conquest brought a terrible carnage to that society. Given their small numbers, the Spanish conquerors could not control it but only managed to terrorize the Indigenous population. The people superstitiously regarded the invaders' guns and horses as supernatural beings. The political and economic organization of the colony, which came after the conquest, continued to exterminate the Indigenous race. The viceroyalty established a system of brutal exploitation. Spanish greed for precious metals led to economic activities geared toward mining. The Inkas had worked those mines on a very small scale because the Indians, who were largely an agricultural people, did not use iron and only used gold and silver as ornaments. To work the mines and textile sweatshops, the Spanish established a system of forced labor that decimated the population. They created not only a system of servitude—as might have been the case had the Spanish limited the exploitation to the use of land and retained the agricultural character of the country—but also a system of slavery. Humanitarian and civilizing voices called for the king of Spain to defend the Indians. More than anyone, Father Bartolomé de Las Casas stood out in their defense. The Laws of the Indies were intended to protect the Indians. It recognized their traditional community organizations. But in reality, the Indians were at the mercy of a ruthless feudalism that destroyed the Inka economy and society without replacing it with something that could increase production. The tendency of the Spanish to settle on the coast drove away so many aboriginals from the region that the result was a lack of workers. The viceroyalty wanted to solve this problem through the importation of enslaved Africans. These people were appropriate to the climate and challenges of the hot valleys and plains of the coast but were inappropriate for work in the mines in the cold sierra highlands. Enslaved Africans reinforced the system of Spanish domination. In spite of Indigenous depopulation, the Indians still outnumbered the Spanish. Even though subjugated, the Indians remained a hostile enemy. Blacks were devoted to domestic service and other jobs. Whites easily mixed with Blacks, producing a mixed type characteristic of the coastal population that had greater adherence to the Spanish and resisted Indigenous influences.

The independence revolution was not, as is known, an Indigenous movement. It was a movement of and for the benefit of creoles and even the Spanish living in the colonies. But it took advantage of the support of the Indigenous masses. Furthermore, as illustrated by the Pumacahua uprising, some Indians played an important role in its development. The independence movement's liberal program logically included the redemption of the Indian as an automatic consequence of the implementation of its egalitarian principles. And so, among the republic's first acts, were several laws and decrees in favor of the Indians. They ordered the distribution of land, the abolition of forced labor, and so on. But independence in Peru did not bring in a new ruling class, and all of these provisions remained on paper without a government capable of carrying them out. The colony's landholding aristocracy, the power holders, retained their feudal rights over the land and, by extension, over the Indians. All provisions designed to protect them have not been able to do anything against feudalism, and that is still true today.

The viceroyalty seems less to blame than the republic. The full responsibility for the misery and depression of the Indians originally belonged to the viceroyalty. But in those days of the inquisition, a great Christian voice, that of Friar Bartolomé de Las Casas, vigorously defended the Indians against the colonizers' brutality. No advocate of the aboriginal race as stubborn and effective emerged during the republic.

While the viceroyalty was a medieval and foreign regime, the republic is formally a Peruvian and liberal regime. The republic, therefore, had a duty the viceroyalty did not have. The republic has the responsibility to raise the Indians' status, but contrary to this duty, the republic has impoverished the Indians. It has compounded their depression and exasperated their misery. The republic has meant for the Indians the ascent of a new ruling class that has systematically taken their lands. In a race based on customs and an agricultural soul, as with the Indigenous race, this dispossession has constituted a cause for their material and moral dissolution. Land has always been the joy of the Indians. Indians are wed to the land. They feel that "life comes from the earth" and returns to the earth. For this reason, Indians can be indifferent to everything except possession of their land, which produces because of their conscientious work and encouragement. In this regard, Creole feudalism has been worse than Spanish feudalism. The Spanish *encomendero* (grant holder) often had some of the noble habits of feudal lords. The creole encomendero has all the defects of a commoner and none of the virtues of a gentleman. The situation of Indian servitude, in short, has not improved during the republic. All uprisings, all of the Indian unrest, have been drowned in blood. Indian demands have always been met with a military response. The silence of the cold, desolate highland *puna* region afterward guards the tragic secret of these responses. In the end, the republic restored the *mita* labor system but with the label of the road labor draft.

In addition, the republic is also responsible for the lethargic and feeble energy of the race. Under the republic, the cause of the redemption of the Indians became a demagogic speculation of some strongmen. Creole parties have signed up for their program. And thus, the Indians lost their will to fight for their demands.

In the highlands, the region mostly inhabited by the Indians, the most barbaric and omnipotent feudalism remains largely unchanged. Under the domination of the earth in the hands of the *gamonales* (landowners), the fate of the Indigenous race falls to an extreme level of depression and ignorance. In addition to farming, which is carried out on a very primitive level, the Peruvian highlands also have another economic activity: mining, almost entirely in the hands of two large U.S. companies. Wages are regulated in the mines, but the pay is negligible, there is almost no defense of the lives of the workers, and labor laws governing accidents are ignored. The system of *enganche* (debt peonage), which enslaves workers through false promises, puts the Indians at the mercy of these capitalist companies. The misery of agrarian feudalism is so great that Indians prefer the lot that the mines offer.

The spread of socialist ideas in Peru has resulted in a strong movement in support of Indigenous demands. The new Peruvian generation knows that Peru's progress will be fictitious, or at least will not be Peruvian, if it does not benefit the Peruvian masses, four-fifths of whom are Indigenous and peasant. This same trend is evident in art and in national literature in which there is a growing appreciation of Indigenous forms and affairs, something that the dominance of a Spanish colonial spirit and mentality had previously depreciated. **Indigenista** literature seems to fulfill the same role of *Mujika* literature in prerevolutionary Russia. Indians themselves are beginning to show signs of a new consciousness. Relationships between various Indigenous settlements that previously had no contact because of great distances grow day by day. The regular meeting of government-sponsored Indigenous congresses initiated these linkages, but as the nature of their demands became revolutionary, they were undermined as advanced elements were excluded and representation was made apocryphal. Indigenista currents press for official action. For the first time, the government has been forced to accept and proclaim indigenista views and, because of this, has decreed some measures that are ineffective because they do not touch gamonal interests. For the first time, the Indigenous problem, which disappears in the face of ruling-class rhetoric, is posed in its social and economic terms and is identified more than anything as a land problem. Every day more evidence underscores the conviction that this problem cannot find its solution in humanitarian actions. It cannot be the result of a philanthropic movement. The patronage of Indigenous chieftains and phony lawyers is a mockery. Leagues such as the former Pro Indigenous Association provide a voice clamoring in the wilderness. The Pro Indigenous Association did not arrive in time to become a movement. Their activities were gradually reduced to the generous, selfless, noble, personal actions of Pedro S. Zulen and Dora Mayer. As an experiment, the Pro Indigenous Association served to contrast, to measure, the moral callousness of a generation and an era.

The solution to the problem of the Indian must be social. The Indians themselves must work it out. This understanding leads to seeing the meeting of Indigenous congresses as a historical fact. The Indigenous congresses, misguided in recent years because of their bureaucracy, have not yet formed a program, but their first meetings indicated a route for Indians in different regions. The Indians lack a national organization. Their protests have always been regional. This has contributed in large part to their defeat. Four million people, conscious of their numbers, do not despair of their future. These same four million people, if they are nothing more than an inorganic mass or a dispersed crowd, will be unable to chart their historical course.

Source: José Carlos Mariátegui, "Sobre el problema indígena," *Labor: Quincenario de información e ideas* 1, no. 1 (November 10, 1928): 6 (translation by author).

COMMUNIST INTERNATIONAL

Even as international currents influenced leftist ideologies in Latin America, revolutionaries debated what relationship they should have with those larger transnational trends or whether they should root their movements primarily or even exclusively as responses to their local situations. The most significant external influence was the October 1917 Bolshevik Revolution that set Russia on the path of a rapid transition to socialism. Inspired by the Bolshevik drive to move a rural, marginalized society toward a modern, industrialized one that was more egalitarian, many socialist and anarchist activists in Latin America formed communist parties in the 1920s. Under the leadership of Vladimir Ilyich Ulyanov (alias Lenin) (1870–1924), the Bolsheviks organized the Communist or Third International (Comintern) in 1919 to lead this international movement to world **communism**.

Previous attempts to organize an international socialist organization had failed. Militants founded the International Workingmen's Association (1864–1877), often called the First International, in London to revive the European labor movement after their defeats in the 1848 socialist uprisings. Karl Marx led and dominated the First International, but sectarian divisions collapsed it. Activists subsequently established the Second International (1889–1914) in Paris. Although it was less torn by internal disputes, its passivity in the face of the First World War led to its decline. The Second International later gathered together mainstream social democratic parties into the Socialist International.

The First and Second Internationals were federations of different national groups and political parties, whereas the Comintern was designed as a single, centrally organized party, radiating out from its base in Moscow. Advocates envisioned it as leading a worldwide socialist revolution that would transcend capitalism. Since capitalism was a global system, the response would similarly need to be transnational. The Peruvian Marxist José Carlos Mariátegui observed that whereas the Second International was an organizational machine, the Third International was a combat machine with the express goal of transforming society.

Initially, the Comintern dedicated its efforts to what it thought would be an imminent revolution in Europe. No Latin Americans attended the Comintern's first congress in Moscow, and few participated in the next several congresses. It was not until the sixth congress, in 1928, that the Comintern "discovered" Latin America and began to play an active role in the region. At the same time, the Comintern entered its "third period," during which it adopted an aggressive and militant strategy of engaging in a class-against-class struggle. Communist leaders optimistically believed that capitalism was entering its final and terminal phase of collapse. In an ultimately futile attempt to hasten the revolution, they turned against moderate left-wing parties whose reforms they believed were only sustaining an existing and unjust system.

The Comintern recognized the revolutionary potential of anticolonial struggles and defended the rights of self-determination for national minorities, including the right to secede from oppressive, colonizing state structures. The policy led to advocating for the establishment of "independent native republics" for Blacks in South Africa and the United States, and a proposal to carve out an Indigenous Republic of the Quechua and Aymara peoples in South America. Mariátegui adamantly maintained that an independent republic would only replicate the existing class contradictions in society. He argued that communists should focus instead on a class struggle that would force changes in the land tenure system that impoverished rural dwellers. Elsewhere, including in neighboring Ecuador, communists picked up the slogan of the rights of Indigenous nationalities and used it as a rhetorical device to advance their struggles. As a result, communism became associated with the liberation struggles of African-descent and Indigenous peoples.

Revolutionaries organized uprisings across Latin America in a futile attempt to replicate the success of the Bolshevik Revolution. All of them met with failure and bloody repression. In 1928, labor leaders on a United Fruit Company banana plantation at Santa Marta in Colombia organized a massive workers' strike that they hoped would lead to a revolution. Instead, the government responded with overwhelming force and crushed the movement in a bloody **massacre** that Gabriel García Márquez memorialized in his award-winning novel *One Hundred Years of Solitude*. In this aftermath, some communists distanced themselves from the strike in an attempt to escape culpability, and they blamed each other for strategic failures. In retrospect, however, considering the organizing capacity and high levels of support that the banana workers enjoyed on the eve of the strike, this may have been the closest the communists had come to gaining power in Latin America. The intense fear that the potential of a working-class victory engendered among the ruling class may help explain the iron grip that conservatives held over the country for the next century.

One of the largest international communist campaigns in the 1920s was in defense of Nicaraguan patriot Augusto César Sandino (1895–1934), who was fighting against the U.S. Marines who had occupied his country since 1911. Sandino had previously worked in the oil fields of Tampico, Mexico, where he was caught up in the revolutionary fervor of the Mexican Revolution. The anarchist Industrial Workers of the World (IWW) organized the oil workers and strongly influenced Sandino's ideology. He drew on liberal, socialist, and spiritual ideologies to shape his struggle. The Mexican muralist Diego Rivera and other notable communists, including Mariátegui, organized an international campaign called "Hands Off Nicaragua" in defense of Sandino's anti-imperialist struggle. By 1933, Sandino had fought the marines to a standstill and the United States agreed to withdraw its military forces. In their place, the United States trained and installed a **national guard** that ambushed and killed Sandino in February 1934.

Scholars have long debated the nature of Sandino's motivation and whether his struggle extended beyond a nationalistic struggle to free his country from U.S. occupation. His ideology reflected a mix of liberal, anarchist, and socialist influences, including **anticlericalism**, antiauthoritarianism, and anticapitalism. Sandino embraced policies that emphasized social legislation, **agrarian reform**, and a redistribution of wealth to benefit marginalized people. Sandino's private secretary Agustín Farabundo Martí (1893–1932) attempted to convince him to accept a more explicitly communist position, but Sandino wanted to emphasize the nationalist aspects of his struggle in an effort to gain a wide base of support. He believed it was necessary to avoid anarchist and communist labels in order to launch a successful, broad-based revolution. The benefits and liabilities of linking local and global struggles were a constant theme of debate among these militant activists.

Martí became frustrated with Sandino's reticence at joining a global movement and returned to his native El Salvador, where he organized an armed insurrection with communist support. Martí set up local political councils, denominated "soviets," after the Russian term the Bolsheviks had used. He developed a socialist program that quickly inspired a large peasant mobilization. In January 1932, the Salvadoran military rapidly and brutally suppressed the rural uprising, killing as many as thirty thousand people in the process. The army massacre targeted Indigenous peoples and led to an abandonment of native dress and language because of their association with the communist insurgency. The peasant insurgents simply did not have sufficient arms, training, or popular support to defend themselves. While some condemn Martí for leading a rural population into a massacre, others celebrate him as a hero for launching a struggle against grinding poverty and extreme socioeconomic inequality in the face of overwhelming odds. Scholars continue to debate what role (if any) the Comintern had in organizing the uprising or whether the attempted revolution emerged primarily in response to local peasant demands.

In Brazil, Luís Carlos Prestes (1898–1990) similarly engaged in attempts at insurrection. In 1924, Prestes participated in a military coup in São Paulo. When that failed, he led one thousand junior military officers on a meandering campaign through the Brazilian interior. The group became known as the Prestes Column, and the leader the Knight of Hope. Although both the coup and the column failed in their immediate objectives of defeating the oligarchy and proclaiming national independence, the effort gained Prestes widespread fame and popular support. Prestes subsequently went into exile, where he became radicalized and joined the communist party. He returned to Brazil in 1935, assumed leadership of the party, and organized another military insurrection in Rio de Janeiro. Again, the government quickly put down the uprising and followed it with a wave of intense repression that included executions, torture, arrests, and the jailing of political prisoners. Prestes himself spent the next decade in prison. The uprising failed in part because it had been organized as a military insurrection rather than as a broader mobilization of the worker and peasant masses, and had been conceptualized as a national-democratic movement that relied on the backing of a progressive and modernizing **bourgeoisie** that would join the masses' efforts.

The Comintern held its seventh and final congress in 1935. With the rise of Nazism in Germany, the congress reversed its policy of class struggle adopted seven years earlier and embraced a **popular front** strategy. Communist parties were now instructed to collaborate with other democratic forces that opposed **fascism** rather than basing themselves only in the working class. Chile was the only place in Latin America where a popular front successfully brought the left to power through electoral means. In 1938, communists entered into a center-left coalition with socialists to elect Pedro Aguirre Cerda of the Radical Party as president. That alliance did not result in the implementation of much of the socialist agenda, which highlighted the limitations of a popular-front strategy of collaborating with others who were not committed to a radical transformation of society.

In 1943, in the midst of a battle for the very survival of the Soviet Union during the Second World War, Soviet leader Joseph Stalin (1878–1953) dissolved the Comintern as a way to calm the fears of his British and U.S. allies that communists were attempting to foment a world revolution under the guise of fighting a common fascist enemy. Following Moscow's lead, during the 1940s and 1950s, most Latin American communists opted to work for progressive social changes through existing institutional channels. This meant largely discarding the option of armed struggle in favor of peaceful, gradual, and electoral paths to revolution. A hope was that the resulting transformations would be profound and permanent. As would later emerge in Cuba with Fidel Castro, the most violent and radical options materialized outside of the communist orbit. Even so, conservatives attacked revolutionary movements as emanating out of Moscow rather than responding to local conditions. The issue of whether to collaborate in one unified global communist revolution or to build a local movement of national liberation continued to divide the left.

IDEOLOGIES

The terms "left" and "**right**," "progressive" and "conservative" are central to this book, and it is important to define them even as their precise meanings can become contentious. The use of left and right to refer to political ideologies originated during the French Revolution when, in 1789, commoners who supported the revolution sat to the left of the president in the National Assembly, and the aristocracy and clergy who backed the monarchy were to the right. Subsequently, "left-wing" positions emphasized freedom, equality, fraternity, and progress, while "right-wing" ideologies indicated a belief in established authority, hierarchy, order, and tradition. At its roots, "conservative" means to conserve the status quo, whereas "progressive" implies progress or a struggle for a better future. In Latin America, conservatives were closely associated with colonial traditions that relied on Catholicism, feudalism, and the monarchy to maintain order. In the nineteenth century, liberals responded with claims for individual rights, civil liberties, and a belief that private property and capitalism would lead to the modernization of society.

Socialism emerged in the twentieth century as a response to the shortcomings of both conservatism and **liberalism**. Whereas in North America, "liberal" and "left" have become euphemisms for progressive political positions, in Latin America, they designate quite distinct ideologies. Socialists advocated independence from foreign intervention and the elimination of private property through an organized class struggle of workers and peasants against the local ruling class and its international imperial allies. The goal was an equal distribution of resources through participatory decision-making processes. Broad categorizations of these three ideologies (right/ conservative, liberal/progressive, and left/socialist) gloss over deep divisions within each, including libertarian versus traditional tendencies within conservatism, an emphasis on civil versus social rights within liberalism, and a rift between reformism and revolution within socialism.

The twentieth-century revolutionary left emerged out of three distinct ideological currents in socialism: utopian socialism, anarchism, and Marxism. Advocates of each tendency shared a common vision of a society without oppression and exploitation in which authoritarian structures, including governments, would disappear. The common goal was socialism in which private ownership of the means of production no longer existed and everyone had equal access to sufficient resources to enjoy life to its fullest. The three ideologies differed greatly in their approaches to the realization of this dream. While moderate reformers promoted working for gradual change through existing institutions, radical revolutionaries resorted to armed struggle against what they saw as the inevitable refusal of rulers to hand over power and promote justice for all. Over the past two centuries, each ideology in turn held dominance over the left, and elements of each survive to the present. The boundaries between the different currents were not always established in an entirely clear manner. Aspects of each can be found in the other branches, as they influenced each other's ideas of how best to transform society.

Utopian Socialism

Utopian socialism was the first current of anticapitalist thought to emerge in the nineteenth century. Adherents contended that they could move people in the direction of an ideal society with intellectual arguments. Individuals would voluntarily adopt their program and establish alternative communities that would set an example for others to follow. This transformation would occur without the destruction inherent in a violent class struggle. Those who advocated for these ideas did not identify themselves as utopian socialists. Rather, other socialists subsequently dismissed their ideas as unrealistic and pejoratively labeled their current as a "utopian" or fanciful and unrealizable way to change society.

The English philosopher Thomas More (1478–1535) introduced the concept of utopia through the publication in 1516 of his book *Utopia* (meaning "nowhere"), in which he describes an imaginary socialist society. Three centuries later, the French political theorist Henri de Saint-Simon (1760–1825) formulated ideas that provided the basis of utopian socialism. Saint-Simon was born into an aristocratic society but with his writings sought to guide society away from feudalism and toward social improvements. From his perspective, enlightened leaders would provide technological solutions to improve society. These developments would occur without class conflict. A violent revolution in which the working class overthrew the ruling class and captured control of the political and economic system was not necessary. Rather, with the proper ideas and guidance, society would naturally evolve to a higher and more perfect state of being.

The author Edward Bellamy (1850–1898) did much to popularize the ideas of utopian socialism. His 1888 novel *Looking Backward* provides a Rip Van Winkle–like tale in which the protagonist falls into a deep sleep and wakes up in the year 2000 in a socialist utopia. Bellamy describes a society in which property was held in common, money had ceased to exist, technological advances drastically reduced working hours, and everyone enjoyed a life of plenty. Bellamy's vision inspired the creation of clubs and utopian communities to propagate his ideas. Critics complained that his book failed to explain how such a perfect society could be achieved without class conflict or violent struggle. Would wealthy individuals willingly give up their privileges in the interests of the entire society?

While utopian communities still exist (for example, the Hutterites, an Anabaptist religious sect that practices a communal way of life), utopian socialism largely lost force by the end of the nineteenth century, and only echoes of this ideology survived into the twenty-first century. In Latin America, utopian socialism never achieved a strong presence. Mostly, this tendency attracted members of the aristocracy who became aware of the inequalities and oppression in society and sought to improve the lives of the most marginalized people without sacrificing their own advantages. Other leftists criticized this approach as advocating romantic ideals that could not be realized without addressing underlying class contradictions. Many of the utopian goals of a better society, however, did not disappear but survived under the umbrella of anarchism.

Anarchism

Anarchism is popularly thought of as a lack of order that leads to chaos, and as a result the term acquires negative connotations. Politically, it refers to an antiauthoritarian ideology that opposes hierarchies as unnecessary and fundamentally harmful to the realization of a more just and equal society. The word "anarchism" comes from the Greek word *anarchos,* which means "without rulers." Rather than seeking to reform government policies, anarchists fought to destroy existing institutions, eliminate governments and capitalism, and create a new society. Far from advocating for chaos, anarchism at its core is a philosophy of freedom, both in the sense of gaining freedom from imposed authority as well as being free to celebrate one's full human potential.

The category of anarchism incorporates a wide range of ideas, stretching from extreme individualism to complete collectivism. The two main traditions can be broadly grouped under individualist anarchism and social anarchism. Individualist anarchism emphasizes personal will over external determinants such as groups, society, traditions, and ideological systems. In contrast to this perspective, which opposes state or social control over individuals, social anarchism emphasizes liberty to realize a person's potential. Social anarchists reject private property because it creates inequality; instead, they call for the public ownership of the means of production and democratic control over organizations, without any government authority or coercion.

The French philosopher Pierre-Joseph Proudhon (1809–1865) was the first person to describe himself as an anarchist and in a sense is the founder of anarchist thought. Proudhon asserted in his 1840 book *What Is Property?* that "property is theft," which subsequently became a common slogan for anticapitalist movements. Instead of private property, masters, and hierarchies, Proudhon advocated for worker self-management through mutualistic societies that would allow for individuals to realize their full potential.

The Russian revolutionary Mikhail Alexandrovich Bakunin (1814–1876) was one of the most famous and influential anarchists. He advocated for a collectivist anarchism that favored the abolition of both state structures and the private ownership of the means of production. Instead, workers would collectively own and manage production. Bakunin opposed Marx's strategy of the working class taking control of political power in order to rule from above to implement policies that would benefit the rest of society. Rather than the enlightened rulers of utopian socialism guiding society, Bakunin advocated for the immediate abolishment of government structures because they would inevitably lead to oppression. Socialism remained a shared goal, but intense debates raged over how to arrive at that point.

Emma Goldman (1869–1940) played a pivotal role in the development of anarchist thought at the beginning of the twentieth century. Goldman was born in Lithuania and immigrated to the United States in 1885. She was a renowned writer and lecturer on anarchist philosophy, women's rights, and social issues and was repeatedly imprisoned for her political activism. Goldman was deported to the Soviet Union during the 1919 Red Scare, when Attorney General A. Mitchell Palmer suppressed radical organizations. She soon left the Soviet Union out of disillusionment with the authoritarian nature of the new communist government. Goldman is best known through a quote that is actually a paraphrase of her ideas: "If I can't dance, I don't want to be part of your revolution." That statement embodies an anarchist rejection of vanguard leadership in favor of democratic participation in movement decisions.

Anarchists opposed joining political parties or voting in elections because these systems inevitably reproduced the oppressive and hierarchical elements of the society against which they rebelled. A fear was that their participation would legitimize an authoritarian system. Instead, anarchists favored direct **democracy** in which people would have control over decision-making processes. Many anarchists also advocated for the development of an autonomous working-class culture. They fostered new social institutions through the staging of theater productions, holding lectures, publishing books and newspapers, and engaging in alternative lifestyles. In the process they developed new forms of community.

Adherents agreed on a need to transform society, but they disagreed over what was the best way to achieve that goal. Some favored violent tactics, which led to a largely inaccurate stereotype of bomb-throwing anarchists. In the twentieth century, anarchists became one of the most peaceful camps on the left. Even while some did engage in armed actions, most mobilized workers through strikes, industrial sabotage, or boycotts. In particular, anarchists are associated with general strikes that aim to disrupt the smooth functioning of a capitalist society. Strikes could either take the form of a direct confrontation with business owners or, more commonly, workers peacefully walking away from their jobs in order to force a change in policies.

Anarchism was particularly influential in the labor movement from about 1880 to 1920. The ideology gained broad exposure through the 1886 Haymarket Affair. On May 1, workers in Chicago engaged in a general strike for an eight-hour workday. On May 4, anarchists staged a peaceful rally at Haymarket Square. At the rally, an unidentified person threw a bomb that killed a police officer. Many suspect a police provocateur who sought to justify violent repression of the labor movement, while others contend that the anarchists believed in the necessity of a violent revolution to achieve their goals. In either case, the police opened fire, killing seven police officers and four workers. Authorities arrested eight anarchists and charged them with murder. The anarchists quickly became international political celebrities. Four (Albert Parsons, August Spies, Adolph Fischer, and George Engel) were executed, another died by suicide while in detention, and the rest were sentenced to lengthy prison terms. The Haymarket Affair is celebrated around the world on May 1 as International Workers' Day, but notably not in the United States.

Some anarchists criticized trade unions as inherently reformist and opposed what they saw as their innately vanguardist, hierarchical characteristics. In 1905, militant workers who favored a revolutionary industrial unionism met in Chicago to found the anarcho-syndicalist Industrial Workers of the World (IWW, or the Wobblies). Its members believed that the organization of the working class was a key task. The IWW gained considerable influence during the early 1900s through its engagement in "direct action," which included general strikes, sabotage, and boycotts. Among its most important founders was William D. "Big Bill" Haywood of the Western Federation of Miners, who had led a series of strikes in western mines. IWW organizer Joe Hill became a martyr and folk hero when he was executed in 1915 on a questionable murder charge. He famously proclaimed to his fellow workers, "Don't mourn, organize!"

Anarchism entered Latin America through the influence of Southern European immigrants, particularly in Argentina, Brazil, and Uruguay. At the beginning of the twentieth century, anarchists engaged in repeated strikes to defend workers' rights and to agitate for higher pay. The military frequently repressed the strikes, leading to the massacre of thousands of workers. While the repression temporarily halted labor militancy, extreme abuses soon led to a resurgence of activity and inevitably a new round of strikes and massacres. In Chile, for example, nitrate miners launched 638 strikes between 1901 and 1924. In Ecuador, a massacre of striking workers at the port of Guayaquil in 1922 gave birth to the modern left through a baptism of blood. Through his journalism, Ricardo Flores Magón introduced anarchist ideas that fundamentally influenced the direction of the 1910 Mexican Revolution. In 1926, Sandino returned to his native Nicaragua from exile in Mexico under the influence of these anarchist ideas and launched his own revolution. While utopian socialism expressed aspirations for a better society, anarchism provided an ideology to achieve those goals.

Marxism

Anarchism was the most significant anticapitalist ideology during the first two decades of the twentieth century. The triumph of the Bolshevik Revolution in 1917, however, changed popular perceptions of its relative importance. For the first time, a successful armed insurrection overthrew an established capitalist system and began to construct a new society based on Marxist principles. In the 1920s, many anarchists deserted ranks and joined communist parties in an attempt to replicate the success they observed in the Soviet Union. Whereas utopian socialism expressed aspirations and anarchism provided an ideology, Marxism laid out a concrete path to implement those goals.

While utopian socialism is commonly labeled with its derogatory moniker and schools of anarchism are identified by their core organizational principle, such as anarcho-syndicalism, Marxism and its variations (**Leninism**, **Trotskyism**, **Maoism**, etc.) are named for their founders. Karl Marx was a German philosopher who, with the assistance of his collaborator Friedrich Engels (1820–1895), wrote such notable works as *The Communist Manifesto* (1848) and *Das Kapital* (1867–1894), which critiqued capitalism and developed a vision for societal transformations. Marx looked to the industrialized working class as the agent of change, as a class that had both the power and interest to transcend capitalism. To achieve this goal, the working class needed a revolutionary organization to give structure to an alternative form of state power, to reorganize society, and to repress the inevitable reaction that the ruling class would mount against a socialist revolution.

Marx was the first to articulate a conception of history that has come to be known as historical materialism. It is a methodological approach that seeks scientific explanations in the concrete, material world for developments and changes in human society rather than relying on idealistic notions or the spiritual realm as causal factors. Furthermore, Marx believed that a dominant mode of production, or the way productive forces and the relations of production are combined, would define the nature of social structures. Productive forces include the means of production such as labor, tools, equipment, and land. The relations of production describe property and power relations that govern society and control the way in which humans relate to the forces of production. The mode of production defines the manner in which productive forces are harnessed to meet material needs, how the labor process is organized, and how the products of that labor are distributed to society. Writing in the context of a nineteenth-century positivist framework, Marx implied a linear progression of modes of production through time, from primitive communalism to feudalism, capitalism, socialism, and, finally, full realization in communism, where the scientific management of society through democratic means would establish the maximum good for all without the need for governments or other forms of coercion to mediate the distribution of resources.

According to Marx, society is divided into antagonistic groups called classes, which are locked into conflict with each other. People's relationship to the means of production—specifically, whether they are the capitalists who own the factories or the workers who deliver their labor to the owners—determines their location in the class structure. Marx wrote in *The Communist Manifesto*, "The history of all hitherto existing society is the history of class struggles." The antagonism between the classes is a result of marked differences in wealth, power, and prestige, as different groups compete for access to those resources. That antagonism is called class struggle and, according to Marx, provides the engine for historical change.

People are born into a class structure, whether they realize it or not, and that class position shapes, determines, and constrains their role in society. When people become aware of their location in a class structure, they gain **class consciousness**. Once they have achieved that, they can begin to guide and determine a historical outcome to the benefit of their class. Marx believed that once workers acquired a class consciousness, they would engage in revolutionary activity that would destroy capitalism and usher in a process of radical change that would socialize the means of production and eventually lead to a communist society. That process would end exploitation and injustice, including the elimination of restrictive social classes and authoritarian governing structures.

Related to the issue of class consciousness is an interplay between objective and subjective factors in determining when a revolution would take place. Some interpreters of Marx's philosophy argue that a society would have to meet certain objective economic conditions before a socialist revolution could take place. Specifically, it was necessary for a capitalist mode of production to develop the economy to a sufficient level to meet people's needs before socialism could succeed. In the process, a highly developed capitalist economy would alienate the working class, which would then act to destroy capitalism and push society to the next higher stage of socialism. Only an industrialized working class, through its experience with capitalist production, could develop the consciousness necessary to be able to see the inherent contradictions in capitalism and the necessity for a democratic, socialist state. A competing interpretation is that subjective factors such as political education and organization of the masses were more important than objective economic conditions to move a society to revolutionary action. Those who emphasized objective factors acquired a deterministic view of Marxism that maintained that once capitalist development reached a certain stage, a revolution would inevitably happen, and it would be a serious error to push for revolutionary changes before those basic economic conditions had been met. It would be dangerous to move toward socialism before society could withstand such a transformation.

In contrast, a voluntarist interpretation of Marxism stressed subjective factors that contended that humans could create a socialist revolution even if the proper conditions did not yet exist. From this perspective, no preordained path to socialism existed. Some revolutionaries in Latin America echoed the words of the Spanish poet Antonio Machado that the path is made by walking. Fidel Castro embraced this idea in the Second Declaration of Havana in 1962, when he stated, "The duty of every revolutionary is to make revolution." Revolutionaries should not "sit in the doorways of their homes to watch the corpse of imperialism pass by." Others believed that both objective and subjective factors were necessary for a revolution. This appears to have been Marx's thinking when he wrote in *The Eighteenth Brumaire of Louis Bonaparte* that people "make their own history, but they do not make it as they please."

A common assumption and critique of Marxists is that they are economic reductionists who prioritize a class struggle above all else. A serious study of Marxism and revolutionary movements, however, reveals a more complicated story. Even while dominated by men and struggling with male chauvinist prejudices, socialist movements have long embraced ideals of the social equality of women and opposed the pervasive discrimination to which they and others were subjected. Early communist leaders included the German Marxist theorist Clara Zetkin (1857–1933) and the Russian revolutionary Alexandra Kollontai (1872–1952) who strongly advocated that women's emancipation must be central to the realization of socialism. From their perspective, women's equality required more than eliminating prejudices; it required elimination of the ruling class. Kollontai and Zetkin were critical of what they termed liberal bourgeois feminism that interpreted the struggle in individual rather than structural terms, as one of women against men. Instead, they maintained that working-class men and women shared the same interests and hence needed to join forces in a common struggle for liberation, including for the rights of women. Rather than ignoring gendered discrimination and racial oppression, or delaying its consideration until some indeterminate point in the future that may never come, they contended that a socialist movement must engage the battle on multiple levels. Historically, Marxist revolutionaries have taken the lead in combating oppressions in all of their myriad expressions.

In an essay in 1989, legal scholar Kimberlé Crenshaw famously introduced the concept of intersectionality to reference the overlapping oppressions that people who have multiple marginalized identities face. From her perspective, these "intersecting" identities cannot be separated. Black women, for example, are simultaneously affected by both their race and gender. Similarly, observers have long commented on the "triple oppression" that weighs down on poor, Indigenous women in Latin America because of their class, race, and gender (what scholars refer to as the "big

three" or "contemporary holy trinity"). A Marxist interpretation, however, understands these factors as addressing very different issues. Class is not merely another
type of identity, but instead a social relationship in the productive process that plays
out differently from racial prejudices and sexist practices. Along with other vectors of
oppression, including sexuality, age, and disabilities, they are distinct categories that
require different analytical approaches.

The sociologist C. Wright Mills defined four different kinds of Marxists. First are
the "dead" Marxists, who treat Marx's texts as a sacred authority with answers to all
of life's questions. Second are "vulgar" Marxists, who read for specific ideological
interpretations and extrapolate from those to represent Marx's ideology as a whole.
"Sophisticated" Marxists look to Marxism as a model for how to structure society
and mold Marx's nineteenth-century ideas to fit new situations. Even so, they find
Marxist answers for everything, and their rigidity can hinder their analysis, which
leads to a substitution of dogmatism for serious reflection. Finally, Mills defined
"plain" Marxists as those who work openly and flexibly with Marx's ideas within a
humanist tradition. They reject forcing real and lived realities into an ideological
straitjacket in order to conform to hard-and-fast rules.

Marx is foundational for an understanding of revolutionary theories, even as advocates have used and abused his thoughts in many different ways. Nevertheless, even
in the face of defeats of socialist experiments and with the resilience of capitalism,
Marx's critiques of the inherent shortcomings and contradictions of the capitalist
mode of production remain surprisingly relevant and prescient for understanding
the current state of the world.

Other Tendencies

In addition to these three trends (utopian socialism, anarchism, and Marxism),
in Latin America, left-wing liberals on occasion also joined forces with socialists
to press for radical reforms. Fundamental ideological divisions normally separated
liberals from leftists. Liberals emphasized individual rights, such as those expressed
in the 1789 Declaration of the Rights of Man and of the Citizen, from the French
Revolution, or codified in the Bill of Rights in the U.S. Constitution (freedoms
of speech, the press, religion, assembly, etc.). Leftists, on the other hand, believed
that social rights that benefited an entire community were more important than
individual liberties. These rights include access to healthcare, education, housing,
and an assured, adequate standard of living. A radical wing of liberalism, however,
recognized the importance of these social concerns. In Latin America, their agenda
included a condemnation of U.S. **imperialism**, a call for agrarian reform, protection
of worker rights, and nationalization of the means of production. Liberals embraced
a representative government as a positive force to implement a social agenda from
above, whereas leftists aspired to participatory governance from below and at the
point of production that would empower workers to formulate policies that would
be in their own interests.

In parts of Latin America, a fifth leftist influence was militant Indigenous (and sometimes Black) movements that fought against racial discrimination and economic exploitation (see the biography of Dolores Cacuango and the documents from the Ecuadorian Federation of Indians included in this section). This tendency occasionally predated other leftist movements. In areas of Mesoamerica and the Andes with sizable native populations, rural Indigenous communities had long engaged in struggles for land, ethnic rights, and their very survival. While some observers disregarded their actions as prepolitical, their lived experiences of discrimination and exclusion contributed to a heightened awareness and critique of the inherently unjust nature of the class structure. Their actions challenged Marx's European assumptions that peasants were inherently reactionary and that only the urban working class could form the motor to move society forward. In Latin America, Indigenous and peasant movements emerged in the context of growing labor unions and leftist political parties. Indeed, the rise of these rural movements was often closely related to, and reliant on the support of, other leftists and labor militants even as they influenced the character and demands of their urban counterparts.

During a period in which members of the ruling class typically manifested deeply held racist sentiments toward Indigenous and African-descent peoples, some communist party members constituted a rare group willing to defend their interests. These Marxists did not remain in urban areas removed from local struggles, nor did they manipulate events at a distance. Rather, they worked hand in hand with rural communities and workers on large estates to develop organizational structures and strategies to fight together to advance their common social, economic, and political concerns. From their perspective, the enemy was one and so was their struggle.

BIOGRAPHY: DOLORES CACUANGO, 1881–1971

Dolores Cacuango is one of the primary symbols of Indigenous resistance in Ecuador. She was born in 1881 on the Pesillo **hacienda** in the canton of Cayambe in northern Ecuador. Like most Indigenous peoples in the nineteenth century, she had to work from a very young age and never had the opportunity to attend school or learn how to read or write. When she was fifteen years old, the hacienda's owner sent her to the capital city of Quito to work in his house. She learned Spanish there, but the experience also raised her awareness of the nature and depth of racial

Dolores Cacuango, 1968
Source: Rolf Blomberg, Courtesy of the Archivo Blomberg, Quito, Ecuador

discrimination and class divisions in society. It led her to dedicate her entire life to a struggle for the rights of her people.

Upon her return to Pesillo, Cacuango began to organize hacienda workers, including a historic strike in 1931 that stunned the country. Cacuango gained renown for her fiery speeches, both in her native Kichwa and Spanish, that included demands to respect women and payment for their work on the estates. She rose to a position of leadership in the fight for land rights, the end of compulsory tithe payments to the Catholic Church, and termination of the domestic labor system that forced young women like her to work in the houses of the landowners. Cacuango understood the power of literacy and fought tirelessly for schools for Indigenous communities. She was instrumental in setting up the first bilingual schools in Ecuador. Because of her activism, the government threatened to exile her to the Galápagos Islands. A local priest attempted to bribe her so that she would stop leading protest movements, but she continued her work for a more just society.

Although Cacuango never learned to read or write, she memorized the relevant portions of the 1938 Labor Code in order to fight for the rights of agricultural workers. In 1943, in the midst of World War II, Cacuango formed the first rural anti-fascist committee. She served as delegate to a national anti-fascist conference, where she was singled out as a model for the rest of the country. During a May 1944 revolution, Cacuango led an assault on the army base in Cayambe. She used this political opening to help organize the Federación Ecuatoriana de Indios (FEI, Ecuadorian Federation of Indians), the first successful attempt to establish a national movement by and for Indigenous peoples. From the 1940s through the 1960s, the FEI flourished as the main national organizational expression of Indigenous and peasant groups. Cacuango dominated the first decade of the federation, serving in various capacities including as its secretary-general.

Cacuango brought rural struggles to the attention of urban socialists and gained their support for their movements. In exchange, the Partido Comunista del Ecuador (PCE, Communist Party of Ecuador) named her to their central committee, where she served along with two other women: the educator María Luisa Gómez de la Torre and feminist Nela Martínez. The government imprisoned Cacuango in 1958 for leading the party in Cayambe, but she continued her work after being freed. When she died in 1971, her fellow community members remembered her as a hero who inspired hope for a better future. Landowners, on the other hand, were relieved to be rid of one of the most memorable "agitators." Cacuango had justifiably gained a reputation as a troublemaker and remains as a symbol of a grassroots activist who made a difference in her world.

DOCUMENTS: ECUADORIAN FEDERATION
OF INDIANS (FEI), 1946

After the founding of the Ecuadorian Federation of Indians (FEI) in 1944, rural activists dramatically accelerated the intensity of their political activism. Cacuango played a central role in defining the mission and setting the agenda for the new federation. The federation dedicated its labors to agricultural workers who were bound to large estates through a system of debt peonage that bordered on enslaving labor even as the FEI attempted to give organizational expression to all Indigenous peoples in the country. The following two documents provide insights into how local grassroots activists translated larger political demands into immediate and concrete objectives. These documents are from the FEI's newspaper Ñucanchic Allpa ("Our Land"), which urban communist allies helped publish in both Spanish and Kichwa, the Ecuadorian variant of the pan-Andean Quechua language.

"Mission of the Ecuadorian Federation of Indians"

The creation of the Ecuadorian Federation of Indians is a result of the need to group together all the Indigenous inhabitants of Ecuador so that as a single block they will be better able to defend their rights.

The defense of Ecuadorian Indians is therefore the central mission of the federation. This work will in essence include the following:

1. Organization of the Indigenous masses into unions, communes, and cooperatives.
2. Ideological orientation of all affiliated organizations.
3. Promulgation of laws that favor the Indians.
4. Promoting the culture of Indigenous groups by all means possible.
5. Protection of Indigenous cultural values, especially in the arts.
6. Technical instruction of Indians, particularly in relationship to anything related to agriculture.
7. Raising the economic standards and improving the living conditions of the Indians.
8. Denouncing abuses and violations committed against Indigenous peoples.

The Ecuadorian Federation of Indians is slowly implementing all of these tasks. To achieve this, the federation has, as one of its most important and effective means of communication, its newspaper Ñucanchic Allpa.

It is of utmost necessity that the federation receives economic support so that it is able to carry out its work on a larger scale and so that Ñucanchic Allpa can appear on a regular basis. This support can only come from the Ecuadorian Indians, and especially from their organizations. For this reason, we request your financial help for the work in which the federation is engaged. Only with your determined cooperation can it successfully fulfill its noble and selfless mission.

Source: "Misión de la Federación Ecuatoriana de Indios," *Ñucanchic Allpa* IV, no. 18 (October 5, 1946): 4 (translation by author).

"Demands of the Ecuadorian Indians"

For Indians on haciendas

1. Fight so that landowners do not take garden plots away from their workers or reduce their size.
2. Fight to defend their rights to graze their animals and collect water and firewood for their own needs on the hacienda lands.
3. Fight so that the peons are not forced to work more than three days a week on the owner's land.
4. Fight so that women, noncontracted peons, and children are not forced to work on the estates. Their work should be voluntary.

5. Fight so that the daily wages of the contracted peons are not less than one sucre fifty cents a day. On other days, the salary should be three sucres. If the number of hours exceed the legal working day, they must be paid in accordance with the overtime provisions of the Labor Code.
6. Fight so that the salary of those who are not contracted peons may be higher than what the contracted peons receive and be paid in accordance with that paid in each region of the country.
7. Fight so that herders are not charged for the death of animals for which they are not responsible.
8. Fight so that workers are not charged for the shrinkage in the weight of grain due to the natural drying that occurs between harvesting and threshing.
9. Fight against the obligatory charging of tithes.
10. Fight so that administrators on the haciendas do not insult or mistreat the peons.
11. Fight for the provision of schools.
12. Fight for the provision of hygienic housing in accordance with the law.
13. Fight to ensure that they are not prevented from organizing.

For Indians on communes and in villages

1. Fight to prevent landowners from taking land and water from communes.
2. Fight so that the government addresses community demands quickly and fairly.
3. Fight so that tribes that have not yet formed villages are guaranteed the land necessary for their current needs and for their future expansion.
4. Fight for the incorporation of these tribes into civilized life and the creation of stable villages that favor the development of their agriculture and livestock.
5. Fight for the creation of a Department of Indian Affairs to help improve the living conditions of the Indians.
6. Fight for the increase and improvement of Indian schools.
7. Fight so that the Federation of Journalists intensifies its literacy campaign.
8. Fight for a campaign to improve the living conditions of the Indians, including provision of housing, healthcare, and public assistance.
9. Fight so that the government supports the formation of cooperatives, either on private or unused land.
10. Fight for the promotion of courses to provide technical instruction in Indigenous methods of agriculture and the raising of livestock.
11. Fight for the promotion of Indigenous manual arts (weaving, woodworking, clay, sculpture, painting, etc.).
12. Fight to encourage the development of Indigenous music, song, and dance.
13. Fight so that development banks provide credit, machinery, and tools to Indigenous communities.
14. Fight for the implementation of laws that favor Indians.

Source: "Programa de reinvindicaciones para los indios ecuatorianos," *Ñucanchic Allpa* IV, no. 18 (October 5, 1946): 3 (translation by author).

GENDER

Throughout the twentieth century, revolutionary leadership remained overwhelmingly urban, male, of European descent, and from privileged backgrounds. Often a good deal of sexism and even racism coursed through revolutionary movements, with leaders relegating women to secondary or domestic roles. Women were to participate in underground communications networks, shelter militants, feed political prisoners, and provide secretarial services, but all of these were an extension of traditional domestic roles. Some male revolutionaries subordinated women's interests to broader emancipatory objectives, or they assumed that women were inherently conservative. Others criticized feminism as inherently a liberal bourgeois value and ignored gender discrimination in favor of focusing on higher priority issues of class struggle.

On occasion, revolutionaries emphasized the need to denounce gendered violence (as well as racial discrimination) and embraced women's contributions as equal to those of men. Such activists recognized that socialism and feminism were not opposed to each other and understood the need to oppose oppression in all of its forms. A genuine social transformation cannot happen without the emancipation of women, Indigenous peoples, those of African descent, and others trapped in marginalized situations. A true revolution requires the conquest of their rights in all social spheres. Furthermore, these militants came to realize that a socialist revolution alone would not automatically result in their liberation, nor could they wait for the achievement of socialism to solve these immediate, everyday problems.

Integrating more women (and others of marginalized identities) into a movement was not sufficient to make a revolution, nor would doing so automatically lead to a feminist consciousness or a change in gender hierarchies. Women, Indigenous peoples, and those of African descent were not inherently revolutionary; just as with men, they could reproduce dominant ideologies. These activists also understood that simply incorporating women and others into capitalist institutions would not address underlying issues of exploitation. Instead, doing so would simply re-create and entrench existing class contradictions and assure the continuation of oppression. Gaining access to a bigger piece of the pie is not the same as liberation. Furthermore, because of their different positions within the class structure, not all women—nor all Indigenous peoples nor those of African descent—shared the same interests. A critique of class relations that is integral to a capitalist mode of production set socialism apart from liberal bourgeois feminism.

These concerns are not just a footnote to revolutionary movements even as they generally have not been adequately recognized. The incorporation of women and others shaped revolutionary ideologies and mobilizations even as revolutions slowly reshaped gender roles and expectations.

NECESSARY CRITERIA FOR A REVOLUTION

Many people assume that revolutions emerge out of oppression, but Russian revolutionary Leon Trotsky (1879–1940) famously observed that if exploitation alone caused an insurrection, the masses would constantly be in revolt. Rather, as historian Crane Brinton (1898–1968) argues in *The Anatomy of Revolution*, revolutions develop when a government is not able or willing to deliver on its promises, which leads to a failure to meet society's rising expectations. Sociologist Theda Skocpol argues that revolutions are not made but come when certain conditions are met. Political scientist Eric Selbin challenges that assertion and instead contends that revolutions do not just happen but are made as a result of leaders' conscious decisions and plans. While social and economic inequalities appear to be prerequisites for a revolution—and perhaps even a given in Latin America—these alone are not enough to move people to action. Human intervention, particularly in the form of leadership and ideology, is also necessary. Furthermore, even though socialist revolutions can acquire characteristics of a civil war or a mass revolt, they are rooted in a quite different process. Socialist revolutions require a vision and a plan for moving forward to a better future and are fundamentally different than fearful reactions against change.

Several factors are necessary for a successful revolution. These include:

Ideology. Some scholars present peasant revolts as negative reactions in which a dispossessed population seeks to hold on to the benefits of a quickly disappearing past. Socialist revolutions, on the other hand, are forward looking, with a program and vision for a new and better future. They have a coherent *ideology* and are successful when revolutionaries convince others to join in a struggle to implement those ideas. In Latin America, this ideology assumes a revolutionary discourse that is typically anti-imperialist and anticapitalist, and forwards a vision of a more equal and just society without class divisions. It advocates for changes in the political culture and includes influences such as **liberation theology**, which relies on religious reflections to advance social struggles. An ideology distinguishes revolutions from other violent affairs.

Leadership. Successful revolutions typically require charismatic, vanguard leaders who set agendas and mobilize and inspire others to support their vision and ideology. As human beings, these leaders often have complicated and contradictory motivations and sometimes can work to advance their own personal interests rather than those of the broader society.

Resources. Successful revolutions rely on the mobilization of significant organizational and material resources, both to challenge U.S. support for the previous government and to overcome opposition to the new regime. In an armed revolution, this includes access to weapons, through either capturing them from the local military or setting up networks to import them from outside the country. General strikes only succeed with organizational pressure. In the electoral realm, political campaigns require the mobilization of human capital and the distribution of propaganda. It is impossible to rally the population without access to resources as well as a hope that proper use of those resources will lead to success.

Discredited previous government. Revolutions only succeed with the collapse of a weakened and discredited ancien régime (the preexisting political system) that has lost popular support. Often revolutions triumph not so much because of external pressure on a government but because the current regime is rotten to the core and collapses in on itself. Personalistic regimes with a weak infrastructure are especially vulnerable. A new revolutionary government can then emerge in that political vacuum, with new and better proposals for how to structure society.

Other avenues for change are closed. Dissidents turn to extraconstitutional means to change a government when it *appears* that all institutional or democratic avenues are closed. It is not necessarily important that other avenues are actually closed. Rather, the revolutionaries must capture the narrative and create in the public mind the idea that a revolution is the best, and perhaps only, path forward. This includes the creation of what might be termed "revolutionary scripts," the transmission of revolutionary traditions, discourses, and practices that influence public perceptions of the political landscape.

Revolutions are rare events, and multiple conditions and factors must coalesce to create a suitable environment for the eventual success of such a movement. Revolutions are volatile and unpredictable, and their emergence, course, development, and outcome are by no means predictable.

DOCUMENT: ORGANIZATION OF AMERICAN STATES (OAS), "THE PRESERVATION AND DEFENSE OF DEMOCRACY IN AMERICA," 1948

The U.S. government has long employed anticommunist rhetoric to combat revolutionary movements. "The Preservation and Defense of Democracy in America" is a key document that codified this policy. It was unanimously adopted in April 1948 at the ninth Pan-American Conference in Bogotá, Colombia. That conference, which led to the formation of the Organization of American States (OAS), represented a pivotal shift in U.S.–Latin American relations, particularly with the onset of the Cold War with its intensification of opposition to communism. As soon as the delegates approved the resolution, U.S. secretary of state George Marshall left Bogotá, highlighting that his primary purpose was to gain its approval. Both the U.S. government and the Latin American ruling class subsequently exploited anticommunist paranoia to justify opposition to left-wing movements and governments that challenged capitalism's hegemonic control over Latin America.

Whereas:

In order to safeguard peace and maintain mutual respect among states, the present situation of the world demands that urgent measures be taken to proscribe tactics of totalitarian domination that are inconsistent with the tradition of the countries of America, and prevent agents at the service of international communism or of any totalitarian doctrine from seeking to distort the true and the free will of the peoples of this continent;

The Republics Represented at the Ninth International Conference of American States

Declare:

That by its anti-democratic nature and its interventionist tendency, the political activity of international communism or any totalitarian doctrine is incompatible with the concept of American freedom, which rests upon two undeniable postulates: the dignity of man as an individual and the sovereignty of the nation as a state;

Reiterate:

The faith that the peoples of the New World have placed in the ideal and in the reality of democracy, under the protection of which they shall achieve social justice, by offering to all increasingly broader opportunities to enjoy the spiritual and material benefits that are the guarantee of civilization and the heritage of humanity;

Condemn:

In the name of the Law of Nations, interference by any foreign power, or by any political organization serving the interests of a foreign power, in the public life of the nations of the American continent,

And resolve:

1. To reaffirm their decision to maintain and further an effective social and economic policy for the purpose of raising the standard of living of their peoples; and their conviction that only under a system founded upon a guarantee of the essential freedoms and rights of the individual is it possible to attain this goal.
2. To condemn the methods of every system tending to suppress political and civil rights and liberties, and in particular the action of international communism or any totalitarian doctrine.
3. To adopt, within their respective territories and in accordance with the constitutional provisions of each state, the measures necessary to eradicate and prevent activities directed, assisted, or instigated by foreign governments, organizations, or individuals, that tend to overthrow their institutions by violence, to foment disorder in their domestic political life, or to disturb, by means of pressure, subversive propaganda, threats or by any other means, the free and sovereign right of their peoples to govern themselves in accordance with their democratic aspirations.
4. To proceed with a full exchange of information concerning any of the aforementioned activities that are carried on within their respective jurisdictions.

Source: Pan American Union, "The Preservation and Defense of Democracy in America," in *Final Act of the Ninth International Conference of American States, Bogotá, Colombia, March 30–May 2, 1948* (Washington, D.C.: Pan American Union, 1948), 46–47.

CENTRAL AND PERENNIAL ISSUES

A series of issues underlay revolutionary efforts across the twentieth century and highlight ongoing fractures within the left proceeding forward into the twenty-first century. These ever-present tensions are not easily resolved, and engagement with these concerns characterizes the inherent dynamism that defines a successful revolutionary movement.

Reform versus Revolution

A key debate is how swiftly revolutionaries can or should make changes in society. If a revolution moves too quickly, it threatens to destabilize society, trigger a reaction, and risk losing the gains it had made. A negative reaction may remove a leftist government from power, eliminate its potential for making any further positive socioeconomic advances, and create lingering negative sentiments that make future progress difficult. On the other hand, if revolutionaries move too slowly, they may lose the support of those who are impatient to enjoy the benefits of a radical transformation of society. A slogan that some reformers have taken up is social evolution, not violent revolution, with the associated goal of realizing a permanent transformation of society without its destabilizing side effects.

Peaceful Roads versus Armed Struggle

The guerrilla leader Ernesto Che Guevara argued that one cannot make an omelet without breaking eggs, that a certain amount of destruction is an inevitable byproduct of a radical transformation of society. Chinese revolutionary Mao Tsetung famously observed that a revolution is not a dinner party but rather an act of violence by which one class overthrows another. More radical groups—such as the Shining Path, in Peru—believed that violence would help purify society, similar to John Brown's religious notion on the eve of the Civil War in the United States that the evil of slavery could only be purged with the shedding of blood. Others, such as Chile's socialist president Salvador Allende, contended that violence was entirely unnecessary to make fundamental changes in society and that socialism could be ushered in through existing institutions, an attitude that many communists in the post–World War II period also shared. Resorting to violence, from this perspective, shortcut longer and more complicated political processes and inevitably only contributed to more strife and instability without any concrete and positive gains. In reality, few give up their privileges willingly, and force may therefore become necessary to create a more equal society. Guevara thought that resistance to change from domestic ruling-class opponents and external imperial forces (such as that embodied in the document "The Preservation and Defense of Democracy in America," included with this section) was a strong indicator that a radical social transformation was taking place.

Institutional versus Extraconstitutional Means

While Allende and subsequent leaders, such as Venezuelan president Hugo Chávez, gained office via electoral means and began to implement socialist changes through existing institutions, others contended that elections only served to reinforce ruling class interests and strengthen capitalist structures. In *The Paris Commune*, Marx famously complained that elections were simply a way to select which members of the ruling class would misrepresent and repress workers in parliament. In a functioning electoral system, a conservative **oligarchy** is largely left intact and can undermine positive social reforms. Rather, the argument goes, revolutionaries should mobilize people on the streets to take power directly and eliminate any possibility of turning back progressive advancements. Marxists have typically been more willing to engage in electoral contests as a means to gain control over the reins of government, while anarchists favor a general strike to destroy capitalism at its roots.

Mass Participation versus Vanguard Leadership

Are political changes better made through mass mobilizations, or with a tightly focused and organized cadre that will lead the revolution to victory? A hierarchical and authoritarian structure can be much more efficient in accomplishing desired goals than the messy and chaotic method of attempting to work with the often-contradictory ideas of a broad range of individuals or interest groups, but that tactic comes with the danger of alienating the very people the revolution intends to benefit. This division between horizontal and vertical forms of organization lies at the heart of the rift between anarchists and communists. A movement's leadership is inevitably male dominated, which further distorts its perspective and priorities.

Role of the State

Related to the issue of vanguard leadership and an issue that also divides anarchists and communists is whether revolutionaries should gain control over government structures or destroy those structures. Communists argue that governments can be used to implement positive programs and that it is necessary to assume authoritarian methods as a transitory phase in the struggle against the entrenched opposition of those who benefited from the previous system. Anarchists, on the other hand, argue that governments are inherently authoritarian and prevent the realization of a more equal society. In interpreting Marx's ideas in a Russian context, Bolshevik leader Vladimir Lenin envisioned a "dictatorship of the proletariat" in which a vanguard only briefly takes power and imposes its will over the rest of society before state structures would become unnecessary and wither away. In practice, an individual or group that takes power tends to be reluctant to give up that privilege. Even among Marxists, ferocious debates proliferated as to whether entrenched leaders and political parties ruled for the benefit of themselves or in the interests of the broader society.

Urban versus Rural Base

Marx envisioned that a social revolution would first develop among the working class in the highly industrialized economies of Germany and England. Ironically, many of his ideas gained a larger following in countries peripheral to the capitalist mode of production. All twentieth-century revolutions, including those in Russia, China, and Cuba, emerged in countries with underdeveloped, precapitalist, and peasant-based economies. Dogmatic Marxists argue that successful socialist revolutions require the alienation that workers experience under advanced capitalism and that the shortcomings of these revolutions arose because society did not meet the necessary objective economic conditions to move on to socialism. Voluntarist Marxists disagree that revolutions require an urban working class and maintain that in Latin America, revolutionary movements should be rooted in rural areas where most of the population has lived and engaged in agricultural production. A related debate is whether a primitive communal, feudalistic, or capitalist mode of production prevailed in Latin America. Some contend that Cuba on the eve of its 1959 revolution, for example, was not a feudal but an advanced capitalist society, albeit with a rural proletariat that experienced alienation and gained a class consciousness through its work on sugar plantations rather than on an urban factory floor. From this perspective, Marx was correct in predicting the necessary objective conditions for a revolution, but in twentieth-century Latin America they occurred in rural environments that he could not have foreseen in his nineteenth-century, industrialized European world.

Class Alliances

Was the working class the primary motor for revolutionary change, or do intellectuals, professionals, and others also have a role to play in the process? Sometimes Marxists looked to bourgeois nationalists to develop a capitalist economy as a necessary precondition for a subsequent move to socialism. Many revolutionary leaders came from the ruling class but gained a social consciousness of the unjust nature of society and brought their privilege to bear in a struggle against their own class interests. Can these leaders be trusted to work on behalf of marginalized people, or will their contributions be inherently paternalistic and self-serving? On a larger level, Marxists have often struggled with the issue of developing a popular front to run electoral campaigns in alliance with progressive liberals against common enemies in the conservative oligarchy. The disagreement is whether to maintain an ideological purity or engage in strategic and even opportunistic alliances to advance common (and often short-term) goals.

Catholic Church

The Catholic Church hierarchy, together with military leaders and wealthy landowners, formed part of a trilogy that has dominated Latin America's social, political, and economic order since the advent of European colonization. After independence, a common, nineteenth-century liberal demand was for the separation of church and state. Anticlerical liberal reformers sought to roll back the institutional power of the church, which was deeply associated with colonialism and conservatism. Many leftists followed in this liberal tradition. The association of the phrase "religion is the opium of the people" with Marx contributed to an assumption that socialists were atheists, even though that idea predated Marx and his ideas on alienation are more complicated than the quote implies. Mariátegui found liberal anticlericalism to be a bourgeois preoccupation that distracted from more important underlying issues regarding the class structure of society. Furthermore, Central American revolutionaries in the 1980s turned to religion in the form of liberation theology as an inspiration for action. Debates over whether religion was a positive or negative force in society, including whether it could serve to enhance or retard liberatory struggles, were more complicated than what might initially appear to be the case.

Nationalism versus Internationalism

Should a revolution be led on a local level and in response to local conditions, or should revolutionaries fight against injustice wherever and whenever it occurs? In Latin America, socialist revolutions typically acquired characteristics of a nationalist revolt against outside (usually U.S.) imperialism. Militants appealed to nationalist images and historic leaders to advance their struggles. Others contend that the overwhelming power of capitalism and imperialism will inevitably defeat a successful revolution if it is attempted in only one country, and for this reason international alliances to build a global revolution are necessary. From the 1920s until its dissolution in 1943, the Comintern served this purpose, and leftists subsequently debated whether they should form a new international. Disagreements over joining an international revolutionary movement or struggling for national liberation in only one country divided the Marxist left into socialist and communist camps, with the former accusing the latter of receiving their instructions from Moscow rather than organizing according to local conditions and needs. On the issue of internationalism, communists tended to agree with anarchists who, as part of their opposition to governments and state structures, believed in the power of an international working-class movement. As Marx and Engels urged in *The Communist Manifesto*, workers of the world should unite because they have nothing to lose but their chains.

All of these complicated issues create challenges for revolutionaries who seek to implement their vision for a transformation of unequal and unjust societal structures. None of them has a simple resolution, but how the left engages them defines possibilities for success.

SUMMARY

This chapter has briefly charted the central social, political, and economic issues that Latin America has confronted and the struggles that the left faces to address these concerns. The Americas have immense natural resources, yet that wealth has not served the interests of the majority of the region's population. Observers commonly highlight factors such as poverty, corruption, and overpopulation to explain Latin America's underdevelopment. Instead, the chief problems that the region faces are persistently high rates of inequality, and these are related to an imperial extraction of wealth to the detriment of internal development.

Revolution is a broad and vague term to refer to movements that have sought to address societal problems. Beginning with the European colonialism of Latin America more than five hundred years ago, conditions of oppression and the exploitation of labor led activists to rise up in defense of their rights. In the twentieth century, these movements become ever more powerful. Latin Americans joined international efforts to reshape the world in a way that would benefit common people rather than a small group of wealthy and privileged individuals.

Revolutionaries employed many different ideologies to advance their goals. While a progressive or even radical agenda (in the sense of going to the roots of a problem) is central to defining a movement as revolutionary, these events also require other aspects to be successful. Revolutions need strong and charismatic leadership, access to material resources, a failed opponent, and the appearance that other avenues for a fundamental transformation of society are closed. Revolutionaries have had to engage a wide range of issues, including how fast and how best to transform society, how much to rely on authoritarian structures to achieve change, and what roles women, peasants, and religion should play in advancing a struggle.

Revolutions are inherently messy and complicated businesses. As the case studies examined in this book will demonstrate, one should not engage in the undertaking of revolutionary actions lightly.

DISCUSSION QUESTIONS

What role does the individual play in a revolution?

What are the relative strengths and weaknesses of basing a revolution in an urban proletariat or a rural peasantry?

Is nationalism a positive or negative factor in a revolution?

Does a movement have to be successful to be considered a revolution? What defines success?

Are social, economic, or political changes most important in a revolution?

FURTHER READING

A very large body of literature exists on theories of revolution. This selected list includes some of the more important works both on revolutions and on Latin American Marxism.

Becker, Marc, Margaret Power, Tony Wood, and Jacob Zumoff, eds. *Transnational Communism across the Americas.* Urbana: University of Illinois Press, forthcoming. A collection of essays that explore the connections communist parties in Latin America had with each other and with their counterparts throughout the world.

Brinton, Crane. *The Anatomy of Revolution.* Rev. and expanded ed. New York: Vintage, 1965. A classic comparative study of the English, U.S., French, and Russian revolutions. Originally published in 1938.

Burns, E. Bradford. *The Poverty of Progress: Latin America in the Nineteenth Century.* Berkeley: University of California Press, 1980. Argues that attempts at modernization in the nineteenth century underdeveloped Latin American economies.

DeFronzo, James. *Revolutions and Revolutionary Movements.* 6th ed. New York: Routledge, 2022. Broad sociological study of revolutionary movements.

Foran, John, ed. *Theorizing Revolutions.* New York: Routledge, 1997. Edited collection of essays with a range of theoretical approaches to understanding revolutions.

Galeano, Eduardo. *Open Veins of Latin America: Five Centuries of the Pillage of a Continent.* New York: Monthly Review Press, 1973. A classic work that condemns European colonialism for underdeveloping Latin American economies.

Goldstone, Jack A. *Revolutions: A Very Short Introduction.* Oxford: Oxford University Press, 2014. Brief but chronologically and geographically broad sociological study of revolutions.

Harmer, Tanya, and Alberto Martín Álvarez, eds. *Toward a Global History of Latin America's Revolutionary Left.* Gainesville: University of Florida Press, 2021. An edited collection of outstanding research on the transnational connections of revolutionary movements in Latin America during the Cold War.

Laforcade, Geoffroy de, and Kirwin R. Shaffer, eds. *In Defiance of Boundaries: Anarchism in Latin American History.* Gainesville: University Press of Florida, 2015. Outstanding edited volume of new scholarship on Latin American anarchism.

Liss, Sheldon B. *Marxist Thought in Latin America.* Berkeley: University of California Press, 1984. Encyclopedic treatment of Latin American Marxist thinkers.

Löwy, Michael, ed. *Marxism in Latin America from 1909 to the Present: An Anthology.* Atlantic Highlands, NJ: Humanities Press, 1992. An exceptional collection of Latin American Marxist documents, with an excellent introductory overview of Latin America's revolutionary tradition.

Mariátegui, José Carlos. *Seven Interpretive Essays on Peruvian Reality.* Austin: University of Texas Press, 1971. Originally published in Spanish in 1928, a classic work by a pathbreaking Latin American Marxist.

Marx, Karl. *Capital: A Critique of Political Economy.* 3 vols. New York: Vintage Books, 1977. A foundational theoretical text that presents a detailed critique of the capitalist mode of production.

Marx, Karl, and Friedrich Engels. *The Communist Manifesto.* London: Verso, 1998. A compelling statement of communist aspirations.

Prashad, Vijay. *Washington Bullets*. New York: Monthly Review Press, 2020. A short, accessible book based on a lifetime of study that paints a broad picture of U.S. imperialism.

Selbin, Eric. *Modern Latin American Revolutions*. 2nd ed. Boulder, CO: Westview, 1999. Applies classic theories on revolution to the Latin American examples of Bolivia, Cuba, Nicaragua, and Grenada.

Shaffer, Kirwin R. *Anarchists of the Caribbean: Countercultural Politics and Transnational Networks in the Age of US Expansion*. Cambridge: Cambridge University Press, 2020. A leading expert on anarchism paints a broad picture of transnational connections across the Americas and in the process provides an excellent introduction to the subject.

Skocpol, Theda. *States and Social Revolutions: A Comparative Analysis of France, Russia, and China*. Cambridge: Cambridge University Press, 1979. A landmark study that has become a theoretical reference point for subsequent studies on revolutions.

Young, Kevin A., ed. *Making the Revolution: Histories of the Latin American Left*. Cambridge: Cambridge University Press, 2019. An outstanding collection of essays that moves well beyond simplistic narratives to consider the roles of race, ethnicity, and gender and in the process contributes a much deeper understanding of the complex and diverse history of the Latin American left.

FILMS

The Baader Meinhof Complex. 2010. Red Army faction fights a guerrilla war against the rise of fascism in the Federal Republic of Germany in the 1960s and 1970s.

The Battle of Algiers. 1966. Dramatization of the conflict between Algerian nationalists and French colonialists that culminated in Algerian independence in 1962.

Burn! 1969. Depicts a fictional revolution loosely based on the Haitian Revolution under Toussaint Louverture's leadership.

The Comrade: The Life of Luís Carlos Prestes. 1997. Documentary on the legendary leader of the Communist Party of Brazil (PCB).

The Internationale. 2000. Chronicles the history of the song that was written in 1871 at the fall of the Paris Commune and later became the anthem of the communist movement.

Katherine (a.k.a. *The Radical*). 1975. Loosely based on the story of Diane Oughton, who joined the Weather Underground and was killed when the bomb she was building exploded.

Reds. 1981. Re-creation of the life and work of journalist John Reed, including his eyewitness account of the Russian Revolution and his efforts to found a communist party in the United States.

Rosa Luxemburg. 1986. Biopic of the revolutionary.

The Weather Underground. 2003. Documentary on the eponymous group that engaged in urban violence in the United States in the 1970s.

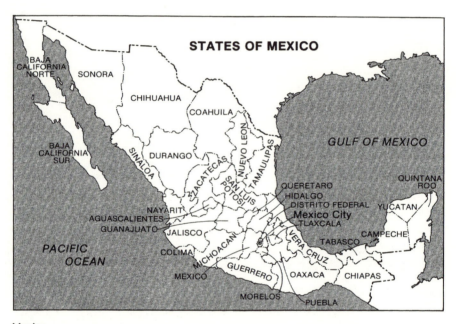

STATES OF MEXICO

BAJA CALIFORNIA NORTE

SONORA

CHIHUAHUA

COAHUILA

BAJA CALIFORNIA SUR

DURANGO

NUEVO LEON

TAMAULIPAS

GULF OF MEXICO

ZACATECAS

SAN LUIS POTOSI

SINALOA

QUINTANA ROO

QUERETARO

HIDALGO

DISTRITO FEDERAL

YUCATAN

NAYARIT

AGUASCALIENTES

GUANAJUATO

JALISCO

Mexico City

TLAXCALA

PACIFIC OCEAN

COLIMA

MICHOACAN

VERA CRUZ

TABASCO

CAMPECHE

MEXICO

GUERRERO

OAXACA

CHIAPAS

MORELOS

PUEBLA

Mexico

2

Mexican Revolution, 1910–1920

KEY DATES

1876–1911	General Porfirio Díaz's entrenched dictatorship known as the *Porfiriato*
1910	Francisco Madero's Plan of San Luis Potosí launches Mexican Revolution
1911	Emiliano Zapata issues his Plan of Ayala in support of agrarian reform
1913	Assassination of Madero
1917	Promulgation of a new constitution under Venustiano Carranza's control
1919	Death of Zapata in an ambush
1920	Assassination of Carranza; end of fighting
1922	Ricardo Flores Magón dies in the Leavenworth Penitentiary in Kansas
1923	Assassination of Pancho Villa
1926–1929	Conservative Cristero Rebellion
1928	Assassination of President Alvaro Obregón
1929	President Plutarco Elías Calles forms the National Revolutionary Party, the forerunner of the Institutional Revolutionary Party (PRI) that rules Mexico for the next seventy years
1934–1940	Lázaro Cárdenas's administration implements progressive reforms
1968	Massacre of protesting students at Tlatelolco in Mexico City
1994	The Zapatista Army of National Liberation (EZLN) launches an uprising in Chiapas
2000	Electoral defeat of the ruling PRI

The anthropologist Eric Wolf included Mexico together with Russia, China, Vietnam, Algeria, and Cuba as the primary examples of rural revolts in his classic book *Peasant Wars of the Twentieth Century*. Many scholars follow his lead in treating the Mexican Revolution, which predates Russia's 1917 Bolshevik Revolution, as the first great social uprising of the twentieth century. The Mexican Revolution is part of an autochthonous revolutionary tradition in Latin America. The revolutionary promises from Mexico provided a model and inspiration for social reformers elsewhere on the continent throughout the twentieth century. Scholars who argue for the domestic roots of Latin American political uprisings often interpret subsequent revolutions through the lens of the Mexican experience. In contrast, opponents point instead to outside influences to explain the appearance of revolutionary movements. During the Cold War, conservatives invariably blamed the Bolshevik example and the Soviet Union for unrest in Latin America.

Historians have long debated whether the Mexican Revolution was a social revolution, a peasant revolt, a civil war, a nationalist movement, a struggle for unrealized liberal ideals, or a mindless bloodletting. Most agree it began in 1910 with Francisco Madero (1873–1913) and his liberal Plan of San Luis Potosí that called for free elections in the face of Porfirio Díaz (1830–1915) and his seemingly entrenched thirty-five-year dictatorship. A popular uprising forced Díaz to resign and leave for exile in Europe the following year, but a decade of chaotic warfare continued in his wake. On Madero's left, Emiliano Zapata (1879–1919) and Francisco "Pancho" Villa (1878–1923) demanded deeper social and political changes. Zapata's Plan of Ayala called for agrarian reform and introduced one of the revolution's most noted slogans: "Land and Liberty." These peasant demands, together with a wide-reaching labor code and liberal anticlerical reforms that curtailed the power of the Catholic Church, were institutionalized into a progressive 1917 constitution. Many of these promised reforms were not realized until the 1930s under the Lázaro Cárdenas (1895–1970) administration, which is best known for nationalizing the country's petroleum reserves.

The Mexican Revolution was extremely violent, with one million killed in a country of only fifteen million people. Armed groups roamed the countryside, forcing people to join them as combatants, and the fighting displaced millions of civilians. Previously isolated communities came in contact with one another, which contributed to the sense of a unified Mexican identity. The revolution also transformed Mexico's economic system, as a new government broke up the large landed estates known as haciendas, where peasants worked in feudalistic conditions; nationalized the foreign-owned oil industry; established public schools; advanced workers' rights; and broke the Catholic Church's hold over the country. Nevertheless, instead of a worker and peasant government taking power, a new ruling class emerged that was dedicated to capitalism cloaked with a nationalist ideology and a **populist** style of governance. Despite its broad historical significance, the promises and potential of the Mexican Revolution were never completely realized.

PORFIRIATO

The Mexican Revolution overthrew General Porfirio Díaz's well-established government, the Porfiriato, which lasted from 1876 to 1911. Díaz rose through the political ranks as a liberal leader in the southern state of Oaxaca, one of the most Indigenous areas in Mexico. He gained national recognition when he stopped the advance of Napoléon III's French army at the battle of Puebla on May 5, 1862, a feat still celebrated as the *cinco de mayo*. The military became Díaz's principal avenue for social advancement. In 1876, Díaz overthrew the previous president, Sebastián Lerdo de Tejada, under charges that he was using fraudulent means to stay in office. Díaz then used the same systems of fraud and patronage to gain reelection seven times and remain in power for thirty-five years. The result was one of the longest dictatorships in Latin America.

In contrast to the anticlericalism of most nineteenth-century liberals, Díaz developed close relations with the Catholic Church and relied on conservative politicians and the ruling class to guarantee his political survival. Díaz governed with a positivist ideology that emphasized the scientific administration of the state based on the social Darwinist ideal of "survival of the fittest." This racist ideology argued for the inherent inferiority of Indigenous peoples and mestizos. Although Díaz was part Mixtec, one of the main ethnic groups in Oaxaca, he disparaged Indigenous peoples, who constituted the majority of the Mexican population. His government sold rebellious natives into slavery in Cuba or simply killed them. Díaz encouraged European immigration to "whiten" Mexico and powdered his own face to appear lighter in complexion. He believed only those of European heritage could lead Mexico out of its feudal backwardness and toward a capitalist modernity. The **científicos** who advocated this ideology found natural allies among foreign investors and the Catholic Church.

Díaz emphasized economic development as a mechanism to keep himself in power while simultaneously creating a large and expensive administrative bureaucracy based on a patronage system. He also used his control over the judiciary to deprive Indigenous communities of their territory. Wealth and land became concentrated in fewer hands, with the majority of the population suffering under impoverished living conditions. The large estates were inefficient and oriented toward the export market, causing domestic food production to decline. Workers labored on the haciendas in situations of permanent indebtedness, while those in textile mills and mines toiled long hours for low pay without the protection of labor unions. They were commonly paid in scrip that could only be redeemed in company stores, which further undermined their economic status. Diets for workers and peasants were inadequate and living conditions unsanitary, which resulted in high infant mortality rates and short life expectancies.

Díaz revised laws to make the country more attractive to international investors. Foreigners bought many of the country's landed estates and owned much of its industry. Railroad building boomed during the Díaz years, but foreign (largely U.S.) companies laid tracks to extract raw materials rather than to encourage internal development. Foreigners owned the telephone and telegraph companies, mines, factories, department stores, and petroleum operations. U.S. companies had more investments in Mexico than in any other country, and during the Porfiriato, those companies came to own more than did the Mexicans themselves. Foreign domination became so pervasive that Mexicans asserted the country was the "mother of foreigners and the stepmother of Mexicans."

Díaz's feared police forces (the *rurales*) viciously suppressed dissent, but equally important, Díaz used the mechanisms of a large (and expensive) government bureaucracy to gain popular backing. Those who supported him received awards of public office, land grants, promotions, and pensions. Díaz significantly reduced the size of the military so that it would be less of a threat to his rule and the generals who remained would be personally loyal to their leader. This dual strategy of *pan o palo*—literally, "bread or the club," implying a largesse for his supporters combined with a vicious repression of his opponents—successfully eliminated any significant opposition. As Díaz acquired more power, elections became farcical. With Díaz loyalists entrenched in political positions from the local to federal level, few possibilities for advancement existed for politically ambitious individuals. Despite the image of modernity that Díaz projected to the outside world, his government was rotten to the core and on the verge of imploding.

MAGONISTAS

The earliest and most significant opposition to the Díaz dictatorship emerged as a critical current within the Partido Liberal Mexicano (PLM, Mexican Liberal Party). The brothers Ricardo, Enrique, and Jesús Flores Magón were social reformers who founded the party to criticize the dictatorship for its lack of democracy. They organized a series of working-class strikes and uprisings against Díaz. Despite the name of their party, they were staunch anarchists who denounced governments as authoritarian, declared private property to be theft, and advocated violent direct action instead of engaging in electoral politics as the best way to achieve change. The Flores Magón brothers organized with the Industrial Workers of the World (IWW) and published a journal called *Regeneración* (Regeneration) in which they advanced their anarchist ideas. Facing persecution, the brothers fled to the United States, where they were promptly imprisoned for their political activities.

Ricardo (1874–1922), the oldest and primary leader of the three brothers, spent the entire revolution in exile in the United States. From that distance, his ideas of worker and peasant power influenced the ideology of other revolutionaries, who came to be known as Magonistas. In 1906, workers in the mining town of Cananea in the northern Mexican state of Sonora struck for higher wages and better working conditions. The U.S.-based owners of the Cananea Consolidated Copper Company sent in armed troops to suppress the strike, resulting in a massacre of twenty-three people, the injury of twenty-two, and the arrest of more than fifty. The workers did not achieve any of their demands, but the strike represented the emergence of vocal and visible opposition to Díaz's government.

From exile in the United States, Ricardo Flores Magón continued his agitation against the Díaz regime. In particular, on the eve of the revolution, he wrote an essay titled "Land and Liberty" that contributed a slogan to Emiliano Zapata's agrarian revolt. Francisco Madero attempted to include the Magonistas in his revolt against Díaz, but Flores Magón refused to join. The Magonistas viewed Madero as part of a "revolution of the rich" that was far removed from their anarchist ideals. Many supporters, nevertheless, viewed both through the same lens—as opposing Díaz—and eventually followed Madero when he emerged as the stronger leader.

In 1918, Ricardo Flores Magón was sentenced to twenty years at the Leavenworth Penitentiary in Kansas for "obstructing the war effort," a violation of the U.S. Espionage Act of 1917. His health deteriorated in prison, a condition that medical neglect exacerbated. When Flores Magón died in 1922, his supporters were convinced that prison guards had murdered him. Although the Flores Magón brothers were never incorporated into the official pantheon of revolutionary heroes, their anarchist ideology provided an important ideological influence for the radical left wing of the anti-Díaz opposition.

FRANCISCO MADERO

In a 1908 interview with the U.S. journalist James Creelman, Díaz indicated that Mexico was ready for a multiparty democratic system and that he would welcome opposition in the 1910 elections. The statement was only meant to improve his image abroad, but local dissidents jumped at the chance to remove Díaz from his stranglehold on power. Francisco Madero, a wealthy landowner from the northern state of Coahuila who had studied in the United States and France, emerged as the leading opposition candidate. Hardly a revolutionary, Madero favored social control that would allow capitalism to flourish. Madero championed a liberal democratic ideology and pushed for open, fair, and transparent elections. For him, democracy meant ruling-class governance, not rule by what he saw as the ignorant masses.

Recognizing the threat Madero posed, Díaz arrested and imprisoned his opponent before the June 1910 elections. As he had done in previous elections, Díaz rigged the vote and won nearly unanimously. The blatant fraud led Madero to conclude that peaceful electoral opposition was not going to remove the dictator. Against the advice of many of his supporters, he reluctantly decided to opt for armed struggle. When released from prison, Madero fled north to Texas, where he drafted his Plan of San Luis Potosí. The document made vague references to agrarian and other social reforms but primarily advocated for political modifications to the established system. Most significantly, Madero declared the 1910 elections null and void, proclaimed himself provisional president, and called for free elections.

With this plan in place, Madero returned to Mexico to launch a guerrilla war with the support of agrarian rebels, including Emiliano Zapata, in Morelos, to the south of Mexico City. After Madero's forces won decisive victories in May 1911, Díaz resigned the presidency and set sail for Europe. His reported parting words were, "Madero has unleashed the tiger; let's see if he can tame it." In 1915, the former dictator died peacefully in Paris at the age of eighty-five. Ironically, he was the only significant figure in the Mexican Revolution not to meet a violent death. With Díaz gone, in November 1911, the Mexican people formally elected Madero as president. Once in office, however, he faced intense pressure from both the left and the right. As members of the old regime blocked his policies, and popular demands for more radical reforms continued, his dreams of implementing a liberal democracy proved elusive.

BIOGRAPHY: EMILIANO ZAPATA, 1879–1919

General Emiliano Zapata in 1911, posing in Cuernavaca with a rifle, a sword, and a ceremonial sash across his chest
Source: Library of Congress, George Grantham Bain Collection, Bain News Service

Emiliano Zapata was the Mexican Revolution's leading advocate of agrarian issues. He was born on August 8, 1879, to a family that had long enjoyed privileged positions of leadership in their community of Anenecuilco in the southern state of Morelos. They lost their lands under the dictatorship of Porfirio Díaz, which led to a decline in their economic fortunes and social prestige. Recognizing Zapata's organizing skills, the community elected him to a leadership position in 1909. When legal negotiations for land titles with landowners collapsed, Zapata impelled community members to occupy their haciendas. He became an armed revolutionary, and his followers were known as Zapatistas.

On November 25, 1911, Zapata issued the famous Plan of Ayala (named after his local municipality). The declaration demanded agrarian reform, including a return of communal lands and **expropriation** of hacienda lands—without payment if the owners refused to accept the plan. The plan highlighted Zapata's most famous slogan, "Tierra y Libertad" (Land and Liberty), which he borrowed from, and which reflected the ideological influence of, the anarchist Ricardo Flores Magón. Over the next decade the plan became the guiding principle for Zapata's forces.

Zapata fought for the rights of rural farmers against overwhelming odds. With his prospects for victory declining and desperately short of weapons, on April 10, 1919, government troops lured Zapata into an ambush at the Chinameca hacienda in Morelos. Revealing their fear of Zapata's leadership and symbolism, they riddled his body with bullets and dumped his corpse in Cuautla's town square. Supporters refused to accept Zapata's death, claiming that someone else had taken his place and that he had escaped to the mountains. Nevertheless, with Zapata gone, the Liberation Army of the South began to fall apart.

After his martyrdom, Zapata became one of Mexico's most renowned and legendary heroes. The iconic image of Zapata dressed in a broad sombrero with a black mustache and cartridge belts across his chest appeared throughout the country. Contemporaries and subsequent scholars have alternatively interpreted Zapata as a common bandit or a social revolutionary. The distance between rural supporters who viewed Zapata as their champion and urban dwellers who denounced him as the Attila of the South points to persistent social divisions that run through the country.

Over the years, Mexico's subsequent political leaders incorporated Zapata into the pantheon of the country's revolutionary leaders, even though he most certainly would have opposed many of their policies. Although politicians invoked Zapata's name for a variety of causes, his image and fame gained renewed interest in 1994 when the Ejército Zapatista de Liberación Nacional (EZLN, Zapatista Army of National Liberation) launched an armed uprising in the southern state of Chiapas. Although Chiapas was isolated from the Mexican Revolution and Zapata never organized in that area, the neo-Zapatistas campaigned for many of the same issues that their namesake had fought for almost a century earlier. Paralleling the situation in Morelos, Indigenous communities in Chiapas had lost their lands to large landowners and faced a corrupt and repressive regime with a political chokehold on local communities. Zapata's slogan "Land and Liberty" summarized their ongoing struggle and highlighted how few of Zapata's dreams had been realized.

DOCUMENT: EMILIANO ZAPATA, "PLAN OF AYALA," 1911

Mexican revolutionary Emiliano Zapata drafted the Plan of Ayala in November 1911 as a call for agrarian reform in response to Francisco Madero's moderate Plan of San Luis Potosí. The plan denounces Madero for not following through on his promises.

> Liberating plan of the children of the state of Morelos, affiliated with the insurgent army that defends the realization of the Plan of San Luis, with the reforms that it has considered necessary to improve the welfare of the Mexican homeland.
>
> The undersigned, constituted into a revolutionary **junta** to support and carry out the promises made by the November 20, 1910, revolution solemnly declare before the civilized world that judges us and the nation to which we belong and love, the propositions that we have formulated to end the tyranny that oppresses us and to redeem to

the homeland of the dictatorships that are imposed on us, which are outlined in the following plan:

1. Considering that the Mexican people, led by Francisco I. Madero, shed their blood to reconquer liberties and vindicate their rights that had been violated, and not so that one man could seize power and violate the sacred principles he vowed to defend under the slogan "Effective Suffrage and No Reelection," thereby offending the faith, cause, justice, and liberties of the people; taking into consideration that the man we are referring to is Francisco I. Madero, the same one who initiated the aforementioned revolution, who imposed by governmental rule his will and influence on the provisional government of the former president of the republic, Francisco León de la Barra, causing repeated bloodshed and multitudinous misfortunes to the homeland in an overlapping and ridiculous manner, having no other purpose than satisfying his personal ambitions, his inordinate tyrant instincts, and his deep contempt for the fulfillment of the preexisting laws emanating from the immortal 1867 constitution written with the blood of the Ayutla revolutionaries.

   Bearing in mind that the so-called head of Mexico's liberating revolution, Francisco I. Madero, due to his lack of strength and complete weakness, did not bring to a successful conclusion the revolution that gloriously began with the support of God and the people, since he left most of the governmental powers and corrupt elements of oppression of the dictatorial government of Porfirio Diaz standing, which are not, nor can they be in any way the representation of national sovereignty, and that, being bitter adversaries of ours and of the principles which until today we defend, are provoking the discomfort of the country and opening new wounds to the bosom of the country to make it drink its own blood; bearing in mind that the aforementioned Francisco I. Madero, the current president of the republic, tries to avoid the fulfillment of the promises made to the nation in the Plan of San Luis Potosí, with the aforementioned promises being deferred to the Ciudad Juárez agreement; already nullifying, persecuting, imprisoning, or killing the revolutionary elements that helped him to occupy the high position of president of the republic, through false promises and numerous intrigues to the nation.

   Bearing in mind that repeatedly Francisco I. Madero has tried to conceal with the brute force of bayonets and to drown in blood the people who ask him, request, or demand the fulfillment of his promises in the revolution, calling them bandits and rebels, condemning them to a war of extermination, without granting any of the guarantees that reason, justice, and the law prescribe; taking into consideration that the president of the republic Francisco I. Madero has made a bloody mockery of Effective Suffrage for the people, and by imposing against the will of the same people, in the vice presidency of the republic, the lawyer José María Pino Suárez and by designating state governors such as the so-called general Ambrosio Figueroa, executioner and tyrant of the people of Morelos; and entering into scandalous conspiracy with the científico party, feudal landowners, and oppressive *caciques* [local political bosses], enemies of the revolution proclaimed by him, in order to forge new chains and follow the mold of a new dictatorship more opprobrious and more terrible than that of Porfirio Díaz. It has been patently clear that he has undermined state sovereignty, violating laws without any respect for life or interests, as has happened in the state of Morelos and other states, leading to the most horrible anarchy registered in contemporary history. By these considerations we declare the aforementioned Francisco I. Madero incapable of realizing the promises of the revolution of which he was author, for having betrayed the principles with which he mocked the will of the people in his rise to power. He is unable to govern and because he has no respect for the law and for the justice of the people, and is a traitor to the country, humiliating Mexicans in blood and fire because they want liberties, in order to please the científicos, *hacendados* [landowners], and caciques who enslaved us. Today we continue the revolution he began until we overthrow the existing dictatorial powers.

2. Francisco I. Madero is disavowed as head of the revolution and as president of the republic for the reasons expressed above, procuring the overthrow of this official.

3. We recognize General Pascual Orozco, second in command to Francisco I. Madero, as head of the liberating revolution, and in case he does not accept this delicate post, we will recognize General Emiliano Zapata as head of the revolution.

4. The Revolutionary Junta of the State of Morelos manifests to the nation, under formal protest, that it endorses the Plan of San Luis Potosí, with the additions that are expressed below for the benefit of the oppressed peoples, and will become defender of the principles that they defend until victory or death.

5. The Revolutionary Junta of the State of Morelos will not accept transactions or agreements until they succeed in overthrowing the dictatorial elements of Porfirio Díaz and Francisco I. Madero, since the nation is tired of false men and traitors who make promises as liberators and, when they come to power, forget them and become tyrants.

6. The lands, mountains, and waters that hacendados, científicos, or caciques have usurped in the shadow of venal justice will enter into the possession of the villages or citizens who have titles for those properties, of those who have been dispossessed of them by the bad faith of our oppressors—who keep the aforementioned possessions at all costs with weapons in hand—and by the usurpers who consider themselves entitled to them, to be decided before special tribunals that will be established upon the triumph of the revolution.

7. Because the vast majority of Mexican villages and citizens own no more land than that upon which they tread and are unable to improve their social status or be able to dedicate themselves to industry or agriculture because the lands, forests, and waters are monopolized in only a few hands, for this reason, a third of these monopolies will be expropriated from the powerful owners with previous indemnification so that Mexican villages and citizens can obtain **ejidos**, colonies, legal funds for the villages, or fields for sowing and working, so as to improve the lack of prosperity and benefit the well-being of the Mexicans.

8. Hacendados, científicos, or caciques who oppose this plan directly or indirectly will have their property nationalized, and two-thirds will be used for war reparations and for pensions for widows and orphans of the victims who are killed in the struggle to achieve this plan.

9. In order to carry out the procedures regarding the aforementioned properties, the laws of confiscation and nationalization will be applied as appropriate. The laws against ecclesiastical properties, which punished the despots and conservatives who have always wanted to impose on us the ignominious yoke of oppression and retrogression, that the immortal [Benito] Juárez implemented can be used as a norm and an example.

10. The insurgent military chiefs of the republic who rose up in arms to the voice of Francisco I. Madero to defend the Plan of San Luis Potosí and to oppose with force the present Plan will be deemed traitors to the cause that they defended and to the country, since at present many of them for a handful of coins or for

bribes please the tyrants and are shedding the blood of their brothers who claim the fulfillment of the promises that Francisco I. Madero made to the nation.

11. War expenses shall be taken in accordance with Article XI of the Plan of San Luis Potosí, and all procedures employed in the revolution shall be in accordance with the instructions established in that plan.

12. After the triumph of the revolution becomes a reality, a meeting of the chief revolutionary leaders from the different states will appoint an interim president of the republic, who will call elections for the organization of federal powers.

13. The principal revolutionary leaders of each state, in a meeting, will designate the governor of the state, and this high official will call for elections for the proper organization of the public powers, in order to avoid forced appointments that bring misfortune to the people, as with the well-known appointment of Ambrosio Figueroa in the state of Morelos and others, who condemn us to the precipice of bloody conflicts sustained by the dictator Madero and the circle of científicos and hacendados who have suggested this to him.

14. If President Madero and other dictatorial elements of the present and former regime want to avoid the immense misfortunes that afflict the country, and have a true feeling of love toward it, they must immediately renounce the positions they occupy, and by so doing they will staunch the grave wounds that they have opened in the bosom of the homeland. If they do not do so, the blood and anathema of our brothers will fall on their heads.

15. Mexicans: consider the cunning and bad faith of a man who is scandalously shedding blood because he is unable to govern. Consider that his system of government is seizing the homeland and trampling on our institutions with the brute force of bayonets. As we raised our weapons to bring him to power, we now turn against him for his lack of commitment to the Mexican people and for having betrayed the revolution he initiated. We are not personalists; we are supporters of principles and not of men!

Mexican people, support this plan with weapons in your hands, and bring prosperity and well-being to the homeland.

*   *   *

Liberty, Justice, and Law. State of Morelos, November 28, 1911.
[General] Emiliano Zapata [and other signatures.]

Source: Emiliano Zapata, "Plan de Ayala (1911-11-28)," *Wikipedia*, last updated January 26, 2013, https://es.wikisource.org (translation by author).

PEASANTS

Madero had stirred the passions of agrarian rebels who wanted the return of their communal *ejido* lands, and in office he grew increasingly repressive in the face of their unrelenting petitions. When Madero deposed the dictator in 1911, Zapata and others asked the new president to return communal lands. Madero, however, insisted on following institutional procedures and demanded that Zapata's Liberation Army of the South disarm. Madero, responding to his ruling-class interests and liberal bourgeois sensibilities, opposed radical reforms and encouraged his rural supporters to regain their lands through legal and institutional means. The agrarian guerrillas refused to disarm, arguing that they could achieve their goals only through military force. Zapata continued to confiscate estates and distribute land to poor peasants. His demand for more radical reforms led him to break with Madero.

On November 25, 1911, Zapata issued his Plan of Ayala (see the document included with this chapter) that called for agrarian reform and popularized one of the revolution's most noted slogans: "Land and Liberty." Zapata demanded that land stolen from Indigenous communities be returned and threatened that hacienda owners who refused to accept this would have their lands expropriated without compensation. The plan also denounced Madero as a tyrant and a dictator worse than Díaz because of his unwillingness to make the necessary deep-seated changes that the revolutionaries demanded. Zapata called for his supporters to arm themselves and continue the revolution by overthrowing Madero.

In the north, Zapata's counterpart Francisco "Pancho" Villa also demanded deep sociopolitical changes. According to legend, Villa became an outlaw when he killed a local wealthy landowner who had raped his sister. The lines between bandit and revolutionary, between criminal and political action, are not always clearly delineated, and during a war they blur even more. In contrast to the agrarian economy of southern Mexico, which was based on small peasant landholdings, large cattle ranches dominated northern Mexico. With fewer peasants and less demand for land redistribution, Villa advocated expropriating ranches and using the revenue to finance his revolutionary struggle. Although he was mostly illiterate, he supported schools in order to raise the standard of living and provide for more opportunities for his followers. Villa's actions in favor of the local population earned him a great deal of popular support.

SOLDADERAS

During the Porfiriato, women formed organizations that shaped subsequent developments. Working-class women founded associations that advocated for revolution as the best way to realize social change and improve conditions for women. Middle-class women, often primary school teachers, forwarded a reformist agenda that advocated for the expansion of educational opportunities to improve economic opportunities. Feminist organizations published journals that opposed Díaz's government and promoted women's rights.

Women participated in a variety of roles in the revolution, most notably as *soldaderas* who accompanied their husbands into battle. Although warfare is historically thought of as a male affair, women have long partaken in war. Military conflicts fundamentally altered their roles in society. Before the advent of modern military operations, women offered support services to male fighters that the military did not provide. Their roles included cooking meals, washing laundry, handling ammunition and other supplies, caring for the injured, burying the dead, and scavenging battle-fields for usable items. The word "soldadera" dates at least to the Spanish conquest of the Americas and refers to soldiers using their pay (the "soldada") to employ women as domestic servants ("soldaderas").

All sides in premodern conflicts used women in support roles, and their involve-ment in the Mexican Revolution was not unique. Elsewhere in the Americas, women who provided cooking, cleaning, medical, sexual, and other services to a premodern army were called *cholas, juanas,* or *rabonas.* Even so, soldaderas have become most commonly recognized for their participation with the insurgents in the Mexican Revolution. At this time, the meaning of "soldadera" shifted from "soldier's pay" to "woman of the soldier," and they were stereotypically seen as women of compro-mised moral standards. Soldaderas usually came from the working class or peasant communities, and their employment was at best informal. For many, it was their first experience with wage labor. Their pay and working conditions varied according to supply and demand. For men, joining the military provided an avenue for social advancement. Earning a wage and marrying an upwardly mobile soldier could also benefit women.

While some women were forced into servitude, others willingly accompanied the men into battle for the economic opportunities it offered, out of an ideological com-mitment to the struggle, or because of a lack of better alternatives. Association with a male soldier provided women with a means of economic survival and protection from rape and other abuses. Premodern warfare led to massive folk migrations as men were pressed into roving armed bands, leaving their families with no other op-tion than to accompany them. In a strict patriarchal society, it was difficult for single mothers to feed and care for their families without male guardians. It could be more dangerous for a woman to remain alone at home during an armed conflict than to join her husband in a war. If another armed band raided her village for supplies, she could be forced to provide domestic and sexual services to other men. Accompanying her spouse would be the surest defense against being raped by strangers.

Death rates during the Mexican Revolution were high. If a woman's partner, known in common parlance as her "Juan," was killed, she would inevitably be obligated to pair up with another soldier. In such a patriarchal society, it could be difficult and even dangerous to remain an unattached soldadera, but that reality hides other motivations that women might have had for joining revolutionary bands. Undoubtedly, as with their male counterparts, women might participate out of ideo-logical motivation, a desire for economic gain, a search for adventure, or an escape from the constraints of traditional village life. Although less common, some women became experienced combatants and, on rare occasions, even rose to positions of military leadership. Their multiple roles made the revolution possible.

During the Mexican Revolution, Pancho Villa came to see the women and children accompanying his fighters as a hindrance rather than a benefit for his cause. Sometimes more than a quarter of a military force could be comprised of women and children, and they interfered with rapid troop movements. Villa attempted to modernize his military forces, including providing for all of the soldiers' necessities in order to sidestep reliance on soldaderas. In one of Villa's more famous acts of brutality, one of the soldaderas was implicated in an attack on his life. When none of them would admit culpability or identify the culprit, he executed an entire group of ninety soldaderas. Villa was also a famous womanizer and rapist who left a large number of children behind in the wake of his "conquests." Reflecting his misogynistic attitudes, he told the journalist John Reed that he did not think women should have the right to vote. Zapata had a reputation for treating women better, and some generals would allow women to accompany their troops because it discouraged male soldiers from deserting.

After the Mexican Revolution, soldaderas were remembered in a variety of ways, ranging from heroic participants to parasitic camp followers or even as traitors. Whereas a "Juan" was a common soldier, a famous *corrido*, or folk song, venerated an "Adelita" as a brave and beautiful sweetheart who accompanied her male partner into battle. In contrast, "Juana Gallo" referred to a fierce fighter, and "La Cucaracha" was a derogatory term for a base camp follower. This final stereotype led the military to see women as the chief cause of vice, disease, crime, and disorder among their troops, and it sought to circumscribe their role. Given the levels of sexism and an entrenched patriarchal system, women had to fight hard to gain their proper recognition after the end of the war.

In addition to working-class participation as soldaderas, privileged women also actively contributed to the Mexican Revolution. Like the English social reformer Florence Nightingale, who is remembered for nursing injured soldiers in the Crimean War, wealthy Mexican women sometimes worked with the Red Cross. Professional women contributed intellectually to the revolution. Nellie Campobello (1900–1986) published a semi-autobiographical novel *Cartucho* ("cartridge," referring both to the ammunition belts Mexican revolutionary soldiers worn as well as the nickname of one of the book's characters), one of few chronicles of the revolution written from a woman's perspective. It narrates her experiences as a young girl in northern Mexico, and she published it in 1931 in part to vindicate her childhood hero Pancho Villa. Dolores Jiménez y Muro (1848–1925) was a schoolteacher, poet, and political radical. She admired Zapata, and her socialist convictions influenced his political thinking. The feminist Hermila Galindo (1886–1954) was a public advocate of the revolutionary leader Venustiano Carranza (1859–1920). Some critics complained that Carranza kept Galindo as an ally only to gain women's support for his political positions and aspirations. As revolutionary movements were inherently male-dominated affairs, women always struggled to have their voice heard and their interests represented in them.

BIOGRAPHY: HERMILA GALINDO, 1886–1954

Hermila Galindo
Source: Centro de Estudios de Historia de México (CEHM)

Among the most renowned women to participate in political debates at the time of the Mexican revolution was Hermila Galindo. During the war, she edited and wrote articles for the feminist journal *La mujer moderna* (The Modern Woman) as well as speaking to many women's groups. Galindo openly attacked the Catholic Church, supported sex education in schools, and demanded equal rights for women, including women's **suffrage**. She ran unsuccessfully for a seat in the Mexican congress and employed tactics that later feminists would use. Galindo was one of the most important voices to introduce new and radical feminist ideas into Mexico, and her activities set an agenda for subsequent generations.

Galindo was born in Durango in northern Mexico to a relatively well-off family and had the good fortune to attend an industrial vocational school in Chihuahua, something that was still relatively uncommon at the time. She learned accounting, shorthand, telegraphy, and typing and subsequently taught these skills to others. In 1911, she moved to Mexico City, where she became a public supporter of Venustiano Carranza and his campaign against Porfirio Díaz. Carranza brought her into his inner circle to rally support for his liberal ideologies. She represented his interests across Mexico and around Latin America. Although Galindo is remembered as a feminist, almost all of her activities helped in some way to advance Carranza's political agenda.

Even as Galindo campaigned in support of Carranza, Carranza also supported her crusade for the rights of women. Even though Galindo did not attend the assembly that drafted a new constitution in 1917 (only men participated), Carranza allowed her to submit a proposal for women's equality. She contended that if women paid taxes and could be convicted of crimes, then they should also be able to vote and run for office. Her arguments did not convince those gathered at the constitutional convention, and delegates refused to act on her proposal. Facing these barriers, she took matters into her own hands and in 1917 filed as a candidate for deputy to congress from Mexico City. It was the first time in Mexico that a woman had attempted to run for elected office. Even though some records indicate she won the election, officials rejected her bid on the grounds that the law only allowed men to hold public offices.

Galindo is best known for publishing *La mujer moderna* from 1915 to 1919. The periodical intended to advance feminist ideas, but as with all of her work, it also served as propaganda organ in support of Carranza. Galindo used the journal to express her disapproval of the Catholic Church and its attempts to control women. She urged women to leave their traditional roles in the home and become educated. Galindo was notorious for addressing uncomfortable topics that others did not necessarily want to discuss in public. She raised issues that others considered to be private, such as abortion, prostitution, divorce, and sexual intercourse. Galindo promoted sex education in schools and contended that a lack of sex education led to women's dependency on men and decreased their social mobility.

Galindo's activism encouraged Salvador Alvarado, the governor of Yucatán, to convene a feminist congress in 1916, the first one held in Mexico. Among the topics of discussion were education, social culture, public measures, identity, and, more broadly, women's rights. That meeting is credited with launching the suffrage movement in Mexico. Although Galindo did not attend the meeting, organizers read a speech she had prepared, and it caused quite a stir.

Galindo was not always popular, because she had the strength to state her views on unpopular issues that might otherwise have been ignored. Nevertheless, she addressed important topics and had the means and the energy to make feminist perspectives public and to bring them to the attention of other leaders. Although not always successful, Galindo was important in advancing a revolutionary agenda.

DOCUMENT: HERMILA GALINDO, "THE SUFFRAGE QUESTION: WHY DO WOMEN WANT THE VOTE?," 1916

Women did not receive the right to vote on a federal level in Mexico until 1953, but the issue had long been debated. In November 1916, as male delegates assembled to write a new constitution, Hermila Galindo published a strong call for women's suffrage in her feminist journal La mujer moderna. *The arguments are not unlike those that others have made, both in Mexico and around the world.*

The suffrage question may be called the battleground question of feminism. There are many men of good will who seem to sympathize with the feminist movement; there are many women of understanding who seem to be interested in the struggle for women's demands, and both are frightened of something inconvenient and antifeminine such as when the right to vote is mentioned. This is not strange, especially in Spain. Here, the words politics, suffrage, elections, voting, parliament, bill, royal decree, royal order, etc., etc. almost always mean something unpleasant, violent, immoral: despotism, cronyism, irregularities, cheating, intrigue, support of petty interests, flagrant injustice, dilapidation, deceitful oratory, buying and selling of opinions, insincerity, fictitious patriotism, selfishness, and, in a word, baseness. Those who think that women are a signifier of dignity and purity cannot understand that women should pretend to be interested in the petty and tragic game of governing and administering the country.

Why do women want to vote?, they ask with sincere and fearful amazement. And they cannot understand a female hand dropping a ballot in a ballot box. So low is the innocent piece of paper in the public mind that the woman's friends fear that just by touching it, her hands will be sullied.

And women, good housewives first and foremost, and as housewives who want the country to be as clean as the home, ask for the right to vote precisely for that reason: to get a little sunshine and clean air into the dark corners of the country's administration, to fight for the moral and material health of the country, to stop wastefulness, to put spending in order, to seek a more equitable distribution of resources that belong to everyone. . . . For another portion of other things, archfeminine and archmaternal: we have already agreed that women who love their homeland love it like a child.

In response to the antisuffragist arguments, I begin today to excerpt for you from the papers on this question that were presented at the Tenth International Women's Congress which we have already referenced in previous publications. The questions dealt with are two, namely: Why, from the threefold legal, economic, and moral point of view, do women need to have a share in national sovereignty? And secondly, what is the influence of women's suffrage on questions of hygiene, morality, education, etc., and what are the results obtained in the countries where they have the right to vote?

*   *   *

Why do women need to have a say in national sovereignty?

We often hear it asked with astonishment, sometimes mingled with indignation: Why do women need the right of suffrage? Do they not already have everything they need? Men make the laws, women make the home: their weakness is protected by men's strength; men's love spares them from rough contact with public life. They do not know what they are asking for when they ask for participation in government; they have much to lose and nothing to gain if they leave their sphere!

To these and other objections we respond:

Women need the right to vote for the same reasons as men; that is, to defend their particular interests, the interests of their children, the interests of the country and of humanity, which they often look upon quite differently from men.

To those who accuse us of wanting to go outside our sphere, we reply that our sphere is in the world, because what questions concerning humanity should not concern a woman, who is a human being, a woman herself, and the mother of women and men?

What problem, what question can be discussed in the world whose solution will not have an impact on women's lives, directly or indirectly?

What laws can there be that do not favor or harm her or hers, and therefore should not and cannot interest her?

The sphere of women is everywhere, because women represent more than half of the human race, and their lives are intimately linked to those of the other half. The interests of women and men cannot be separated. The sphere of woman is, therefore, wherever that of man is, that is to say, in the whole world.

The laws that govern and regulate marriage contracts, the rights of spouses, parental authority, are made by men, and are clearly unjust. Why should women not be involved in the writing of laws that decide the most important part of their lives?

Legally, the married woman does not exist. If in fact some wives have an important place in marriage, they owe it to their own exceptional merits or to the no less exceptional feelings of justice and love of their husbands; but the laws and customs seem to treat women as enemies, and not as mothers of the human race. And that should not be, because the majority of women are not superior women, capable of conquering the position that justly belongs to them by force of ability, but vulgar and mediocre women, as are vulgar and mediocre the majority of men. The exceptional cases are not included, and above all the laws should not take them into account, because the laws are made for the majority.

The woman especially needs suffrage rights, and she asks for it principally from a moral point of view because of the use she can make of the vote. She needs it imperatively to fight against alcoholism, against prostitution, against the criminality of children and youth, against pornography and all that demoralizes her children. She needs it to ensure hygiene and public health, to improve workers' housing, city life, schools, marketplaces, etc., etc., etc.

To this, some retort that not all women will concern themselves with these moral and social questions; that many of them will be utterly indifferent to the progress of humanity. This is true; but there are also an infinite number of men responsible for the same guilty indifference, and no one has thought of taking away the use of their right in spite of their incompetence, in spite of their alcoholism, in spite of a publicly immoral and depraved life. There will be indifferent women, but there will be many of enthusiastic heart and clear intelligence: all those who today would like to and cannot put their effort and their will at the service of their neighbors and their country. Through the influence of their vote, many will be able to tip the balance and obtain the just laws which they judge indispensable and which they have been demanding for so long.

Just as the human couple is necessary to give life to a being, in order to create an appropriate environment in which the being that has been born can fully develop, the woman is as indispensable as the man.

Ask men of all social classes in the countryside and in the cities, and they will tell you that a house without women is the worst thing in the world. And yet, these same men do not want to acknowledge that a municipality or a state without women is much more pitiful than a house in which women are missing, because, in a house, the evil falls on only a few individuals, but in a state, the entire population suffers.

For the individual and the collective to be complete, the first condition is that all the organs of the human body and of the social body function normally. A state without women is as reduced in functionality as an individual who has had an arm or a leg amputated.

People who have two eyes to see and two feet to walk diminish their possibilities of progress by insisting on seeing only through men's eyes the difficulties that must be solved for the good of all humanity, and to walk only with a masculine step toward the goal of perfection that must be achieved.

What is decided in public assemblies by the minority of one sex cannot be in the interest of the whole nation that is made up of both men and women.

Women, who are subject to laws, must contribute to their formation.

Clairvoyant men realize this, and every day the number of those increases who dare to propose the collaboration of women in the establishment of the social arrangement.

Considering this necessity, the Tenth International Congress of Women, placing itself in the point of view of the dignity of women and of the justice due to them, judging their intervention indispensable to fight in all countries against the evils of alcoholism and immorality, issues the following wish: "That in all countries women be granted the right of suffrage and eligibility."

However, in order to avoid too abrupt a shock to the state, the congress is of the opinion that this suffrage should be granted in stages and that it should begin with municipal suffrage, by means of which women will be able to prove their ability before claiming a broader right of suffrage.

Source: Hermila Galindo, "La cuestión sufragista: Para qué quieren el voto las mujeres," *La mujer moderna* 54 (November 25, 1916) (translation by author).

REACTION

Madero's legalization of labor unions and his inability to prevent peasant revolts alienated conservatives. U.S. ambassador Henry Lane Wilson favored political stability and economic development over democracy and henceforth threatened to invade Mexico to protect U.S. property. With Wilson's tacit approval and with the support of Mexican conservatives, General Victoriano Huerta launched a coup against Madero in February 1913. A ten-day battle (called the *Decena Trágica*) heavily damaged Mexico City and resulted in high civilian casualties, culminating in Madero's overthrow and assassination. Huerta's time in office ushered in a period of chaos and extreme political violence, with the conflict assuming aspects of a civil war rather than an ideologically driven revolutionary struggle. New weapons, including machine guns, brought an unprecedented level of carnage to the battlefield. Various armies moved across the country, drafting people and stealing food along the way. These great migrations broke through Mexico's provincial isolation and contributed to the creation of a national identity.

Wealthy landowner and former Madero supporter Venustiano Carranza merged the forces of Zapata, Villa, and Alvaro Obregón (1880–1928) into the Constitutionalist Army to fight the new dictator. Together, they defeated Huerta and forced him to flee the country. With their common enemy gone, the revolutionaries turned their guns on each other. Carranza wanted to construct a new and modern capitalist state. His rival, Villa, proposed more radical social policies, including land reform, labor rights, and education. For the next five years, the moderate and radical wings of the revolution fought each other for control of the country's future.

In October 1914, delegates representing Villa and Zapata met at a convention at Aguascalientes to unify their forces and drive Carranza from power. Together, Zapata and Villa occupied Mexico City. Zapata, however, was more interested in solving issues in his home state of Morelos than in governing the entire country. His alliance with Villa fell apart, and Carranza recaptured the capital. Under the impression that the United States was supporting Carranza, Villa raided the border town of Columbus, New Mexico. In response, U.S. president Woodrow Wilson sent General John J. "Black Jack" Pershing into Mexico to capture Villa. Pershing's pursuit was a fiasco, and Villa's popularity increased. Nevertheless, under Obregón's military leadership, Carranza gained the upper hand.

DOCUMENT: AMBASSADOR HENRY LANE WILSON TO SECRETARY OF STATE PHILANDER KNOX, 1913

On the ninth day of the tragic ten-day battle for control of Mexico City, Victoriano Huerta and Félix Díaz, a nephew of the former dictator Porfirio Díaz, met with Ambassador Henry Lane Wilson at the U.S. embassy. The three agreed to orchestrate a coup against Madero. Four days later, Huerta ordered the ambush and assassination of Madero—with Wilson's complicity and encouragement. Following is Wilson's message to Secretary of State Philander Knox at the State Department in Washington regarding his meeting with Huerta and Díaz.

File No. 812.00/6246. American Embassy, Mexico, February 18, 1913—midnight.

Apprehensive of what might ensue after the downfall of President Madero, I invited General Huerta and General Díaz to come to the Embassy to consider the preservation of order in the city. I discovered after their arrival that many other things had to be discussed first; but, after enormous difficulties, I got them to agree to work in common on an understanding that Huerta should be the Provisional President of the Republic and that Díaz should name the Cabinet, and that thereafter he should have the support of Huerta for the permanent Presidency. They thereupon left the Embassy to put into effect common order, which they had agreed upon for the public peace. I expect no further trouble in the city, and I congratulate the Department upon the happy outcome of events, which have been directly or indirectly the result of its instructions.

Wilson.

Source: Papers Relating to the Foreign Relations of the United States, With the Address of the President to Congress December 2, 1913, edited by Joseph V. Fuller (Washington, D.C.: U.S. Government Printing Office, 1920), 720–21, Document 836, https://history.state.gov/historicaldocuments/frus1913/d836.

1917 MEXICAN CONSTITUTION

Once in power, Carranza convened a constitutional convention and was subsequently elected president of the republic. The assembly debated many key issues of the revolution, including the roles of the church and state, property rights, agrarian reforms, labor policies, education, foreign investments, subsoil rights, and the political participation of Indigenous peoples and women. Carranza wanted a conservative document, but delegates drafted a more radical constitution that embodied the aspirations of revolutionaries who attacked wealthy landholders, the church, and foreign capitalists. Even though many of its provisions were only slowly, if ever, implemented, it was a surprisingly progressive document that influenced subsequent social reforms in other Latin American countries.

The constitution codified much of the revolution's nationalist ideology. In a reversal of policies from the Díaz regime, the constitution tightly restricted foreign and church ownership of property and returned communal ejido lands to rural communities. Even though Carranza did not invite Zapata to the assembly, the latter's Plan of Ayala influenced Article 27, which codified an agrarian reform program and claimed mineral rights for the state. The constitution's defense of communal landholdings attempted to propose a third way between communists, who favored state ownership of property, and capitalists, who argued that land should continue to be held in private hands.

With Article 123, the constitution created a detailed and progressive labor code that presented a lasting model for other Latin American countries. The Mexican labor code instituted an eight-hour workday, set a minimum wage, abolished company stores and debt peonage, established the right to organize and strike, outlawed child labor, and provided for generous maternity leaves. This lengthy article also expanded government powers over foreign capitalists, thereby laying the groundwork for the nationalization of natural resources.

Article 130 declared that the congress could not dictate laws establishing or prohibiting any religion, and as a result mandated freedom of religion and the separation of church and state. During the colonial period, the Spanish only permitted the practice of Catholicism in their territory, which left much of Latin America—Mexico included—with a strong religious tradition. The new constitution significantly curtailed the power of the Catholic Church over society. Marriage would now be a civil rather than a religious affair. Only Mexicans could be religious ministers, and they were prohibited from engaging in political acts, wearing their clerical garb in public, or conducting religious processions or outdoor masses. Other articles extended the constitution's liberal anticlericalism, including provisions in Article 3 that outlawed religious control over education, and Article 27, which restricted the church's landholdings.

The 1917 constitution was very progressive in terms of its attack on large landholders, the Catholic Church, and foreign ownership of the economy, even though the ideals written into the law were not always implemented. The constitution assumed a procapitalist perspective that protected the rights of private property even as it placed limits on those rights and sought to control, rather than eliminate, foreign ownership. In that sense, it was a liberal document that attempted to move Mexico from a feudalistic to a capitalist economy, rather than a communist manifesto that envisioned socializing the means of production. Nevertheless, it was forward-looking and influenced the ideology of future revolutions in Latin America. Notably, the constitution was drafted before the Bolsheviks came to power in Russia, which highlights the importance of internal rather than external factors in Latin America's revolutionary tradition.

While progressive in many aspects, the constitution subjugated women's rights to the expansion of land and labor rights. Furthermore, while conservative delegates in the all-male constitutional assembly had favored giving women the right to vote out of an assumption that they would support their interests, liberals and leftists opposed that provision out of fear that doing so would strengthen the church's influence in society. Meanwhile, feminists had met in a congress in the frontier state of Yucatán a year before the constitutional convention met. Three positions emerged in the meeting, and they characterized ideological divisions throughout the first half of the twentieth century. Conservative Catholic women wanted to maintain their traditional roles as wives and mothers. Moderate liberal women believed that expanding educational opportunities was the best way to gain political and civic rights. Leftist radicals advocated for treating women equally in all aspects of life, including access to the franchise. Although the constitution expanded women's legal and social rights, it limited citizenship rights, including suffrage and holding office, to men.

AFTERMATHS

In May 1917, Carranza assumed power under the new constitution as the first constitutionally elected president since Madero. Two years later, he rid himself of one of his primary enemies by killing Zapata. Carranza had moved significantly to the right by then and attempted to manipulate the electoral apparatus to remain in power. In response, Obregón, who had become more liberal, overthrew Carranza, who was then killed in an ambush. With Carranza gone, Obregón won the 1920 elections and made concessions that largely brought the ten years of fighting to an end.

With the war over, Villa retired to a comfortable estate in the northern state of Chihuahua. As a result of the revolution, he had transitioned from a landless peon to a powerful landowner. In 1923, Villa was assassinated in an attack that seemed to trace back to old feuds between revolutionary leaders. Neither the identity of his assassins nor their motivation was ever clearly established.

In the first peaceful transfer of power since the revolution began, Plutarco Elías Calles (1877–1945) became president in 1924. His time in office witnessed increased conflict between the government and the church hierarchy, leading to the 1926–1929 Cristero Rebellion. In reaction to the constitution's vast anticlerical provisions, priests went on strike and refused to celebrate masses, perform baptisms, or provide last rites for the dying. Conservative guerrilla bands organized under the slogan "¡Viva Cristo Rey!" (Long Live Christ the King!). In opposition to the new public socialist education system, they burned government schools and killed teachers. In retaliation, the government killed one priest for every dead teacher. The military looted churches and converted them into stables. Similar to the previous decade's soldaderas, women's brigades played a crucial role in sustaining the Catholic army. The conflict culminated with a Cristero partisan assassinating Obregón, who had been reelected president in 1928, before he could take office.

Facing endless violence that seemed to be claiming the lives of all the revolutionary leaders, politicians devised a system that would ensure their continued hold on power. In 1929, Calles formed the National Revolutionary Party, the forerunner of the Partido Revolucionario Institucional (PRI, Institutional Revolutionary Party), which ruled Mexico for the next seventy years. The consolidation of a new political party allowed revolutionary general Lázaro Cárdenas to ascend to the presidency. During his time in office (1934–1940), Cárdenas not only implemented progressive agrarian and social reforms but also consolidated his control over the country. The first significant distribution of land occurred under his government. In what some view as the high point of the revolution, in 1938 Cárdenas used the provisions of the

1917 constitution to nationalize Standard Oil and other foreign companies and establish the government-owned Petróleos Mexicanos (PEMEX, Mexican Petroleum). By the time Cárdenas handed power to his conservative successor Manuel Ávila Camacho, the governing party had formed a corporate state that held more absolute control than even Díaz had at the height of his power.

The government introduced successful reforms in education and healthcare and created political stability, but for many marginalized peoples, the revolution brought few changes. Indigenous peasants were still confronted with authoritarian political structures and rampant racial discrimination. For all the effort women put into the Mexican Revolution, as soldaderas as well as in other roles, they ultimately had little to show for their involvement. The military expelled women from the army at the end of the war and, in 1925, banned them from their barracks altogether. Soldaderas engaged in a protracted battle for the recognition and pensions that their male counterparts enjoyed. Many liberal men had long feared women as a conservative force in society with the perception that they fell under the undue influence of the Catholic Church. As a result, in the anticlerical atmosphere of the postwar period, women did not receive suffrage rights on a federal level until 1953 (although the franchise came sooner on a local level, particularly in frontier regions). Even with these limitations, the revolution fundamentally changed the lives of many women. The disruptions of war provided women with a perspective of a society that extended beyond their family, village, and church. Some women emerged more empowered, which led to rebellions against arranged marriages and for access to more educational and economic opportunities. Although the revolution delivered little in terms of tangible gains for women, it did contribute to growing demands for equality.

The failures of the 1910 Mexican Revolution led to ongoing social protest, most notably as exhibited in a neo-Zapatista revolt in the impoverished southern state of Chiapas. On January 1, 1994, as the North American Free Trade Agreement (NAFTA) that was to eliminate trade barriers between Canada, the United States, and Mexico came into force, the launch of the guerrilla war caught the world by surprise. The EZLN announced its opposition to neoliberal economic policies that favored the wealthy to the detriment of marginalized Maya farmers. Under the leadership of the charismatic, masked Subcomandante Marcos, the EZLN conceptualized the struggle as a continuation of that which its namesake, Emiliano Zapata, had launched at the beginning of the twentieth century.

INTERPRETING THE REVOLUTION

Scholars disagree on when the Mexican Revolution ended or on whether it is still an ongoing process. For some, the drafting of the 1917 constitution marks the revolution's culmination. Those who view revolution as a military action rather than the consolidation of an ideological agenda consider the cessation of hostilities in 1920 as the endpoint. Others point to 1940, when, after a period of deep social reforms, the progressive Cárdenas passed power to the conservative Ávila Camacho. The new government largely terminated the revolution's social policies, though not necessarily its populist rhetoric. For others, a massacre of protesting students at Tlatelolco in Mexico City on the eve of the 1968 Summer Olympics demonstrated that Mexico had left its revolutionary heritage behind. In political terms, the electoral defeat of the ruling PRI at the hands of the conservative Partido Acción Nacional (PAN, National Action Party) in 2000 brought an end to the hegemonic legacy of the early revolutionaries. Nonetheless, some contend that Mexico continues to be shaped by various legacies of the 1910 popular uprising against Porfirio Díaz's dictatorship and that the revolution is an interrupted or still-ongoing process.

The Mexican Revolution was a seemingly chaotic, incoherent series of events, leading scholars to interpret it in a myriad of ways. It had aspects of a struggle for unrealized liberal ideals, a seemingly meaningless rebellion, a civil war, a nationalist movement, a peasant revolt, or a failed social revolution. These historiographic debates are ongoing and likely will never be resolved.

Liberal Movement

Those who see the revolution as a liberal bourgeois reform movement emphasize Madero's initial goals of democracy, an embrace of individual liberties, and the positive outcomes of social reforms, such as expanded access to education. Many of these liberal aspects were embodied in the 1917 constitution, particularly in its anticlerical provisions, which were the most restrictive anywhere in a historically Catholic region. Another liberal reform was to professionalize and depoliticize the military and place it under civilian control. The government curtailed military expenditures to the point where Mexico had one of the smallest armies in Latin America. In contrast to Porfirio Díaz, after Cárdenas's presidency no military leader would leverage personal renown gained from military exploits into a position of political power.

Great Rebellion

Historian Ramón Eduardo Ruiz refuses to call the events in Mexico a revolution but instead labels it a "great rebellion" that pitted rebel factions against each other for control of the country. Leaders, including Madero, Zapata, Villa, Carranza, and Obregón, fought each other because they did not have a unified plan. The result was a disorganized rebellion rather than a revolution with a coherent ideology. At best, one faction of the bourgeoisie simply replaced another as the owners of the means of production. The winners only wanted a larger share of the spoils rather than the outright destruction of capitalism. As evidence that it failed to rise to the level of a revolution, Ruiz points out that the 1917 constitution is best understood as codifying nineteenth-century liberal ideals that stressed continuity over radical change. It merely affirmed the principles of private property and the sacred rights of the individual that were already present in Juárez's 1857 liberal constitution. The great expenditure of lives ultimately accomplished or changed little.

Civil War

The level of violence and seeming lack of ideology that led parties to change sides to gain the upper hand have led some to interpret the events as little more than a civil war that devolved into a particularly senseless bloodbath. During the fighting, novelist Mariano Azuela published *Los de abajo* (*The Underdogs*), which became the most famous novel of the revolution. The story is based on the author's experiences with Villa and paints a rather dismal picture of the lack of changes that came out of these events. Toward the end of the novel, Azuela writes, "If a man has a rifle in his hands and a belt full of cartridges, surely he should use them. That means fighting. Against whom? For whom? This is scarcely a matter of importance." His protagonist proclaims, "Villa? Obregón? Carranza? What's the difference? I love the revolution like a volcano in eruption; I love the volcano because it's a volcano, the revolution because it's the revolution! What do I care about the stones left above or below after the cataclysm? What are they to me?" Although Azuela captures the brutality of the war, those who would argue it was a nationalist movement, a peasant revolt, or a failed socialist revolution would disagree with his nihilistic portrayal of events.

Nationalist Movement

Some scholars see the revolution as a nationalist movement and point to attacks on foreign economic ownership as evidence of its anti-imperialist aspects. From this perspective, the high point of the revolution came in the 1930s with Cárdenas's nationalization of Standard Oil—well after the fighting had ceased. The March 18, 1938, decree that expropriated seventeen companies became a cause célèbre throughout Latin America. Many scholars and activists embraced the confiscation as a declaration of economic independence from the United States that they wished to replicate in their own countries.

Peasant Revolt

Anthropologist Eric Wolf interprets the Mexican events as a peasant revolt. A key question is whether the protagonists were looking forward to positive social changes or gazing back to an idyllic and highly romanticized past that never existed. For agrarianists such as Zapata, a key demand was for rural communities to regain control over their communal ejido territories. Was this an attempt by Indigenous communities to cling to a quickly disappearing past? Or was it an effort to define a better future that would benefit the masses rather than a small number of wealthy landholders? Many disagree on whether Mexico's economy on the eve of the uprising was feudalist or capitalist and on whether the necessary objective economic conditions were present for a socialist revolution.

Failed Socialist Revolution

Others argue that Mexico indeed did experience a revolution, although it was a liberal bourgeois democratic revolution that, some Marxists argue, is a necessary precondition for a socialist revolution. Unlike those who see it as a peasant revolt, Marxists portray Porfirio Díaz's regime as leading to the consolidation of capitalism and not as a period of semifeudalism. From this perspective, the revolution represented the victory of a middle-class bourgeoisie and the development of capitalism. Alternatively, the events could be interpreted as an aborted or unfulfilled proletarian revolution, because the workers and peasants lacked the advanced class consciousness necessary to achieve positive social changes. In this case, it was a failed socialist revolution in which a class struggle attempted but failed to alter the mode of production. Through this lens, the progressive aspects of land and labor reforms in Articles 27 and 123 of the 1917 constitution are seen as attempts to advance a socialist agenda rather than to codify liberal ideals or embrace nationalist sentiments. The scholar Adolfo Gilly retains an optimistic tone in that he interprets the events as an interrupted but ultimately not defeated revolution. He presents Zapata's peasant army as the vanguard of socialism and argues that his assassination in 1919 did not end but merely delayed a longer political process. Eventually, the peasant and worker masses will break free and conclude the revolution.

SUMMARY

Even though the Mexican Revolution has been commonly included in the pantheon of significant twentieth-century revolutions, historians continue to debate interpretations of what these events mean. The revolution began as a revolt against an authoritarian government and ended with an entrenched one-party state that held more power than Porfirio Díaz ever could have imagined. The revolution expressed the aspirations of peasants who had lost their land base, but they failed to achieve a socialist transformation of society. Women and others made great sacrifices but received little reward for their efforts. The violence killed one million people and resulted in extensive destruction, but the fighting also contributed to the birth of a modern Mexican identity. Heroes such as Emiliano Zapata emerged out of the war, even though few of their goals had been achieved. Nevertheless, the revolution, and particularly its codification in the 1917 constitution, created a model that subsequent revolutionaries throughout Latin America sought to emulate.

DISCUSSION QUESTIONS

Was it necessary to use violence to remove Díaz from power?

Was mass discontent or charismatic leadership more important in determining the direction of the Mexican Revolution?

Was the Mexican Revolution a peasant reaction against the modernizing encroachment of capitalism, or a social revolution that envisioned a better future?

Was the Mexican Revolution a democratic or social revolution?

In what ways was the Mexican Revolution a true revolution?

FURTHER READING

More historical works have been published on Mexico than on any other Latin American country, and many of these focus on the Mexican Revolution. Newer works challenge interpretations presented in older works. The list below includes classic works on which subsequent interpretations build.

Azuela, Mariano. *The Underdogs: A Novel of the Mexican Revolution.* New York: Penguin, 1963. Based on the author's experiences fighting with Pancho Villa and originally published during the war, this novel paints a vivid but dismal picture of the revolution.

Baitenmann, Helga. *Matters of Justice: Pueblos, Agrarian Reform, and Judiciary in Revolutionary Mexico.* Lincoln: University of Nebraska Press, 2020. A detailed comparison of Emiliano Zapata's and Venustiano Carranza's competing agrarian reform programs, contending that they favored liberal notions of private property rather than cooperative, communalist, socialist, or anarchist solutions.

Flores Magón, Ricardo. *Land and Liberty: Anarchist Influences in the Mexican Revolution.* Montreal: Black Rose Books, 1977. A collection of writings of the leading anarchist in the Mexican Revolution.

Gilly, Adolfo. *The Mexican Revolution.* New York: New Press, 2005. A stirring, bottom-up account that argues that the revolution was interrupted and failed to achieve its socialist goals.

Joseph, Gilbert M., and Jürgen Buchenau. *Mexico's Once and Future Revolution: Social Upheaval and the Challenge of Rule since the Late Nineteenth Century.* Durham, NC: Duke University Press, 2014. A broad introductory survey of the revolution.

Katz, Friedrich. *The Life and Times of Pancho Villa.* Stanford, CA: Stanford University Press, 1998. Lengthy and masterful biography of one of the main peasant leaders of the revolution.

Knight, Alan. *The Mexican Revolution.* 2 vols. Cambridge: Cambridge University Press, 1986. An ambitious, comprehensive, excellent synthesis of the Mexican Revolution.

Mitchell, Stephanie, and Patience A. Schell, eds. *The Women's Revolution in Mexico, 1910–1953.* Lanham, MD: Rowman & Littlefield Publishers, 2007. Collection of essays that delves beyond stereotypes to explore what the Mexican Revolution meant to women.

Olcott, Jocelyn, Mary K. Vaughan, and Gabriela Cano, eds. *Sex in Revolution: Gender, Politics, and Power in Modern Mexico.* Durham, NC: Duke University Press, 2006. Collection of essays that draws on decades of feminist scholarship to place women at the center of state formation in Mexico.

Purnell, Jennie. *Popular Movements and State Formation in Revolutionary Mexico: The Agraristas and Cristeros of Michoacán.* Durham, NC: Duke University Press, 1999. A key work on the 1926–1929 Cristero Rebellion.

Ruiz, Ramón Eduardo. *The Great Rebellion: Mexico, 1905–1924.* New York: Norton, 1980. Argues that the events in Mexico did not rise to the level of revolution.

Salas, Elizabeth. *Soldaderas in the Mexican Military: Myth and History*. Austin: University of Texas Press, 1990. Fascinating study that challenges the stereotypes of the roles women played in the Mexican Revolution.

Wolf, Eric R. *Peasant Wars of the Twentieth Century*. New York: Harper & Row, 1969. Includes a chapter that presents the Mexican Revolution as a peasant revolt.

Womack, John, Jr. *Zapata and the Mexican Revolution*. New York: Vintage, 1968. A classic work that examines the Mexican Revolution from the perspective of Emiliano Zapata and the peasants of Morelos.

FILMS

And Starring Pancho Villa as Himself. 2004. The story of how Mexican revolutionary Pancho Villa allowed a Hollywood crew under the leadership of D. W. Griffith (of *Birth of a Nation* fame) to film him in battle, altering the course of film and military history in the process.

Mexico in Flames. 1982. A chronicle of the Russian and Mexican revolutions in the early twentieth century.

Mexico, Part 1: Revolution, 1910–1940. 1989. A PBS/WGBH documentary that provides a narrative overview of the Mexican Revolution.

Viva Villa! 1934. An early Hollywood depiction of Pancho Villa in the Mexican Revolution.

Viva Zapata! 1952. Marlon Brando stars as Emiliano Zapata in a classic Cold War–era Hollywood film on the Mexican Revolution.

Guatemala

3

Guatemalan Spring, 1944–1954

KEY DATES

1820	Atanasio Tzul crowned king of the K'iche'
1821–1838	Guatemala made capital of the United Provinces of Central America
1838–1865	Conservative Rafael Carrera rules Guatemala
1872–1885	Liberal Justo Rufino Barrios rules Guatemala
1898–1920	Liberal Manuel Estrada Cabrera rules Guatemala
1902	United Fruit Company arrives in Guatemala
1931–1944	Liberal Jorge Ubico rules Guatemala
July 1, 1944	Ubico resigns, opening the way to the Guatemalan Spring
October 20, 1944	October Revolution establishes a progressive provisional government
March 11, 1945	Promulgation of new constitution
March 15, 1945	Inauguration of Juan José Arévalo as president
February 8, 1947	Promulgation of labor code
November 11, 1950	Jacobo Arbenz Guzmán elected president
June 17, 1952	Land reform (Decree 900) redistributes large landholdings
December 1953– July 1954	CIA's Operation PBSUCCESS to remove communist influence from Guatemalan government
June 16, 1954	Colonel Carlos Castillo Armas launches military coup against Arbenz's elected government
June 27, 1954	Arbenz resigns presidency, bringing revolutionary changes to an end

Similar to Porfirio Díaz in Mexico, Guatemala's pro-U.S. dictator Jorge Ubico (1878–1946) appeared to be deeply entrenched in power (1931–1944) but quickly fell when the public withdrew its support of his government. That political opening led to the election of Juan José Arévalo (1904–1990), who governed for six years (1945–1951). During that time, he implemented moderate labor, social security, and agrarian reforms. Jacobo Arbenz Guzmán (1913–1971) won the 1950 presidential election and dramatically increased the pace of reforms. Most notably, a 1952 land reform program known as Decree 900 expropriated unused United Fruit Company (UFCo) land. In response, U.S. secretary of state John Foster Dulles (1888–1959) and Central Intelligence Agency (CIA) director Allen Dulles (1893–1969), both of whom had close relations with the UFCo, authorized a 1954 military coup that overthrew Arbenz and implemented a long and bloody military dictatorship that undid most of the previous decade's progressive reforms. The extreme measures taken to stop and reverse those policies indicate that a fundamental shift threatened to take hold that would have transformed Guatemala's archaic socioeconomic structures.

MAYA

Guatemala is home to one of the highest concentrations of Indigenous peoples in Latin America. Most of these people speak one of twenty-two Maya languages and are descendants of the builders of the classic Maya civilization that flourished a thousand years ago. That civilization had largely disappeared by the time the Spanish conquistadors arrived in the early sixteenth century.

Few European immigrants came to Guatemala during the Spanish colonial period, and most wealthy landholders and political leaders had some Maya heritage. In most of Latin America, those of mixed European and Indigenous descent are called *mestizos*, but in Guatemala they are known instead as *ladinos*. The term generally refers to those who have abandoned a Maya ethnic identity and assimilated into a Western culture. The Maya primarily lived in rural areas and engaged in subsistence agriculture, while ladinos resided in cities and worked in a cash economy. The Maya had little access to education, healthcare, and proper nutrition and, as a result, had much higher infant mortality rates and shorter life expectancies than ladinos did. At the beginning of the twentieth century, illiteracy rates hovered around 90 percent in rural Maya communities, with an infant mortality rate of 50 percent and life expectancies of less than forty years. These socioeconomic indicators were even lower for women.

Throughout the colonial period and even after independence, the Maya launched repeated uprisings against Spanish efforts to subjugate them as a labor force. The largest and best known of these uprisings came in 1820 on the eve of independence from Spain. The Maya evicted the Spanish governor and instead crowned Atanasio Tzul as king of the K'iche', one of the largest Maya groups. Tzul's independent kingdom did not last long, and the following year the Spanish empire collapsed.

Nevertheless, that revolt highlights the persistence of a Maya identity and aspirations for autonomous control over their own affairs.

NINETEENTH CENTURY

For almost three hundred years, the Spanish administered Guatemala as part of its viceroyalty of New Spain. When Mexico gained its independence in 1821, the rest of the viceroyalty separated as the United Provinces of Central America, with Guatemala as its capital. A small, powerful, and wealthy ruling class dominated the newly independent federation's political and economic systems. A liberal government implemented reforms that reduced the power of the Catholic Church and privatized communal Indigenous landholdings. In 1838, the conservative Rafael Carrera led a revolt that reversed these reforms and, in the process, tore the Central American federation apart into five separate countries. Carrera became the first of only four presidents who dominated the first century of Guatemala's existence. These leaders had a tendency to come to power legally and then stay in office through fraudulent means in a process known as *continuismo*.

As the first president of an independent Guatemala, Carrera implemented conservative policies that revived the authority of the Catholic Church, returned church and Indigenous-held lands to their previous owners, reintroduced Indigenous forced labor, and reinstated colonial political offices. In 1854, he had the congress name him president for life and attempted to exert control over the rest of Central America. Carrera died in 1865, an 1871 liberal revolt defeated the conservatives, and the liberals resumed their earlier efforts at modernization.

The liberal Justo Rufino Barrios took office in 1872. He was a positivist who came to be known as "Little Porfirio Díaz," his contemporary counterpart in neighboring Mexico who implemented similar types of policies. During Barrios's government, Guatemala became a coffee republic. By the end of his time in office in 1885, coffee comprised 75 percent of the country's exports.

In 1898, after a period of unrest, Manuel Estrada Cabrera succeeded Barrios in office. Estrada Cabrera also ruled as a liberal who attempted to modernize Guatemala's economy by integrating it into the global capitalist system. Foreign owners, particularly Germans, dominated coffee production and by 1914 controlled half of the country's exports. In an attempt to balance out coffee production and to move away from a monoculture export economy, in 1902 Estrada Cabrera invited the UFCo to begin banana production. His plan to lure the company away from Colombia and Cuba, where it already had established production, faced no serious organized opposition in Guatemala. In fact, his supporters championed the benefits of his plan. The government was located in Guatemala City, in the highlands, but since bananas were a tropical crop, the UFCo would economically develop lowland regions of the country. In addition, the scheme would personally benefit members of his government.

Turning Guatemala into a banana republic caused a dramatic change in labor relations. Highland Maya migrated to the lowlands to toil on the banana plantations. They often worked on a seasonal basis and returned to their homes in the highlands to engage in subsistence agriculture when there was no work on the plantations. They provided cheap labor that ensured high profits for the foreign-owned company. While the UFCo flourished, the president who had invited them stumbled. Estrada Cabrera was famous for his cruelty to his opponents and eventually alienated even his own handpicked legislative assembly. In 1920, the congress declared him insane and removed him from office. Political unrest plagued the decade that followed, but it was also a period critical to the formation of intellectual and political ideas that emerged after 1944 in the Guatemalan Spring.

JORGE UBICO

In 1931, Jorge Ubico was elected president and soon consolidated his control over the country. He abolished labor unions, persecuted workers, and embraced a rigidly patriarchal society. Similar to Barrios and Estrada Cabrera before him, Ubico ruled as a liberal and implemented a series of modernizing reforms. He rejected the Catholic Church's control over society in favor of the scientific administration of the country. These reforms included the secularization of education in a society in which the Catholic Church had previously dominated instruction. A lack of funding, however, restricted his efforts, and 86 percent of the country's inhabitants remained illiterate. Ubico also limited the control of the Catholic Church in other realms, including nationalizing church lands, ending the special privileges the church enjoyed, and establishing freedom of religion and civil marriage.

Despite these traditional liberal, anticlerical stances and similar to Porfirio Díaz in Mexico, Ubico slowly moved toward a position of greater reliance on the Catholic Church. The president shared conservative political and social ideologies with the archbishop Mariano Rossell y Arellano, who was installed in 1939. Both hated communism and favored an authoritarian government, social stability, and respect for a hierarchical society. The government also permitted the return of religious orders, including the Jesuits, who had previously been expelled. Ubico's admiration of Spain's fascist leader Francisco Franco earned him the support of conservative Spanish priests, which further helped bolster his authoritarian rule.

While Ubico was not particularly concerned with human rights or the economic exploitation of Maya workers, he was fascinated with their folklore and traditions. He was the first president to visit Maya villages and celebrate their cultures. Ubico liked anthropologists and encouraged scholars to come to Guatemala to study Maya societies. In this aspect, the influence of his Mexican counterpart Lázaro Cárdenas (1934–1940), who implemented similar types of *indigenista* policies that celebrated native cultures, is apparent. In 1934, Ubico ended debt peonage structures that trapped rural workers in a system of semislavery on large landed estates. At the same time, however, he implemented a vagrancy law that required people to work 150 days each year or face a threat of jail. Ubico intimidated his opposition and manipulated constitutional bans on reelection with a fraudulent **plebiscite** to maintain himself in power.

Ubico assumed a very strong, pro-U.S. political position. Particularly with the Boston-based UFCo firmly planted in the country, the U.S. government gained a large degree of control over the country's economic and political decisions. Previously Ubico had openly identified as a fascist and expressed admiration for Adolf Hitler, Benito Mussolini, and Francisco Franco, but in the midst of the Second World War, he altered his professed political preferences to match the prevailing winds. Guatemala was one of the first Latin American countries to join the Allies in the fight against Germany. Ubico exploited the war as an opportunity to confiscate German-owned coffee lands, not to benefit the Allied cause but to sell them at a profit to his friends. His government remained repressive and tolerated no outspoken opposition. Ubico executed labor leaders, students, political dissidents, and others who dared to challenge his hold on power. The Guatemalan president embodied an irony found elsewhere in the region in that he was a dictator allied with democratic powers in a war against dictators. The contradictions of fighting fascist military governments in Europe while supporting authoritarian administrations in Latin America contributed to a growth in domestic opposition and eventually led to a loss of support from the U.S. government.

REVOLUTIONS OF 1944

In 1944, civilian pressure, especially from students and urban professionals as well as younger, disgruntled army officers, led to Ubico's fall from power. In June 1944, students started a nonviolent *huelga de brazos caídos*, or sit-down strike, to demand autonomy for their university. Ubico refused to concede to their demands, and the protest expanded into a general strike. Ubico declared a state of siege, which led prominent Guatemalans to petition for a return of constitutional guarantees. The president sent in troops to suppress the nonviolent demonstrations, and they killed a young woman named María Chinchilla Recinos in the process. Her death, and the injuring of four others (Aída Sándoval, Hilda Balaños, Esperanza Barrientos, and Julieta Castro de Rólz Bennett) who were participating in a teachers' march dressed completely in black as if in mourning, shocked the country and undermined the ruler's legitimacy. Soldiers fired on other protesters, injuring or killing dozens. In response, shopkeepers closed their establishments despite government orders to remain open. External factors, including the economic disruption of the war and a deterioration in Ubico's health, contributed to a weakening of his power. But more than anything, a withdrawal of popular support for his government led to its collapse. Finally, this growing movement forced the president to resign on July 1.

The toppling of Ubico's government was part of a broader regional phenomenon in Latin America, as the public's refusal to support strong-armed leaders forced their resignations. This movement began in neighboring El Salvador in May with a general strike that removed the military dictator Maximiliano Hernández Martínez. His fall on May 9 had repercussions throughout the region, with his departure inspiring uprisings in Honduras, Nicaragua, Costa Rica, and Ecuador. Student strikes in Nicaragua attempted but ultimately failed to remove Anastasio Somoza García from power. In Ecuador, a May 28 general strike ushered in a period of progressive reforms known as the Glorious May Revolution. Protest in one country encouraged uprisings in others.

Support for these antigovernment movements extended beyond the small leftist political parties and labor unions that advanced working-class interests. Instead, these strikes appealed to students, professionals, shopkeepers, and white-collar workers who formed part of a growing urbanized population. They occurred during a period of economic crisis combined with a repressive government that had closed off possibilities for constitutional solutions. The general public shared a common fear that leaders would establish themselves as permanent fixtures in power and thereby lose democratic accountability. Furthermore, these strikes lacked an individual charismatic leader who set an ideological agenda and became the public face of the movement. Instead, representatives from a broad coalition made decisions that influenced the direction of the movement. Although the strikes appeared to emerge spontaneously, in reality they followed months or even years of underground organizing that was largely hidden from public view.

Even though governments employed violence to repress these strikes, the activists did not employ armed force as their principal strategy to topple the governments. Rather, activists relied on mass demonstrations, marches, sit-ins, petitions, letter-writing campaigns, and work stoppages. Consequently, governments fell not so much as a result of external pressure but rather by a loss of popular support and legitimacy that caused them to implode. An organized movement could then take advantage of the power vacuum to advance an alternative political project. These massive civic strikes are part of a rich but largely neglected Latin American tradition of nonviolent political struggles. In a region and at a time where many assumed that change could only result from armed struggle, these events illustrated the relevance of nonviolence as a means of political action.

The most famous and longest lasting of these civic strikes was the one in Guatemala. As with other uprisings in 1944, the movement in Guatemala was mostly an urban affair that emerged in response to a specific crisis. It had little unifying ideology beyond removing Ubico from office, and the movement lacked clear leadership. Generally, its goals resembled those of nineteenth-century liberalism rather than expressing the aspirations of a socialist or agrarian revolution. The leading reformers were primarily intellectuals and professionals who wanted greater personal liberty, a political voice in society, more economic opportunities, and improvements in their social status. They also wanted more respect from the United States and Great Britain on the world stage. They were tired of Guatemala being kicked around and wanted global powers to treat it as an independent, sovereign power rather than a banana republic. Their efforts opened a path toward more radical reforms.

OCTOBER REVOLUTION

When Ubico resigned the presidency, he left a military triumvirate under the leadership of General Federico Ponce Vaides in control. Those military officers promised to hold presidential elections, but these never materialized. Ponce continued Ubico's repressive policies, including assassinating the newspaper editor Alejandro Córdova, who had become an outspoken critic of the government. His death and funeral revitalized revolutionary sentiments. Opposition groups began to conspire with sympathetic and reform-minded military leaders to launch a coup and remove Ponce from office.

On the night of October 20, 1944, Colonel Jacobo Arbenz and Major Francisco Javier Arana led a force that captured a military base, distributed weapons to workers and students, and attacked the National Palace in what became known as the October Revolution. Hundreds of workers joined the movement that stormed military garrisons and police barracks. They tore up paving stones to create barricades. During the brief but intense fighting, women provided food and emergency medical care to the insurgents, and they opened their houses to those fleeing the fighting, including sheltering defecting soldiers who were hungry and terrified. Women also exploited gendered stereotypes that they were apolitical, to facilitate passing messages surreptitiously among the insurgent forces.

Two days later, the revolutionaries defeated the remnants of the military that had remained loyal to Ubico. Arbenz and Arana established a provisional junta that wrote a new, progressive constitution and prepared for general elections. The new constitution curtailed executive power and granted greater autonomy to the judiciary. It also ended censorship, outlawed racism, legalized labor unions, required equal pay for equal work, and provided for civil equality for men and women.

Opposition leaders selected the educator and scholar Juan José Arévalo as their presidential candidate for the December 1944 elections. Arévalo had spent the last decade in exile in Argentina and over the years had fallen out of touch with Guatemala. Rather than returning immediately, he slowly and cautiously traveled north from South America, testing the waters. Along the way he talked to Guatemalans about the political changes currently under way in the country and consulted with opposition leaders about the feasibility of a presidential run. The public warmly welcomed the outsider as a breath of fresh air, and he easily won the election with 85 percent of the vote. He took office in March 1945 under the new constitution.

Arévalo was not a charismatic leader, but his campaign launched a process of social change. He had social-democratic tendencies and embraced an ideology of "spiritual socialism" that was closer in nature to nineteenth-century utopian socialism than a Marxist call for class struggle. His goal was not a revolutionary transformation of society or a redistribution of wealth but, rather, psychological liberation. His government, however, did usher in a climate of political freedom, economic opportunity, and social justice.

Arévalo's political platform included three main programs that championed labor, social security, and agrarian reform. Influenced by Mexico's 1917 constitution, in 1947 Arévalo implemented Guatemala's first modern labor code. The reforms encouraged the organization of labor unions in both rural and urban areas, implemented an eight-hour workday, established a minimum wage, guaranteed social security payments, provided for vacations for workers, and allowed for collective bargaining. Arévalo also abolished Ubico's vagrancy laws and outlawed racial discrimination in the workplace. The new labor code spurred on worker organization in urban areas, on banana plantations, and among railroad workers. Comparatively, however, the labor code was quite moderate. It forbade, for example, rural organizations on farms with fewer than five hundred people out of fear that such organizations would foster ethnic conflicts. The limitations of the labor code highlighted the persistence of racism among the governing ruling class and the isolation of the country's majority Maya population. Similarly, the legislation assumed that men were the primary wage earners and failed to address the majority of women workers who labored overwhelmingly in the informal sector.

The more controversial policies in Arévalo's government included a shift from private to public enterprises, including nationalization of the insurance industry and the creation of a social security institute. Arévalo's social security program emphasized the construction of schools, hospitals, and houses as well as a national literacy campaign that increased educational opportunities. He expanded suffrage rights to all men and literate women but still excluded nonliterate women. Many of the moderate reforms primarily benefited privileged urban sectors of society rather than the poor urban working class and rural peasantry. Overall, the programs largely failed to address underlying structural inequalities.

The new government implemented a land reform program that embraced agrarian capitalism as a path to modernizing Guatemala's economy. The desire was to diminish the control the UFCo held over the economy, with an ultimate goal of ending economic **dependency** and feudalism. Again, Mexico's example was present in the Guatemalan path to agrarian reform. Despite ample talk, Arévalo's government did not engage in much concrete action, and existing landholding patterns largely remained intact.

Women played an important but largely unrecorded role in this process of political change. University students who had mobilized against Ubico formed the Unión de Mujeres Democráticas (UMD, Union of Democratic Women) to continue a fight for women's rights. In the context of the optimism that these political openings fueled, the UMD sponsored the First Inter-American Congress of Women that brought political activists from across the Americas to Guatemala City in 1947. Arévalo's wife, Elisa Martínez, welcomed delegates to a country that she proclaimed was a shining example of expanded citizenship rights and civil liberties that allowed for a free discussion of ideas. The congress advocated for greater democracy and human rights and declared a woman's right to speak on these and other political issues.

Although for the most part educated women from the ruling class had organized the congress, working-class women participated as representatives of trade unions and the educational profession.

Notwithstanding the aspirations emerging out of both the 1944 revolution that removed Ubico and the promises of Arévalo's new government, the resulting reforms were more moderate than radical. Economic policies emphasized regulation rather than the nationalization of the means of production. Government policies attempted to assimilate the majority Maya population into the political and social life of the country. This goal was achieved in part through the establishment of schools in rural communities. In 1945, the government founded an indigenist institute within the ministry of education. Although active with cultural programs, the institute remained largely ineffective at solving the persistent structural problems of racial discrimination and economic marginalization that the Maya people faced. Urban ladino fears of rural ethnic revolts slowed the pace of more radical reforms.

Arévalo did not draw on an organized political party or a mass movement as his base of support. He did, however, allow more political space for the communist party that Ubico had banished during his dictatorial regime. That party became Arévalo's most dependable ally, in part because its rigidly controlled hierarchical structure resulted in it being the least corrupt political grouping in the country. Arévalo also took this action in the context of the Allies cooperating with the Soviet Union in the Second World War against the fascist powers. Since 1935, the Comintern had followed a moderate popular-front policy of setting aside an agenda of a revolutionary class struggle. Instead, it collaborated with other liberal and left groups to work on a common reform agenda. In 1943, the Soviet Union had shuttered the Comintern to emphasize that communism would not present a threat to capitalist powers. In this context, the communist party no longer appeared as dangerous to the established order as it had previously.

The Arévalo administration encouraged urban workers and rural peasants to work together on common objectives. Conflicting agendas and identities made that elusive goal a constant struggle. In rural areas, Maya ethnic identities and a history of intense racial discrimination clashed with the rationale of a peasant class struggle for economic development. Politicized Maya communities formed new organizations to alter the lived realities they had suffered under systems of structural oppression. In urban areas, the working class was divided between those who adhered to their ladino identities and others who favored a more explicitly revolutionary agenda that incorporated the demands of Maya communities.

Arévalo's reform agenda triggered significant resistance from the wealthy ruling class and others who benefited from the previous oligarchical system of government. This reaction led to thirty coup attempts against his government, primarily from liberal military officers. Despite those odds, he managed to finish his term in office and, for the first time in the country's history, peacefully passed power on to another elected leader.

BIOGRAPHY: JACOBO ARBENZ GUZMÁN, 1913–1971

Jacobo Arbenz Guzmán campaigning for the presidency with his spouse, María Cristina Vilanova, about 1948–1949

Source: Government of Guatemala, María Cristina Vilanova

Guatemalan president Jacobo Arbenz rose to national prominence through the military. He was born in the provincial town of Quetzaltenango to a wealthy Swiss German pharmacist who had immigrated to Guatemala in 1901. Arbenz took advantage of a scholarship to attend a military academy in the capital, Guatemala City, where he excelled as a student. After graduating with high honors, he steadily rose through the military ranks and taught in the academy for several years. Although traditionally the military formed part of the bedrock of Latin America's con-

servative society, Arbenz is an example of a dissident leftist tradition within that institution. His wife, María Cristina Vilanova, introduced him to Marxist writings, including *The Communist Manifesto*, which influenced his progressive ideas and the policies he subsequently implemented as president.

As a soldier, Arbenz observed how Jorge Ubico's dictatorship in the 1930s used the military to repress agrarian workers. This experience radicalized him, and he began to form links with the labor movement. He became deeply involved in military conspiracies against Ubico and, in 1944, helped lead the revolution that removed Ubico from power. He served as defense minister in the subsequent elected government of Juan José Arévalo, which provided him with broad public exposure and growing popular support. He leveraged that position to election to the presidency in 1950 with 65 percent of the vote.

In 1952, Arbenz implemented a new agrarian reform program that redistributed land to the peasants who worked it. The program particularly targeted the UFCo, which led its supporters in the United States to encourage the CIA to overthrow his government. Arbenz worked closely with Guatemala's small communist party although he was not a member of the party and his government had only minimal relations with the Soviet Union. In June 1954, Colonel Carlos Castillo Armas launched a military coup that forced Arbenz to seek political asylum in the Mexican embassy and finally exile. His family wandered from one country to another as they sought an amenable political environment. Arbenz eventually joined the Guatemalan communist party in 1957, three years after he had been deposed from office. By then, it was too late to solidify the types of reforms he envisioned for the country.

In 1960, after the triumph of the Cuban Revolution, Fidel Castro invited Arbenz to move to Cuba. In exile, his family fell apart, his daughter developed a drug addiction and eventually died by suicide, and Arbenz descended into alcoholism. In 1970, Arbenz moved to Mexico City, where a year later he drowned in his bathtub. In 1995, Arbenz's remains were returned to Guatemala. In 2011, Guatemalan president Alvaro Colom publicly apologized for the government's role in ousting him from power. In retrospect, the reforms that Arbenz had launched were the best possibility that Guatemala had to address the country's deep-seated problems.

DOCUMENT: "DECREE 900," 1952

On June 17, 1952, the Guatemalan congress promulgated a wide-ranging agrarian reform law known as Decree 900 that provided the base for the expropriation of large estates, including foreign-owned banana lands. These excerpts of the law demonstrate its roots in the government's determination to modernize the country's economy in a way that would benefit small local farmers rather than wealthy individuals or multinational corporations.

The Congress of the Republic of Guatemala,

WHEREAS that one of the fundamental objectives of the October Revolution is the need to make a substantial change in the relations of ownership and in the forms of exploitation of land as a measure to overcome Guatemala's economic backwardness and to improve significantly the standard of living for the large masses of the population;

WHEREAS that the concentration of land in a few hands not only undermines the social function of property but produces a considerable disproportion between the many peasants who do not possess it, despite their ability to produce, and a few landowners who own excessive amounts, without cultivating it to its full extent or in proportion that justifies its tenure;

WHEREAS that according to Article 90 of the constitution, the state recognizes the existence of private property and guarantees it as a social function, with no more limitations than those determined in the law, for reasons of public necessity or utility or national interest;

WHEREAS that the expropriation and nationalization of German assets as compensation for war must be the first step to modify the relations of agricultural property and to introduce new forms of production in agriculture;

WHEREAS that the laws passed to ensure the forced leasing of idle land have not fundamentally satisfied the most urgent needs of the vast majority of the Guatemalan population;

BE IT THEREFORE RESOLVED that based on Articles 67, 88, 90, 91, 92, 93, 94, 96, and sections 15 and 25 of Article 137 of the republic's constitution, that the following agrarian reform law be decreed.

TITLE I: General Disposition

ARTICLE 1. The agrarian reform of the October Revolution aims to liquidate feudal property in the countryside and the relations of production that originate in it to develop a capitalist form of exploitation and method of production in agriculture in order to prepare the way for Guatemala's industrialization.

ARTICLE 2. All forms of slavery are abolished, and therefore the gratuitous personal benefits of the rural settlers and agricultural workers are prohibited, as is payment for labor in the form of land leases and the division of Indigenous labor in whatever form it exists.

ARTICLE 3. The essential objectives of the agrarian reform include:

A) Development of the peasant capitalist economy and of the capitalist agriculture economy in general;

B) Granting of land to peasants, colonists and agricultural workers who do not own any, or who own very little;

C) Facilitation of the investment of new capital in agriculture through the capitalist lease of nationalized land;

D) Introduction of new forms of cultivation, providing livestock, fertilizer, seeds and necessary technical assistance, especially to less well-off peasants; and

E) An increase in agricultural credit for all peasants and capitalist farmers in general.

ARTICLE 5. The expropriation referred to in this law that is decreed by social interests shall be consummated prior to indemnification, the amount of which shall be covered by "agrarian reform bonds" that are redeemable in the manner that the law determines.

ARTICLE 6. The amount of compensation shall be established based on the declaration of the fiscal registration of rural lands on May 9, 1952, and shall be paid in proportion to the expropriated land.

In case the property does not have a tax return, the compensation will be calculated according to the average of the declared value in tax registrations of adjoining or nearby land.

ARTICLE 8. For the purposes of this law, different rural estates registered under different numbers in the property registry but in the name of the same owner shall be considered a single property.

TITLE II: Adjudication, Usufruct, and Lease

CHAPTER I: Affected Goods

ARTICLE 9. Affected by the agrarian reform:

A) Wasted land;

B) Land that is not cultivated directly or at the owner's expense;

C) Land leased in any form;

D) Land necessary to form the urban populations to which the present law refers;

E) State farms denominated "national farms" or the national rural real estate, except for exceptions as established by law;

F) Municipal lands as established in the law;

G) Excesses from previous denunciations of private and municipal private property; and

H) Surplus water that the owners do not use in the irrigation of their lands or for industrial purposes, as well as those that surpass the rational volume necessary for their crops.

ARTICLE 10. Notwithstanding the provisions of the previous article, the agrarian reform does not affect the following properties:

A) Rural properties up to ninety hectares whether cultivated or not;

B) Rural properties greater than ninety hectares and less than two hundred hectares with two thirds cultivated;

C) Lands of agricultural communities commonly called Indigenous or peasant communities;

D) Owned or leased land on which agricultural enterprises operate with technical or economic crops such as coffee, cotton, citronella, lemon tea, banana, sugarcane, tobacco, rubber, quinine, fruit, pasture, beans, cereals, or other articles whose production is destined to satisfy needs of the internal or external market;

E) Industrial or commercial installations or establishments of agricultural enterprises of private individuals, of the state, of the nation, or of a municipality as well as the model farms that the National Agrarian Department will determine;

F) Pasture land used by cattle companies, provided that the permanent and rational use of the same for that purpose is verified;

G) Lands within five kilometers of the capital city, or of departmental and municipal capitals if entered into mutual agreement with the National Agrarian Department and the corresponding municipality, taking into account its absolute and relative population. Exceptions are national or municipal land that may be disposed of in accordance with the Law; and

H) Forest reserves.

ARTICLE 12. For the purposes of this law, as far as affectability is concerned, there shall be no difference between natural or juridical persons who own or lease land, even if they have entered into contracts with the state previous to the date of the promulgation of this law.

CHAPTER IV: Feudal latifundios and municipal lands

ARTICLE 32. Privately owned landholdings larger than two hundred hectares that are not cultivated by or on behalf of their owners or that have been leased in any way or exploited for personal benefit or to replace or supplement deficient wages during any of the last three years shall be considered **latifundia** and shall be expropriated in favor of the nation or in favor of the peasants and workers referred to in this article. Once expropriated, agricultural workers, farm laborers, or peasants without land will be granted the land as private property, if the majority of them so decide, or if once nationalized if a majority makes that decision in a democratic matter.

Once the needs mentioned in the previous paragraph are fulfilled, and if there is still land available on such farms, they may be leased to peasants, farm laborers, or agricultural workers, or to Guatemalan capitalist farmers under the conditions and proportions that this law establishes.

The usufructuaries will pay 3 percent of the value of each harvest to the National Agrarian Department, but the owners will pay 5 percent of the value of each harvest.

ARTICLE 33. If there are land conflicts between municipalities and agrarian communities, they will be adjudicated to the latter, in the place that the communities choose, in perpetual usufruct and to the extent that they need it.

If the conflict is between individuals and agrarian communities on uncultivated land, it will be resolved in favor of the latter.

CHAPTER V: Leases

ARTICLE 34. Any person, whether or not a farmer, who has access to capital has the right to request the lease of nationalized lands, provided they guarantee a percentage of the investment necessary to exploit them, which will be fixed by the National

Agrarian Department, and in no case will the percentage be less than 15 percent or more than 25 percent.

ARTICLE 35. Also, if they so request, peasants, settlers, and agricultural workers may acquire the right to rent small parcels of land nationalized under this law, provided that they have not obtained any others in usufruct.

ARTICLE 36. No natural or juridical person may lease more than two hundred and seventy-nine hectares, and will not pay more than 5 percent of the annual crop for it. The payment to the state must always be made in money. It is the responsibility of the National Agrarian Department to grant the contracts referred to in this chapter.

ARTICLE 37. The term of the lease shall not be less than five years nor more than twenty-five and may be extended at the end of each period. Tenants are prohibited from entering into sublease agreements. If, at the end of the second year, the tenant did not produce crops that demonstrate the proper use of the land, the National Agrarian Department may terminate the contract, without liability, by awarding it to another applicant.

CHAPTER VI: Provisions in common to the previous chapters

ARTICLE 38. Lands granted in accordance with Articles 4 and 32 may not be alienated or embargoed for a term not greater than twenty-five years, from the date of the award; but their owners can lease them.

The usufructuaries of national or nationalized lands will lose their right if within two years they do not dedicate themselves to the cultivation of the parcels awarded. The claimed lands may be given in usufruct to other applicants.

ARTICLE 39. The usufructuaries cannot assign their rights to a third party, but they can lease the lands provided they have the approval of the National Agrarian Department. The usufruct of the national or nationalized lands granted in favor of private individuals expires upon death. Children, widows, or others who depended economically on the usufructuary will have preferential right to acquire the same lands in usufruct.

TITLE III: Agrarian Debt

CHAPTER III: Technical support, credits, and spare parts

ARTICLE 49. The National Agrarian Department may, in consultation with the National Agrarian Council, dispose of a portion of the agrarian debt fund to provide the necessary economic or technical assistance to the usufructuaries and tenants of Article 34 and to the agrarian communities. The economic aid may consist of awarding livestock, seeds, implements, or agricultural machinery at a fair price and with as favorable conditions of payment as possible. In order to provide technical assistance, the Ministry of Agriculture must be consulted and supported. The Institute for the Promotion of Production and other analogous institutions, autonomous of the State, must provide all kinds of facilities for this purpose.

ARTICLE 50. In due course, in accordance with available resources and as demand so requires, the National Agrarian Bank will be created, with the primary purpose of authorizing and granting credits mainly for the small peasant economy and supplies and spare parts for the farmers, to the extent that the law determines.

Guatemala, June 17, 1952, eighth year of the Revolution.

Source: Ley de reforma agraria: Decreto número 900 (Guatemala: Departamento Agrario Nacional, 1952) (translation by author).

ARBENZ ADMINISTRATION

Arbenz won the 1950 presidential elections without significant opposition. As minister of defense in Arévalo's government, he had put down a military coup in 1949 that led to the death of Colonel Francisco Javier Arana in an ambush near Guatemala City. Arévalo had placed Arana at the head of the armed forces and promised that he would be the official candidate in the next presidential elections. Arbenz and Arana had collaborated in the 1944 revolution, but political divisions between the two leaders highlighted the different visions for the direction that revolutionaries wanted to take the country. Conservative forces favored Arana, while the left grouped around Arbenz. The removal of Arbenz's chief rival fed rumors that he had played a role in his assassination, although such a conspiracy was never proven. In any case, the ascendancy of Arbenz to power opened a path for more radical reforms.

Arbenz took office on March 15, 1951. In a dramatic change from Arévalo's administration and under the influence of his wife, María Cristina Vilanova (1915–2009), Arbenz spent less time talking about spiritual socialism and placed more emphasis on concrete material transformations. Vilanova was a strong feminist who was not content to be confined to the traditional ceremonial role of first lady. Some observers compared her to Eva Perón, her contemporary in Argentina, who similarly assumed an unusually public role in advancing social policies. Arbenz's government significantly sped up the pace of reforms, including expanding voting rights, extending the ability of workers to organize, and legalizing political parties. More than anything, he pursued a goal of ending neocolonial relations with the United States and converting Guatemala into an economically independent country.

In the mid-1940s, in the context of Soviet collaboration with the Allies in the Second World War, Arévalo had been able to work with Guatemala's small communist party with a minimum amount of political fallout. By the 1950s, however, relations between the United States and the Soviet Union had cooled significantly as the Cold War heated up. In this international context, charges of communist influence in Arbenz's government came to be seen as much more of a menace. In 1952, Arbenz formally legalized the communist party, which had adopted the less threatening name of the Partido Guatemalteco del Trabajo (PGT, Guatemalan Workers Party) in order to gain more public support. The PGT advocated for quite moderate policy objectives. Rather than attempting to move directly to socialism, it sought to develop the country's backward feudal economic situation. Following orthodox Marxist interpretations, party leaders believed that capitalism must first be fully developed in the country before conditions would be right to move on to socialism.

The PGT remained tiny, with fewer than two hundred active members. The party failed to gain much influence in the army, workers' unions, or student organizations. They held no cabinet posts in government and only five of fifty-eight seats in the congress. Nevertheless, the well-known communist José Manuel Fortuny (1916–2005) was one of Arbenz's main advisers and exercised a strong influence over government policy. Fortuny was a staunch nationalist who sought to improve living conditions in Guatemala. In short, the communist influence on Arbenz's government was small, but because of the party's disciplined structure and connections with international communist movements, some opponents argued that it represented a significant threat. Those in the traditional oligarchy opposed the government because popular support for social reforms extended well beyond the confines of a small leftist party and thereby challenged their grasp on sociopolitical power.

Women in the communist party formed the Alianza Femenina Guatemalteca (AFG, Guatemalan Women's Alliance) that supported Arbenz's leftist turn. In contrast to the established, ruling-class women who had supported Arévalo, many of the women in the AFG were younger and often the first in their families to gain a university education and aspire to professional careers. They were also effective labor organizers who reached beyond the urban borders of Guatemala City to include agricultural and textile workers from the rural periphery in their movement. The AFG championed agrarian reform and Indigenous rights, and it challenged the traditional gender roles that women were expected to play in Guatemala. Their gains and challenges to the status quo were in part what fueled a conservative backlash against the Arbenz government.

BIOGRAPHY: ESTER CASTELLANOS DE URRUTIA, 1892–1964

Ester Castellanos de Urrutia speaking in public in the early 1950s
Source: Courtesy of the Urrutia family archive

Women tend to be written out of popular narratives and political analyses of male-dominated revolutionary movements. Repression after the 1954 military coup in Guatemala further suppressed and erased organizations like the AFG from public memory. Activists burned their papers to avoid being caught with incriminating evidence, which has further complicated the process of reconstructing these histories. Scraping below the surface, however, immediately reveals the key roles that women played in revolutionary movements, and their contributions to the Guatemalan Spring is no exception. Scholars have only recently begun to recover their stories. Historian Patricia Harms movingly tells of meeting eighty-three-year-old Julia Urrutia, who had participated in those earth-shaking events sixty years earlier. When Harms asked Urrutia why she had agreed to meet with a complete stranger to discuss her involvement, she responded, "Because everyone has forgotten us." Approaching revolutions from the perspective of women and others who have been marginalized in their retelling fundamentally shifts how we understand and interpret their significance.

Julia Urrutia and her mother, Ester Castellanos de Urrutia, were among the hundreds of women who joined a march on June 25, 1944, that led to the collapse of the Ubico dictatorship. Both threw themselves wholeheartedly into the revolutionary movement and exploited the opportunity to participate in a wide variety of activities to improve the lives of all Guatemalans. During the October 1944 insurrection that led to Arévalo's election as president, they opened their house to people fleeing the fighting, including hungry and terrified soldiers who no longer wanted to support an oppressive regime. Together they actively campaigned for women to gain suffrage rights in the constitution that the new government promulgated in March 1945.

During the next decade, their activism only increased and included advocating for structural changes to benefit rural and Indigenous peoples, whom the previous regime had oppressed and marginalized. This included advocating for the extension of the franchise to rural, nonliterate women who had been excluded from the 1945 constitutional reforms. Although many early feminists in Latin America enjoyed lives of privilege, Ester Castellanos de Urrutia came from a working-class family, and that perspective encouraged the growth of a class consciousness among other members of the AFG. She only had a sixth-grade education, but recognizing her skills in 1953, the AFG promoted her to the position of secretary-general. Urrutia used the alliance as a way to battle structural inequalities in society, including forming civic education centers to teach others to read and write. Reflecting her important role as a leading activist, Guatemalan newspapers called Urrutia "doña"—a mother of the revolution.

Urrutia was a natural leader and a good speaker. As part of a campaign for peace and against imperialism, she opposed the Korean War that broke out in 1950 and celebrated when an armistice agreement was signed three years later. Urrutia represented Guatemalan women in international conferences that addressed problems of poverty, oppression, racism, and world peace. This included representing the AFG at the Second Inter-American Congress of Women in Mexico City, in 1951, and at a Women's International Democratic Federation (WIDF) meeting in Copenhagen, in 1953. Urrutia's activism earned her the enmity of the Catholic Church hierarchy, who denounced her as a communist.

After the military coup against the Arbenz government in June 1954, the Urrutia family joined about two hundred others who took refuge in the Argentine embassy. Among those was Ernesto Guevara who later become known as Che and played a leading role in the Cuban Revolution. While Che sought exile in Mexico, after three months the Urrutia family received asylum in Che's native Argentina. The family returned to Guatemala in 1956, where they remained committed political activists, which included helping organize market women into cooperatives. Even as a seventy-year-old grandmother, Ester Castellanos de Urrutia would go out at night to post antigovernment propaganda around Guatemala City. She also served as a courier to carry messages to exiles in Mexico. When she died in

1964, communist party leaders came out of hiding to pay their respects. She had remained a political activist to the end.

Decades later, Urrutia's granddaughter, Maritza Urrutia, continued her activist tradition and joined the Ejército Guerrillero de los Pobres (EGP, Guerrilla Army of the Poor). In 1992, the military police kidnapped and tortured her in a secret prison, a story that Dan Saxon compellingly relates in *To Save Her Life*. Although not widely known, the women in the Urrutia family played important roles in advancing a revolutionary agenda.

DOCUMENT: GUATEMALAN WOMEN'S ALLIANCE, "APPEAL TO THE WOMEN OF GUATEMALA," 1950

Although literate women won the right to vote in 1945, the 1950 presidential election was the first time they were able to exercise the franchise on a federal level. As the following statement makes immediately apparent, the AFG was determined to exploit that opportunity to advance their political agenda. The statement is a surprisingly forward-looking document that argues for a more inclusive feminism. As a manifesto for a women's movement, it advances ideas that still have to be realized.

For the first time in the history of Guatemala, women, whom the constitution of the republic elevated to the category of citizens with full capacity to exercise the right of suffrage, will participate broadly and democratically in the presidential election. This means a great responsibility for the country and Guatemalan women are obliged to fulfill such a high function in a conscious way: free of fanaticism, free of prejudices, with civic fervor and revolutionary sentiments.

The October Revolution has elevated women to a position of well-deserved dignity. Relegated to the background in the past, doubly oppressed and vexed by the dictatorship that dismissively discriminated against them—insulting their noblest feelings, denying them the recognition of their most legitimate rights, and making them the victims of the most violent exploitation—they have been vindicated by the great emancipatory movement that began in 1944. This means that if the advanced laws of the republic have raised women from the plane of inferiority, to which past regimes have subjected them, to a higher degree of political, economic, and social equality, they must recognize in the October Revolution the instrument of their liberation and fight for its consolidation in the next administration. With this responsibility they must go to the polls to cast their votes for the October Revolution, for the candidate who represents the interests of the revolutionary citizens of Guatemala, and never for the candidate or candidates who represents interests contrary to democracy, independence, and the country's progress.

We have heard the strange thesis that it is unworthy and indecent for women to participate in politics, meaning in its electoral and partisan manifestations. But being involved in politics is more than partisanship and electoral issues. It is to participate actively in the debates and in solutions to national problems that men and women face daily. It is to fight for an effective and popular democracy; it is to fight for social institutions that allow women to develop freely, facilitating involvement in the tasks that life imposes on them. It is to fight for women's equality with men to be effective in practice and for their rights to be extended in a consistent manner. It is to fight against customs, traditions, and prejudices that hinder the free development of their personalities and confine them to the four walls of the house, condemning them to domestic servitude. It is to fight for the right to obtain a salary equal to that of men under equal working conditions. It is to fight for the organization of special maternity centers to assist them with childbirth and with raising their children, to help them better withstand the adversities of life in their condition as working women. It is to fight for legislation that recognizes the rights of children in all its breadth and that abolishes the shame of the so-called reformatories for minors. Instead of redeeming children who have strayed from good habits, those institutions are preparing future delinquents, thanks to their ignominious and inhuman prison regulations. It is to fight for Social Security to be extended to maternity to benefit all women directly, and especially the workers and peasant women, who need it most. It is to fight for housing. It is to fight against the high cost of living that enriches speculators to the detriment of the interests of the household. We women know well what it is to face household expenses with a meager budget, what it is to go to the market with little money and return with little food that is not enough to satisfy the minimum needs of the family. We know how terrible it is for housewives to find themselves in the market with high prices for basic necessities while hoarders fill their pockets. That is why we advocate for an agrarian reform that will increase agricultural production and improve the living conditions of the people. That is why we need to intervene in politics, shaking off the indifference that overwhelms us and that is clearly negative. To participate in politics is, in short, to fight for peace, for the independence of Guatemala, for democracy and progress. It is to learn the lesson of civility that Dolores Bedoya, the enlightened patrician of our national independence, the heroine who mixed with her people and helped them to free themselves, taught us. The heroine of the purest revolutionary values whose example should inspire us. It is also to follow the worthy path of María Chinchilla who, illuminated by a glorious ideal, went to meet death.

Male egoism feeds the strange thesis of "women's apoliticalism" that does not want to see that times have changed. Some women with a slave mentality whom old chains still restrict still believe they are inferior beings, helpless and incapable of making up their own minds.

It is necessary to understand that when women intervene positively in public debates, when they enter the revolutionary movement en masse, there will no longer be a force capable of stopping the social advance of humanity. And what this means in general terms in Guatemala is that the October Revolution trusts in the democratic clarity, in the faith, and in the patriotism of Guatemalan women to save themselves in this historical dilemma. The question is whether it will push forward its victorious movement, or whether antidemocratic forces are stronger in Guatemala and will defeat it in the November elections. If progressive ideas penetrate into homes and enlighten female consciences, Guatemala will be saved by virtue of its women whose influence controls and decides the acts of men. This is the responsibility that the country places in the hands of Guatemalan women who must honor the patriotic symbol of the quetzal that encourages ideals of freedom.

We call upon the women of Guatemala without distinction of social categories, religious creeds, political parties, or ideological tendencies in the sense that they prepare to fulfill their civic duties by casting their vote at the polls for the candidate of national unity, for the candidate that the democratic forces of Guatemala support, for the candidate that guarantees the development of the October Revolution so that the laws of social protection that it has been able to give us, the feminist laws that it has granted us, are maintained and consolidated. For the candidate who knows how to maintain revolutionary unity and carry out agrarian reform and fulfill the program of revolutionary citizenship.

The Guatemalan Women's Alliance, a grassroots organization with strong revolutionary convictions, proudly proclaims that it does not hesitate to join the struggle of the workers with whom it fully identifies in its aspirations and efforts to vindicate them. The feminist struggle contributes to contemporary social struggles because it understands that it now has a new message. Since women are doubly oppressed, its place is at the side of the oppressed, with whom it will play a decisive historic role.

In turn, the Guatemalan Women's Alliance, which is a firm standard-bearer of national unity because it is the just and patriotic slogan for Guatemala, calls on all democratic women of the country, without sectarianism of any kind, to strengthen the United Front of the October Revolution and tip the electoral balance in favor of the conquests of the people and against the anti-Guatemalan, anti-feminist, pro-imperialist feudal reaction, the liberal-conservative and Ubico-Poncist reaction.

Source: Alianza Femenina Guatemalteca, "Llamamiento a las Mujeres de Guatemala," 1950, Guatemalan Documents (GD), Manuscript Division, Library of Congress, Washington, D.C. (translation by author).

LAND REFORM

Land reform, meaning a redistribution of land from an entrenched and privileged oligarchy to the peasants who actually work it, became the Arbenz administration's signature issue. The president hesitated for a year after taking office to implement broad-ranging reforms because he was unable to obtain funding from the United States or the World Bank. Finally, on June 17, 1952, Arbenz enacted a groundbreaking land reform program known as Decree 900 (the document included earlier in this chapter). The legislation faced stiff resistance from the Catholic Church and opposition political parties, including a large number of urban ladinos. Despite this hostility, on August 7 the government began to redistribute land as part of an ambitious program to remake rural Guatemalan society. In a highly unequal society, 2 percent of the population owned 72 percent of all arable land, whereas 88 percent of the population was crowded onto only 14 percent of the land. The legislation expropriated landholdings over ninety hectares in size and compensated the previous owners with twenty-five-year bonds. Under this program, even revolutionary leaders, including Arbenz, lost land. In two years, one hundred thousand peasants received land as well as credit and technical assistance. Despite its reach, the program was not particularly radical. U.S. development officials considered the land reform program to be relatively moderate, similar to programs the United States was currently sponsoring in Japan and Taiwan.

The agrarian program faced controversies over whether to redistribute expropriated land into cooperatives or whether to give peasants private titles to their individual plots. A concern was that small subsistence farms would aggravate agrarian problems in the country and fail to produce food efficiently for urban markets. At the same time, the liberal supporters of Ubico's former government did not want to lose their control over labor in the export economy, which is what could transpire if peasants were given their own land to farm and hence no longer needed to migrate to work on banana plantations. Arbenz faced significant challenges in shifting production to a sustainable, domestic agricultural model.

To win backing for his program, Arbenz built a base of support in the rural population. His government encouraged the formation of peasant unions and legally recognized hundreds of them. The ministry of agriculture assisted in the creation of hundreds of credit and marketing cooperatives that dramatically expanded agrarian opportunities. Arbenz's radicalization of the agrarian reforms that Arévalo had begun assured peasant support for his government, alienated some middle-class moderates, and weakened the power of wealthy conservative landowners. Speeding up the pace of these policies solidified working-class support for Arbenz and the PGT, especially since many farmers with small holdings now owed their ownership of land and livelihood to the PGT's influence in the government.

As Arbenz consolidated his revolutionary gains, he began to take on the UFCo. In particular, the government expropriated large, unused estates that hindered the expansion of agricultural production. When the UFCo had moved operations to Guatemala, it had banked land so that when the intensive cultivation of bananas exhausted the soil's fertility or if a disease swept through a plantation, the company would not have to move operations to another country, as had previously been the case. The UFCo only used 15 percent of its extensive landholdings, while many Guatemalan farmers lacked access to sufficient land to earn a living.

In 1953, the government expropriated one hundred thousand hectares of UFCo land and almost an equal amount the following year. In total, the land the government took from the UFCo represented a seventh of all arable land in Guatemala. The government reimbursed the UFCo with bonds equal to the value that the company had declared on Guatemala's public tax rolls rather than a much higher privately assessed value listed in the company's internal records. In response, the UFCo cried foul and called on the U.S. government to intervene on its behalf. Meanwhile, the UFCo was already under Justice Department investigation in the United States over antitrust issues. The State Department called off an overt intervention into the UFCo's internal affairs because of the foreign policy implications of doing so. The larger consideration of containing a perceived expansion of communism in the hemisphere won out over domestic policy concerns or respect for the internal affairs of another sovereign country.

Guatemala's agricultural production rose as a result of Arbenz's reforms. At the same time, corruption flourished in the distribution of land. Some large landholders attempted to avoid expropriation of their estates by breaking them up into smaller plots so that they would fall under the ninety-hectare threshold. Nevertheless, the success of the agrarian reform program contributed to the growth of significant opposition to Arbenz's government from wealthy conservative individuals.

Arbenz's opponents condemned his policies as communist inspired, but his supporters declared that fears of ties to the Soviet Union were highly exaggerated. In fact, the Soviet Union had no formal relations with the Guatemalan government. The only contact the Soviets had made with Arbenz was an attempt to buy bananas, but the deal fell through when the Guatemalan government could not arrange for transportation without the help of the UFCo, which controlled the shipping infrastructure. In the Cold War era, fear rather than reality drove perceptions.

Compared to other revolutions, the reforms that Arbenz implemented were not all that radical. Arbenz's social programs were not very extreme, and communists had only a very small influence in his government. An open and unknown question was whether Arbenz was an opportunist who attempted to play the current environment in a way that would consolidate his own personal position of power, or a dedicated revolutionary with much larger plans for a radical transformation of society. Although by 1954 the Guatemalan revolution had not taken that radical of a turn, Arbenz's domestic and international opponents feared the potential expansion and deepening of his reforms. If he remained in office, what kind of policies might he implement in the future?

DOCUMENT: CENTRAL INTELLIGENCE AGENCY, "PRESENT POLITICAL SITUATION IN GUATEMALA AND POSSIBLE DEVELOPMENTS DURING 1952," 1952

The following document provides a relatively balanced and dispassionate assessment of the political situation in Guatemala but also reveals an exaggerated fear of a communist threat and an underlying concern for the economic interests of U.S.-based corporations. National Intelligence Estimates (NIEs) were high-level U.S. governmental interdepartmental reports that intended to present authoritative appraisals of vital foreign policy problems to the president and other key officials. In the case of this estimate, officers from the intelligence organizations of the Department of State, the Army, the Navy, the Air Force, and the Joint Staff collaborated with the CIA in its preparation.

National Intelligence Estimate
NIE–62, Washington, March 11, 1952

The Problem

To analyze the present political situation in Guatemala and possible developments during 1952.

Conclusions

1. The Communists already exercise in Guatemala a political influence far out of proportion to their small numerical strength. This influence will probably con-

tinue to grow during 1952. The political situation in Guatemala adversely affects US interests and constitutes a potential threat to US security.

2. Communist political success derives in general from the ability of individual Communists and fellow travelers to identify themselves with the nationalist and social aspirations of the Revolution of 1944. In this manner, they have been successful in infiltrating the Administration and the pro-Administration political parties and have gained control of organized labor upon which the Administration has become increasingly dependent.

3. The political alliance between the Administration and the Communists is likely to continue. The opposition to Communism in Guatemala is potentially powerful, but at present it lacks leadership and organization. So far Communist-inspired Administration propaganda has succeeded in stigmatizing all criticism of Communism as opposition to the Administration and to the principles of the still popular Revolution of 1944.

4. Future political developments will depend in large measure on the outcome of the conflict between Guatemala and the United Fruit Company. This conflict is a natural consequence of the Revolution of 1944, but has been exacerbated by the Communists for their own purposes.

5. If the Company should submit to Guatemalan demands the political position of the Arbenz Administration would be greatly strengthened. It is probable that in this case the Government and the unions, under Communist influence and supported by national sentiment, would exert increasing pressure on other US interests, notably the Railway.

6. If the Company should withdraw from Guatemala a worsening economic situation would probably result. It is unlikely, however, that the economic consequences during 1952 would be such as to threaten political stability unless there were a coincident and unrelated decline in coffee production, prices, or markets.

7. Any deterioration in the economic and political situations would tend to increase the Administration's dependence on and favor toward organized labor, with a consequent increase in Communist influence. However, it is unlikely that the Communists could come directly to power during 1952, even though, in case of the incapacitation of President Arbenz, his present legal successor would be a pro-Communist.

8. In present circumstances the Army is loyal to President Arbenz, although increasingly disturbed by the growth of Communist influence. If it appeared that the Communists were about to come to power in Guatemala, the Army would probably prevent that development.

9. In the longer view, continued Communist influence and action in Guatemala will gradually reduce the capabilities of the potentially powerful anti-Communist forces to produce a change. The Communists will also attempt to subvert or neutralize the Army in order to reduce its capability to prevent them from eventually taking full control of the Government.

Discussion

The Arbenz Administration

10. The present political situation in Guatemala is the outgrowth of the Revolution of 1944. That Revolution was something more than a routine military coup. From it there has developed a strong national movement to free Guatemala from the military dictatorship, social backwardness, and "economic colonialism" which had been the pattern of the past. These aspirations command the emotional loyalty of most politically conscious Guatemalans and the administration of

President Arbenz derives corresponding strength from its claim to leadership of the continuing national Revolution.

11. President Arbenz himself is essentially an opportunist whose politics are largely a matter of historical accident. Francisco Arana, the principal military leader of the Revolution of 1944, became Chief of the Armed Forces under President Arévalo and Arbenz, a lesser member of the military junta, became Minister of Defense. As the Arévalo Administration turned increasingly leftward in its policies Arana opposed that trend. His possible election to the Presidency in 1951 became the one hope of moderate and conservative elements in Guatemala. In view of Arana's political position, Arbenz, his personal rival for military leadership, became the more closely associated with Arévalo and the leftist position in Guatemalan politics. The assassination of Arana in 1949 cleared the way for Arbenz' succession to the Presidency in 1951.

12. By 1951, the toleration of Communist activity which had characterized the early years of the Arévalo Administration had developed into an effective working alliance between Arévalo and the Communists. Arbenz, to attain the Presidency, made with the Communists commitments of mutual support which importantly affect the present situation. He did not, however, surrender himself completely to Communist control.

Communist Strength and Influence

13. The Communist Party of Guatemala has no more than 500 members, of whom perhaps one-third are militants. The Party, however, has recently reorganized and is actively recruiting, especially in Guatemala City, on the government-owned coffee plantations, and among United Fruit Company workers. It is in open communication with international Communism, chiefly through the Communist-controlled international labor organizations, the Latin American CTAL and the world-wide WFTU.

14. The Communists have achieved their present influence in Guatemala, not as a political party, but through the coordinated activity of individual Communists in the leftist political parties and labor unions which emerged from the Revolution of 1944. The extension of their influence has been facilitated by the applicability of Marxist clichés to the "anti-colonial" and social aims of the Guatemalan Revolution.

15. With the assistance of the Government, Communist and Communist-influenced labor leaders have been the most successful organizers of Guatemalan labor, especially among the United Fruit Company and government plantation workers. Their formation of the General Confederation of Guatemalan Workers in 1951 and Government pressure for labor unity have facilitated the extension of their control over all organized labor. They have been less successful in converting to political Communism the mass of labor, which is illiterate and politically inert. In the important railway workers' and teachers' unions there is opposition to association with Communism.

16. Through their control of organized labor and their influence within the pro-Administration political parties the Communists have been successful in gaining influential positions within the Government: in Congress, the National Electoral Board, the Institute of Social Security, the labor courts, the propaganda office, and the official press and radio. Their influence is extended by the presence of an indefinite number of Communist sympathizers in similar positions. The Communists do not fully control the Administration, however. Over their protests

President Arbenz has recently dismissed a pro-Communist Minister of Education and appointed a non-Communist Minister of Communications.

17. If President Arbenz should become incapacitated his legal successor would be Julio Estrada de la Hoz, the President of Congress, an ardent nationalist but a Communist sympathizer. In this event, however, the Army would probably seize power itself in order to prevent the Communists from gaining direct control of the Government.

The Anti-Communist Potential in Guatemala

18. Various elements in Guatemala, including many loyal adherents of the Revolution of 1944, view with misgiving the rapid growth of Communist influence in that country. The principal elements of this latent anti-Communist potential are:

   a. The Catholic hierarchy, implacably opposed to Communism. While its influence has been considerable, the Church has been handicapped by the small number of priests and by a lack of a constructive social program.

   b. Guatemalan landholding and business interests. These interests, which are now enjoying prosperity, resent increasing taxes and labor costs, but so far have not been subjected to direct attack, as have corresponding foreign interests. They may shortsightedly hope for advantage at the expense of these foreign interests.

   c. The strong railway workers' union, which has repudiated its adherence to the Communist-controlled Confederation and has ousted its former leaders.

   d. A large proportion of university students and an important segment of leadership in the teachers' union.

   e. The Army, which has shown some concern over the growth of Communist influence. The Army command is loyal to President Arbenz and to the Revolution of 1944, but is probably prepared to prevent a Communist accession to power.

19. So far, Communist-inspired Administration propaganda has been successful in stigmatizing all criticism of the Administration as opposition to the principles of the Revolution of 1944. So long as it remains possible to discredit opposition to Communism by identifying it with opposition to the Revolution of 1944 and with support of foreign "colonialism," it is unlikely that a coherent, sustained, and effective opposition to Communism will develop. Moreover, political dissatisfaction in Guatemala has been strong enough to unify the pro-Administration parties, and to prevent members of these parties from openly opposing the Communists. For the period of this estimate, therefore, it is likely that the alliance between the Administration and the Communists will continue, and that the potentially powerful opposition to Communism will remain ineffective.

The United Fruit Company Crisis

20. The United Fruit Company, which conducts extensive operations in nine Latin American countries, dominates Guatemalan banana production. The Company controls the only effective system of internal transportation, the International Railways of Central America. Through its merchant fleet the Company has a virtual monopoly of Guatemalan overseas shipping. It owns or leases large tracts of land in Guatemala and is second only to the Government as an employer of Guatemalan labor.

21. The important position of the United Fruit Company in their economy has long been resented by Guatemalan nationalists, regardless of the fact that the wages

and workers' benefits provided by the Company were superior to any others in the country. When the Revolutionists of 1944 undertook to "liberate" Guatemala from "economic colonialism" they had the Company specifically in mind. The Government can therefore count on the support of Guatemalan national sentiment in its conflict with the Company.

22. The present crisis had its origin in the virtual destruction of the Company's principal Guatemalan plantation by wind storms in September 1951. In view of previous Communist-inspired labor troubles, the Company unsuccessfully demanded Government assurances against future increased labor costs before it would undertake to rehabilitate the plantation. Meanwhile the Company suspended some 4,000 out of the 7,000 workers at that plantation. With Government support, the Communist-led union demanded that these workers be reinstated with pay for the period of suspension and the labor court ruled in favor of the union. The Company refused to comply with the court's decision and in consequence certain of its properties have been attached to satisfy the workers' claim for back pay. The scheduled sale of these properties has been postponed, however, in circumstances which suggest the possibility of a compromise settlement of the dispute.

23. The Communists have an obvious ulterior purpose in forcing the issue with the Company. The Government, however, probably does not desire to drive the Company from Guatemala at this time, preferring that it remain in the country on the Government's terms. The Company's employees also have an interest in the continuation of its operations. For its part, the Company has an interest in preserving its investment in Guatemala.

Possible Future Developments

24. Future developments will depend in large measure on the outcome of the struggle between the United Fruit Company and the Guatemalan Government.

25. If the Company should submit to Guatemalan demands the political position of the Arbenz Administration would be greatly strengthened. The result, even if it were a compromise agreement, would be presented as a national triumph over "colonialism" and would arouse popular enthusiasm. At the same time the Company would continue its operations, paying taxes and wages. The Government and the unions, under Communist influence and supported by national sentiment, would probably proceed to exert increasing pressure against other US interests in Guatemala, notably the Railway.

26. If the Company were to abandon its investment in Guatemala there would also be a moment of national triumph, but it would soon be tempered by realization of the economic consequences of a cessation of the Company's operations. It is unlikely, however, that these consequences during 1952 would be severe enough to threaten the stability of the regime unless there were a coincident and unrelated decline in coffee production, prices, or markets.

27. Any deterioration in the economic and political situations would tend to increase the Administration's dependence on and favor toward organized labor, with a consequent increase in Communist influence. However, it is unlikely that the Communists could come directly to power during 1952, even though, in case of the incapacitation of President Arbenz, his present legal successor would be a pro-Communist.

28. If during 1952 it did appear that the Communists were about to come to power by any means, the anti-Communist forces in Guatemala would probably move to prevent that development. In particular, the Army command would probably withdraw its support from the Administration and seize power itself.

29. In the longer view, continued Communist influence and action in Guatemala will gradually reduce the capabilities of the potentially powerful anti-Communist forces to produce a change. The Communists will also attempt to subvert or neutralize the Army in order to reduce its capability to prevent them from eventually taking full control of the Government.

Source: U.S. Department of State, *Foreign Relations of the United States, 1952–1954, Guatemala*, edited by Susan Holly (Washington, D.C.: U.S. Government Printing Office, 2003), 6–12, Document 6, https://history.state.gov/historicaldocuments/frus1952-54Guat/d6.

U.S. GOVERNMENT INTERVENTION

Worried about the direction in which Arbenz was taking Guatemala, in April 1952, the strongly pro–U.S. ruler of Nicaragua, Anastasio Somoza García, proposed to U.S. president Harry Truman that they work together to overthrow Arbenz. They made an initial attempt in October 1952, but their cover was blown and they abandoned their efforts.

In August 1953, newly installed U.S. president Dwight D. Eisenhower authorized a $2.7 million budget for a psychological warfare and political action plan known as Operation PBSUCCESS. The plan called for a propaganda campaign against Arbenz, the recruitment of members of the Guatemalan military, and the "disposal" or assassination of fifty-eight leftist leaders. Together with Secretary of State John Foster Dulles and CIA director Allen Dulles, Eisenhower authorized a military coup against Arbenz's government. In the context of the Cold War, the declared justification was Soviet influence on the Guatemalan government. The administration exploited this fear to rally international support for an anticommunist resolution at the Tenth Inter-American Conference of the Organization of American States in Caracas in March 1954 that isolated Guatemala. An immediate trigger for the coup was that in the face of a U.S. arms **embargo** and confronting a growing military threat to his government, in May 1954, Arbenz secretly arranged an arms shipment from Czechoslovakia.

Not coincidentally, John Foster Dulles was part of a law firm that represented the UFCo in Central America, and his brother, Allen, also did legal work for the UFCo and sat on its board of directors. These flagrant conflicts of interest have led to charges that they were not motivated by honorable and high-minded foreign policy objectives but rather by crass and personal economic concerns directly related to their financial interests in the banana company. Critics charge that the Eisenhower administration responded in a heavy-handed fashion to what in reality was a rather moderate nationalist reform movement in order to advance U.S. corporate interests.

MILITARY COUP

With U.S. backing that included provision of supplies and training, on June 16, 1954, Colonel Carlos Castillo Armas launched a military coup against Arbenz's constitutionally elected government. The coup was not a popular reaction to Arbenz's policies but a military action that was planned and executed in the United States. Radio propaganda and political subversion were more effective tools in overthrowing the government than was direct military force. The CIA launched an effective psychological campaign that undermined Arbenz's ability to rule. U.S. pilots flew CIA planes over Guatemala City that struck fear in the hearts of the residents of the capital. In a completely fictitious action, CIA operatives taped radio programs in the United States and beamed them into Guatemala from a transmitter across the border in Honduras that declared that they were Guatemalan patriots broadcasting live from liberated Guatemalan territory. This "Voice of Liberation" radio station, featuring Sonia and Sara Orellana, the young daughters of the anticommunist leader Manuel Orellana, engaged in a disinformation campaign with false reports of popular unrest and military rebellions. Right-wing military regimes in Nicaragua, Venezuela, and the Dominican Republic also actively conspired against the Arbenz government, with the collaboration of the CIA and the State Department.

The Guatemalan military refused to defend Arbenz, because leading officers opposed him. Other factors also played a role in their decision. With all of the saber-rattling coming from Washington, military officers did not want to face a direct U.S. invasion that would easily overwhelm their small force. The military also had its own economic interests. It wanted more arms, and with Guatemala isolated with the U.S. embargo, it was difficult to procure weapons. Their failure to protect Arbenz was not so much an issue of ideological opposition to a progressive government as a practical defense of their institutional concerns.

Some of Arbenz's supporters advocated arming workers and peasants to defend his administration. The plan encountered several problems. The army prevented the distribution of weapons to militias, and some supporters did not want to take on a much better armed military. To do so would have very likely resulted in a bloodbath with little hope of success. Wishing to avoid such an outcome, Arbenz refused to arm workers and peasants to defend his government. In the face of what initially appeared to be overwhelming opposition and the threat of a U.S. invasion, on June 27, Arbenz resigned the presidency, denounced U.S. involvement in the coup, and took refuge in the Mexican embassy. In reality, Castillo Armas had only 150 troops under his campaign. The coup succeeded not because of its strength or support, but due to propaganda and simple bravado.

After a brief period of turmoil, Castillo Armas assumed office. Far from the flourishing of freedom and democracy, the new regime subjected Guatemalans to intense persecution. The military engaged in an all-out campaign of terror against Arbenz's supporters. Seven hundred people sought refuge in the Mexican and Argentine embassies. Castillo Armas outlawed political parties and labor unions and drove their operations underground. The repression was particularly fierce in the countryside, with massacres claiming the lives of as many as eight thousand people. The military promptly reversed all of the revolution's reforms and reverted landholding patterns back to the earlier Ubico period. The new government restricted voting rights to those who knew how to read and write, once again disenfranchising the vast majority of Guatemalans. It also reopened the country to foreign corporations, with the wealth pouring outward rather than leading to internal development.

Even so, Castillo Armas and his allies in the UFCo were not entirely successful in turning the clock back to the Ubico regime. Antitrust cases in the United States led to legal action that broke up the company. The coup had stirred right-wing nationalist sentiments with the result that, unlike other domestic private landowners, the UFCo was not able to regain control over its land. Nevertheless, even though the UFCo lost direct ownership of much of its property, it still effectively controlled the international market and price of bananas. In 1970, the UFCo became United Brands and after 1984 did business as Chiquita Brands International. Despite its diminished presence in Guatemala, it still was a global economic force.

At the time of the Guatemalan coup, it had been two decades since the United States had last intervened in such an overt and direct military fashion in the internal affairs of another American republic. Franklin Delano Roosevelt declared a so-called Good Neighbor policy at the start of his presidential administration that included a withdrawal of the marines from countries that the United States had occupied for decades, including Haiti, the Dominican Republic, and Nicaragua. Roosevelt was not an anti-interventionist, but he did think that economic penetration of the hemisphere was a more effective foreign policy tool than placing boots on the ground. U.S. support for the 1954 military coup in Guatemala was a dramatic reversal of that policy and came at a cost to democratic forces across the hemisphere.

The coup was not a passing period of intense violence but introduced a long and bloody series of military dictatorships. Castillo Armas's own competitors assassinated him three years later, and decades of militarization and civil strife followed in his wake. Right-wing administrations with xenophobic and fascist tinges that were antagonistic to the United States ruled the government for decades. Intense repression led to the emergence of leftist guerrilla movements in the 1960s and one of the bloodiest counterinsurgency campaigns in Latin American history to suppress them. The military engaged in a scorched-earth policy that sought to deprive the guerrillas of their base of support. Soldiers moved rural dwellers into "model villages" that resembled concentration camps where the military could monitor the civilian population. Peasants were forced into civil defense groups, and **paramilitary death squads** targeted those who refused to cooperate. The result was a highly militarized society that ensured the continuance of an extremely unequal and exclusionary society that led to the genocide of as many as 250,000 Maya. It was not until 1985 that Guatemala returned to civilian rule, but even then, it remained apparent (as it is today) that the military calls the shots in the country. The country still suffers from a high degree of illiteracy, low life expectancies, high infant mortality rates, and an inordinate number of human rights violations. The 1954 coup provides a cautionary tale as to the negative consequences of an outside force intervening in the internal affairs of another sovereign country to advance its own imperial interests.

WHY DID THE GUATEMALAN REVOLUTION FAIL?

Scholars have long debated why, after a brief political opening, the Guatemalan Spring came to a tragic end in 1954. Stephen Schlesinger and Stephen Kinzer argue in *Bitter Fruit: The Untold Story of the American Coup in Guatemala* that the decision to collapse Arbenz's government was made in Washington, D.C. U.S. policy makers feared Arbenz's move to economic and foreign policy independence, as well as his growing reliance on communist supporters. Some scholars question whether, given the history of U.S. domination of the region, Castillo Armas would have dared to revolt without overt U.S. support and approval. They point to the UFCo's commercial enterprises in the country and its close alliance with the Dulles brothers to explain the Eisenhower administration's actions. In addition to economic interests, Cold War ideological concerns drove the CIA's intervention. Washington's bipolar foreign policy led officials to depict all reformist elements as communists and thereby greatly exaggerate the threat that Guatemala posed to the international order. Those sympathetic to this perspective seek to portray Eisenhower and the Dulles brothers as noble-minded but misguided anticommunists who overreacted to a perceived danger with unforeseen and undesirable consequences.

Other scholars, such as Jim Handy in his book *Revolution in the Countryside*, highlight domestic rather than international factors that led to Arbenz's fall. Instead of pointing to the role of the UFCo and the CIA, Handy emphasizes the conservative opposition of Guatemalan landholders and how agrarian reform legislation undermined their economic investments. From this perspective, Arbenz's principal failure was not integrating the Maya peasants fully into his revolution, since they could have provided his most solid and steadfast base of support in the face of conservative reaction. The country was predominantly agricultural and lacked a large urban working-class movement that was properly positioned to introduce political, social, and economic changes. The base of the movement needed to be in the countryside.

The revolution also lacked a clear and coherent political ideology, such as what the communist party could have provided had not a fear of communism been so pervasive. In addition, Arbenz failed to provide strong leadership in the face of Castillo Armas's coup. At the time, it appeared that Arbenz was confronting overwhelming opposition, but later it became apparent that most of that was bluster. The country faced deep divides, with most of the opposition based in the capital city. Urban ladino professionals and market women launched numerous demonstrations against the president. Limiting the vote to wealthy, literate women who tended to vote conservative reinforced the power of antirevolutionary politicians on a municipal level.

With more willpower, and a willingness to rely on peasants and workers as his base, Arbenz probably could have survived the coup and continued his reform program. On a strategic level, in hindsight it was a mistake not to eliminate the army that represented the strength of the previous regime and provided an institutional framework of opposition to his reforms. Cuban revolutionaries only five years after Arbenz's fall were determined not to repeat this same mistake. Rather than working within the confines of existing institutions, the Cubans decided to abolish the army, decapitate the landholding class, and expel foreign-owned corporations. Unlike in Guatemala, that decision ensured the longtime survival of the Cuban Revolution.

Highlighting internal factors does not mean that external factors did not play a significant role. Obviously, a foreign military power could guide and determine the nature and direction of events. Given a fear of communism and hostility to agrarian reform policies, however, Arbenz's domestic foes had enough reason to remove him from power whether or not an antagonistic foreign imperial power existed. It does a disservice to Guatemalans to remove agency from their actions and assume that they acted only at the behest of a foreign power, even if for a time their interests did align with those of that imperial agent.

SUMMARY

Guatemala was home to the second great social revolution in Latin America, but its history also provides a cautionary tale of the difficulties and liabilities of attempting profound transitions in the context of an underdeveloped economy dependent on external imperial interests. A pattern of strong and repressive caudillo leaders seemingly would make Guatemala an unlikely location for a social revolution. The collapse of Jorge Ubico's dictatorship in the midst of the Second World War that relied on the rhetoric of fighting for democracy, however, opened up the possibilities for deep reform.

Jacobo Arbenz assumed the presidency in 1951 and dramatically accelerated the pace of reforms begun under his predecessor, Juan José Arévalo. At first the new governments made substantial progress in expanding access to resources for the majority of the country's marginalized peoples. Arbenz, nevertheless, encountered significant difficulties when he attempted to expropriate UFCo property to provide land to peasants. Those redistributive policies ran him afoul of wealthy individuals in Guatemala and the U.S. government, both of which charged him with pursuing communist-influenced policies. The Guatemalan Spring ended with a military coup and a reconcentration of wealth and power into the hands of a small and privileged group of people. A more thorough dismantling of the previous regime, stronger leadership in the face of opposition to the reforms, and a reliance on grassroots support might have ensured the revolution's success.

DISCUSSION QUESTIONS

Why did Jorge Ubico's government fall?

Why is it so difficult to unify workers and peasants in a common struggle for social justice?

Why was the military's support so important for Arbenz to remain in power?

What was the relative importance of domestic as opposed to international opposition to the Arbenz government?

Does land reform inherently present a threat to capitalism?

Did the Cold War justify the anticommunism that brought down the Arbenz government?

What would have been the logical result of Decree 900 had Arbenz not been overthrown?

In retrospect, what could Arbenz have done differently to prevent the overthrow of his government? Was the collapse of his government inevitable?

FURTHER READING

Almost all of the writing on the Guatemalan Spring has been sympathetic to the Arbenz government. The great divide is between authors who concentrate on domestic opposition to his reforms and those who point the finger at the CIA and the UFCo for intervening in the country.

Arévalo, Juan José. *Anti-Kommunism in Latin America: An X-Ray of the Process Leading to New Colonialism.* New York: L. Stuart, 1963. Former Guatemalan president attacks U.S. policy in Latin America as myopic and misguided.

Cullather, Nick. *Secret History: The C.I.A.'s Classified Account of Its Operations in Guatemala, 1952–1954.* Stanford, CA: Stanford University Press, 1999. Declassified CIA history of its covert operations in Guatemala.

Doyle, Kate, and Peter Kornbluh, eds. *CIA and Assassinations: The Guatemala 1954 Documents.* Electronic Briefing Book 4. Washington, D.C.: National Security Archive, 1997. http://nsarchive.gwu.edu. Declassified CIA documents on covert operations in Guatemala.

Forster, Cindy. *The Time of Freedom: Campesino Workers in Guatemala's October Revolution.* Pittsburgh, PA: University of Pittsburgh Press, 2001. Examines Guatemala's revolution from the peasants' perspective.

Gibbings, Julie, and Heather A. Vrana, eds. *Out of the Shadow: Revisiting the Revolution from Post-Peace Guatemala.* Austin: University of Texas Press, 2020. A collection of essays that discuss the social and political reforms of the Guatemalan Spring from a variety of disciplinary perspectives.

Gleijeses, Piero. *Shattered Hope: The Guatemalan Revolution and the United States, 1944–1954.* Princeton, NJ: Princeton University Press, 1991. Defends Arbenz's reforms, though he argues that Arbenz moved too quickly in implementing them.

Grandin, Greg. *The Last Colonial Massacre: Latin America in the Cold War*. Chicago: University of Chicago Press, 2004. A probing examination of rural organizing during and after the Guatemalan Spring.

Handy, Jim. *Revolution in the Countryside: Rural Conflict and Agrarian Reform in Guatemala, 1944–1954*. Chapel Hill: University of North Carolina Press, 1994. Outstanding study of Guatemala's 1952 land reform program.

Harms, Patricia. *Ladina Social Activism in Guatemala City, 1871–1954*. Albuquerque: University of New Mexico Press, 2020. An important work that approaches the Guatemalan Spring from the perspective of progressive urban women and in the process demonstrates how incorporating a gender analysis changes our understandings of revolutionary changes.

Immerman, Richard H. *The CIA in Guatemala: The Foreign Policy of Intervention*. Austin: University of Texas Press, 1982. Critique of CIA-inspired overthrow of Arbenz.

Saxon, Dan. *To Save Her Life: Disappearance, Deliverance, and the United States in Guatemala*. Berkeley: University of California Press, 2007. A compellingly written account of the kidnapping of the political activist Maritza Urrutia in 1992 that details connections of that event to the 1944 October revolution and 1954 military coup.

Schlesinger, Stephen C., and Stephen Kinzer. *Bitter Fruit: The Untold Story of the American Coup in Guatemala*. Garden City, NY: Doubleday, 1982. Passionate denunciation of the CIA's involvement in the overthrow of Arbenz's government.

Schneider, Ronald M. *Communism in Guatemala, 1944–1954*. New York: Praeger, 1958. An extensively documented Cold War history that argues that communists played a significant role in the Arbenz administration.

FILMS

Devils Don't Dream! 1995. In 1950, Guatemalans elected Jacobo Arbenz president. When he began to give farmers their own land, the CIA helped overthrow his government.

Men with Guns. 1998. A fictional depiction of villagers caught between guerrilla fighters and military violence, broadly based on Guatemala in the 1980s.

El Silencio de Neto (*The Silence of Neto*). 1994. Portrays the 1954 coup in Guatemala from the point of view of a young boy.

Bolivia

4

Bolivia's Nationalist Revolution, 1952–1964

KEY DATES

1932–1935	Bolivia loses the Chaco War with Paraguay
1941	Formation of the Revolutionary Nationalist Movement (MNR)
1942	Strike at the Catavi tin mine leads to massacre
1943	A civilian–military coup brings Major Gualberto Villarroel to power with cooperation of the MNR
1945	National Indigenous Congress
1946	Popular protest leads to the hanging of Villarroel
1946	The Union Federation of Bolivian Mine Workers (FSTMB) drafts "Pulacayo Theses"
1951	Electoral fraud appears to close the MNR's constitutional path to power
April 9–11, 1952	An armed insurrection brings the MNR to power
October 31, 1952	MNR government nationalizes the tin industry
August 3, 1953	Agrarian reform breaks up old hacienda system
November 4, 1964	General René Barrientos Ortuño leads military coup that ends MNR rule
October 9, 1967	Ernesto Che Guevara killed while leading a guerrilla uprising in Bolivia
1971–1978	Hugo Banzer Suárez holds power as military dictator
1985	Víctor Paz Estenssoro returns the MNR to office through electoral victory
2005	Leftist labor leader Evo Morales elected president

During Easter week in 1952, a popular uprising brought a new government to power in Bolivia that turned the poorest country in South America upside down, obliterated traditional landholding structures, and modernized the economy. Urban professionals formed the base of support for the Movimiento Nacionalista Revolucionario (MNR, Revolutionary Nationalist Movement) that took over the reins of government. As with all successful revolutionary movements, it was not a spontaneous uprising but a well-organized, carefully planned, and skillfully executed insurrection that counted on popular backing and participation. Workers and peasants exploited this political opening to demand radical structural changes. Popular pressure led to the nationalization of tin mines, an agrarian reform that broke up large landed estates, and the elimination of restrictions on suffrage rights. The 1952 revolution opened space for some of the most militant labor and peasant unions in Latin America.

Notably, the MNR's radical reforms did not trigger U.S. military intervention, as had Jacobo Arbenz's policies in Guatemala. Historians have debated these contrasting responses, with explanatory factors including Bolivia's greater distance from the U.S. sphere of influence, domestic rather than foreign ownership of the nationalized commodities, and the MNR's willingness to adjust its policies to U.S. demands. Accommodation, however, did not ensure long-term survival. A military coup brought the MNR's rule to an end in 1964. When the MNR returned to office through electoral means two decades later, it was a much more conservative political force.

Many scholars regard the MNR as a failed or unfinished revolution. For a brief period in the 1950s, it unleashed social forces that appeared to be positioned to transform society in favor of previously dispossessed miners and peasants. Its failure to bring these aspirations to completion points to the limitations of being able to achieve revolutionary changes in an impoverished country with an economy dependent on external political forces.

LANDLOCKED BOLIVIA

Bolivia was Spain's most valuable colony during the European power's almost three-hundred-year presence in the Americas. Europeans extracted immense wealth from the silver mines at Potosí, yet today Bolivia is South America's poorest country. This contrast is not coincidental but provides a key example of how extractive enterprises underdevelop an economy and leave it worse off than if it had no natural resources at all.

Bolivia is currently the fifth-largest country in Latin America, yet it lost every war it fought and today is only half the size it was when it gained independence from Spain in 1825. In the War of the Pacific (1879–1882), Bolivia forfeited its coast and nitrate fields to neighboring Peru and Chile. Half a century later, the country suffered another humiliating defeat, to Paraguay in the Chaco War (1932–1935), and in the process lost much of its population, territory, and oil fields. The result is that

Bolivia is one of only two of the thirty-five republics in the Americas that do not have a coastline (the other is neighboring Paraguay). Although located in the heart of South America, it has few connections with its five neighboring countries. These losses combined with geographic isolation contributed to Bolivia's impoverishment.

Like Guatemala, many of Bolivia's inhabitants are of Indigenous descent. Present-day Bolivia was once known as Qullasuyu, a region that made up the southern quadrant of the Inka Empire (or Tawantinsuyu). In the 1950s, many people still primarily spoke the Indigenous languages of Quechua, Aymara, or Guaraní. Most lived in rural areas and worked in agriculture. They suffered the lowest life expectancies, highest infant mortality rates, and highest illiteracy rates in South America. Bolivia was a large country, but it was also one of the least densely populated in the Americas—its poverty was not the result of overpopulation.

Bolivia is the most politically unstable country in the Americas. Since gaining independence from Spain, it has averaged about one irregular and extraconstitutional change of government per year. Most were palace coups with little corresponding alteration in wealth and power relations. Instead, the struggles were between rival conservative and liberal factions, with both representing wealthy economic interests far removed from the majority of the population. The conservatives were rooted in silver mining in the southern part of the country as well as in large landed estates on which they held peasants in servile and feudalistic relationships. During the nineteenth century, wealthy landowners seized much of the land from autonomous Indigenous communities. By 1950, 6 percent of landowners held 92 percent of the land. They only worked a very small part of it, and even that they farmed inefficiently. In contrast, half of the rural population owned 0.13 percent of the land with holdings of three hectares or less. As a result of this unequal distribution of land, Bolivia imported one-fifth of its food.

By the end of the colonial period, Bolivia's silver deposits had largely been exhausted, leaving the country with a stagnant economy. In the 1880s, the economic center of the country shifted away from the silver mines at Potosí and the conservative stronghold at Sucre and toward new tin mines at Oruro and their corresponding liberal stronghold in La Paz. The liberals won an 1899 civil war against the conservatives and used their newfound dominant position to set the country on a course of economic development and modernization based on the exploitation of tin. Soon, the Bolivian economy became almost exclusively dependent on tin exports, leaving it extremely vulnerable to international fluctuations in demand and price. Three corporations controlled 80 percent of the tin trade, and the owners acquired much more power than the Bolivian government. Tin barons imposed policies that played to their personal benefit but functioned to the detriment of the country as a whole and particularly hurt rural communities.

Bolivia had a dual and polarized society, its aggregate parts rarely intersecting with each other. About one-third of the population lived in urban areas and was dependent on the tin economy. During the first half of the twentieth century, an increase in access to education in urban areas led to a jump in literacy from 17 to

31 percent. This contributed to rising expectations for urban professionals, but with the decline of the tin industry and an almost total lack of industrialization, they had few possibilities to improve their economic situation. In contrast, rural peasants who worked on traditional haciendas and lacked political rights constituted two-thirds of the population. Formally, Bolivia was a democracy, but literacy and property require-ments excluded the rural Indigenous masses and urban working class from political participation.

Of the three tin barons, Simón Patiño (1862–1947) was the wealthiest and most powerful (the other two were Mauricio Hochschild and Carlos Victor Aramayo). Patiño came to be known as the "Andean Rockefeller." By the Second World War, he was one of the five richest men in the world. His annual income exceeded that of the country's budget, and his son's allowance was larger than the allotted funding for education. Even though he was Bolivian, he extracted wealth from the country to live opulently in Europe. Economic development did little to benefit the coun-try. By the 1930s, the tin barons dedicated little new investment in mining. At the same time, the quality of the ore dropped, production declined, and profit margins shrank. The 1929 Great Depression hit the industry particularly hard, leading to a collapse of the tin-based export economy. The oligarchy that had formed around tin interests began to lose its grip on the country.

CHACO WAR

In 1932, as Bolivia was sinking into an economic crisis, the country became involved in a protracted war with neighboring Paraguay over the arid and sparsely populated Chaco region that lay between the two countries. Some attribute the conflict to a dispute between oil companies for access to petroleum in the Chaco, with Royal Dutch Shell backing Paraguay and Standard Oil supporting Bolivia. By the time the fighting ceased in 1935, tens of thousands of soldiers lay dead on each side. Bolivia was the loser, both in terms of the number of dead and the amount of territory ceded to Paraguay. Most soldiers died from natural causes such as dehydration and dysentery, and many more were captured or deserted. The devastating loss caused Bolivians to reflect critically on their society and ponder who was at fault for the country's failures. Many blamed political leaders who self-servingly gained power only to benefit themselves rather than to improve society. Bad governing decisions meant that public institutions were in a process of fragmentation and collapse. As a result, corrupt and self-interested civilian administrators as well as the military lost credibility in the eyes of the general public.

The Chaco War introduced isolated rural communities to a broader political system with which they had not previously interacted. Drafting peasants into the military brought them into contact with an urban working class that was also im-poverished and dispossessed. The organizational structure of the army re-created the caste structure of society and contributed to the growth of a class consciousness among the Quechua and Aymara combatants. Those of European descent populated the upper-level officer corps, while the lower-level officers were mostly mestizos. The rank-and-file soldiers who bore the brunt of deaths in the war were from rural Indigenous communities and had the least to gain from a war that was not fought in their interests. After the war, many of these involuntary recruits refused to return to their previous serf-like lives. They wanted change.

In this context, Indigenous activists organized grassroots movements to advocate for their rights. A complex network of communal authorities known as the *cacique* (or local chiefdom) movement bargained with government authorities to seek justice for their communities. They demanded a return of their land and appealed for aid for Indigenous instruction. Their activism led to the formation of government-funded rural schools alongside private and religious institutions. Scholars previously interpreted these early movements as prepolitical, meaning they did not fundamentally challenge the structure of society. In reality, they provided the roots for later political actions. These activists formed the first peasant **syndicates** or rural labor unions. These new organizational structures gained support from leftist political parties, miners, workers, and anarchists. They learned new forms of struggle from external contacts, such as the sit-down strike, that contributed to their political influence. As their strength grew, rural communities demanded abolition of compulsory feudalistic service relations on haciendas. The syndicates attacked oppressive hacienda structures, which increased pressure for agrarian reform and profound changes in society.

SOCIALISM

The economic and political crises resulting from the Great Depression and the Chaco War led to a proliferation of political parties and a growth in socialist ideologies. Leftist parties included the Trotskyist Partido Obrero Revolucionario (POR, Revolutionary Workers Party) and the pro-Soviet Partido de la Izquierda Revolucionaria (PIR, Party of the Revolutionary Left). Their emergence reflected popular aspirations for systemic change. On the other side of the political spectrum was the Falange Socialista Boliviana (FSB, Bolivian Socialist Falange). Even though it used the word "socialist," similar to the National Socialist or Nazi Party in Germany it was a far-right fascist party that appealed to reactionary and chauvinistic nationalist sentiments (see table 4.1).

In the late 1930s, in the aftermath of the Chaco War, military leaders David Toro and Germán Busch capitalized on leftist sentiments to implement self-styled socialist regimes that combined progressive labor initiatives with resource nationalization policies. The most significant move was Toro's March 1937 decree that expropriated Standard Oil's holdings. His action was the first major nationalization of a natural resource in Latin America, and it happened a full year before Lázaro Cárdenas took a similar but much better-known step in Mexico. Popular pressure for change drove Toro and Busch's economic and labor policies, but the leaders also ruled in an

Table 4.1. Political Groups

COB	Central Obrera Boliviana (Bolivian Workers Confederation). Founded in 1952 following the MNR revolution. Under the control of FSTMB secretary-general Juan Lechín Oquendo, the COB became Bolivia's chief trade union federation.
COMIBOL	Corporación Minera de Bolivia (Bolivian Mining Corporation). State mining corporation created in 1952 when the MNR nationalized the country's tin mines. Controlled by organized labor.
FSB	Falange Socialista Boliviana (Bolivian Socialist Falange). Founded in 1937. A far-right political party that drew inspiration from Benito Mussolini's fascism and Francisco Franco's falangism. The FSB adopted a strongly anticommunist stance.
FSTMB	Federación Sindical de Trabajadores Mineros de Bolivia (Union Federation of Bolivian Mine Workers). The FSTMB was the first miners' federation in Bolivia. Formed in 1944 under MNR sponsorship, it continually provided the MNR with needed support. It rapidly became the most powerful union in the country. Juan Lechín Oquendo was the organization's secretary-general.
MNR	Movimiento Nacionalista Revolucionario (Revolutionary Nationalist Movement). Founded in 1941 by future presidents Víctor Paz Estenssoro and Hernán Siles Zuazo. The MNR was the leading force in the 1952 revolution. It moved sharply to the right and advocated neoliberal economic policies when it returned to power in 1985.
PIR	Partido de la Izquierda Revolucionaria (Party of the Revolutionary Left). Officially formed July 26, 1940. A party with Marxist-Leninist tendencies, it generally maintained that the Bolivian proletariat was weak in numbers and consciousness due to uneven economic development. It drew its support largely from professional sectors of society. The party adhered to Marx's historical determinism and rejected a permanent revolution on the grounds that before becoming socialist, Bolivia must pass through a capitalist stage. The PIR placed strong emphasis on the role of education in revolutionizing Bolivian society, and it connected with various artisan and labor groups. Its influence was strongest among railway workers. It also showed some interest in the situation of Indigenous peoples.
POR	Partido Obrero Revolucionario (Revolutionary Workers Party). The POR was the Trotskyite sector of the left. The party attacked the student left while pursuing connections with various labor groups. In the early 1940s, it consisted of a mixture of proletarian elements along with privileged intellectuals. It gained considerable influence with miners and was deeply involved with mining syndicates. It was also somewhat interested in the situation of Indigenous peoples.
RADEPA	Razón de Patria (Homeland's Cause). The RADEPA was a secret military society that was influenced by nationalistic, corporatist, fascist, and statist doctrines from both Europe and Latin America. Many of its members were veterans of the Chaco War. The RADEPA wanted control of the government but lacked an organized platform and program. It generally favored direct military seizure of the state.

Republicans	The party officially formed in 1914 when they split off from the ruling liberal party, yet it showed little differentiation from the original liberal party. The Republicans gathered together powerful groups, including the new wealthy mine owners and disgruntled members of the old landed aristocracy. It followed the same traditions of the liberals, drew its strength from the ruling class, and was racist and oligarchic. It first took control in a coup in 1920 and ruled until the military takeover in 1936. After a brief decline in power, the Republicans reemerged in the late 1940s and won the 1947 and 1949 elections. They took a strong stand against the left and the labor movement.

authoritarian fashion that sought to maintain control over society. Their progressive policies reflected widespread discontent with liberal capitalist ideas but also co-opted support from leftist political parties that proposed much more radical alternatives. Busch's death by suicide in 1939 brought the brief era of military socialism to a close. The decrees they had issued remained aspirational symbols rather than achieving the transformation of society through the mobilization of the worker and peasant masses.

The MNR was the largest and most important of the new political parties. At the time of its formation in 1941, the MNR consisted largely of moderate-left, urban intellectuals and professionals who at one point had supported the conservative government of General Enrique Peñaranda but had grown alienated from the general's increasing warmth toward the United States. The example of fascist leaders in Germany and Italy who implemented policies to develop their country's basic industries influenced the MNR's policy objectives. Despite its fascist origins, the MNR was also highly pragmatic. The MNR was more nationalistic and anti-imperialist in its outlook than totalitarian or militarist in its proposed governing strategies. Party leaders resented U.S. and British wealth and power, and that imperial presence made those with an underdeveloped political consciousness susceptible to Nazi criticism of Western allies. At the same time, the MNR made common cause with leftist mine workers who likewise criticized imperialism, although for quite different reasons. The party included mestizo and Indigenous members and leaders who were not particularly attracted to the German Nazi preoccupation with racial purity, or the supposed superiority of the Aryan "race." Nevertheless, tinges of anti-Semitism grew out of resentment toward the economic challenges that an influx of Jewish refugees from Nazi Germany represented for local Bolivian merchants. Other populist expressions in Latin America, particularly Juan Perón's mobilization of workers in Argentina, also influenced the MNR leadership.

The political climate of Bolivia shifted in 1942 when the country officially joined the Allies in the Second World War. The MNR retained its fascist policies but broke its close ties with Germany. The MNR subsequently concentrated its attention on national issues. Eventually, the MNR, and Bolivians in general, abandoned Germany when it became obvious that the Nazis were losing the war. In the 1942 congressional elections, nontraditional, largely leftist parties gained more votes than did the established liberal and conservative parties. This outcome launched a trend toward the radicalization of Bolivian society, a process that continued until the elections of 1951. The radicalization of urban professionals bled over into the working class, and popular discontent with the oligarchy acquired characteristics of a mass movement.

Repeated attempts to organize the working class bred several conflicts between the government and the laborers, particularly in Patiño's mines. The most intense clash occurred in December 1942, when miners from Catavi mine went on strike to demand better working conditions. With María Barzola in the lead, the women supported the miners in their strike. They were upset that the company had closed the stores on which they relied for food supplies. The government declared the strike illegal and sent in the military to stop it. The troops opened fire on the unarmed miners and their families, killing hundreds in the process. Among those who died were Barzola, who became a symbol of their struggle. The MNR capitalized on the slaughter to attack the Peñaranda government. Under the leadership of Víctor Paz Estenssoro (1907–2001), the party increased its support for the miners, thus gaining the backing of workers. As the left grew stronger, popular support for the government declined.

With a weakened government, the military became restless with its lack of progress at addressing societal problems. A number of secret societies formed within the military, the most important being Razón de Patria (RADEPA, Homeland's Cause), which materialized as part of a longer tradition of progressive, nationalist military leaders in Latin America. In 1943, RADEPA allied with the MNR in a successful civilian–military coup against the Peñaranda government. The previously unknown Major Gualberto Villarroel (1908–1946) emerged as the leader of the military junta that governed for three years. The majority of other Latin American countries and the United States refused to recognize the new regime until it removed the extremist leaders of the MNR. Despite the official displacement of these leaders, the actual ties between the Villarroel government and the MNR remained close. The MNR's influence largely defined the reformist policies the new government implemented.

Villarroel's government worked to draw the Indigenous masses into national politics for the first time in Bolivian history. In 1945, the government organized a National Indigenous Congress that gathered one thousand delegates to discuss rural problems and to improve the lives of people in peasant communities. The regime issued a series of decrees that abolished labor service obligations for Indigenous agricultural workers, required consent and payment for their labor, and established rural schools. The regime's actions could have led to a revolutionary transformation that would have destroyed the large landholding system (known as latifundia) and freed Indigenous peoples from centuries of servitude, but the decrees were never enforced, thus little changed. The scholar James Kohl presents the Villarroel administration as an early, moderate phase of the Bolivian revolution that radicalized when the MNR took power almost a decade later and followed through on these promised reforms.

The Villarroel regime continued the MNR's support for mine workers' demands. The MNR collaborated closely with Juan Lechín Oquendo, a mine leader and member of the Trotskyist POR. Miners formed the Federación Sindical de Trabajadores Mineros de Bolivia (FSTMB, Union Federation of Bolivian Mine Workers), with Lechín as its head. The FSTMB took over leadership of the labor movement and provided the MNR with essential support.

BIOGRAPHY: JUAN LECHÍN OQUENDO, 1914–2001

Juan Lechín Oquendo was Bolivia's foremost labor leader. He worked in the Catavi and Siglo XX tin mines, where he gained awareness of the desperate conditions under which the majority of workers suffered. He became involved in the labor movement and joined the Trotskyist Revolutionary Workers Party (POR). In 1944, Lechín organized a miners' congress that led to the formation of the Union Federation of Bolivian Mine Workers (FSTMB). Members elected him as the federation's executive secretary, a position he held until 1987.

Even as Lechín continued to work with the leftist POR, he also became involved with the more moderate MNR. After the 1952 revolution, Lechín was named minister of mines and petroleum. He also led the founding congress of the Bolivian Workers Confederation (COB) in 1952 and remained its executive secretary until 1987.

Lechín was the most radical of the central MNR leadership. He advocated arming the workers' militias to prevent a conservative backlash against the revolution's progressive reforms. He was a charismatic leader who became popular with the working class. His leftist positions led him into conflict with the more moderate

Juan Lechín Oquendo
Source: Gente y la actualidad, Buenos Aires, Argentina, September 15, 1970

leadership of Víctor Paz Estenssoro and Hernán Siles Zuazo. Militants, however, complained that he compromised the interests of labor in favor of consolidating the MNR's hold on power, including supporting austerity measures as the economy began to spin out of control.

In order to reduce tensions within the MNR, Paz Estenssoro returned to the presidency in 1960 and named Lechín vice president, a position he held until 1964. Lechín initially was to be the MNR's presidential candidate in 1964, but he split with the party when leadership passed over him for the nomination. Instead, he joined a coup that toppled the MNR, mistakenly thinking that the military would let him share power. Rather than keeping its promise, the military government forced the labor leader into exile.

When Bolivia returned to civilian rule in 1982, Lechín resumed his previous position as leader of the FSTMB and the COB. As a labor leader, he opposed the economic measures of his former colleagues in the MNR—Siles Zuazo (1982–1985) and Paz Estenssoro (1985–1989)—who now introduced draconian neoliberal policies that privatized tin mines and undermined the livelihoods of miners and other members of the working class.

In 1987, Lechín left his positions as head of the FSTMB and the COB. He had never risen to the position of president of Bolivia, but he did represent the most significant left-wing political force in the country.

DOCUMENT: THE UNION FEDERATION OF BOLIVIAN MINE WORKERS, "PULACAYO THESES," 1946

Mine workers adopted this document at a November 1946 meeting in the city of Pulacayo. Its drafters contended that because of Bolivia's economic backwardness, no national bourgeoisie was present to carry forward a revolutionary movement, so this responsibility fell to a proletarian vanguard. It is based on the Trotskyist concept of permanent revolution and became the most important expression of the demands of Bolivia's labor movement.

I. Basic principles

1. The proletariat, in Bolivia as in other countries, constitutes the revolutionary social class par excellence. The mineworkers, the most advanced and the most combative section of this country's proletariat, determine the direction of the FSTMB's struggle.

2. Bolivia is a backward capitalist country; within its economy different stages of development and different modes of production coexist, but the capitalist mode is qualitatively dominant, the other socio-economic forms being a heritage from our historic past. The prominence of the proletariat in national politics flows from this state of affairs.

3. Bolivia, even though a backward country, is only one link in the world capitalist chain. National peculiarities are themselves a combination of the essential features of the world economy.

4. The distinctive characteristic of Bolivia resides in the fact there has not appeared on the political scene a bourgeoisie capable of liquidating the latifundia system and other pre-capitalist economic forms, of achieving national unification and liberation from the imperialist yoke.

   These unfulfilled bourgeois tasks are the bourgeois democratic objectives that must unavoidably be realized. The central problems facing the semi-colonial countries are: the agrarian revolution, that is, the elimination of the feudal heritage, and national independence, namely, shaking off the imperialist yoke. These two tasks are closely inter-linked.

5. The specific characteristics of the national economy, important as they may be, are more and more becoming an integral part of a higher reality known as the

world economy. This is the basis for proletarian internationalism. Capitalist development is characterized by a growing interlinking of international relations, expressed in the growing volume of foreign trade.

6. The backward countries are subjected to imperialist pressure. Their development is of a combined character. These countries simultaneously combine the most primitive economic forms and the last word in capitalist technology and civilization. The proletariat of the backward countries is obliged to combine the struggle for bourgeois democratic tasks with the struggle for socialist demands. These two stages—democratic and socialist—are not separated in struggle by historic stages; they flow immediately from one another.

7. The feudal landowners have linked their interests with those of world imperialism and have become unconditionally its lackeys.

From this it follows that the ruling class is a veritable feudal bourgeoisie. Given the primitive level of technology, the running of the latifundia would be inconceivable if imperialism did not support them artificially with scraps from its table. Imperialist domination is inconceivable without the aid of the national governments of the elite. There is a high degree of capitalist concentration in which three firms control mining production, the heart of the country's economic life. The class in power is puny and incapable of achieving its own historic objectives, and so finds itself tied to the interests of the latifundists as well as those of the imperialists. The feudal-bourgeois state is an organ of violence destined to uphold the privileges of the landowners and the capitalists. The state, in the hands of the dominant class, is a powerful instrument for crushing its enemies. Only traitors or imbeciles could continue to maintain that the state can rise above the classes and paternally decide what is due to each of them.

8. The middle class or petit bourgeoisie is the most numerous class, and yet its weight in the national economy is insignificant. The small traders and property owners, the technicians, the bureaucrats, the artisans and the peasantry have been unable up to now to develop an independent class policy and will be even more unable to do so in the future. The country follows the town and there the leading force is the proletariat. The petit bourgeoisie follow the capitalists in times of "class peace" and when parliamentary activity flourishes. They line up behind the proletariat in moments of acute class struggle (for example during a revolution) and when they become convinced that it alone can show the way to their own emancipation. In both these widely differing circumstances, the independence of the petit bourgeoisie proves to be a myth. Wide layers of the middle class obviously do possess an enormous revolutionary potential—it is enough to recall the aims of the bourgeois democratic revolution—but it is equally clear that they cannot achieve these aims on their own.

9. What characterizes the proletariat is that it is the only class possessing sufficient strength to achieve not only its own aims but also those of other classes. Its enormous specific weight in political life is determined by the position it occupies in the production process and not by its numerical weakness. The economic axis of national life will also be the political axis of the future revolution.

The miners' movement in Bolivia is one of the most advanced workers' movements in Latin America. The reformists argue that it is impossible for this country to have a more advanced **social movement** than in the technically more developed countries. Such a mechanical conception of the relation between the development of industry and the political consciousness of the masses has been refuted countless times by history.

If the Bolivian proletariat has become one of the most radical proletariats, it is because of its extreme youth and its incomparable vigor, it is because it has remained practically virgin in politics, it is because it does not have the traditions of parliamentarism or class collaboration, and lastly, because it is struggling in a country where the class struggle has taken on an extremely war-like character. We reply to the reformists and to those in the pay of La Rosca [the oligarchy] that a proletariat of such quality requires revolutionary demands and the most extreme boldness in struggle.

II. The type of revolution that must take place

1. We mineworkers do not suggest we can leap over the bourgeois democratic tasks, the struggle for elementary democratic rights and for an anti-imperialist agrarian revolution. Neither do we ignore the existence of the petit bourgeoisie, especially peasants and artisans. We point out that if you do not want to see the bourgeois democratic revolution strangled then it must become only one phase of the proletarian revolution. Those who point to us as proponents of an immediate socialist revolution in Bolivia are lying. We know very well that the objective conditions do not exist for it. We say clearly that the revolution will be bourgeois democratic in its objectives and that it will be only one episode in the proletarian revolution for the class that is to lead it.
2. The proletarian revolution in Bolivia does not imply the exclusion of the other exploited layers of the nation; on the contrary, it means the revolutionary alliance of the proletariat with the peasants, the artisans and other sectors of the urban petit bourgeoisie.
3. The dictatorship of the proletariat is the expression at state level of this alliance. The slogan of proletarian revolution and dictatorship shows clearly the fact that it is the working class who will be the leading force of this transformation and of this state. On the contrary, to maintain that the bourgeois democratic revolution, as such, will be brought about by the "progressive" sectors of the bourgeoisie, and that the future state will be a government of national unity and concord, shows a determination to strangle the revolutionary movement within the framework of bourgeois democracy. The workers, once in power, will not be able to confine themselves indefinitely to bourgeois democratic limits; they will find themselves obliged—and more so with every day—to making greater and greater inroads into the regime of private property, in such a way that the revolution will take on a permanent character.

Before the exploited, we, the mineworkers, denounce those who attempt to substitute for the proletarian revolution, palace revolutions fomented by various sections of the feudal bourgeoisie.

III. The struggle against class collaboration

1. The class struggle is, in the last analysis, the struggle for the appropriation of surplus value. The proletariat that sells its labor power struggles to do this on the best terms it can and the owners of the means of production (capitalists) struggle to seize the product of unpaid labor; both pursue opposite aims, which makes their interests irreconcilable.

We must not close our eyes to the fact that the struggle against the bosses is a fight to the death, for in this struggle the fate of private property is at stake.

Unlike our enemies, we recognize no truce in the class struggle.

The present historical stage, a period of shame for humanity, can only be overcome when social classes have disappeared and there no longer exist exploiter and exploited. Those who practice class collaboration are playing a stupid game of words when they maintain that it is not a question of destroying the rich but of making the poor rich. Our goal is the expropriation of the expropriators.

2. Every attempt to collaborate with our executioners, every attempt to make concessions to the enemy in the course of the struggle, means abandoning the workers to the bourgeoisie. Class collaboration means renouncing our own objectives. Every conquest by the workers, even the most minimal, is obtained only at the price of a bitter struggle against the capitalist system. We cannot think about reaching an understanding with our oppressors because, for us, the program of transitional demands serves the goal of proletarian revolution.

    We are not reformists, even when putting before the workers the most advanced platform of demands; we are above all revolutionaries, for we aim to transform the very structure of society.

3. We reject the petit bourgeois illusion according to which the state or some other institution, placing itself above the social classes in struggle, can solve the problems of workers. Such a solution, as the history of the workers' movement, nationally and internationally, teaches us, has always meant a solution in accord with the interests of capitalism at the expense of the impoverishment and oppression of the proletariat.

    Compulsory arbitration and legal limitations of workers' means of struggle, in most cases mark the onset of defeat. As far as is possible, we fight to destroy compulsory arbitration.

    Social conflicts should be resolved under the leadership of the workers and by them alone!

4. The realization of our program of transitional demands, which must lead to proletarian revolution, is always subject to the class struggle. We are proud of being the most intransigent when there is talk of making compromises with the bosses. That is why it is a key task to struggle against and defeat the reformists who advocate class collaboration, as well as those who tell us to tighten our belts in the name of so-called national salvation. There can be no talk of national grandeur in a country where the workers suffer hunger and oppression; rather we should really talk of national destitution and decay. We will abolish capitalist exploitation.

    War to the death against capitalism! War to the death against the reformist collaboration! Follow the path of class struggle towards the destruction of capitalist society!

Source: Excerpt from the Union Federation of Bolivian Mine Workers, "Pulacayo Theses," Oxford University Press, 1946, https://global.oup.com/us/companion .websites/9780195375701/pdf/SPD8_Bolivian_Revolution.pdf.

DOCUMENT: ANTONIO MAMANI ALVAREZ, "CARANGUILLAS THESIS," 1947

In December 1947, the Indigenous leader Antonio Mamani Alvarez organized a second Indigenous congress at Caranguillas. At the congress, the Indigenous intellectual Asto Warachi Condorcanqui presented a lengthy manifesto that called for an agrarian revolution and presented a blueprint for an Indigenous revolution. This document includes a critique of foreign ideologies (including fascism and communism), capitalism, and imperialism and proposed a new multiethnic society based on traditional Andean practices. The Caranguillas thesis provides an Indigenous response to the Trotskyist Pulacayo thesis and in ways is more radical than Emiliano Zapata's Plan of Ayala from the Mexican Revolution. Included here are only short sections of a very lengthy document.

The Revolution: Its Basic Objectives

The basic objectives on which our Revolution is founded can be condensed into these three points:

1. The conquest of political power. . . .
   One thing is certain: for us, the Indians, electoral fraud is not the best way to come to power. We have already realized that peaceful means are out of the question for us. Even if we were to obtain the most resounding electoral triumph, La Rosca would never allow us to assume command nor to develop our thesis. Our complicity with electoral fraud would give fuel for the oligarchy to continue bragging about their false "democratic" practices. The only accessible path that we Indians have for the conquest of political power is revolutionary action. When this becomes a palpable reality, then, and only then, will we be able to agree to truly democratic elections. In the meantime, we should not hallucinate about any "demorosquero" [demo-oligarchical] mirage, nor should we be diverted from our objective, which is definite: revolution or nothing. . . .
2. Demand for land
   The occupation that we have been exercising over Indo-American soil since time immemorial grants us sufficient right of ownership over these lands, just as humanity's antiquity makes it the owner of the earth. This right is universally recognized. But it is surprising how we Indians are deprived of exercising it as owners of these lands. On the contrary, we find ourselves reduced to servility within our own domains, which have been usurped from us in the most violent and unjust manner by an idle caste, which abhors work and which feeds, today as yesterday, on the sweat of our brow. . . .

   When we advocate that the land will be returned to its original owners, we do not mean that the possession of the land will return to the sole and exclusive power of the peasantry. No. To say that the land will be returned means that feudal property, as well as the latifundia, will be abolished; that all Bolivian soil will again become the property of the entire Bolivian nation, united in a powerful association where all the laboring classes meet: the peasantry, the proletariat, artisans, etc. It will not mean, however, that the land will return to the peasants or proletarians individually, but to a conglomerate of organized workers. And it does mean that the usurpers of our lands will be destroyed and that the old individualistic forms of land possession will be definitively suppressed. Those who want to possess it will only have to fulfill the obligatory requirement to organize themselves and cultivate the land that the nationality gives them, the social tree of the cooperative community, and fertilize it with effort, work, and common loyalty to the new social order. . . .
3. The possession of economic power
   There should not be "those who reap what they did not sow," and under a just law, only those of us who work should reap the fruits of our efforts. But unfortunately in Bolivia, as in the world, this is the paradox. While we Indians kill ourselves by working the land, hungry and under the whip, it is the feudal

rosquería [oligarchy] that builds palaces, buys cars, enjoys luxuries, and leads a life of debauchery with the fruit of our unpaid labor. While we Indians are subjected to bloody exploitation and systematic extermination in the mines and on the haciendas, it is the feudal–mining oligarchy that with the fruit of our sweat and blood fills its coffers, erects sumptuous skyscrapers, and maintains powerful factories in foreign countries. While the nation itself is drowning in the blackest misery and in the most dreadful backwardness as a result of the actions of that clique of abject rich people, with more fury they sink their murderous claws into the entrails of our country that is immensely wealthy and dreadfully poor. . . .

We Indians, as serfs, are the ones who create the value of the land for the feudal oligarchy, and as proletarians, the surplus value for the industrial oligarchy. From here it follows that we Indians, as an exploited labor force, are the creators of capital, and as a mass of exploited consumers, the sustainers of all the capitalist power that emerges out of our efforts. Now then, if capital is the result of our labor, then money must serve our needs and not be something that enslaves us. We, the worker-consumers, as creators of wealth, should be the masters and lords over capital and not the property of a few ambitious people who had the ability to accumulate it at the expense of the poor. . . .

At the triumph of our Revolution not a single object of capitalist power should be left standing. The lands, the mines, the factories, the railroads, the banks, the public services, everything must be entirely confiscated and placed in the hands of our nationality, by means of a cooperativist system.

Source: Antonio Mamani Alvarez, "Tesis de Caranguillas," Caranguillas, Bolivia, 1947, in James V. Kohl, *Indigenous Struggle and the Bolivian National Revolution: Land and Liberty!* (New York: Routledge, 2021), electronic appendix, https://s3-eu-west-1.amazonaws.com/s3-euw1-ap-pe-ws4-cws-documents.ri-prod /9780367471392/Kohl_eResources.pdf (translation by author).

The Villarroel regime lasted from 1943 until 1946 and collapsed in part as a result of it resorting to police violence and repression to remain in power. In 1944, the government responded to opposition electoral gains by jailing and assassinating their leaders. In July 1946, a protest march devolved into a revolt, and a mob hanged Villarroel. The pro-Soviet PIR opportunistically participated in the government that followed Villarroel's death. Over the next several months, unions took advantage of the political unrest to organize numerous strikes for better wages and working conditions in the Patiño mines. Indigenous workers in alliance with urban leftist activists also led strikes on haciendas for their rights. Ideological divisions among the MNR, POR, and PIR prevented their coalescence into one powerful political force, even though they generally shared policies of opposition to the traditional oligarchy and support for labor reforms.

Following the collapse of the Villarroel government, the MNR spent the next six-year period between 1946 and 1952 (called the *sexenio*) in exile. During this time, women were crucial in organizing resistance, including supporting political prisoners, sheltering dissidents, building communication networks, and smuggling weapons. As in other revolutionary movements, women proved to be effective agitators, because in a patriarchal society they were less likely to arouse suspicion than men were. As the MNR engaged in clandestine activity, it re-created its image and defined what its future would be. The party rid itself of all its remaining fascist elements and adopted a nationalist program that advocated a program of strong economic stabilization. Under the guiding hand of Paz Estenssoro and a new leader, Hernán Siles Zuazo, the son of a previous president of the same name, the MNR attempted to broaden its base of support, particularly among urban professionals. It sought to emulate the success of Mexico's Institutional Revolutionary Party (PRI) that had ruled in that country since 1929 by rooting itself in various sectors of society rather than just operating as an expression of the working class. Nevertheless, in a time of rising rightist forces, continual labor unrest, and repression, the MNR became the left's best hope for social justice.

Three factions emerged in the MNR. One continued with its traditional rightist, protofascist program that emphasized national dignity, harmony, and anti-Semitism. Wálter Guevara Arze became the primary leader of this conservative wing. A second, centrist tendency with pragmatic nationalists formed the core of the MNR. Paz Estenssoro and Siles Zuazo, with their national-developmentalist values, led this faction. Their leadership was more reformist than radical. Labor leader Lechín led a third faction that advocated a leftist program of political, social, and economic change. This group supported universal suffrage, the nationalization of the tin industry, and agrarian reform to dismantle the latifundia system. This broad and diverse coalition led to the need to negotiate awkward and fragile alliances. The MNR was organized not on the basis of a class struggle but as a broad, multiclass movement of urban activists, with young people—and especially university students—in the lead. Workers with tenuous ties to leftist unions and some organized peasant communities joined them as well.

The PIR made a tactical error in ignoring rampant popular demand for change in Bolivian society, siding instead with the country's traditional parties. In the elections of 1947 and 1949, the PIR lost to the Republicans but refused to relinquish power. The two parties, however, became political bedfellows, with the Republicans slowly replacing the PIR in power. They relied heavily on military force in an attempt to contain demands for change and in the process created a repressive situation much like that under the previous Villarroel administration. The PIR used violence to suppress the mine workers and fraud to reduce the number of electoral votes the MNR received. The pressure for change became so strong that the FSTMB publicly called for a violent, armed struggle. This demand came out of the POR wing of the FSTMB, but the MNR desired to keep control of the labor movement and as a result was forced to move its position even further to the left. At the same time, a drastic decline in international tin prices left the country in dire economic straits, which placed even more pressure on the government. All of these episodes combined to lead the MNR to commit itself to an armed overthrow of the PIR regime.

In September 1949, the MNR organized a civilian revolt under the leadership of Siles Zuazo. After two months of fighting, the Bolivian army firmly defeated the MNR. Despite earlier cooperation between the RADEPA and the MNR, the military now supported the PIR government against the rebels. In 1951, the MNR tried for the last time to gain control through electoral means. Paz Estenssoro and Siles Zuazo ran for the presidency and vice presidency, respectively, on a political platform that emphasized central issues of universal suffrage, nationalization of the tin mines, and agrarian reform that labor movements and leftist parties had long embraced. The goal of the MNR leaders was to destroy the oligarchy, open up the country's resources for economic development, and advance social justice. They sought to nationalize the tin mines with the aim of diversifying the economy and breaking the country's dependence on a single export commodity.

The MNR ticket won a plurality of the vote in the 1951 election, and congress should have certified its victory. Military leaders and the established political oligarchy, however, voided the outcome and prevented the MNR from taking office. Conservative political leadership declared the MNR to be communist and dangerous and turned control over to the military. Facing this reality, the MNR leadership considered its alternatives. First, they attempted to organize another civil–military coup as they had done in 1943, but the army was unwilling to join them. Tensions intensified until Paz Estenssoro and other MNR leaders decided that civilians must be armed in order to defeat the army. The final revolt of the MNR began on Ash Wednesday, April 9, 1952, and lasted only three days. On Good Friday, the old regime fell, and the miners marched victoriously into La Paz, the Bolivian capital.

INSURRECTION

The brief but bloody insurrection from April 9 to April 11, 1952, brought the MNR to power. The MNR enjoyed support from part of the army, but its victory was due in large part to the tin miners who, fueled with revolutionary rhetoric, had stepped into the political vacuum that the old system's collapse had created. MNR militants distributed arms to urban and rural militias, and together they overwhelmed the police power of the state. About six hundred people died in the fighting, but the old regime collapsed due more to its lack of popular support than to the armed blow that the insurgents were able to deliver. The uprising opened the way to a social revolution, although one that urban reformers rather than workers or the rural peasantry led. Reflecting this orientation, the MNR leaders' ideology remained more nationalist than socialist in its outlook.

Despite leading the revolt, the MNR quickly began to lose control over the political process that it had set in motion. The creation of new and open political spaces led to the popular mobilization of workers and peasants, who demanded more radical structural changes than the moderate MNR had proposed. Paz Estenssoro and Siles Zuazo were reluctant leaders who attempted to engage in a legal and constitutional process, but leftist revolutionaries took the movement in a much more radical direction. MNR leaders feared that mobilizing the peasantry might release a revolutionary movement with unforeseeable consequences. Working-class and peasant pressure had been building since the Chaco War, and their efforts contributed to the slogan, "Mines to the state and land to the people." Those aspirations came to characterize the movement and quickly outpaced what the leadership had initially proposed.

The political establishment at the time of the insurrection presented limited organized resistance to the MNR. The tin mines, which provided the vast majority of Bolivia's national income, were unproductive and expensive to run. As the mines' once-rich veins ran dry, the owners failed to invest in new technology. Most years, the mining industry barely covered its own costs. For this reason, with proper recompense, the tin barons did not complain about a national takeover of their industry. Likewise, absent hacienda owners offered little opposition to land confiscation if provided with sufficient compensation. In short, the traditional ruling class was economically weak and offered little opposition to the MNR.

The MNR quickly instituted a program of profound changes that altered the social, economic, and political landscape of the country. The three most important reforms were in line with the political program that the radical wing of the party had pressed: nationalization of the tin mines, agrarian reform, and universal suffrage. The overall goal of these reforms was to modernize the economy, with a resulting downward redistribution of income and wealth from the ruling to the working class. The new government also curtailed the power of the military by closing the national army college and purging five hundred members from the officer corps. As a result, the civilian militias were better armed than the police (known as carabineros) and army and therefore helped determine the direction of the country.

Women played important economic and social roles in Bolivian society and in the insurrection, but the revolution did little to improve their status. The MNR never drafted a program or statement on women's rights. Leaders organized a women's branch of their party, but with the goal of advancing the government's interests rather than addressing gender issues or changing women's domestic status. Even so, the women's branch did help create political space for women. Poor urban women formed a grassroots group called the Barzolas, named after the leader of the 1942 Catavi strike, to mobilize support for the revolution. The women's involvement included participation in the armed militias that solidified MNR control over the country, with Lidia Gueiler Tejada as one of the commanders. The Barzolas denounced antigovernment activity, particularly that of ruling-class members of society in whose houses they worked as domestic servants. On a level of policy, however, the government conducted reforms along class lines to the exclusion of condemning sexual violence and gender discrimination. Male chauvinistic attitudes continued to be strong, and women remained dependent on men. In failing to incorporate women and Indigenous peoples into the cabinet or other high government offices, the MNR maintained the same exclusionary practices of previous conservative administrations.

The revolution failed to deliver on promises of a more thoroughgoing social transformation of society. It was a lost opportunity for an oppressed majority to overthrow their masters and take power for themselves.

BIOGRAPHY: LIDIA GUEILER TEJADA, 1921–2011

Although women played a significant role in the Bolivian revolution, they have received little academic study and their contributions have largely faded from view. That exclusion has only reinforced a top-down and male-centric perception of the movement.

Lidia Gueiler Tejada is mostly remembered for briefly serving as an interim president of Bolivia from November 1979 to July 1980. She was the first woman to be head of state of that country and only the second in all of the Americas, after Isabel Perón in Argentina from 1974 to 1976. Gueiler was also one of the first women to win election to congress in Bolivia.

Gueiler was born to a well-off family in Cochabamba, and had the privilege of studying accounting at the American Institute in that city. In addition to Spanish, she spoke Quechua, English, and German. She was working at the Central Bank in the capital of La Paz in

Lidia Gueiler Tejada
Source: Wikimedia Commons/Jorge ga

1946 when Villarroel was overthrown. These events led her to become politically active, starting with participating in a strike at the Central Bank in defense of their labor rights. She joined the MNR in 1948 when she was twenty-seven years old and was closely allied with the labor leader Juan Lechín. In the middle of the 1951 electoral campaign, she took part in a hunger strike of twenty-seven women who demanded the release of political prisoners and the return of the MNR leader Víctor Paz Estenssoro, who was in exile in Buenos Aires. They achieved their objective after eight days, which contributed to the MNR's victory in that election—even though the military prevented the party from taking office.

Gueiler actively participated in the insurrection in April 1952 that brought the MNR to power, in particular rallying women to the cause. Under the new government, Gueiler first worked at the Bolivian consulate in Hamburg, Germany, and subsequently at the legation in Bonn. Upon her return to Bolivia, she first worked with the municipal government in La Paz and then, between 1956 and 1964, served two terms in congress. Gueiler took advantage of her post to champion legislation that benefited women and children. The election in 1956 that brought her to office was the first time in Bolivia that women, Indigenous peoples, and those who did not know how to read and write had the opportunity to exercise the franchise.

In 1963, Gueiler, together with Lechín, was one of the founders of the Partido Revolucionario de la Izquierda Nacionalista (PRIN, Revolutionary Party of the Nationalist Left), a left-wing breakaway from the MNR. She went into exile when a military coup toppled the MNR government in 1964, and it was fifteen years before she would return to the country. She spent much of that time in Chile, where she became close to the socialist Salvador Allende, who was elected president in 1970.

When Gueiler returned to Bolivia in 1979, she again ran for congress with the MNR and was elected president of the chamber of deputies. Since no candidate in the concurrent presidential contest received the required 50 percent of the vote, the congress was tasked with certifying the winner. When the body could not reach a consensus, they offered the position to the former conservative MNR leader Wálter Guevara, who was now president of the senate. Guevara was soon overthrown in a military coup. When that coup collapsed, as leader of the lower congressional house and with the support of military as well as political and union leaders, Gueiler became the new provisional president. She called new elections for June 1980, but before the victors could assume their positions, General Luis García Meza Tejada overthrew her government in a bloody right-wing coup. Gueiler went into exile in France until the fall of the dictatorship in 1982. After the return to civilian government, she served as ambassador to Colombia, the Federal Republic of Germany, and Venezuela. Gueiler spent a long, rich life both as a feminist and as a political activist.

Nationalization of Tin Mines

The most import initiative to come out of the MNR revolution was an October 31, 1952, decree that nationalized 80 percent of the tin mines, Bolivia's key industry. With this legislation, the new MNR government assumed control over the big three tin companies. The MNR created a state mining corporation called the Corporación Minera de Bolivia (COMIBOL, Bolivian Mining Corporation) that administered tin production under joint labor–government management. Radicals demanded confiscation of the mines without indemnification, but in the end, moderate forces prevailed. The owners received $20 million from the proceeds of subsequent tin sales for their former properties.

The nationalization of the mines provided opportunities for popular organizations to flourish. Under Lechín's leadership, the Central Obrera Boliviana (COB, Bolivian Workers Confederation) formed within a week of the MNR triumph. The COB demanded a system of co-government with the MNR and became one of the strongest labor movements in Latin America. The COB gained an increase in wages for the miners, better working conditions, a social security system, and subsidies for goods that laborers purchased in company stores. In addition, workers who were fired in the 1942 Catavi strike returned to their jobs. The COB also assisted highland Aymara and Quechua Indigenous communities with the organization of peasant unions in order to agitate for land reform.

Unfortunately, the workers inherited a costly and run-down industry, and at the same time the price of tin fell on the world market. Furthermore, MNR leaders were more interested in mobilizing miners, peasants, and women in support of the government than in liberating and transforming their lives. The Trotskyists soon lost control of the COB to moderate sectors of the MNR, and in the process the façade of co-governance contributed to an erosion of radical worker expressions. The MNR revolution was intensely nationalist, but it did not lead to a socialist revolution that envisioned a more equitable society with workers directly in control of the means of production. Conservatives, nevertheless, viewed the extensive nationalization program as a threat and denounced the labor activists as communists. All of these factors limited the effectiveness of the nationalization program.

Agrarian Reform

The second significant MNR reform was an August 2, 1953, decree that broke up the old hacienda system and redistributed land to the Aymara and Quechua peasant masses. Rural communities previously had been largely excluded from the MNR movement, but with the agrarian reform decree, the 1952 revolution spread to the countryside. Rural workers destroyed work records on the estates and killed and expelled landowners and the abusive overseers they employed to maintain order on the estates. The result was the forcible seizure of land through the occupation of haciendas and the division of large estates (latifundia) into very small individual holdings (*minifundia*). The confiscation of land was relatively easy because many of the wealthy proprietors were absentee landowners who lived in the cities. Only later did legislation formalize the expropriations.

The agrarian reform legislation also legalized rural syndicates that peasants subsequently used to advance their agenda, including the formation of armed militias to press for the redistribution of land. The COB attempted and failed to direct the process under way. Instead, peasant leaders pushed aside government officials and came to control entire regions of the country. Despite the relatively moderate reforms, conservatives and moderates in urban areas viewed the mobilized rural masses with alarm. A good deal of racism toward Aymara and Quechua peasants heightened that level of fear.

The redistribution of land away from large and inefficient estates led to an expansion of local internal markets and a corresponding slow rise in peasant living standards. As with most agrarian reform initiatives in Latin America, however, the program fell short of its intent. It is not enough to provide people with land; they

also need resources and training. In Bolivia, government programs to educate peasants in modern farming techniques floundered. Farmers lacked access to financing
and credit that would have increased their levels of production. Administration of
the program was slow, irregular, and underhanded. As a result, agricultural production lagged. Furthermore, under the patriarchal system, primarily men received land
because they were considered to be heads of households, thereby excluding most
women and ensuring a continuation of gender inequality. Some critics subsequently
complained that the intent of the legislation was to assimilate Indigenous peoples
in a Western, capitalist economy and thereby erase their ethnic identities. In part
this was reflected in the substitution of the word "*indio*" ("Indian") with its strongly
pejorative connotations with the less onerous "*campesino*" ("peasant"). Nevertheless, government policies did transform rural dwellers into active participants in the
country's political life. Indigenous militants would later reclaim the term "indio"
with the declaration that they were colonized with that label and hence would seek
their liberation with it.

The rapid pace of land seizures quickly overwhelmed the MNR government's
ability to administer the agrarian reform process. Conservative MNR members condemned the unauthorized seizures of land and urged officials to crack down on rural
militants in order to stop the violence against wealthy estate owners. What emerged
apparent was that the redistribution of land was not a gift from the government but
the result of the organized pressure of rural syndicates that pushed hard for it. In an
attempt to moderate and control the process, the government succeeded in co-opting
some Indigenous leaders and communities. Paz Estenssoro used these local leaders
to maintain his power, which included inducing rural communities to side with his
administration against labor unions. Under this pressure, by the 1960s the radical
reform process in the countryside had moderated and shrunk in size and significance. Once some peasants gained access to land, they became extremely conservative and no longer wished to organize and advocate for further changes. Rather, they
wanted to be left alone to live their own lives. Providing peasants with their primary
demand—land—effectively neutralized them as a political force.

Universal Suffrage

Until 1952, literacy and gender restrictions limited the vote to wealthy, landowning males and left the vast majority of the country's population outside of the country's formal political process. In the 1920s, privileged women from the ruling class
began to organize for their civil and political rights. They faced opposition from the
Catholic Church that held a conservative influence over society and opposed women
participating actively in the public realm. At the same time, these early feminist
movements held little appeal for working-class and peasant women. Men in their
communities did not enjoy the rights for which the feminists fought, making their
participation in such battles meaningless. For them, the struggle was against racial
discrimination and economic exploitation rather than for gender equality.

The new government eliminated literacy requirements and, in the process, granted voting and other citizenship rights to Indigenous peoples for the first time. In contrast, such political changes did not occur in the neighboring Andean republics of Peru and Ecuador until the late 1970s nor in Colombia until 1991. Although this decree was intended to mobilize poor peasants and miners, women were also unintentional beneficiaries of the expansion of the franchise. The provision of a universal vote brought the women's suffrage movement to a rapid and unexpected conclusion. Only 7 percent of the population had voted in the 1951 election, and as a result of this reform, the number of voters jumped from two hundred thousand to more than one million, of whom about three-quarters could not read and write. Providing women and Indigenous peoples with the vote was a democratic landmark that converted them into an important political force that could influence the outcome of electoral contests. Almost all candidates, however, still came from the male, ruling-class, European-descent sectors of society. Women and Indigenous peoples did not gain a significant direct political presence in government for another half a century.

CONSOLIDATION

Once in control of the government, MNR leaders attempted to emulate the PRI in Mexico to maintain themselves in power. They created political spaces where power could be negotiated between the new forces that had been brought to the forefront: workers, peasants, the middle class, and a new civilian-controlled military. Still, historical divisions persisted within the MNR. The more traditional and conservative wing of the party resisted social and political changes. Moderate pragmatists attempted to achieve economic development through the fostering of state capitalism. Those on the left, particularly in the COB, pushed for more radical changes such as a system of state socialism.

The four main MNR leaders represented separate power bases, and they agreed to a pact to rotate terms in office. The primary leader and 1951 presidential candidate Víctor Paz Estenssoro assumed the presidency for the first four-year period from 1952 to 1956. His vice president, Hernán Siles Zuazo, was elected for the second term from 1956 to 1960. Both wanted to develop a state capitalist system, but nevertheless, passing the presidency from Paz Estenssoro to Siles Zuazo in 1956 represented one of very few peaceful transfers of political power in Bolivian history. According to the agreement, conservative MNR cofounder and the party's third-highest leader, Wálter Guevara Arze, would serve from 1960 to 1964, to be followed by the leftist labor leader Juan Lechín Oquendo.

The MNR's patriarchal leadership never expressed much interest in women's rights or their social agenda. It excluded women from government leadership and decision-making positions. Gueiler was the only woman to lead a militia group during the insurrection, but afterward she was marginalized from political power. The male leadership converted the Barzolas from a grassroots movement into a secret police and shock troop to support government interests, including attacking pro-testers who fought independently for working-class interests. The Barzolas gained control over marketplaces and excluded those who were not part of their group.

The MNR struggled to deliver on promises of redistributing wealth and power more equally across society. The revolution's early years had triggered high expecta-tions from peasants and workers. Facing a dire economic situation, MNR leaders first swung left in their policy decisions and then, after 1956, toward the right. Rather than favoring redistributive programs, the government now pursued policies that benefited the urban professionals and U.S. creditors. Tin still provided Bolivia with its major source of revenue. In the process of consolidating power, the MNR failed to break the country's dependency on its exports or to build an alternative strong domestic economic base. Declines in the mining industry meant that annual per capita income fell from US$118 in 1951 to US$99 in 1959. Agricultural and mineral production also fell. Manufacturing rose during the first years of the MNR government but fell after 1957. With the heavy dependence on mining, half of the country's imports were food, even though the country should have easily been able to feed itself, which led to skyrocketing food prices and increases in the overall cost of living. The result was 900 percent inflation, with corresponding losses in wage gains.

The MNR appealed to the United States for financial backing and eventually be-came dependent on foreign aid, with the United States providing 30 percent of the country's budget. Acceptance of this aid came at the cost of betraying a commitment to national sovereignty and the sacrificing of core principles, most notably in support for an anticommunist resolution at the OAS conference in Caracas in March 1954 that the U.S. government used to justify the overthrow of the Arbenz administration in Guatemala. In retrospect, some scholars have argued that the foreign aid success-fully preserved some of the achievements of the revolution, such as land reform. Others point out that International Monetary Fund (IMF) conditions reduced the MNR's ability to govern the country on behalf of Bolivian interests. A consequence of these economic and social compromises to ensure its survival was that the MNR squandered the support of the miners who originally had placed it in power. Further-more, the MNR increased its persecution of political opponents, and as a result, the labor unions lost even more influence over governmental policies.

DOCUMENT: CENTRAL INTELLIGENCE AGENCY (CIA), "THE OUTLOOK FOR BOLIVIA," 1956

This National Intelligence Estimate reflects how effectively and thoroughly the U.S. government had pulled the MNR government into its orbit in order to control the direction of its policies. Even though communists were few in number, U.S. policy makers feared and attempted to control the potential for the radicalization of the MNR. Printed here are only the conclusions that summarize a lengthy docu-

ment that includes background information on the history of Bolivia, a much fuller analysis of the then-current political and economic situation, and predictions for likely future developments. The entire document is available on the Department of State website.

National Intelligence Estimate
NIE 92–56, Washington, September 11, 1956.

The Problem

To estimate the character and future stability of the present government.

Conclusions

1. As shown in the recent elections, the moderate leftist Nationalist Revolutionary Movement (MNR) regime has successfully consolidated its position and achieved a degree of political stability unusual for Bolivia. However, Bolivia's basic economic problems have been aggravated by the MNR's tin nationalization and land reform policies. These policies led to decreased agricultural output and increased tin mining costs at a time when world tin prices were declining, and they accelerated the inflationary trend. Only US aid has prevented collapse of the regime.

2. The only opposition party capable of even a limited challenge to the MNR is the right-of-center Bolivian Socialist Falange (FSB). The Communists are few in number, and the MNR has succeeded in reducing but not eliminating their influence. Although we do not believe that either the Communists or the FSB can develop sufficient strength to pose a serious challenge to the MNR during the next few years, we believe both the Communists and the rightist parties possess sufficient potential to exploit possible future economic deterioration or a split within the MNR.

3. The strongest internal threat to political stability lies in the possibility of an open break between the moderate and left wings of the MNR. Since 1952 Juan Lechín, the influential leader of the left, has refrained from using his political power to unseat the Paz administration. For reasons of political expediency and party unity he will probably continue this policy toward the Siles government. We believe, however, that Lechín would not hesitate to move against President Siles if he felt that his power or freedom of political action were being seriously circumscribed either by design or by force of events.

4. The stability and political orientation of the MNR will also be strongly influenced by its efforts to control inflation and by the external assistance it receives over the next few years. Withdrawal of US assistance would almost certainly lead to the adoption of more radical and nationalistic policies by the MNR, and would probably cause the repudiation of moderate MNR leadership and bring leftist MNR factions into power. We cannot at present estimate the political course of Bolivia after the emergence of such a regime.

5. In the event of an attempted overthrow of the government from the right, the civilian militia would support the regime and would almost certainly be joined by enough elements of the army and Carabineros to insure the survival of the government. The outcome of a conflict resulting from a left-moderate split within the MNR would be considerably more doubtful. For reasons of self-interest, if not of loyalty, the bulk of the army and the Carabineros would probably support the moderates against the large group of worker militia who would follow leftist

leadership. Under present conditions, it is probable that the army and Carabineros combined could successfully defend the government against an attack by
the militia alone, but any substantial defection from either army or Carabineros
would make the outcome extremely doubtful.

6. Bolivia has shown increasing willingness to follow a pro-US foreign policy. It so far
has manifested little interest in strengthening its negligible ties with the Soviet
Bloc, despite several Bloc overtures. Should the Bolivian government feel that
the country's economic progress were being thwarted, either by deficient export
earnings or inadequate US assistance, strong pressures would be generated
within the MNR to develop and expand economic and other relations with the
Bloc countries.

Source: U.S. Department of State, *Foreign Relations of the United States, 1955–
1957, American Republics: Central and South America, Volume VII, Guatemala*,
edited by Edith James, N. Stephen Kane, Robert McMahon, and Delia Pitts
(Washington, D.C.: U.S. Government Printing Office, 1988), 556–57, Document
270, https://history.state.gov/historicaldocuments/frus1955-57v07/d270.

ROLE OF THE UNITED STATES

The Guatemalan and Bolivian revolutions emerged at the same time and with similar nationalist agendas, but the U.S. government responded in diametrically opposed
ways to the two events. At the same time that the CIA was undermining Jacobo
Arbenz's administration in Guatemala, the State Department was providing funds to
prop up the MNR government in Bolivia. On July 6, 1953, the State Department
announced a one-year contract to purchase tin from Bolivia's nationalized mines.
On October 14, 1953, it followed with an assistance package of $9 million for food,
$2 million for emergency technical assistance, and $2.4 million for road construction. By 1954, the United States had contributed $18.4 million to support Bolivia's
nationalist reformers, while it had spent $20 million to overthrow Guatemala's
progressive government. Why would it support one revolutionary experiment but
simultaneously pour an equal amount of funds and resources into ending another?

The political processes in Bolivia and Guatemala shared several similarities. Both
advanced a modernizing reform program. Leaders in the two countries drew on support from coalitions of urban professionals, workers, and peasants. Both rejected the
traditional oligarchies for their elitism, Eurocentrism, and export-oriented economic
liberalism. Instead, they used state power to redirect economic resources toward
domestic development. Finally, the two countries had the highest concentration
of Indigenous peoples in the Americas, and both attempted to integrate them into
mainstream society.

Still, Bolivia and Guatemala had very significant differences. The Bolivian MNR
represented a more successful case of accommodation due to the country's history,

the personalities of the leaders, their skill at engaging in diplomacy, and differences in perceived national interest. In short, Bolivian leader Paz Estenssoro was willing to collaborate with the United States, while in Guatemala, Arbenz was not. U.S. diplomats excelled at drawing the MNR's pragmatic leadership to their side and in the process suppressed more radical working-class tendencies.

Opponents both domestically and internationally greatly exaggerated the degree of communist influence in the two revolutions. Communists played a small but crucial role in both countries, and it was one that in the milieu of a cold war with the Soviet Union, officials in the United States had trouble understanding. Those policy makers alternatively called the MNR fascist or communist and sometimes both at the same time. That characterization hides more than it reveals. A more accurate assessment would have been that the movement had different wings, and ideologies shifted over time to respond to a changing domestic and international context. Early on, Paz Estenssoro maintained fascist affiliations, and Stalinists opposed the MNR. Communist ideologies in both cases could be described as Marxism filtered through a nationalist perspective.

Although communists had only a small presence in both Guatemala and Bolivia and did not hold any significant positions of power in either country, government leaders responded to those to their left in different fashions. Paz Estenssoro was apprehensive of a powerful left, and as a result the United States did not have as much fear of the MNR. In Guatemala, in contrast, Arbenz needed communist support to counter right-wing opposition to his government. In fact, had he relied more heavily on the communists, he may have been able to withstand both domestic and U.S. opposition and maintain himself in office.

Geography also plays a role in explaining the difference in the U.S. response to the two revolutionary movements. Guatemala is located on the Caribbean basin that the United States has long considered to be at the heart of its geopolitical sphere of influence. In contrast, as a landlocked country deep in the heart of South America, Bolivia was more distant and had less strategic significance for the United States.

Economic concerns cannot be overlooked, and they provide a compelling explanation for the contrasting responses to reform movements in the two countries. The Dulles brothers and others in the Eisenhower administration had significant financial and personal interests in the United Fruit Company, whose lands Arbenz had expropriated in Guatemala. On the other hand, the Bolivian tin mines that the MNR nationalized were the property of Simón Patiño and other Bolivians. Furthermore, the United States had a surplus of tin and did not have an immediate concern with supply, while consumer demand for bananas continued to grow. Consequently, the expropriation of the tin mines did not have as much of an impact on U.S. economic interests as Arbenz's policies in Guatemala did.

Bolivia also had the advantage of witnessing U.S. actions against Arbenz as he launched a reform program in Guatemala. Learning that lesson in the context of the 1950s Cold War, MNR leaders were careful not to alienate the United States, and in fact they actively sought out diplomatic recognition from the colossus of the north. The MNR government deliberately did not move against medium-sized U.S.-owned mines and other economic interests that were not related to the key tin-mining sector.

Unlike Guatemala, the MNR significantly reduced the size of the military and allowed the growth of militias—a force that perhaps could have kept Arbenz in office in the face of a military coup. A weak military meant the United States could not turn to it to remove the MNR from office. The alternatives to the MNR were more radical Marxist groups, and none of them was preferable to the United States over the MNR. A return of U.S. military aid after 1957 allowed a strengthening of the armed forces to the point where in 1964 they were able to overthrow the MNR government and retake control. An important lesson for a successful revolution is to dismantle elements of the previous regime—in particular, the military—that could present a threat to the new administration's hold on power.

In the end, however, explaining variations in U.S. foreign policy actions is not always an exercise in evaluating a rational thought process. U.S. officials had a limited understanding of Latin America, and they failed to develop a clear, logical, or consistent policy toward the region. Those shortcomings were evident in Cuba after the triumph of their revolution in 1959 and most directly led to the failure of the Bay of Pigs invasion in 1961.

COUP

Fearing threats that the MNR might lose its grip on power, Paz Estenssoro violated the power-sharing agreement that stipulated that Guevara Arze would become president in 1960; instead, he returned to office himself. Guevara Arze denounced Paz Estenssoro as a dictatorial caudillo, as someone who had become too enamored with power, which led the MNR to expel the challenger. Guevara Arze subsequently formed his own party. Paz Estenssoro's goal was to prevent the collapse of the MNR government, but the result of his actions was a fracturing of the MNR coalition.

In his second term, Paz Estenssoro offered generous compensation to former mine owners. He also invited new foreign investment into the country on favorable terms. He ended the participation of labor unions in the management of the governmental tin company and reduced welfare benefits to miners. Paz Estenssoro also restored the U.S.-trained army to offset peasant and worker militias and in the process gained the support of the military, which helped him maintain his rule, but this also became a two-edged sword. What could have become a socialist revolution instead emphasized a nationalist agenda, which ironically included increased dependence on the United States. By the end of Paz Estenssoro's second term, the revolution had experienced a reversal of its initial radical orientation.

The original 1952 MNR pact called for the Trotskyist labor leader Lechín to assume the presidency in 1964, but Paz Estenssoro sought to retain his position so that financial aid from the United States would continue to flow into the country. Unlike

Paz Estenssoro and Siles Zuazo, who favored a capitalist model, Lechín advocated taking Bolivia in a socialist direction. Neither the United States nor the Bolivian military wanted an avowed Marxist as president. In response to his exclusion from office, Lechín followed Guevara Arze's lead and also left to form his own party, the PRIN. When Paz Estenssoro's thirst for power led him to attempt to change the constitution so that he could be reelected for a third time in 1964, the military stepped in and brought the MNR's twelve years in government to a close. Paz Estenssoro's desire to keep everyone happy led to no one being satisfied and his eventual downfall.

Coup leader General René Barrientos Ortuño (1919–1969) had been one of the original supporters of the MNR revolution. In power, a now more conservative Barrientos decapitated worker and peasant organizations through the imprisonment and exile of their leadership. The army occupied the mines, fired many workers, and slashed the wages for those who remained, although not for the administrators. The MNR had turned to moderate reformist policies to head off more profound, transformative revolutionary changes, but the result was a repressive military dictatorship that emphasized export-oriented trade at a detriment to internal economic development that would favor workers' interests. The left's failure to mobilize and empower the peasants as part of a revolutionary movement's popular base opened them to manipulation first by the MNR and then by Barrientos for their own political ends. Paz Estenssoro's decision to retain the military intact after the 1952 revolution and then become dependent on it for his survival proved to be a tragic mistake that ultimately led to his downfall.

In 1966, the famous guerrilla leader Ernesto Che Guevara arrived in Bolivia to launch a hemispheric revolution, but he failed to connect with leftist miners or rally peasants to his cause. Barrientos brought in a U.S.-trained military force that captured and executed Guevara in October 1967. Barrientos was killed in a plane crash in 1969, and a series of other military dictators followed him in power. The most significant, and the most brutal, was Hugo Banzer Suárez (1971–1978), who repressed labor and peasant organizations and tripled Bolivia's foreign debt. In 1979, Gueiler was appointed as the interim head of state, the first woman in Bolivia to have that role and only the second in Latin America, before being overthrown in a right-wing military coup. Despite her previous affiliation with the progressive wing of the MNR, her short time in office did not result in any lasting changes.

Bolivia did not return to a civilian government until 1982 with the election of Siles Zuazo. The former MNR leader had broken with Paz Estenssoro in 1964, when he had attempted to maintain himself in office. Siles Zuazo claimed the presidency at the head of a leftist alliance, but Bolivia descended into significant economic difficulties. Reversing his earlier political stances, Siles Zuazo responded with neoliberal economic measures that weighed most heavily on the working class. Society was deeply fragmented, and a tiny minority of politicians and business people made policy decisions that benefited their own economic interests.

In 1985, Paz Estenssoro once again won election to the presidency and returned the MNR to power. He was now older and more conservative than during his first terms in office. He implemented harsh neoliberal austerity measures that slashed government subsidies for public services and privatized the mines and state-owned companies that he had helped nationalize thirty years earlier. The government understated the value of the industries and then sold them at fire-sale prices to politically connected members of the ruling class. One economic objective was to stop hyperinflation through the destruction of labor unions that could advocate for working-class interests. The outcome instead was a decline in living standards for most Bolivians, an increase in the country's indebtedness, an upward redistribution of wealth, and an accompanying rise in socioeconomic inequality.

A series of MNR and other conservative governments ruled Bolivia for the next twenty years. Their neoliberal economic policies undermined working-class interests, which led to powerful protests that repeatedly rocked the country. Critical observers note that democracy requires much more than elections; it also requires broad public participation. Although the MNR had implemented universal suffrage during its first time in office, it subsequently ruled against the economic interests of the majority of the country's population. The MNR in power during the 1980s and 1990s was distant from that which had led the 1952 insurrection.

In 2005, leftist labor leader Evo Morales rode waves of protests against the MNR's neoliberal policies in a successful campaign to become the first person of Indigenous descent to win the presidency in Bolivia. In office, Morales redirected Bolivia's natural resources to meet local needs rather than to benefit foreign economic interests. His government began to fulfill the long-delayed and betrayed promises of the 1952 MNR revolution.

SUMMARY

Some scholars point to the 1952 MNR revolution as the second great revolution in Latin America, after the Mexican Revolution. Observers debate to what extent it was a social or political revolution. Some describe it as an unfinished or incomplete process, and in particular emphasize the failures of leadership to consolidate a progressive political transformation. It followed a path similar to that of revolutionaries in Guatemala and initially appeared to have learned from some of the shortcomings that their counterparts in Central America had experienced. The MNR was more successful in dismantling previous political structures and courting the support of the U.S. government. After about a decade in power, however, both experiments ended in military coups.

Moderates in Bolivia co-opted the socialist promises of the 1952 revolution, and the 1964 military coup terminated any hopes for additional progressive changes to benefit the country's impoverished and marginalized people. Continual problems of fragmentation and division plagued the MNR during its twelve years in office. The party suffered from a legacy of vertical forms of leadership that fell short of consolidating popular participation in the revolutionary project. At the same time, radicals failed to advance their revolutionary agenda of pressing for the creation of a new society. Once workers and peasants gained their immediate goals of better salaries, working conditions, and access to land, they stopped fighting for more profound transformations of society, the revolution stalled, and eventually reversed course.

DISCUSSION QUESTIONS

How did the Chaco War spark the MNR revolution?
Was the MNR conservative, centrist, or leftist?
Was the MNR revolution a grassroots movement or one of urban professionals?
Was U.S. involvement in Bolivia significant in determining the direction of MNR policies?
How do the Guatemalan and Bolivian revolutions compare?

FURTHER READING

Bolivia's MNR is the most understudied of the Latin American revolutions. The best works examine broader issues rather than the revolution itself. Although we still lack a good contemporary synthetic overview of the Bolivian revolution, Kohl's *Indigenous Struggle and the Bolivian National Revolution* takes us a good way toward realizing the goal of a readily accessible book that frames out the broad outline of the movement and places it within a wider imperial and historiographic context.

Alexander, Robert J. *The Bolivian National Revolution.* New Brunswick, NJ: Rutgers University Press, 1958. An early study by a leading political scientist while the MNR was still in power.

Barrios de Chungara, Domitila. *Let Me Speak! Testimony of Domitila, a Woman of the Bolivian Mines.* New York: Monthly Review Press, 1978. Story of a woman who became politically active through her work in the mines.

Dangl, Benjamin. *The Five Hundred Year Rebellion: Indigenous Movements and the Decolonization of History in Bolivia.* Chico, CA: AK Press, 2019. Emphasizes the contributions of Indigenous peoples in reshaping Bolivia's social and political landscapes.

Field, Thomas C. *From Development to Dictatorship: Bolivia and the Alliance for Progress in the Kennedy Era.* Ithaca, NY: Cornell University Press, 2014. Examines how U.S. aid defined Bolivia's internal policies, including thwarting leftist movements and justifying authoritarian military regimes.

Gotkowitz, Laura. *A Revolution for Our Rights: Indigenous Struggles for Land and Justice in Bolivia, 1880–1952.* Durham, NC: Duke University Press, 2007. An important study that examines how Indigenous peasants influenced the MNR revolution.

Grindle, Merilee, and Pilar Domingo, eds. *Proclaiming Revolution: Bolivia in Comparative Perspective.* Cambridge, MA: Harvard University David Rockefeller Center for Latin American Studies, 2003. Collection of essays on the causes of the MNR revolution on its fiftieth anniversary.

Hylton, Forrest, and Sinclair Thomson. *Revolutionary Horizons: Popular Struggle in Bolivia.* London: Verso, 2007. Highly readable overview of Bolivia's history with a particular emphasis on Indigenous perspectives.

John, S. Sándor. *Bolivia's Radical Tradition: Permanent Revolution in the Andes.* Tucson: University of Arizona Press, 2009. An analysis of the origins, internal dynamics, and trajectory of Bolivia's Trotskyist Revolutionary Workers Party (POR).

Kohl, James V. *Indigenous Struggle and the Bolivian National Revolution: Land and Liberty!* New York: Routledge, 2021. Reinterprets the origins and history of the Bolivian National Revolution from an Indigenous perspective, including arguing that it begins with a moderate phase under Villarroel's administration (1943–1946).

Lehman, Kenneth. *Bolivia and the United States: A Limited Partnership.* Athens: University of Georgia Press, 1999. Expert synthesis of U.S.-Bolivian relations.

Lora, Guillermo. *A History of the Bolivian Labour Movement, 1848–1971.* Cambridge: Cambridge University Press, 1977. A classic examination of Bolivian labor written by Bolivia's leading Trotskyist leader.

Malloy, James. *Bolivia: The Uncompleted Revolution.* Pittsburgh, PA: University of Pittsburgh Press, 1970. A standard study of the MNR that argues that the 1952 revolution has yet to be completed.

Shesko, Elizabeth. *Conscript Nation: Coercion and Citizenship in the Bolivian Barracks.* Pittsburgh, PA: University of Pittsburgh Press, 2020. Examines how Bolivian governments used compulsory military conscription to shape and assimilate Indigenous peoples into the nation-state.

Smale, Robert L. *"I Sweat the Flavor of Tin": Labor Activism in Early Twentieth-Century Bolivia.* Pittsburgh, PA: University of Pittsburgh Press, 2010. Provides background on labor movements that led to the MNR revolution.

Soliz, Carmen. *Fields of Revolution: Agrarian Reform and Rural State Formation in Bolivia, 1935–1964.* Pittsburgh, PA: University of Pittsburgh Press, 2021. An important new book that reexamines Bolivia's land redistribution program from the perspective of the peasants.

Young, Kevin A. *Blood of the Earth: Resource Nationalism, Revolution, and Empire in Bolivia, 1927–1971.* Austin: University of Texas Press, 2017. Analyzes the role of popular mobilizations in determining government resource-extraction policies.

FILMS

Blood of the Condor (*Yawar Mallku*). 1969. A dramatization of an incident in which foreign development workers sterilized Quechua women without their consent as part of a birth-control program.

The Courage of the People. 1971. This film reenacts a 1967 miners' strike in the company town of Siglo XX, using many of the original strikers and their families.

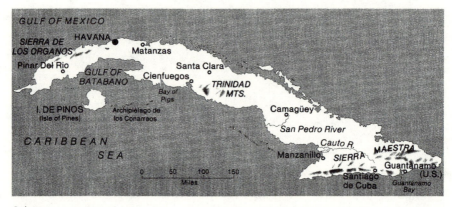

Cuba

5

Cuban Revolution, 1959–

KEY DATES

1898	Cuban independence from Spain
1933	Revolt of the Sergeants
1934–1944	Fulgencio Batista in power
March 10, 1952	Batista returns in a military coup
July 26, 1953	Fidel Castro leads failed attack on Moncada Barracks
August 1955	Founding of the 26th of July Movement
November 25, 1956	Castro arrives in Cuba on the *Granma* with eighty-two fighters
March 13, 1957	Failed Revolutionary Directorate attack on presidential palace in Havana
January 1, 1959	Batista leaves for exile in Miami
January 8, 1959	Guerrillas enter Havana
May 17, 1959	Agrarian reform law
April 15–19, 1961	Failed U.S.-backed Bay of Pigs invasion
April 16, 1961	Castro proclaims socialist character of revolution
December 2, 1961	Castro publicly embraces Marxism-Leninism
February 4, 1962	Organization of American States (OAS) expels Cuba
October 1962	Cuban Missile Crisis
1965	Refounding of Communist Party of Cuba
1970	Ten-million-ton sugar harvest
1975	Family Code
1980	Mariel boatlift
1992	Cuban Democracy (Torricelli) Act
1996	Helms-Burton Act

July 31, 2006	Fidel Castro temporarily transfers powers due to illness
February 24, 2008	Raúl Castro replaces brother Fidel as Cuban president
December 17, 2014	Cuba and United States reestablish diplomatic relations
November 25, 2016	Fidel Castro dies after long illness
2018	Miguel Díaz-Canel elected president

The 1959 Cuban Revolution was the most successful, longest lasting, and furthest reaching of the twentieth-century revolutions in Latin America. On July 26, 1953, Fidel Castro (1926–2016) led an attack on the Moncada Barracks in Santiago in eastern Cuba that he hoped would spark a popular uprising against the corrupt Fulgencio Batista (1901–1973) dictatorship. The assault coincided with the centennial of the birth of independence hero José Martí (1853–1895), and Castro exploited that timing to appeal to nationalist sentiments. After the uprising failed, Castro went into exile in Mexico, where he met the Argentine Ernesto "Che" Guevara (1928–1967), who had just witnessed the coup against Jacobo Arbenz in Guatemala. Guevara, who subsequently became the Americas' most renowned guerrilla leader and theoretician, argued that revolutionaries should arm the masses and not hesitate to execute opponents who had repressed the population. His policies ensured Cuba's survival even as the new revolutionary government's extensive land reform program and expropriation of foreign industries led to the failed 1961 U.S.-backed Bay of Pigs invasion.

As revolutionary leaders consolidated their control over the island, they radicalized and extended reforms, often with dramatic results. Gains in education and healthcare led to socioeconomic indicators that rivaled those of the industrial world, sometimes surpassing those of the United States. Critics complained, however, that this was done at the cost of individual liberties. Although strong by developing world standards, Cuba failed to reach its goal of an industrialized economy.

INDEPENDENCE

Cuba has an ideal climate for growing sugar, and this commodity has long provided a cornerstone of the island's economy. Sugar production began on the island during the Spanish colonial period, but it did not become an important export crop until the end of the eighteenth century. The dramatic growth of sugar in Cuba is intimately tied to the history of Haiti. Enslaved people launched a revolution on the neighboring island in 1791 that destroyed its sugar economy (see discussion in chapter 1). Before that revolution, sugar production had made Haiti the most valuable colony in the world. With Haiti's independence from France in 1804, many French planters moved to neighboring Cuba in order to continue profiting from the sugar industry.

The increase in sugar exports from Cuba meant that it did not face economic pressure to separate itself from European control. In addition, as Spain lost the rest of its American empire, its military and political infrastructure became entrenched as officials retreated to their home base on the Caribbean island. As a result, unlike Spain's other colonial possessions, Cuba did not gain independence in the early nineteenth century. Various attempts to free Cuba from Spanish control throughout the nineteenth century all failed.

By 1850, Cuba produced one-third of all the sugar in the world. Even though it remained a Spanish colony, it became thoroughly dependent on the United States. Seventy percent of Cuba's trade was with its neighbor to the north, and three-fourths of that was in sugar. Since large plantations were more economical than small ones, sugar production stimulated centralization of the industry. Sugar also required a large capital outlay, a small skilled managerial class, and a large unskilled labor force. These dynamics led to a reliance on the labor of enslaved peoples from Africa. As a result, slavery persisted in Cuba until 1886, more than twenty years after the Civil War in the United States and well after the institution's disappearance in most of the rest of the world.

Martí led the Cuban struggle for independence, both in a political sense from Spain and in an economic sense from the United States. He was the child of a Spanish colonial official but came to identify with Cuban nationalists. Martí spent much of his time in exile, including working as a journalist in the United States, where he was radicalized by the 1886 Haymarket Square massacre in Chicago that led to the execution of a group of anarchists. Martí returned to Cuba to fight for independence, only to be killed in battle on May 19, 1895. He was subsequently seen as a revolutionary nationalist who worked against economic dependency and for political independence. Martí famously proclaimed, "Revolution is not what we begin in the jungle but what we will develop in the republic." Had he survived, he would have guided subsequent developments in Cuba in a more positive direction.

U.S. intervention in 1898 to ensure that the island remained within its sphere of influence thwarted Martí's dream of a politically and economically independent Cuba. Although the United States pledged not to annex the island, as some territorial expansionists had long desired, the United States controlled Cuba's internal affairs through the addition of the Platt Amendment (so named for its creator, the conservative Republican senator Orville Platt, from Connecticut) to its constitution. This legislation gave the United States "the right to intervene for the preservation of Cuban independence, the maintenance of a government adequate for the protection of life, property and individual liberty." The growth of radical student movements and leftist political parties eventually led to the abrogation of the Platt Amendment in 1934.

BATISTA REGIME

A September 1933 coup d'état known as the Revolt of the Sergeants or the Cuban Revolution of 1933 established Fulgencio Batista as head of the military and launched his long period of influence on Cuban politics. The global economic collapse of 1929 and the authoritarian policies of President Gerardo Machado had led to growing popular discontent. Opposition from the U.S. government forced him from power. A new provisional government under Carlos Manuel de Céspedes y Quesada assumed control but soon collapsed because it, too, was unable to satisfy the demands of enlisted members of the military who had allied with student activists. For the next four months, a new revolutionary government under the leadership of Ramón Grau attempted to push forward a radical program of social and nationalistic reforms that included establishment of an eight-hour workday, cuts to utility rates, land grants to poor peasants, and limits to foreign ownership of the economy. U.S. ambassador Sumner Welles denounced the government as communistic, and the United States refused to recognize it. In January 1934, Batista conspired with Welles to force Grau to resign, thereby ending a radical phase of the revolution and establishing Batista as the power behind the throne. Many Cubans viewed this as a lost opportunity to eliminate corruption, redistribute wealth, and free the country from external control.

For the next six years, Batista ruled Cuba through puppet presidents and then as an elected leader from 1940 to 1944 before temporarily stepping down. The Partido Ortodoxo (Orthodox Party) campaigned in the 1952 elections against the massive corruption and political patronage of the previous two elected administrations. When the populist reform party appeared positioned to win, Batista once again took power in a military coup. Back in office, Batista oversaw a period of uneven modernization and growing social inequalities. His base of support was in the army, but he gradually lost backing from the broader public. Batista censored the media and executed thousands of political opponents to quell discontent with his corrupt and repressive administration. The United States provided Batista with financial, military, and logistical support in his battle against a perceived communist threat.

In the 1950s, Cuba was trapped in a sugar-based, monoculture export economy that was dependent on the cyclical nature of external, particularly U.S., markets. Furthermore, Cuba's sugar industry had stagnated. It suffered from structural unemployment and underemployment due to the nature of a four-month harvest that left workers without a steady income for the other two-thirds of the year. While many urban dwellers were fairly well off, those in rural areas suffered grinding poverty. The extreme inequalities in the country fueled a sense of social injustice.

The Cuban economy suffered from extreme U.S. corporate control. Foreigners owned more than 80 percent of the country's utilities, mines, cattle ranches, and oil refineries, as well as half of the public highways and 40 percent of the sugar industry. Similar to Mexico on the eve of its revolution, in 1958, U.S. investment on the island reached $1 billion. The situation was ready to explode.

MONCADA BARRACKS

On July 26, 1953, Fidel Castro led an attack of mostly young people on the Moncada army barracks in the eastern Cuban city of Santiago. He had engaged in the audacious and arguably foolhardy action with the hope that it would spark a popular uprising across the island. Militarily, the attack was a miserable failure. Of the 160 participants, 80, including Fidel and his brother Raúl Castro (1931–), were captured within three days. More than 60 were killed, some in the attack and others after being brutally tortured in prison. The assault on Moncada took place on the centennial of José Martí's birth. Castro referenced the independence leader twelve times in his courtroom defense, which supporters smuggled out of prison and published as *History Will Absolve Me*. He concluded the speech with the famous proclamation, "Condemn me—it does not matter. History will absolve me." He successfully turned his defeat into a clarion call for revolution.

The Cuban government sentenced Castro and his coconspirators to lengthy prison terms. For Castro, it was a time of reading, reflecting, and developing ideas. Castro argued that political independence was not sufficient for the island to realize its potential. Rather, as Martí had advocated, Cuba also needed to gain its economic independence from the United States. This led the revolutionary leader to examine issues of imperialism and colonialism. Castro's interpretation foreshadowed the 1960s dependency-theory critique that the flow of natural resources from the periphery to an industrial core would underdevelop Latin America's economies. A political revolution was necessary to change this economic situation.

After an intense international campaign for Castro's release, the Cuban government freed him on May 15, 1955, along with the rest of his coconspirators. The former political prisoner left for exile in Mexico, where he continued to develop his plans to overthrow Batista's government. Together with his brother Raúl and Che Guevara, Castro founded the Movimiento 26 de Julio (M-26, 26th of July Movement), named after the date of the attack on the Moncada Barracks. The rebels began preparations for an armed revolt. Their ideology included an embrace of democracy, humanism, pluralism, anti-imperialism, and nationalism.

In December 1956, Castro returned to Cuba with eighty-two fighters on the yacht *Granma*. Frank País (1934–1957), a leader of the urban underground in Santiago, led an uprising that was to coincide with the arrival of the boat. Unfortunately, the yacht did not arrive on time due to a rough sea and the sailors' inexperience. Without the coordinated activity, Batista's troops crushed País's uprising. When the guerrilla force finally landed, it came under intense fire from the Cuban military. It was almost defeated, and only eighteen of the original fighters survived. Those who did, however, took to the remote mountains of Sierra Maestra, where they gathered strength as local peasants joined their struggle.

The pro-Soviet Communist Party of Cuba initially criticized Castro's guerrillas as misguided, adventurous, and lacking theoretical cohesion and a proper ideology. The communists did not believe that Cuba had the necessary level of capitalist economic development for a socialist revolution. They argued that launching an armed struggle in this context was irresponsible and reckless and would inevitably lead to futile bloodshed. Instead, they favored working within the system for structural changes. In fact, some communists had accepted cabinet posts in Batista's first government in the 1930s, a fact that led to their being discredited in the eyes of the guerrillas. Many communists did not join forces with the guerrillas until it was clear they could militarily defeat Batista.

A parallel resistance to the Batista regime grew out of students and professionals organized into an urban underground called the *llano*, or plains, in contrast to the rural guerrillas in the *sierra*, or mountains. A March 13, 1957, attack by the Directorio Revolucionario (Revolutionary Directorate) on the presidential palace in Havana, which mimicked the previous assault on Moncada on the other side of the island, failed to kill Batista. In response, Batista increased his repression of dissidents, including the murder of País on July 30, 1957. His death was a severe blow to the 26th of July Movement.

A planned general strike for April 1958 also failed, which shifted more attention to the rural guerrillas fighting in the eastern Sierra Maestra. As they gained strength, the guerrillas began a march toward Havana in the west with the goal of cutting the island in two. At the end of December 1958, Guevara defeated Batista's forces in the battle of Santa Clara in the middle of the island. In one of the war's most famous actions, the guerrillas derailed and captured an armored train with weapons and reinforcements that the regime had sent against the insurgents. For the first time, the rebels controlled a major city, and this achievement signaled the end of Batista's regime. On January 1, 1959, Batista fled into exile in Miami. A week later, rebel army troops rolled into Havana. They occupied key military posts, and the guerrillas called for a general strike to put down any remaining support for the dictatorship. Castro arrived in Havana to the cheers and open embrace of the general public that was ready to see Batista ousted.

The guerrilla forces won due to their persistence and disciplined nature. They had gained the sympathy of the masses, including the peasants, workers, and urban professionals, thanks in part to the corrupt and repressive nature of Batista's military. Although the military was brutal, naked force alone was not enough to maintain control over the country. Rather, the military disintegrated when it faced a well-organized opposition. Weak conservative institutions, including a Catholic Church that played less of a public role in Cuba than elsewhere in Latin America, meant fewer barriers to the revolution's success. The guerrillas enjoyed the advantages of strong, competent, and motivated leadership. In addition to being idealistic, capture would have meant certain torture and possible death. That potential fate made members of the guerrilla force even more determined to stand firm in their struggle.

BIOGRAPHY: FIDEL CASTRO, 1926–2016

Fidel Castro led the guerrilla 26th of July Movement that toppled the pro–U.S. Fulgencio Batista dictatorship in Cuba in 1959. He was born in 1926 to a wealthy Spanish farmer in northwestern Cuba. His childhood helped him see the vast differences between social classes. Castro attended a Jesuit school, where he received a fine education and excelled as an athlete. He studied law at the University of Havana in the 1940s, where he gained a reputation as a student activist. During his time as a student, he had his first taste of an armed revolution when he participated in an ill-fated invasion of the Dominican Republic in an attempt to remove the strongman Rafael Trujillo from power.

As a student in the 1940s, Castro studied the writings of Karl Marx and the Cuban communist party founder Julio Antonio Mella. Nevertheless, his political activities in the 1950s were those of a revolutionary nationalist and not a

Fidel Castro at a September 22, 1960, meeting of the UN General Assembly
Source: Photo by Warren K. Leffler, Library of Congress Prints & Photographs Online Catalog

Marxist. Castro's justification for the July 26, 1953, assault on the Moncada army barracks highlights the native roots of the Cuban Revolution. In his courtroom defense *History Will Absolve Me*, Castro referred frequently to Cuban independence hero José Martí. Although Martí's social and political program of national reform is evident in this speech, Castro's ideology also shows the influence of other thinkers. Castro read the Peruvian Marxist José Carlos Mariátegui, among others, while in prison from 1953 to 1955. Consistent with Mariátegui's thought, Castro approached Cuba's problems in a nondoctrinaire manner, with a flexible attitude as to how to foment a revolutionary consciousness in an underdeveloped country. Not only was Castro an anti-imperialist and a revolutionary nationalist in the tradition of Martí but he also, like Mariátegui, understood the revolutionary potential of the peasantry and affirmed the value of African and Indigenous cultural expressions.

Despite these intellectual influences, Castro was better known for his organizing skills and charismatic leadership than his political theory or his strength as an ideological thinker. He studied and learned the military strategy that he carried out in his guerrilla warfare in the Sierra Maestra mountains from Augusto César Sandino's fight against the U.S. Marines in Nicaragua in the late 1920s. Like

Sandino, Castro relied on a strategy of flexible organization that could adapt to changing conditions. Both guerrilla leaders depended on a sympathetic peasant base to support their fight.

Castro emphasized that a new Communist Party of Cuba, formed in 1965, would be built on Cuban ideas and methods. At the same time, the party drew on a mixture of both Latin American and European influences. Although Cuba developed close economic ties with the Soviet Union, it refused to submit political control of its communist party to a foreign ideology. In spite of parallel interests with Moscow, Cuba maintained an independent foreign policy.

DOCUMENT: "FIRST DECLARATION OF HAVANA," 1960

In August 1960, a meeting of the Organization of American States (OAS) in Costa Rica declared that Cuba's revolutionary government presented a threat to the Americas because of its links with the Soviet Union. Several days later, more than a million people gathered in Havana's Revolutionary Square to demonstrate their approval of the following declaration in support of the revolution.

Close to the monument and to the memory of José Martí in Cuba, free territory of America, the people, in the full exercise of the inalienable powers that proceed from the true exercise of the sovereignty expressed in the direct, universal and public suffrage, has constituted itself into a national general assembly.

Acting on its own behalf and echoing the true sentiments of the people of our America, the national general assembly of the people of Cuba:

1. Condemns in all its terms the so-called "Declaration of San José," a document dictated by North American imperialism that is detrimental to the national self-determination, the sovereignty and the dignity of the sister nations of the continent.

2. The national general assembly of the people of Cuba energetically condemns the overt and criminal intervention exerted by North American imperialism for more than a century over all the nations of Latin America, which have seen their lands invaded more than once in Mexico, Nicaragua, Haiti, Santo Domingo, and Cuba; have lost, through the voracity of Yankee imperialism, huge and rich areas, whole countries, such as Puerto Rico, which has been converted into an occupied territory; and have suffered, moreover, the outrageous treatment dealt by the marines to our wives and daughters, as well as to the most exalted symbols of our history, such as the statue of José Martí.

    This intervention, based upon military superiority, inequitable treaties and the miserable submission of treacherous rulers throughout one hundred years has converted our America—the America that Bolívar, Hidalgo, Juárez, San Martín, O'Higgins, Sucre, and Martí wanted free—into an area of exploitation, the backyard of the political and financial Yankee empire, a reserve of votes for the international organization in which the Latin America countries have figured only as the herds driven by the "restless and brutal North that despises us."

    The national general assembly of the people declares that the acceptance by the governments that officially represent the countries of Latin America of that continued and historically irrefutable intervention betrays the ideals of independence of its peoples, negates its sovereignty and prevents true solidarity among our nations, all of which obliges this assembly to repudiate it in the name of the people that echoes the hope and determination of the Latin American people and the liberating patriots of our America.

3. The national general assembly of the people of Cuba rejects likewise the intention of preserving the Monroe Doctrine, used until now, as foreseen by José Martí, "to extend the dominance in America" of the voracious imperialists, to better inject the poison also denounced in his time by José Martí, "the poison of the loans, the canals, the railroads. . . ."

Therefore, in the presence of a hypocritical **Pan-Americanism** that is only the dominance of Yankee monopolies over the interests of our people and Yankee manipulation of governments prostrated before Washington, the assembly of the people of Cuba proclaims the liberating Latin-Americanism that throbs in Martí and Benito Juárez. And, upon extending its friendship to the North American people—a country where Negroes are lynched, intellectuals are persecuted and workers are forced to accept the leadership of gangsters—reaffirms its will to march "with all the world and not with just a part of it."

4. The national general assembly of the people declares that the help spontaneously offered by the Soviet Union to Cuba in the event our country is attacked by the military forces of the imperialists could never be considered as an act of intrusion, but that it constitutes an evident act of solidarity, and that such help, offered to Cuba in the face of an imminent attack by the Pentagon, honors the government of the Soviet Union that offered it, as much as the cowardly and criminal aggressions against Cuba dishonor the government of the United States.

Therefore, the general assembly of the people declares, before America and before the world, that it accepts and is grateful for the support of the Soviet Union's rockets, should its territory be invaded by military forces of the United States.

5. The national general assembly of the people of Cuba categorically denies the existence of any intent whatsoever on the part of the Soviet Union and the Chinese People's Republic to "use Cuba's political and social situation . . . to break the continental unity and endanger the unity of the hemisphere." From the first to the last shot, from the first to the last of the twenty thousand martyrs who died in the struggles to overthrow the tyranny and win revolutionary control, from the first to the last revolutionary law, from the first to the last act of the revolution, the people of Cuba have acted with free and absolute self-determination, and therefore, the Soviet Union or the Chinese People's Republic can never be blamed for the existence of a revolution which is Cuba's firm reply to the crimes and wrongs perpetrated by imperialism in America.

On the contrary, the national general assembly of the people of Cuba maintains that the policy of isolation and hostility toward the Soviet Union and the Chinese People's Republic, promoted and imposed by the United States government upon the governments of Latin America, and the belligerent and aggressive conduct of the North American government, as well as its systematic opposition to the acceptance of the Chinese People's Republic as a member of the United Nations, despite the fact that it represents almost the total population of a country of over six hundred million inhabitants, endanger the peace and security of the hemisphere and the world.

Therefore, the national general assembly of the people of Cuba ratifies its policy of friendship with all the peoples of the world, reaffirms its purpose of establishing diplomatic relations with all the socialist countries and, from this moment, in the full exercise of its sovereignty and free will, expresses to the government of the Chinese People's Republic that it agrees to establish diplomatic relations between both countries, and that, therefore, the relations that Cuba has maintained until now with the puppet regime, which is supported in Formosa [Taiwan] by the vessels of the Seventh Fleet, are hereby rescinded.

6. The national general assembly of the people reaffirms—and is certain of doing so as an expression of a view common to all the people of Latin America—that democracy is incompatible with the financial oligarchy, racial discrimination, and the outrages of the Ku Klux Klan, the persecutions that prevented the world from hearing for many years the wonderful voice of Paul Robeson, imprisoned in his own country, and that killed the Rosenbergs, in the face of the protests and the horror of the world and despite the appeal of the rulers of many countries, and of Pope Pius XII, himself.

The national general assembly of the people of Cuba expresses its conviction that democracy cannot consist only in a vote, which is almost always fictitious and manipulated by big land holders and professional politicians, but in the right of the citizens to decide, as this assembly of the people is now deciding, its own destiny. Moreover, democracy will only exist in Latin America when its people are really free to choose, when the humble people are not reduced—by hunger, social inequality, illiteracy, and the juridical systems—to the most degrading impotence.

For all the foregoing reasons, the national general assembly of the people of Cuba:

Condemns the latifundium, a source of poverty for the peasants and a backward and inhuman agricultural system; condemns starvation wages and the iniquitous exploitation of human labor by immoral and privileged interests; condemns illiteracy, the lack of teachers, of schools, of doctors and hospitals, the lack of protection of old age that prevails in Latin America; condemns the inequality and exploitation of women; condemns the discrimination against the Negro and the Indian; condemns the military and political oligarchies that keep our peoples in utter poverty and block their democratic development and the full exercise of their sovereignty; condemns the handing over of our countries' natural resources to the foreign monopolies as a submissive policy that betrays the interests of the peoples; condemns the governments that ignore the feelings of their people and yield to the directives of Washington; condemns the systematic deception of the people by the information media that serve the interests of the oligarchies and the policies of oppressive imperialism; condemns the news monopoly of the Yankee agencies, instruments of the North American trusts and agents of Washington; condemns the repressive laws that prevent workers, peasants, students and intellectuals, which form the great majority of each country, from organizing themselves and fighting for the realization of their social and patriotic aspirations; condemns the monopolies and imperialistic organizations that continuously loot our wealth, exploit our workers and peasants, bleed and keep in backwardness our economies, and submit the political life of Latin America to the sway of their own designs and interests.

In short, the national general assembly of the people of Cuba condemns both the exploitation of man by man and the exploitation of under-developed countries by imperialistic finance capital.

Therefore, the national general assembly of the people of Cuba proclaims before America:

The right of the peasants to the land; the right of the workers to the fruit of their work; the right of children to education; the right of the ill to medical and hospital attention; the right of youth to work; the right of students to free, experimental, and scientific education; the right of Negroes and Indians to "the full dignity of Man"; the right of women to civil, social and political equality; the right of the aged to a secure old age; the right of intellectuals, artists, and scientists to fight, with their works, for a better world; the right of nations to their full sovereignty; the right of nations to turn fortresses into schools, and to arm their workers, their peasants, their students, their intellectuals, the Negro, the Indian, the women, the young and the old, the oppressed and exploited people, so that they may themselves defend their rights and their destinies.

7. The national general assembly of the people of Cuba proclaims: The duty of peasants, workers, intellectuals, Negroes, Indians, young and old, and women, to fight for their economic, political and social rights; the duty of oppressed and exploited nations to fight for their liberation; the duty of each nation to make common cause with all the oppressed, colonized, exploited peoples, regardless of their location in the world or the geographical distance that may separate them. All the peoples of the world are brothers!

8. The national general assembly of the people of Cuba reaffirms its faith that Latin America soon will be marching, united and triumphant, free from the control that turns its economy over to North American imperialism and prevents its true voice from being heard at the meetings where domesticated chancellors form an infamous chorus led by its despotic masters.

   Therefore, it ratifies its decision of working for that common Latin American destiny that will enable our countries to build a true solidarity, based upon the free will of each of them and the joint aspirations of all. In the struggle for such a Latin America, in opposition to the obedient voices of those who usurp its official representation, there arises now, with invincible power, the genuine voice of the people, a voice that rises from the depths of its tin and coal mines, from its factories and sugar mills, from its feudal lands, where *rotos* [a member of the exploited labor force of Chile, generally of Indigenous and European descent], *cholos* [a member of the exploited labor force of Peru, generally of Indigenous and European descent], *gauchos* [Argentine cowboys, an exploited class that forms the backbone of the cattle industry of that country], *jíbaros* [a member of the much-exploited agricultural labor force of Puerto Rico], heirs of Zapata and Sandino, grip the weapons of their freedom, a voice that resounds in its poets and novelists, in its students, in its women and children, in its vigilant old people.

   To that voice of our brothers, the assembly of the people of Cuba answers: "Present!" Cuba shall not fall. Cuba is here today to ratify before Latin America and before the world, as a historical commitment, its irrevocable dilemma: *Patria* [homeland] or Death!

9. The national general assembly of the people of Cuba resolves that this declaration shall be known as "The Declaration of Havana."

Havana, Cuba, Free Territory of America, September 2, 1960

Source: Fidel Castro, *The Declaration of Havana* (n.p.: 26th of July Movement in the United States, 1960).

ROLE OF WOMEN

Women have long been acknowledged for their important roles in the Cuban Revolution, even though, both in the events themselves and in subsequent retelling, they are relegated to support rather than leadership roles in what has always been an over-whelmingly male-dominated movement. Women participated in urban underground movements that challenged Batista's government even before the 1953 attack on the Moncada Barracks. Their activities included the traditionally gendered domestic tasks of cooking, cleaning, and caring for the wounded. As elsewhere, women were effective spies, couriers, smugglers, and recruiters for the movement. Particularly in rural areas, women faced patriarchal attitudes that proscribed their active involvement.

Nevertheless, the revolutionaries sometimes challenged the limitations women faced. In September 1958, the rebel army created an all-women's platoon named after Mariana Grajales (1815–1893), an icon of Cuba's independence struggles. Grajales's sons José and Antonio Maceo served as generals in the Ten Years' War (1868–1878) that had failed to free Cuba from Spanish control. During that war, Grajales ran field hospitals and provided provisions to the soldiers. She was hailed for her willingness to enter the battlefield to aid wounded soldiers, playing a role similar to the soldaderas in the Mexican Revolution. In the guerrilla insurrection, the Grajales platoon went beyond such support roles to engage in active fighting and in the process challenged the chauvinism of some of their male counterparts. Their example inspired other women to join the revolution.

Two women, Haydée Santamaría (1922–1980) and Melba Hernández (1921–2014), participated in the assault on the Moncada Barracks. Similar to Castro's father, Santamaría's Spanish parents were small-scale sugar planters. Santamaría participated in almost every step of the revolutionary process, beginning with her capture and imprisonment in the aftermath of the Moncada attack. She told her prison guards that if her brother Abel and fiancé Boris Luis Santa Coloma, who had been tortured and killed after their arrests, would not speak, neither would she. In May 1954, the government released Santamaría from prison, and she continued her work on behalf of the revolutionary movement. She arranged for the publication of Castro's speech *History Will Absolve Me* as a pamphlet and assisted in its distribution as a propaganda tool.

In 1956, Santamaría helped organize the November 30 Santiago uprising with Frank País that was to coincide with the arrival of the *Granma* on the Cuban coast. Even though she had never before left the island, in 1958, revolutionary leaders sent her to Miami to organize on behalf of the M-26 and to buy guns for the guerrillas. Despite having only a sixth-grade education, after the triumph of the revolution, Santamaría founded and ran the publishing house Casa de las Américas. She built it into one of the most important cultural institutions in Latin America, one that was renowned for publishing literary works. When militants formed the Communist Party of Cuba in 1965, she was selected as a member of its central committee and remained at the highest levels of leadership for her entire life. In 1967, she presided over the Organización Latinoamericana de Solidaridad (OLAS, Latin American Solidarity Organization). Until her death in 1980, she played a key role in fostering the development of the revolution.

Celia Sánchez (1920–1980) was another key founder of the Cuban Revolution. Her father's occupation as a doctor provided her with the necessary cover and connections to work effectively as a member of the 26th of July Movement in her native province of Manzanillo. She made arrangements for the landing of the *Granma* and was responsible for organizing their reinforcements in Cuba. She helped supply the rebels with weapons, food, and medical supplies. In 1957, she was the first woman to join the guerrilla army and rose through the ranks to become a member of the rebel army's general staff.

Sánchez was Castro's closest companion. After the triumph of the revolution, she served as secretary to the presidency of the Council of Ministers and in the Department of Services of the Council of State. Together with Santamaría, in 1965, Sánchez was named to the communist party's central committee. With her death from lung cancer in 1980, Castro lost a close confidante. Some observers say he was never the same afterward.

GUERRILLAS IN POWER

The war ended when Batista fled in the face of the guerrillas closing in on Havana on New Year's Day 1959. That triumph was only the beginning of the revolution. The task of radically transforming the country's political and economic structures now lay before them. The guerrillas enjoyed enormous popular backing, but supporters had widely divergent views on what should happen next. Castro embraced a Pan-Americanist ideology, much like that which Latin American independence leaders Simón Bolívar and José Martí had previously expressed. In addition, he was an anti-imperialist. He argued that property should not be seen as a right but should serve a social function in society. This ideology led to a nationalization of subsoil rights and public services, as well as an agrarian reform that included the expropriation of large estates and the formation of cooperatives. The revolutionaries wanted to remake the country so that the island's resources benefited common people rather than foreign capitalist enterprises.

DOCUMENT: CENTRAL INTELLIGENCE AGENCY (CIA), "COMMUNIST INFLUENCE IN CUBA," 1960

As in Guatemala and Bolivia, U.S. government officials were preoccupied with a communist presence in the Cuban Revolution. During the insurrection and immediately after the triumph of the revolution, the Central Intelligence Agency (CIA) scrambled to make sense of the situation. While they identified communists in the government (most notably Raúl Castro and Che Guevara), they did not think that Fidel Castro was a communist, nor did they think the revolution would come under communist control.

Special National Intelligence Estimate
SNIE 85–60, Washington, March 22, 1960.

The Problem

To estimate present and probable future Communist control or influence over the leadership and policies of the Castro regime in Cuba.

The Estimate

1. The trend of events in Cuba is a source of deep satisfaction to the leaders of international communism. Fidel Castro is embarked on a bitter and virulent anti-US campaign directed not only at the Cuban population but also at public opinion throughout Latin America. In the domestic field, Castro is pursuing an increasingly radical program employing techniques used by the Communists themselves in other countries. The government has expropriated without adequate arrangements for compensation or has otherwise assumed control over a wide range of business enterprises, ranging from sugar plantations and cattle ranches to mines, factories, airlines, and hotels, in many of which US investors have had a considerable stake. Castro has declared that his goal is the elimination of private enterprise, foreign or domestic, from all major sectors of the economy. He recently stated that private foreign capital will henceforth be accepted for investment in Cuba only if delivered to the government to be used as it sees fit. Economic power has become centralized in the recently established Central Planning Board, the National Bank, and the National Institute for Agrarian Reform (INRA). The Central Planning Board is headed by Fidel Castro himself. The Bank is directed by "Che" Guevara, a staunch pro-Communist, the INRA by Núñez Jiménez, a known Communist. The INRA is a virtual state within a state and has sweeping powers over agriculture, industry, and commerce.

2. Local Communists have been readily accepted by the regime as participants in the process of remaking Cuba. At the same time, the administration has been purged of anti-Communist elements, including not only professional personnel who had served under Batista, but also even those adherents of the 26th of July Movement who have sought to moderate the pace of change and to curb Communist influence. Under the direction of Fidel Castro's brother Raúl, and under the influence of "Che" Guevara, the armed services, police, and investigative agencies have been brought under unified control, purged of Batista professionals as well as other outspoken anti-Communist elements, and subjected to Communist-slanted political indoctrination courses; a civilian militia composed of students, workers, and peasants is being trained and armed. At least nine of the most prominent anti-Communist leaders of the Confederation of Cuban Workers (CTC) have been eliminated from the labor organization and others effectively silenced. Although Communists probably constitute a small proportion of the CTC membership, at least five active pro-Communists have been elevated to the 13-man CTC Executive Committee, some in key positions. Although CTC Secretary General David Salvador was "expelled" from the Popular Socialist (Communist) Party (PSP) in 1951, he has been active in promoting Communist influence in the labor movement and has become a prominent spokesman for the government's policies.

3. All the old-line, non-Communist political parties have been disrupted or cowed. The PSP now is the only effective political body in Cuba except for Castro's own 26th of July Movement, a loosely organized vehicle of popular support for Castro which lacks most of the characteristics of a political party. Relegalized in effect

by Castro on his assumption of power, the PSP occupies no official role in the government and has deliberately avoided the appearance of seeking power for itself. Although the party has openly sought to develop its base in labor, education, and the entertainment industry, its overt apparatus, press, and front organizations have generally concentrated on drumming up support for Castro and his policies; top PSP leaders have generally remained in the background, and party strength has probably not risen significantly above its estimated June 1959 total of 17,000. However, the PSP has had considerable success in penetrating the military, INRA and other parts of the government, and the 26th of July Movement—and in utilizing the government's tendency to equate anticommunism with counterrevolution and treason. Fidel Castro's chief lieutenants, Raúl Castro and "Che" Guevara, have long records of association with Communists and a marked affinity for Communist economic and political concepts; they are strong pro-Communists if not actual Communists.

4. Meanwhile, the Castro regime has also developed significant contacts with the Bloc. Although formal diplomatic relations have yet to be established with any of the Communist powers, a $100 million Soviet credit to Cuba and a five-year trade agreement were concluded during Soviet Deputy Premier Mikoyan's visit to Cuba to open the Soviet exposition in February 1960. The agreement calls for Soviet purchases of one million tons of Cuban sugar annually, at world prices, of which 20 percent is payable in hard currency and the rest in merchandise and services. Early in March banking arrangements for the exchange of over $4 million in commodities with East Germany were concluded. Czechoslovakia has also expressed interest in a trade deal. The joint Cuban-Soviet statement issued upon Mikoyan's departure from Cuba called for close collaboration by the two countries in the UN. Cuba is currently seeking a seat in the Security Council and will probably receive considerable support from the Soviet Bloc as well as from the Afro-Asian countries. The Cuban-sponsored Latin American news agency, *Prensa Latina*, which is a major vehicle of anti-US propaganda, has working relations with news agencies from the Sino-Soviet Bloc as well as from neutralist countries and is using Bloc materials in its output. The Chinese Communist news agency has established a branch in Havana. In contrast to Cuban fulminations against the US, official statements in the press have been generally favorable to the Bloc.

5. These developments obviously raise serious questions as to the degree to which Cuba may now be or may become subject to international Communist control. Certainly the local Communists have taken advantage of the opportunities afforded them to influence the course of government policy and to develop their own position within the armed forces, INRA, and other key elements of the Cuban political structure. Prolongation of the present situation will result in even greater Communist influence in Cuba and will further encourage Communists and other anti-US elements throughout Latin America.

6. However, Fidel Castro remains the dominant element in the regime and we believe that he is not disposed to accept actual direction from any foreign source. His susceptibility to Communist influence and suggestion and his willing adoption of Communist patterns of action spring from the parallelism of his revolutionary views with the current Communist line in Latin America, from his conviction that Communism offers no threat to his regime, and from his need for external support. He almost certainly has no intention of sharing his power or of abandoning his announced objective of developing a neutralist "third force" position for Cuba and other nations of Latin America in association with the Afro-Asian world. Moreover, his fanatic determination to direct the course of the revolution and the preponderant popular support he commands would

make it difficult at this time for the Cuban Communists or their Bloc supporters to force Fidel Castro in a direction contrary to that of his choice. We consider it extremely unlikely that the PSP, which has little broad support among the Cuban people, could soon develop sufficient strength to make openly an effective bid for power on its own. Although development of pro-Communist strength in the armed forces and elsewhere may eventually give them such a capability, we believe that Fidel Castro's appeal to the Cuban masses, rather than the coercive power of the armed forces, represents the present mainstay of the regime. In the event of Fidel Castro's death, Raúl Castro and "Che" Guevara would assume the leadership of the regime. Under these two, the Communists would be given an even greater opportunity to perfect their organization and to influence the policy of the government. Raúl Castro and "Che" Guevara, however, would not command the popular support which Fidel Castro now inspires.

7.   We believe that for some time Communist leaders will continue to concentrate on influencing the formulation and implementation of policy and on covert infiltration of the government—and that they will avoid any challenge to Fidel Castro's authority or any claim to formal PSP participation in the government. Particularly in the light of Soviet experiences with Kassim and Nasser, the Soviet leaders are well aware of the need for caution in dealing with messianic national-ist leaders. They probably believe that the present state of affairs is weakening the US position and advancing their interests, not only in Cuba, but throughout Latin America. The Communists probably also believe that the US will lose in-fluence and prestige so long as Castro's successful defiance of the US (including his acceptance of bloc assistance) continues, and that the US is faced with the dilemma of tolerating an increasingly Communist-oriented Cuba or of arousing widespread Latin American opposition by intervening. Above all, the Soviets probably wish to avoid a situation in which the US could secure broad Latin American support for action to curb Castro. While Castro's regime has lost pres-tige in Latin America, particularly among government officials and the upper and middle classes, few popular leaders in the area are prepared to dismiss Castro as merely a pro-Communist demagogue. For many Latin Americans, especially the masses, Castro remains an important symbol as a destroyer of the old order and as a champion of social revolution and of anti-US and anticapitalist feeling.

8.   We believe that Fidel Castro and his government are not now demonstrably under the domination or control of the international Communist movement. Moreover, we believe that they will not soon come under such demonstrable domination or control. We reach this conclusion in part because we feel that under present circumstances international Communism does not desire to see a situation arise in which it could be clearly demonstrated that the regime in Cuba was under its domination. Yet, we believe that the Cuban regime is in practice following the line set for Latin American Communist Parties at the time of the 21st Party Congress in Moscow in February 1959 and that it will continue to pur-sue policies advantageous to the Communists and to accept Communist assis-tance and advice in carrying them out. Cuba may give increasing appearances of becoming a Communist society. Although Castro may for tactical reasons seem at times to moderate his relations with the US, he appears intent on pressing ahead with his anti-US campaign, which might come to involve attempted ex-pulsion of the US from its Guantánamo Base, abandonment of Cuba's privileged position in the US sugar market, a complete diplomatic rupture, and danger to the lives of American citizens. The more he becomes embroiled with the US, the more he will look to the Bloc for support, including provision of military equip-ment, although both the Bloc and the Cubans would probably seek to avoid

any accusation that Cuba was being made into a Soviet base. Should the Castro regime be threatened, the USSR would probably do what it could to support it. However, the USSR would not hesitate to write off the Castro regime before involving itself in a direct military confrontation with the US over Cuba, or, at least during the present state of Soviet policy, in a major diplomatic crisis with the US.

Source: Central Intelligence Agency, "Communist Influence in Cuba," March 22, 1960, https://www.cia.gov/readingroom/document/0000132455.

Destruction of the Old Regime (1959–1962)

The initial goal of the guerrillas once they took power was to consolidate their domestic political position. The leaders sought to centralize power as well as to crack down on their political opposition and a conservative press that could challenge their hold on power. The guerrillas engaged in public trials and executed thousands of Batista's henchmen. They purged conservatives and strengthened their alliances with communists in order to fortify their political position. These moves created a polarized split between moderate and radical supporters of the revolution. Moderates only wanted to remove Batista from power and disagreed with implementing far-reaching social reforms based on a leftist ideology.

One of the first policy objectives of the new revolutionary government was to socialize the economy. Similar to the Guatemalan and Bolivian revolutions earlier in the decade, a centerpiece of the agenda was an expansive agrarian reform program that was designed to alter extreme inequalities in landholding. A May 1959 decree restricted the size of estates. Property holdings were so concentrated that the law affected 85 percent of the farms on the island. The government distributed the land in small plots to individual farmers for subsistence agriculture in addition to creating agricultural cooperatives for commercial purposes. Much of this land distribution took place in Oriente (eastern) province, where the guerrillas had enjoyed early peasant support for their struggle.

The government kept some of the large estates intact and converted them into state farms. The same workers continued to work the land, but now they were paid better wages and labored under improved working conditions. The government sought to diversify agricultural production in the country. An elusive goal was to gain agricultural self-sufficiency through the transfer of farmland from sugarcane production to cotton, rice, soybeans, and peanuts.

The new revolutionary government prioritized a redistribution of income. They achieved this goal through lowering rents and utilities and providing free social services to the public. As a result, wages rose 40 percent, purchasing power rose 20 percent, and unemployment disappeared because all members of society were assured of a job. The revolutionaries also sought to gain economic independence from the United States. They achieved this through the nationalization of foreign industries, including telephone companies, oil refineries, factories, utilities, sugar mills, banking, and urban housing. The redistributive policies later targeted Cuban-owned businesses.

One of the greatest triumphs of the revolution was the 1961 literacy campaign, when more than one hundred thousand workers taught almost a million people to read and write. It built on such slogans as, "If you know, teach; if you don't know, learn"; "Every Cuban a teacher; every house a school"; and "The people should teach the people." It followed in the footsteps of José Martí's statement, "To know how to read is to know how to walk." That initiative raised literacy levels from 76 percent before the revolution to 96 percent in 1962, the highest in Latin America and a level that equaled that of wealthy, industrialized countries. This high percentage of people who could read and write indicated that the island was essentially free of illiteracy. The campaign was such a success that it became a model that other countries subsequently followed.

The revolutionary government converted military barracks into schools and hospitals to liberate rather than oppress the population. They opened private beaches and social clubs to the general public. The Cuban revolutionaries developed new organizations to solidify support for their political project. The government founded neighborhood vigilance committees called Comités de Defensa de la Revolución (CDR, Committees for the Defense of the Revolution) to promote social welfare and report on counterrevolutionary activity. The Organizaciones Revolucionarias Integradas (ORI, Integrated Revolutionary Organizations), founded in March 1962, unified Castro's 26th of July Movement, the communist party, and the Revolutionary Directorate. At the end of 1963, revolutionaries formed the Partido Unificado de la Revolución Socialista (PURS, United Party of the Socialist Revolution) to replace the traditional communist party. Rather than a mass party, it had a selective membership, and joining the party was a privilege. In 1965, PURS became the new Communist Party of Cuba. Youth organizations also flourished after the triumph of the revolution. Founded in October 1960, the Association of Young Rebels grouped youth in the ORI. In April 1962, the association was changed to the Unión de Jóvenes Comunistas (UJC, Union of Young Communists).

In 1960, Vilma Espín (1930–2007), a wealthy chemist from the privileged sectors of society who was married to Raúl Castro, founded the Federación de Mujeres Cubanas (FMC, Federation of Cuban Women) with official support. Early goals of the FMC included domestic programs such as teaching women household skills. As with other early, second-wave feminist organizations, the FMC emphasized the importance of education and an eradication of misogynist ideas. As the revolution advanced, the FMC sought to involve women in society, on both an economic and a political level. The FMC drew women out of the home and into the workforce and also involved them in the political formation of a collective society. The FMC emphasized the importance of daycare for children so that women could join the labor force.

The revolution produced important gains for women. Many young women left their homes to teach in the famous 1961 literacy campaign, and for the first time, they experienced a broader world. More than half of those who learned to read and write in the campaign were women, and with these new skills they joined medical and biological fields in large numbers. Even so, women remained responsible for domestic labor in the house, so-called second-shift work. This incentivized young and poor women to demand more, and they criticized the FMC leadership for approaching women's problems from the perspective of privileged sectors of society. They wanted mutual respect from their husbands and equally shared responsibilities in domestic tasks and the care of children. The FMC leaders wanted to preserve the nuclear family, but many poor women saw the traditional family structure as a source of oppression. Furthermore, as with the Barzolas in Bolivia, the FMC was organized from the top down to consolidate women's support for the revolution instead of being dedicated to transforming gender relations.

BIOGRAPHY: VILMA ESPÍN, 1930–2007

Throughout her entire life, Vilma Espín was one of the most committed feminists and revolutionaries in Cuba. She helped organize and supply the 26th of July Movement during the insurrection in the 1950s, and after the triumph of the revolution until her death in 2007, she took an active role in advancing the revolutionary agenda. Espín is best known for founding the Federation of Cuban Women (FMC) in 1960 and was instrumental in passing the Cuban Family Code in 1975, but those are only two of the many roles that she played in Cuba.

Vilma Espín
Source: Wikimedia Commons/Public Domain

Espín was born in Santiago de Cuba, in eastern Cuba, to a wealthy Cuban lawyer who was an executive for the Bacardi rum company. She studied chemical engineering at the Universidad de Oriente (University of Oriente), in Santiago, and in 1954 was one of the first women to graduate from that program. She subsequently studied for a year at the Massachusetts Institute of Technology (MIT) in Cambridge, Massachusetts. Upon her return to Cuba in 1956, she joined Frank País as part of the 26th of July Movement in Oriente province to launch an uprising that was to coincide with the landing of the *Granma*. One of her jobs was to carry messages between País, in Cuba, and Fidel and Raúl Castro, who were in exile in Mexico. Espín's fluency in both English and Spanish allowed her to represent the revolutionary movement internationally and to translate for the *New York*

Times reporter Herbert Matthews when he interviewed Fidel Castro in 1957. That report proved that Castro was still alive, and presented his band of guerrillas as a formidable force. Espín joined the Rebel Army in July 1958, one of only a handful of women combatants.

In addition to founding the FMC and leading it until her death in 2007, Espín also played other roles in the Cuban revolutionary government. She was a member of the Central Committee of the Communist Party of Cuba from its refounding in 1965 until 1989, of the Council of State after 1976, and of the Political Bureau after 1980. She also worked with a variety of other Cuban organizations and commissions on food, children, and health issues. Internationally, Espín headed Cuban delegations to meetings of the Women's International Democratic Federation (WIDF) and in 1973 became a vice president of the organization. She also served as Cuba's representative to the United Nations General Assembly.

Espín's advocacy for gender equality and the transformation of the roles of women and others in Cuba influenced the activities of her family members. Her daughter, Mariela Castro Espín, is the director of the Centro Nacional de Educación Sexual (CENESEX, National Center for Sex Education). In addition to fostering a sex-positive climate and promoting reproductive rights, the center advocates for acceptance of sexual diversity and marriage equality in what traditionally had been a very homophobic society. It has significantly advanced gay and lesbian issues and has campaigned for the rights of transgender persons. Both Mariela Castro and her mother, Vilma Espín, worked hard to make Cuba one of the most progressive countries in Latin America on gender issues.

DOCUMENT: VILMA ESPÍN,
"A REVOLUTION WITHIN A REVOLUTION," 1988

The following is a brief extract of an interview with Vilma Espín by Claudia, a Brazilian women's magazine, in 1988. It describes how the Cuban Revolution advanced women's rights.

> For the Cuban family, especially the woman, socialism has meant an enormous improvement to the quality of life and personal development. We should remember that until January 1, 1959, in our country hunger, poverty, exploitation, repression, and dependence reigned. The revolution opened up new horizons in the economic, political and social fields and amongst its key principles is the defense of equal rights for all human beings.
>
> The constant struggle to make ends meet disappeared, and with it the antagonism between people competing for the crumbs that could help them escape the tragic destiny that awaited the majority. Thus the family, the basic cell of society, could develop in a rounded way.
>
> Our revolution assured all Cubans the chance to exercise each one of their inalienable rights. Each citizen is assured that food prices are reasonable and that education and medical services are free. The state makes a systematic effort to improve living standards, to the extent that it is permitted by the tense battle for development we wage under blockade and constant imperialist threats.

Childcare facilities have been created to provide care for the children of tens of thousands of working women from the age of three months to six years. Services to lighten domestic work have also been created; hundreds of thousands of students also receive free lunch at day school and all their meals at boarding school.

Hundreds of thousands of workers also receive their meals at a moderate price in their workplace. More industrial laundries and dry cleaners have been established, and more domestic labor-saving devices are available with preference in acquisition and cheaper prices for workers.

Huge resources are dedicated to housing construction in urban and rural zones. We also try to guarantee recreational facilities and spiritual enjoyment to all the population.

Of course the possibilities are exciting, but also what we have achieved to date, considering our limitations, is already vastly superior to what families experienced in the past. Social security provides an income for those who cannot work.

As far as women·are concerned, equal rights have certainly changed their position in the family and in society. A woman's participation in social production, because it implies her financial independence, has altered her dependent position in the marriage and allowed a change in her ideas, in the way she looks at life. The laws that govern family relations, such as the Family Code, are based on equality and guarantee the right of members of the family to participate in society: to work, study and to responsibly educate the children in line with our revolutionary principles. This does not mean that we have achieved all that we aspire to. We still have problems of a material nature to resolve, which are directly related to our economic development. There is still the need to eliminate backward ideas that some people hold, men and women, with respect to the nature of the socialist family and the relationship between a couple, ideas which work against the full participation of women in the building of a new society.

Obviously, the economic security guaranteed by both men and women having access to work, free health care and education; the enormous satisfaction and confidence in oneself that equal opportunity and the chance to fully develop to the extent of one's talents, intelligence and aptitudes offer to each person; the constant motivation and emotional stability that comes from feeling useful, recognized and dignified as a human being—everything that socialism has brought to us—undoubtedly fulfills the deepest desires of a family, particularly the woman who, until just over a quarter century ago, was exploited, oppressed and marginalized in the family and in society.

Source: Vilma Espín, *Cuban Women Confront the Future: Three Decades after the Revolution*, 2d ed. (Melbourne, Australia: Ocean, 1991), 1–3.

The revolutionaries established a new pattern of foreign relations. Some leaders saw the Soviet Union as their most logical ally and protector from their revolution's inevitable conflict with the United States. Cuba resumed diplomatic relations with the Soviet Union, and in turn the Soviets agreed to buy Cuban sugar, although they faced the liability of the long distance in shipping the commodity. In addition, Cuba actively pursued an internationalist foreign policy. The government supported guerrilla movements in Panama, Nicaragua, the Dominican Republic, and Haiti. Scholars have debated whether an idealist drive to spread a socialist revolution motivated the decision to back other insurgencies or whether more pragmatic considerations of gaining international allies and deflecting U.S. attacks away from Cuba inspired those policy choices.

Cuba strongly supported anticolonial movements in Africa. In 1960, Cuba provided military aid and medical personnel to the Algerian National Liberation Front in its fight against French colonialism. The following year, military instructors arrived in Ghana to assist guerrillas fighting in Upper Volta (now called Burkina Faso), and in 1965 Che Guevara led a contingent of two hundred combat troops to join a revolutionary struggle in Congo. Most significant was Cuba's military support in the 1970s for Angolan independence and against the intervention of apartheid South Africa. Operation Carlota, named after an enslaved African woman who led an 1843 uprising on the island, included a massive airlift of Cuban volunteer troops to assist in the defense of the Angolan capital of Luanda. The operation culminated in the fierce battle of Cuito Cuanavale in 1988, in which the Cubans helped roll back the South African advance, thereby contributing to the defeat of apartheid.

The new Cuban government's domestic and international policies soon strained relations with the United States. Some scholars viewed the confrontation as inevitable because of the United States' long-standing desire to control the island's destiny. Expropriation of large estates under the agrarian reform legislation, particularly those estates that U.S. citizens and corporations owned, only heightened these tensions. Relations spun downward when in May 1960, Cuban officials told Texaco, Standard, and Shell to process crude oil that the country had received from the Soviet Union in their refineries. The Eisenhower administration instructed the companies to refuse, and in June the Cubans expropriated the refineries. In response, Eisenhower ended Cuba's sugar quota, which only led the Cuban government to expropriate more U.S.-owned properties. In October, the United States placed a trade embargo on Cuba that included the banning of U.S. exports to the island. The action led to more Cuban expropriations, including Sears, Coca-Cola, and U.S.-owned nickel deposits. In January 1961, shortly before leaving office, Eisenhower broke diplomatic relations with the neighboring republic. It is unclear who started the diplomatic tit for tat between the two countries, but once the downward spiral began, it was very difficult to halt the deterioration of relations.

Soon after Batista's departure, the CIA initiated funding of exile groups to remove the revolutionaries from power. During the summer of 1960, the CIA set up training camps in Guatemala. In March 1961, the newly installed president John F. Kennedy granted approval for the CIA-created force to invade the island. The mercenaries entered at the Bay of Pigs on April 15, 1961, but the Cuban forces were waiting for them on the shore known as Playa Girón. The invasion was poorly planned and executed, and it quickly turned into a rout. By April 19, the Cubans had defeated the invaders. The wealthy anticommunist exiles promised Kennedy that the locals felt betrayed by the direction the revolution had taken and would rise up against Castro's government. The common people, however, had benefited substantially from the revolution's social programs and redistributive policies. They had no desire to return to Batista's repressive and exclusionary regime that the invading mercenary force represented. The Bay of Pigs failure highlighted just how little policy makers in the United States understood Cuban realities.

The U.S. defeat at Playa Girón increased Castro's support and prestige in the country. This led to a quickened pace of reforms and a radicalization of the revolution. The failed invasion provided Castro with a convenient opportunity to announce the socialist nature of the revolution. On December 2, 1961, Castro proclaimed, "I am a Marxist-Leninist, and I will be a Marxist-Leninist until the last days of my life." Observers subsequently debated whether Castro had been a communist from the beginning of the revolution and, as an astute politician, had waited until the proper moment to make such a proclamation or whether the irrational responses of the country's logical trade partner, the United States, had forced him to turn to the Soviet Union. If this were the case, a declaration of the socialist nature of the revolution was merely a ploy to gain Soviet support.

On February 4, 1962, the United States convinced the Organization of American States (OAS) to expel Cuba from its membership. Over the course of the next several years, the U.S. government strong-armed most of the other American republics to break diplomatic relations with the Cuban government. A notable exception was Mexico, and its maintenance of relations with the communist island provided the United States with a convenient backdoor for secret talks with its adversary.

On October 22, 1962, Kennedy ordered a quarantine of the island and demanded the dismantling of missiles that the Soviets were installing to protect the Cubans from a threatened U.S. invasion. The two governments disagreed whether the missiles were of a defensive or offensive nature. During the course of a tense period of thirteen days known as the Cuban Missile Crisis, the U.S. military pressed for an invasion of the island, but instead the two superpowers reached an agreement. The Soviet Union agreed to remove the missiles, and in exchange, the United States pledged not to invade the country and to remove missiles they had installed in Turkey that were targeted at their adversary. For their part, Cuban leaders wanted to be treated as equals to the superpowers on the global stage, and they were bitterly upset when the two Cold War opponents negotiated behind their backs. Although the Cubans and Soviets would subsequently present a public face as warm allies, the betrayal permanently altered their warm diplomatic relations even as their economic ties strengthened.

After the Cuban Missile Crisis, the United States never again attempted to invade the island, but it did continue its attacks against the government, targeting the economy, infrastructure, and even civilians. The CIA repeatedly launched raids against the country's refineries and ports and infiltrated enemy agents onto the island. Most famous were the assassination plots against government leaders. Operation Mongoose included such ludicrous plans as providing Castro with exploding cigars or powder that would make his beard fall off. Although these plots were not successful in overthrowing the Cuban government, fighting off the constant attacks made it more difficult for revolutionaries to advance their progressive social programs.

Period of Experimentation (1962–1966)

The Cuban revolutionaries enjoyed various advantages that allowed them to proceed quickly with the implementation of their socialist experiment soon after they had dismantled the previous regime. The revolutionary war had caused relatively little destruction of life and property, and so they did not need to put as much effort into reconstruction as would have been the case after a long and drawn-out civil war such as Mexico had faced. Cuba had a fairly well-developed infrastructure, which provided a strong groundwork on which to build socialist programs. These factors helped offset the economic damage of the U.S. embargo.

A large portion of the Cuban labor force had been unionized before the revolution, and this provided workers with a good deal of political awareness and organizational structure. Even in the sugarcane fields, Cuba's proletarianized agricultural workforce had a high level of class consciousness. Workers had sympathy with the revolutionary changes sweeping the country, as well as motivation to participate actively in them. For the most part, rather than demanding land, an agrarian proletariat fought for better working conditions and wages. The government used idle farmland and increased industrial capacity to improve living standards. According to some Marxists, on the eve of the revolution, Cuba had not a feudal mode of production but rather an advanced capitalist economy, albeit one based on rural sugar production rather than an urban, industrial workforce. From this perspective, Cuba had witnessed not a peasant revolt but precisely the type of proletarian revolution that resulted from working-class alienation, although in this case it was rooted in a rural rather than urban proletariat. If this were indeed the case, an additional but little-understood advantage that Cuba enjoyed was the presence of the proper, objective economic conditions that orthodox Marxists had long argued were necessary for a socialist revolution. Possibly for this reason Cuba experienced more success while other revolutions failed.

Despite these advantages, the Cuban revolutionaries faced a range of problems. Many of the economic experts and ablest technicians came from the professional class that identified with the previous capitalist system. The implementation of socialist policies led them to leave the country. The inexperience of the revolutionaries who replaced the trained professionals contributed to errors that caused disruptions in the economy and the smooth functioning of society. The revolutionaries pumped money and resources into rural housing and infrastructure, but poor planning resulted in a waste of scarce resources. In a drive to socialize the economy, officials ignored the private sector, which still comprised half of the country's economy. Government policies that favored affordable food for consumers forced farmers to sell their crops at low prices. Those farmers who were motivated by the marketplace had few incentives to increase their production.

The U.S. embargo caused crippling shortages that damaged the economy. With a cutoff of trade with the United States, the Cubans shifted their trade relations to Eastern Europe, which introduced a series of problems. Their new trade partners were geographically more distant than their close neighbors to the north, which added significantly to shipping costs and logistics. Language barriers also introduced challenges. Relying on new suppliers generated unforeseen problems with replacement parts as equipment aged, since the global metric-sized threads and tools were not compatible with the existing machinery manufactured in the United States.

Redistribution of resources from the former ruling to a newly empowered working class created new challenges. A growth in disposable income prompted increases in consumer demands. Before the revolution, meat consumption was largely limited to the wealthy, but now many more people had access to the wages necessary to buy meat. This demand precipitated the overkilling of cattle, which lowered their reproduction rates and soon resulted in scarcities. A lack of imports also caused shortages. A paucity of consumer products forced the introduction of rationing in March 1962. The rationing was to be a short-term measure designed to ensure equal and democratic access to resources until production could rebound and make such distribution systems unnecessary. Half a century later, ration booklets were an institutionalized aspect of the revolution and pointed to one of its major shortcomings.

Even with these limitations, a good deal of idealism motivated the revolutionaries. Che Guevara in particular emphasized what he called the "New Socialist Man" who would be motivated by moral rather than material incentives. Instead of working hard to improve an individual's economic situation, Guevara encouraged people to concentrate on the improvement of society. This goal required a significant shift away from the fundamentally liberal goals of improved wages and working conditions toward a class consciousness that instead fought for a change from a capitalist to a communist mode of production. Guevara set a personal example by sacrificing time with his family on weekends to participate in voluntary work projects. Despite his best efforts, the Cuban public did not respond entirely well to the emphasis on moral incentives. By 1969, the government moved to a more pragmatic mix of engaging both material and moral incentives.

The positive socioeconomic gains of the period of experimentation proved to be quite remarkable. Building on the success of the 1961 literacy campaign, the revolutionaries quickly built a strong education system. By mid-1961, all Cuban schools were public and free. The rapid growth of literacy and educational opportunities introduced a new set of challenges. The government could not keep up with the demand for schools and faced shortages of teachers and classroom materials. Increased access to educational opportunities contributed to a growth in social aspirations. Many people were no longer content to work in agriculture as unskilled laborers. Instead, they sought to put their new education to use in professional fields. Their upwardly mobile aspirations created shortages as previously unskilled workers moved away from productive sectors of the economy.

Government policies that shifted resources from the wealthy to the poor overcame class disparities and significantly shrank income inequalities. The difference in wages between the highest- and lowest-paid individual in a company could not be any greater than four to one. The revolution improved access to affordable and decent housing. By law, every family had the right to one—and only one—dwelling. While the law clamped down on speculation, the country could not meet the demand for housing. At the same time, housing conditions improved dramatically, particularly with access to running water, sewage systems, and electricity.

Revolutionary leaders struggled to overcome persistent social problems such as sexism and racism. Official government policy was to outlaw racial and gender discrimination and to embrace the country's African cultural heritage as an important component of Cuban identity. The result was dramatically increased opportunities for those previously excluded communities. On an informal level, racism continued to be an issue, which showed the limitations of attempting to legislate moral attitudes. Even though discrimination was still a problem, it was not as pronounced as in other countries, such as Brazil. Significant advances were made to attack formal gender inequalities that created new opportunities for women in the public sphere, although, as with racism, those policies often did not reach into private household domains. Furthermore, high-level government and military positions remained overwhelmingly in the hands of men of European descent—the same social class that had always run the country.

One of the greatest accomplishments of the Cuban Revolution was a dramatic expansion and improvement in the medical system. The government increased the healthcare budget tenfold, which allowed for free medical services for everyone. The healthcare system provided for one doctor for every two hundred people, and about half of these doctors were women. The revolution increased the number of nurses by a factor of ten and tripled the number of dentists. Many of these gains were in rural areas, where communicable and preventable diseases were particularly devastating for the local population. As a result of these policies, many diseases such as tuberculosis, malaria, smallpox, diphtheria, and typhoid were eradicated or greatly reduced. Socioeconomic indicators improved dramatically, including lowering infant mortality and raising life expectancy rates to the best levels in Latin America. Those advances led to outcomes that rivaled those of wealthy industrialized countries, often at a fraction of the expense. Its medical system achieved these gains because of a dedication to preventive rather than palliative medicine, which is a much more efficient, cost-effective, and successful method of treatment.

Building on the gains in the field of medicine, Cuba subsequently became a leader in biotechnology research, including pioneering work on coronavirus vaccines. Other Latin Americans turned to Cuba when they could not receive appropriate treatment in their own countries. The export of doctors and medicine became an important generator of hard currency for the country. At the same time, the U.S. embargo made access to some medicine difficult for common people on the island, even as Cuban technicians developed new treatments that could have saved lives in the United States had they been allowed to export them. The Cold War standoff hurt private citizens on both sides of the Florida Straits.

Return to Sugar (1966–1970)

In the 1960s, government experiments with a move to a socialist mode of production took Cuba through a series of policy reversals that ultimately hindered the island's economic development. At first the country made steps away from dependency on an export market toward self-sufficiency, but that came at a cost. Because of favorable weather and because many of the perennial sugarcane stands had been at the peak of their production cycle, Cuba enjoyed good harvests in 1960 and 1961. With the move to experimentation and the push to diversify agricultural production, in 1962 Cubans plowed up the best cane land to plant other crops for domestic consumption. The resulting harvest was the worst since 1955.

In the mid-1960s, government planners reversed course and decided that it would be better to work with Cuba's historic strength as a sugar island. Their plan was to use the earnings from the export of that commodity to purchase needed goods as imports. They hoped that profits from sugar production could be used to fund a desired industrialization of the economy. In pursuit of that goal, the government announced a target of a ten-million-ton harvest in 1970. It was an audacious objective and, if achieved, it would be by far the largest harvest in the country's history. By the late 1960s, Cuba was realistically capable of producing only six million tons of sugar. The goal of ten million tons would be very difficult to meet.

The return to sugar production faced a series of significant challenges. The sugar industry now lacked the administrative and technical expertise that it had enjoyed in the 1950s before the revolution. Many professionals who were the most skilled at running the industry had left the country, and others now worked in different sectors of the economy. Much of the equipment necessary for a large-scale harvest had been abandoned, and a lack of proper maintenance rendered much of it useless. An absence of parts from the United States to repair the old mills meant that bringing them back into operation would be expensive. Little had been invested domestically in maintaining or growing sugar production. For the most part, sugar stands had not been replanted, and those fields that remained were well past their prime.

By 1968, the number of professional cane cutters had fallen by about 80 percent from before the triumph of the revolution. Cutting sugarcane required notoriously difficult and physically demanding manual labor, and, once given the educational and economic opportunities, many of those previously engaged in that backbreaking task left to explore better prospects. To replace this lost labor, the Cuban government redirected people and resources from other sectors of the economy to the sugar industry. Professionals with no skill or experience in cutting sugar were sent to the fields even as they continued to earn their normal salaries, which were higher than what sugar cutters would typically have been paid. Not only did that prove to be an expensive way to harvest the crop but it also caused significant disruption and turmoil in other sectors of the economy. One of the major failings of the sugar policy was the diversion of resources away from other productive industries.

In 1970, Cuba had its largest sugar harvest ever, but rather than a success, that attempt proved to be a significant failure for the government. Rather than producing 10 million tons, Cubans only harvested 8.5 million tons—well short of the goal. The process of reaching so high ruined the industry, and as a result, subsequent harvests were poor. On July 26, 1970, at the annual commemoration of the assault on the Moncada Barracks, Castro admitted defeat and took personal responsibility for the disaster. Even as the failure led to a loss of Castro's prestige, he vowed that the government would make the necessary changes to achieve success in the future. He reemphasized the need for sacrifice and the inevitability of hardships. He pledged that the revolution would go on.

Sovietization of Cuba (1970–1990)

With the bungled attempt to achieve economic self-sufficiency and industrial development through sugar production, Cuba turned to the Soviet Union for support. The island subsequently became heavily dependent on the Soviets. Among other support mechanisms, the Soviet Union increased its subsidies for the Cuban economy through running trade deficits with the island and paying above-market prices for its sugar.

In the 1970s, Cuba also depersonalized and institutionalized its revolution. The military was restructured along traditional hierarchical lines. The government emphasized an increased importance of popular organizations. Workers were more closely involved in the setting of production goals and other workplace policies. The implementation of work quotas helped raise production levels. These changes also meant a move away from Guevara's emphasis on moral incentives to material ones. As a result of this shift, the **gross national product (GNP)** more than doubled to an impressive growth rate of 10 percent a year from 1971 to 1975.

The 1975 Family Code provided landmark legislation that dictated equality in the home, in the workplace, in politics, and in access to educational opportunities. The code stipulated equality in marriage and declared that the husband must share 50 percent of household work and responsibility for raising children. The code's maternity law was the most far reaching in the world. It provided for an eighteen-week paid maternity leave and guaranteed that a woman could return to her previous job after taking a year without pay. The legislation contributed to an increase in access to childcare, educational levels, and opportunities for women in the labor force.

The Communist Party of Cuba's congress in 1975 also engaged gender issues with a statement supporting full equality for women. Critics complained that these policy statements, like earlier ones that outlawed racism, only had a limited effect on changing deeply ingrained cultural mores that played out privately in the domestic sphere. To codify these gains, the party congress drafted the country's first socialist constitution. That document provided legal guarantees for equal rights both inside and outside the home, which led to an expansion of women's participation in the public sphere.

The new constitution also reorganized the country's administrative structures, including the creation of popularly elected assemblies at the municipal, provincial, and national levels. The national assembly elected a Council of State that in turn named the head of government and the first secretary of the communist party. Fidel Castro served in those roles for the next thirty years. Foreign critics complained that this system made little distinction between the government and the party, while supporters countered that it was a Cuban system that worked well in their domestic environment.

In the late 1970s, poor management and quality control led to a shrinking of the GNP from previously high growth rates to about 4 percent a year. Furthermore, consumer goods, such as shoes and TVs, declined in quality. Facing fewer economic opportunities, in 1980, 10,000 people crowded into the Peruvian embassy with the hope of being able to leave the island. After a period of tense negotiations, the United States agreed to admit those who wanted to leave en masse. The resulting exodus of 125,000 people came to be known as the Mariel boatlift, so called for the port from which they departed. The Cuban government took advantage of the opportunity to empty its prisons of criminals as well as to deport others with significant mental illnesses. The government learned to play crises to its benefit. In the 1980s, the government moved to attack economic problems through a diversification of exports. Cuba also gained access to hard currency by reexporting Soviet crude oil that had been brought into the country to be refined. As a result, the economy began to rebound.

Special Period (1990–Present)

The collapse of the Soviet Union in 1991 led to the most significant economic crisis in Cuba's history. The loss of the island's major trading partner meant that average income dropped by 45 percent between 1989 and 1992. Government planners responded with what they denominated "a special period in peacetime" to confront the crisis. The revolution faced the liabilities of not achieving economic self-sufficiency. Many observers thought that the days of the socialists in power were limited, although the next quarter century demonstrated that these pundits had significantly underestimated the revolution's resilience.

In 1992, the Cuban national assembly made sweeping changes to government policies. The alterations included respect for freedom of religion in what was a highly secular society. This opening to religion reflected the influence of liberation theology among revolutionary movements in Central America that broke with the Catholic Church's traditional alliance with a conservative oligarchy. For the first time, the communist party accepted those professing religious beliefs into its ranks. The assembly also made changes to its centrally planned economy, including permitting joint venture enterprises with foreign capital. In particular, this opened up the way for companies in Spain, Canada, and Mexico to invest in the Cuban tourist trade, which had grown into a significant generator of revenue for the government.

Even with all of these changes, Cuba continued to be highly dependent on the production of sugar. The government attempted to modernize production but was hindered by a lack of oil imports that had forced agricultural production to revert largely back to animal traction. In the 1980s, the sugar harvest averaged eight million tons a year, but in 1992 it fell to less than five million tons, the lowest in twenty-five years. A monoculture export economy continued to be an albatross around the island's neck.

POST-CASTRO CUBA

In July 2006, because of an illness, Fidel Castro temporarily passed power to his brother Raúl. Almost two years later, Fidel formally stepped aside to allow Raúl to assume his offices of president and first secretary of the communist party. In February 2013, the national assembly reelected Raúl for another five-year term of office. At the same time, the younger Castro announced that he would not seek reelection in 2018. In office, Raúl liberalized many of the strict policies that his brother had followed. Supporters cheered the changes as necessary to come to terms with the realities of the contemporary world, whereas others worried that those steps would take the island back to capitalism with all of its associated problems of inequality and poverty.

After a long illness, Fidel Castro died on November 25, 2016. Cubans marked his death with solemn tributes, but after having largely been out of the public eye for a decade, his passing had minimal effect on government policy. Perhaps the historic commander had become irrelevant, but more likely observers had overstated the personalized nature of the revolution. Before dying, the legendary leader had instructed that no monuments should be constructed in his honor. The profound social transformations that he had launched had been sufficiently institutionalized that they would survive in his absence, even in the face of continuing opposition from the United States.

As promised, Raúl Castro did not seek reelection as president of Cuba in 2018. This opened the way for the assembly to elect Miguel Díaz-Canel (1960–) to the post. His ascent marked a generational shift as those who fought in the revolutionary war in the 1950s passed from the scene and those born after the triumph of the revolution in 1959 assumed the reins of power. The new generation brought new ideas and perspective to the governance of the island but remained as committed as ever to defending and advancing the gains of the revolution.

Before becoming president, Díaz-Canel had served in a variety of posts, including as a member of the Politburo of the Communist Party of Cuba, minister of higher education, president of the council of ministers, and president of the Council of State. In 2021, he also became the first secretary of the Communist Party of Cuba when Raúl Castro resigned from that post. Previously, in the 1990s, Díaz-Canel had been elected first secretary of the communist party in the central Cuban province of Villa Clara. He gained a reputation for competence in that post and also used the position to advance cultural issues and to champion gay and lesbian rights. As president of Cuba, he continued that trajectory, including promoting constitutional reforms that banned discrimination based on disability, gender, gender identity, race, or sexual orientation.

U.S. POLICY

Through all these changes in Cuba, U.S. policy remained remarkably consistent in its attempts to overthrow the Cuban government. Both Republican and Democratic administrations in the United States continued to put pressure on Cuba even as the country moved toward a normalization of relations with the rest of the world. The original rationalization in 1960 for a blockade of the island was because of its ties to the Soviet Union. After the disappearance of the Soviet Union, Cuba's backing of revolutionary movements justified the policy, even though that support had ended decades earlier. The 1992 Torricelli Act and the 1996 Helms-Burton Act involved an extraterritorial extension of the trade embargo to U.S. subsidiaries in other countries. The legislation barred any ship that had docked in Cuba, even if it was not registered in the United States, from entering the United States for a period of 180 days. In essence, any country that wanted to trade with the United States had to boycott Cuba.

Significant global diplomatic pressure grew against the extraterritorial reach of U.S. policies. Latin American leaders called for the embargo to end, and the United Nations (UN) repeatedly condemned it. In 1992, Cuba introduced a resolution that denounced the embargo as a violation of the UN Charter. That year, 59 countries voted in the General Assembly for the resolution, 3 opposed it, and the rest abstained. In 2015, 190 countries joined Cuba in opposition to the embargo, with only Israel aligning with the United States in support of a policy of isolation.

In a stunning reversal of half a century of estrangement, on December 17, 2014, U.S. president Barack Obama and Cuban president Raúl Castro made simultaneous announcements that the two countries would reestablish diplomatic ties. That was a first step toward a full normalization of relations that included the removal of Cuba from the State Department's list of state sponsors of **terrorism** and an opening of embassies. In March 2016, Obama made a historic visit to the island. For the first time that year, no country voted against Cuba's annual resolution at the UN in opposition to the embargo. Only the United States and Israel abstained from the vote, with all other UN member countries supporting the resolution. Ending the embargo, however, would require legislative action, and the Republican-dominated U.S. Congress gave no indication that it would be willing to take such a step. Meanwhile, the Cuban government continued to insist that the United States end its blockade of the island and return the Guantánamo naval base that it had occupied since 1903. Although significant advances had been made, more work needed to be accomplished before Cuba would realize its long-standing goal of convincing the United States to recognize its rights as a sovereign and independent country.

Obama's openings to Cuba did not represent an embrace of the revolution's gains nor recognition of the country's sovereignty but rather an acknowledgment of the failure of a fifty-year policy of isolation and a belief that engagement would be a more effective mechanism for undermining the government. When Donald Trump assumed the presidency in 2017, he quickly returned to the previous aggressive policies of isolating Cuba, among them, placing the country back on the State Department's list of state sponsors of terrorism during his final days in office. Some activists hoped for a return to Obama's policy of rapprochement with Joe Biden's election, but that was not to be. In 2021, the UN General Assembly once again overwhelmingly approved Cuba's resolution to end the economic, commercial, and financial blockade that the United States had imposed against Cuba. Once again, only the United States and its loyal ally Israel opposed the resolution, 3 countries (Colombia, Ukraine, and the United Arab Emirates) abstained, and 184 countries voted with Cuba.

For a long time, a succession of U.S. administrations pledged not to normalize relations with Cuba as long as Fidel Castro remained in power. Once Fidel stepped aside and Raúl Castro took over his leadership positions, the rhetoric changed to say that normalization would not happen as long as any Castro was in power. When that transpired with the election of Díaz-Canel, the underlying reality that had existed all along became unmistakably apparent: the only Cuban government that would be acceptable to the United States was one that it controlled and one that ruled in its imperial interests.

ASSESSMENT

The Cuban Revolution is often considered a success, both because of its dramatic socioeconomic achievements and because of its ability to survive for more than half a century in the face of intense imperialist pressure from its giant neighbor to the north. Some criticize Cuba for its lack of freedoms, including shortcomings in democratic governance. The debates often revolve around issues of what should be a priority: national sovereignty, individual freedoms, or access to social guarantees such as education and healthcare. A perennial question is why individual freedoms and social rights seem to be mutually exclusive goals and whether they necessarily need to be so.

Opponents of the Cuban Revolution frame their objectives in terms of a return to democratic governance. Historically, however, political participation in Cuba, as in the rest of the Americas, had been limited to a very small base of wealthy, literate, male landholders of European descent. Until the mid-twentieth century, those enjoying full citizenship rights constituted less than 5 percent of the population. Democracy in a broader sense refers not only to elections but also more importantly to equal access to resources and a say in how those are used and distributed. By dramatically expanding access to education and healthcare, Cuba's revolutionary government increased people's ability to enjoy the country's wealth.

Opponents also criticize restrictions on freedom of speech in Cuba. In reality, all societies have parameters and ground rules by which people are expected to play. A common saying in Cuba was, "Within the revolution everything; outside the revolution nothing." Government leaders argued that social advances in the country were due to the revolution and that members of society should not bite the proverbial hand that fed them. The revolution's supporters also contended that crackdowns on dissent were necessary because of the unceasing U.S. attempts to overthrow the Cuban government. Before the revolution, Cuba had neither individual freedoms nor social equality. Many of those opposed to the revolution wanted to return to a prerevolutionary situation in which they controlled everything. A dilemma for supporters was how to increase individual freedoms without strengthening a conservative opposition committed to a rollback of the revolution's progressive advances.

Economically, Cuba faced difficulties in breaking from its historic pattern of dependence on a monoculture sugar-export economy. Critics charged that Cuba simply moved from the orbit of the United States to that of the Soviet Union. After the fall of the Soviet Union, Cuba became increasingly dependent on the tourist trade for hard currency. As a result, foreigners enjoyed privileged access to resources, including better food and internet access, that were largely not available to Cubans. While politically conscious Cubans acknowledged the need for sacrifices to ensure the survival of the revolution, others complained that this system of "tourist apartheid" was in essence a continued form of imperial domination over the island. For the government, the U.S. embargo and its relentless efforts to overthrow the revolution provided a convenient scapegoat on which to blame any and all problems the country faced.

SUMMARY

The Cuban Revolution represents a watershed in twentieth-century revolutions in Latin America and forms a gold standard by which other movements are judged. It was the most thoroughgoing and the most sustainable of the revolutions in Latin America. Cuba was unique in many ways that would seem to make it an unlikely location for a revolution. It was the last Spanish colony to gain its freedom, and it was also close to the United States. Those same factors may also explain its success. As the target of imperialist powers, nationalism was a strong force in Cuba. The nationalist impulses also raise questions of how explicitly a *communist* revolution it was and whether a turn to the Soviet Union was an opportunistic move in the face of U.S. opposition. In any case, the revolution confronted overwhelming odds to survive for more than half a century. It achieved remarkably high health, education, and other socioeconomic indicators that rivaled those of industrialized countries. In the eyes of many in Latin America, Cuba's ability to survive and flourish in the face of imperialist pressures made it a model worthy of respect.

DISCUSSION QUESTIONS

What was the relative importance of the urban underground in the removal of Batista from power?

Was Fidel Castro a humanist, nationalist, socialist, or communist? Did his ideology change after he took power?

Why did the revolution succeed in Cuba?

How important was leadership to the success of the Cuban Revolution? Was it a people's revolution or one of individual leaders? What degree of credit should go to Fidel Castro and Che Guevara for its success?

Did women play a unique role in the Cuban Revolution?

Was the purging and execution of supporters of the old regime justified? Was this necessary for revolutionary success or contrary to the ideals of a revolution?

Did the USSR play an imperial role or one of international solidarity in Cuba?

What does democracy mean for Cuba?

FURTHER READING

A very large body of literature exists on the Cuban Revolution, most of it polemical rather than academic and explicitly partisan in either its support of or its opposition to the revolution. Given the divisive nature of the revolution, it may be impossible— and perhaps even undesirable—to write a neutral account of these events.

Chase, Michelle. *Revolution within the Revolution: Women and Gender Politics in Cuba, 1952–1962*. Chapel Hill: University of North Carolina Press, 2015. Emphasizes the role of women in the Cuban Revolution.

Chomsky, Aviva. *A History of the Cuban Revolution*. 2nd ed. Malden, MA: Wiley-Blackwell, 2015. A highly readable and sympathetic survey of the Cuban Revolution.

Cushion, Steve. *A Hidden History of the Cuban Revolution: How the Working Class Shaped the Guerrilla Victory*. New York: Monthly Review Press, 2016. Argues that the working class played a larger role than did the rural guerrillas in the Cuban insurrection.

Farber, Samuel. *Cuba since the Revolution of 1959: A Critical Assessment*. Chicago: Haymarket Books, 2011. Criticizes the Cuban Revolution from a leftist perspective.

Fitz, Don E. *Cuban Health Care: The Ongoing Revolution*. New York: Monthly Review Press, 2020. Examines how a poor country was able to transform its healthcare system into a first-class institution with outcome indicators that met or surpassed those of the industrialized world.

Geyer, Georgie Anne. *Guerrilla Prince: The Untold Story of Fidel Castro*. 3rd rev. ed. Kansas City, MO: Andrews McMeel, 2001. One of many biographies of the Cuban leader.

Gleijeses, Piero. *Conflicting Missions: Havana, Washington, and Africa, 1959–1976*. Chapel Hill: University of North Carolina Press, 2002. Argues that Cuba acted independently with its involvement in Africa rather than as a Soviet proxy.

Gleijeses, Piero. *Visions of Freedom: Havana, Washington, Pretoria and the Struggle for Southern Africa, 1976–1991*. Chapel Hill: University of North Carolina Press, 2013. A brilliant survey of the Cuban response to the South African invasion of Angola.

Gott, Richard. *Cuba: A New History*. New Haven, CT: Yale University Press, 2004. A broad historical overview of Cuba.

LeoGrande, William M., and Peter Kornbluh. *Back Channel to Cuba: The Hidden History of Negotiations between Washington and Havana*. Chapel Hill: University of North Carolina

Press, 2014. An important book about secret negotiations between Cuba and the United States.

Mahler, Anne Garland. *From the Tricontinental to the Global South: Race, Radicalism, and Transnational Solidarity.* Durham, NC: Duke University Press, 2018. Traces the history and legacy of the Tricontinental, an alliance of liberation struggles from eighty-two countries in Asia, Africa, and Latin America that was founded in Havana in 1966.

Pérez, Louis A., Jr. *Cuba: Between Reform and Revolution.* 3rd ed. New York: Oxford University Press, 2006. Political survey by an eminent historian of Cuba.

Pérez-Stable, Marifeli. *The Cuban Revolution: Origins, Course, and Legacy.* 3rd ed. New York: Oxford University Press, 2012. Presents a negative image of the Cuban Revolution.

Sippial, Tiffany A. *Celia Sánchez Manduley: The Life and Legacy of a Cuban Revolutionary.* Chapel Hill: University of North Carolina Press, 2020. A feminist biography of one of the most important but little-known revolutionary leaders.

Stout, Nancy. *One Day in December: Celia Sánchez and the Cuban Revolution.* New York: Monthly Review Press, 2013. Fascinating biography of Fidel Castro's closest companion.

FILMS

Bananas. 1971. Woody Allen as a fictitious and absurd Castro-esque revolutionary.

Cuba, an African Odyssey. 2008. A remarkable documentary on Cuba's international mission in Africa, beginning with Che Guevara in Congo through the defeat of South African forces in 1988 at the Battle of Cuito Cuanavale in Angola that led to the end of apartheid.

Cuba Va: The Challenge of the Next Generation. 1993. Young people born after the 1959 revolution discuss the challenge of Cuba's economic crisis in the 1990s.

El Che. 2009. Steven Soderbergh's two-part biopic based on the diaries of guerrilla leader Che Guevara, who led the Cuban Revolution and was later killed in Bolivia.

Fidel. 1969. Activist filmmaker Saul Landau's documentary about Fidel Castro portrays his revolution, his relationship with the people of Cuba, his school years, and the Bay of Pigs incident.

Fidel. 2001. Showtime biography of Fidel Castro's rise to power in Cuba, based on Georgie Anne Geyer's biography *Guerrilla Prince* and Robert E. Quirk's *Fidel Castro.*

Fidel: The Untold Story. 1999. Estela Bravo's documentary celebrates the life and political career of Fidel Castro through archival footage, interviews with Fidel, and commentary by family, associates, former guerrilla fighters, politicians, and historians.

IA—Kuba (I Am Cuba). 1964. Soviet film portrays four main stories that depict the rise of the communist revolution in Cuba, including Batista's Havana, the grinding poverty, and the oppression of the Cuban people.

Lucía. 1968. Follows the lives of three different women named Lucía during three different revolutionary periods of Cuba's history: the 1895 Cuban independence war, the failed 1933 revolution, and 1960s revolutionary Cuba.

Maestra (Teacher). 2013. An examination of young women who taught in rural communities in the 1961 literacy campaign.

Memorias del Subdesarrollo (Inconsolable Memories/Memories of Underdevelopment). 1968. A study of Cuban society before and after the revolution as seen through the eyes of a man who is a landlord and self-styled writer.

Salud. 2006. Documentary on Cuba's international medical solidarity program.

Strawberry and Chocolate. 1993. A Cuban film that directly engages issues of homophobia.

Chile

6

Chilean Road to Socialism, 1970–1973

KEY DATES

1952	Salvador Allende campaigns for president for the first time
1958–1964	Presidency of conservative Jorge Alessandri
1964–1970	Presidency of Christian Democrat Eduardo Frei
1967	Partial land reform program designed with the Alliance for Progress to stabilize capitalist agricultural production
September 4, 1970	Allende wins presidential election
November 3, 1970	Allende takes office
July 17, 1971	Chilean government nationalizes copper mines
March 4, 1973	Popular Unity's vote increases in midterm congressional elections
September 11, 1973	General Augusto Pinochet overthrows Allende in brutal, CIA-backed military coup
September 21, 1976	Car bomb kills Pinochet opponent Orlando Letelier in Washington, D.C., the most notorious of many assassinations and disappearances planned and executed as part of Operation Condor
1980	Pinochet promulgates conservative constitution in order to inscribe neoliberal economic policies permanently and assure continued right-wing political control
October 5, 1988	Pinochet loses a plebiscite that would have maintained him in power
March 11, 1990	Pinochet hands power to an elected civilian government
October 16, 1998	Pinochet arrested while recovering from back surgery in a London hospital

| October 2019 | Massive demonstrations against neoliberal economic policies known as the "*estallido social*" or social outburst |
| 2020 | Chileans vote to draft a new constitution |

Chile is unique in many ways. The country appears as a geographic anomaly on maps. Hugging the western coast of South America, it is squeezed between the high Andean mountains and the Pacific Ocean. It averages less than two hundred kilometers wide, and it measures more than four thousand kilometers long. Henry Kissinger, the presidential assistant for National Security Affairs in the Richard Nixon administration, once derogatorily described the country as a dagger pointed at the heart of Antarctica. The northern part of the country is the driest region on earth, with some areas never having received any recorded rainfall. That area also has the world's largest-known copper reserves. Most people live in the fertile central valley that enjoys a moderate Mediterranean-like climate. The cold southern regions are home to the Mapuche, who stopped first Inka and then Spanish encroachment into their territory.

Before 1973, scholars had long seen Chile as the most stable and democratic country in Latin America, a part of the planet that has suffered through its share of military coups and extraconstitutional changes in administration. Whereas governments elsewhere repeatedly drafted new constitutions to suit current political needs, Chile had a single governing document from 1818 until 1925. Chile enjoyed the longest periods of continuous civilian rule of any Latin American republic. After gaining independence from Spain in 1818 until 1973, the only interruptions occurred in 1891 and between 1924 and 1932.

Chile was the first country in the world where an avowed Marxist came to power through constitutional means. Similar to the progressive president Jacobo Arbenz in Guatemala, Salvador Allende (1909–1973) won election as president in 1970 and then dramatically accelerated reforms begun under his predecessor. Allende's goal to transform Chile from a capitalist and dependent country into a socialist and independent one within a democratic and constitutional framework delivered significant gains to the working class at a cost to the ruling class. Unsurprisingly, his policies quickly alienated the U.S. government. Nationalization of U.S.-owned copper mines, as with Arbenz's confiscation of United Fruit Company banana lands in Guatemala, prompted Nixon's support for the brutal September 11, 1973, military coup that Augusto Pinochet (1915–2006) led.

The Pinochet military regime stretched for seventeen long years from 1973 to 1990, bringing standard interpretations of Chile's democratic traditions into question. Historically, the country's electoral process had been corrupt and dominated by a small, conservative minority of wealthy men. Although civilians led most governments, voting restrictions limited the franchise to literate men and excluded the active participation of the vast majority of the population. Given these realities, alternative interpretations attributed Chile's political stability not to the presence of democratic institutions but to its heavy dependence on the export of a single commodity—first nitrate and then copper. A lack of conflict between competing internal economic interests meant that the country did not experience frequent and extraconstitutional changes in administrations as different power blocs struggled to control the central government, a phenomenon common in other countries. Particularly in the nineteenth century, political stability should not be confused with democratic rule, which in reality was limited and largely a mirage. Instead, democratic control emerged out of the fight that leftist political parties and labor unions leveled against the exclusionary economic system that wealthy individuals had imposed on Chile.

Chile returned to civilian rule at the end of Pinochet's dictatorship in 1990, but a new constitution in 1980 left significant power in the military's hands. Pinochet's neoliberal economic policies subjected the country to extreme social and economic inequalities. Even the 2000 presidential election of socialist Ricardo Lagos presented a limited challenge to these exclusionary policies. It took forty years of organized pressure before finally, in 2020, Chileans voted to draft a new constitution that would reflect the needs and aspirations of the majority of the population. The Chilean experiment with a socialist revolution illustrates the restrictions on achieving profound and radical societal changes within an institutional and democratic framework.

LABOR MOVEMENTS

Chile developed an export-oriented economy that, by the latter part of the nineteenth century, had become highly dependent on the export of a single product, nitrate, to British markets. Chile provides a classic example of the liabilities of an export-oriented economy reliant on foreign capital. Nitrate sales funded the development of state structures and enriched the ruling class while leaving the vast majority of the population economically impoverished, politically powerless, and subject to discrimination and repression. The nitrate industry dramatically expanded the working class, and along with its larger size came a proliferation of militant actions to improve their working, living, and social conditions. These workers came to understand that they had class interests distinct from those who owned the mines, controlled the infrastructure, and benefited financially from international trade. The workers became actors in a class struggle that moved beyond issues of pay and working conditions to ones that dealt with ownership and modes of production. This realization was the setting for the emergence and growth of a working-class consciousness in Chile, especially among those in the northern nitrate fields, on the shipping docks at the port of Valparaíso, at the coal mines in southern Chile, and in factories in Santiago.

Workers suffered abject poverty and miserable working conditions that contributed to short life expectancies and high infant mortality rates. Miners worked twelve-hour days and were paid on a piecework basis in scrip that could only be used at company stores, where they were charged inflated prices. Companies actively recruited families, because married men were less likely to revolt or leave the mines than single males, plus their children could be drafted to work in the mines. The miners suffered in a dangerous, unhealthy, and stressful environment that resulted in injury and death from cave-ins and explosions. The miserable working conditions led to strike waves that the mining companies brutally repressed with the slaughter of thousands of protesting workers.

The worst massacre in Chilean history occurred in December 1907 among nitrate workers at Santa María de Iquique. The workers had gone on strike with relatively moderate demands: they called for an end of payment in scrip, a termination of illegal salary deductions, protections for the right to assemble, and improvements in worker safety. The police gave an order to disperse within five minutes but then immediately fired on the crowd, killing thousands of men, women, and children. As with many massacres, it was impossible to determine the exact death toll. The brutality had its intended effect of instilling fear into the survivors, who did not want to admit that their family and friends had been targeted, out of trepidation that they would also fall under the taint of having engaged in subversive activities. The aristocracy applauded the suppression of the strike because it reestablished social order in the country.

Journalist Luis Emilio Recabarren (1876–1924) founded and edited numerous working-class newspapers, which contributed to the development of a working-class consciousness in the early twentieth-century nitrate fields. He was also the founder and chief ideologist of numerous labor unions as well as of the socialist and later the communist party. Recabarren was first elected to congress in 1906, but the conservatives refused to seat him because of his revolutionary views. In 1912, Recabarren formed the Partido Obrero Socialista (POS, Socialist Workers Party) that favored the nationalization of private property and the confiscation of church wealth. Recabarren ran for president in 1920, but the government imprisoned him, thereby preventing him from extending his base of support beyond the northern nitrate regions.

In 1921, Recabarren was again elected to congress as a socialist delegate. In congress, Recabarren countered attacks that blamed working-class agitation on foreign agents. Instead, he concluded that the capitalist regime had fostered revolutionary attitudes among the workers. He maintained that the working class was itself capable of fomenting revolutionary action and that such militancy had its roots in Chilean history. In fact, labor activism predated the Bolshevik Revolution in Russia by fifteen or twenty years. Furthermore, Recabarren contended that socialism entailed more than the redistribution of wealth from the rich to the poor; it also included changes in mentality to abolish the imaginary rights of private property.

At Recabarren's urging, the POS joined the Communist International (Comintern) in 1922 and transformed itself into the Partido Comunista de Chile (PCCh, Communist Party of Chile). In 1923, Recabarren traveled to the Soviet Union for Comintern's fourth congress. The successes of the Russian Revolution impressed him. The following year, he died by suicide in the face of a military coup and infighting in the communist party that had undermined its ability to defeat the dictatorship. The communists remained the dominant leftist force in Chile throughout the 1920s, but leaders brought the party increasingly in line with the strict dictates of Comintern. These restrictions from Moscow incentivized left-wing activists to break off into a separate socialist party in 1932. The socialists subsequently took positions that were sometimes more radical than those of the communists.

ELECTIONS

In 1938, Chile was the first and only Latin American country to elect a popular-front government. Pedro Aguirre Cerda served as president of the center-left coalition that included the radical, socialist, and communist parties. The competing political interests, however, limited the influence that leftists had in the government. Nevertheless, during the 1950s and 1960s, broad sectors of the Chilean left continued to cling to the goal of transforming society through constitutional means.

In 1952, the socialist party ran Salvador Allende as its candidate for president. The socialists had a poor showing, and Allende finished fourth in a field of four candidates. Allende was not bothered by the loss, because his intent was not to win but to lay the basis for future attempts. Six years later, Allende once again ran as the candidate of the socialist and communist parties. This time he made a much better showing and narrowly lost to Jorge Alessandri, who headed a coalition of the traditional liberal and conservative parties. Allende's support had increased fivefold, and only the candidacy of a left-wing splinter party prevented his victory. In Chile's multiparty races, if no candidate won a majority, then congress decided the victor, traditionally certifying the top vote getter. Allende had lost by only 33,500 votes out of the 1.2 million cast. Given the narrow defeat, some leftists pushed for Allende to claim power, by extraconstitutional means if necessary. Allende, however, had faith in Chile's traditions and institutional order. He graciously conceded defeat and encouraged congress to designate his conservative rival as president. He would try again in the next election.

Eduardo Frei

Allende's strong showing in 1958, together with socialist gains in midterm congressional elections, frightened conservatives. As a result, in the 1964 election they abandoned their party and rallied behind the centrist **Christian Democratic** candidacy of Eduardo Frei to prevent a socialist victory. The Christian Democratic Party had only just formed in 1957, and Frei came in third as the candidate for that party in the 1958 election. Now in 1964, with both conservatives and centrists supporting his candidacy, he achieved the rare feat in Chilean politics of winning an outright victory. Even though Frei secured 55 percent of the vote, Allende also boosted his percentage of the vote to almost 40 percent, a significant 10 percent increase from six years earlier.

In office, Frei promised a "revolution in liberty." His reformist government was one of the most progressive administrations in Chilean history. Frei's government featured a series of reforms, including an increase in education spending. Most significant was a 1967 agrarian reform program designed with the assistance of the Alliance for Progress to modernize one of Latin America's most archaic rural structures. A predominance of large, ill-managed agricultural estates that produced little forced Chile to import a quarter of its meat, a third of its milk, and a fifth of its wheat. The government expropriated land from feudal-style estates, legalized peasant unions, and encouraged the formation of cooperatives. For many people, the reforms were moving in the right direction but did not make deep enough changes to satiate their growing demands for profound structural changes.

Frei's second reform entailed a partial nationalization of the copper mines. His goal was to strengthen domestic control over the industry and increase earnings from the exports. After the creation of synthetic alternatives had contributed to the collapse of the nitrate industry during the First World War, Chile had shifted its dependency to copper. Similar to nitrate exports, wild fluctuations of copper prices on the global market complicated the creation of coherent economic policies. A common saying was that as copper went, so went the Chilean economy. The copper industry was concentrated in a few hands, mostly in U.S.-based corporations. The Kennecott Corporation owned the largest copper mine in the world. The mine was very profitable, but its wealth flowed to the United States rather than remaining in Chile. Copper mining was more capital- than labor-intensive, which resulted in fewer economic gains for miners than during the nitrate boom. The dependence on new technology required extensive capital investment, and the importation of equipment and parts undermined the potential industrialization of the country. The departure of most of the copper profits from the country added to the growing resentment toward an industry that failed to contribute to the development of the domestic economy.

Frei decided that paying for an outright nationalization of the copper mines was too expensive. Instead, in a scheme called the "Chileanization" of the copper industry, the government acquired part ownership in the mines with an eye toward reinvesting the profits and doubling production. The Chilean government bought a 51 percent controlling share in the Kennecott mines and 25 percent of Anaconda. The plan was not as successful as Frei had hoped. Because of the nature of the contracts, most of the profits continued to flow to the companies and out of the country.

Many of Frei's reforms were funded with foreign aid, but the loans created a heavy debt burden for the country. In March 1961, John F. Kennedy announced the Alliance for Progress as a type of Marshall Plan for the Americas. A goal was to demonstrate the virtues of capitalism and champion the United States as a model for economic development. An intent was to make moderate reforms in order to prevent another policy disaster such as the Cuban Revolution and to halt Soviet influence in the region by making the region more dependent on the United States. Chile became a showcase for the program and received more per capita funding than any other country. The aid came at the cost of U.S. control over Chile's domestic policies. In 1964, the Central Intelligence Agency (CIA) contributed $3 million to Frei's electoral campaign and spent an additional $17 million in anti-Marxist propaganda. The propaganda was aimed particularly at women in an attempt to convince them that an Allende victory would mean the loss of their children and the breakup of their families.

Despite Frei's best attempts, he failed to satisfy society's growing demands. His moderate reforms were too extreme for the conservatives and not radical enough for the leftists, and as a result he was squeezed between the two extremes. Furthermore, his programs fell short of their announced goals, and a heavy debt load triggered an increase in inflation. Frei's progressive reforms also strained his relations with his conservative allies. In the 1965 midterm congressional elections, the vote for the traditional liberal and conservative parties fell to 12 percent. Their poor showing resulted in the dissolution of their parties and the reconstitution in 1967 of the liberal, conservative, and radical parties as the right-wing National Party. With a new face, the right-wing bloc delivered a stronger showing in the 1969 congressional elections, scoring 20 percent of the vote. Even so, the left was steadily gaining support and rapidly closing a gap with the center.

BIOGRAPHY: SALVADOR ALLENDE GOSSENS, 1909–1973

Salvador Allende was born in the coastal town of Valparaíso, the son of a well-to-do lawyer. His privileged status allowed him to attend medical school. His training as a medical doctor, similar to Che Guevara, made him aware of the deep class divisions in Chilean society. Recognition that a small number of people could afford proper nutrition while the vast impoverished majority could not, contributed to his political consciousness. Rather than the charisma that typically characterized many political leaders, what distinguished Allende was a commitment to making revolutionary changes in society through existing institutional structures.

In 1932, Allende helped found the socialist party. Five years later, at only twenty-nine years old, he was first elected to congress. He spent the rest of his life in government. In 1939, he was named minister of health in the center-left, popular-front government that included socialists and communists. Allende gained recognition for his humanitarian concerns. In that post, he helped thousands of refugees

Salvador Allende at 1973 parliamentary elections

Source: Biblioteca del Congreso Nacional de Chile

from the Spanish civil war resettle in Chile. In 1945, Allende was elected to the senate and served in that body for the next twenty-five years. He used his political position to fight for healthcare and women's rights. Allende gained a good deal of respect in the senate and in 1968 was elected president of the body. In 1970, after three unsuccessful attempts, Allende won the presidency of the country in a three-way race.

Allende argued that Chile's extreme inequalities required rapid changes. Forty percent of the population suffered from malnutrition, and one-third of those who died were children. Three percent of the population earned 40 percent of the income, while half only received 10 percent. The challenge for Allende was, as he said, that "we must make haste—slowly" in order to address these inequalities but within the constraints of the existing institutional order. He wanted to make reforms that would be permanent and irreversible and to implement them in a fashion that would not destabilize the country and bring the entire political project crashing down on itself.

One way to address Chile's problems of poverty and inequality was to end economic dependency on foreigners. Allende noted that Chile was rich in natural resources and could be a wealthy country but instead was plagued by poverty. The country was trapped in dependent relations with foreign powers, first with the Spanish during the colonial period, then with the British in connection with the nitrate industry in the nineteenth century, and finally with the United States and copper exports in the twentieth century. Allende wanted to break those colonial and neocolonial ties and redirect those resources to develop Chile's internal economy.

Allende was a close friend and ally of the Cuban revolutionary leader Fidel Castro. Allende was not opposed to armed struggle, but he argued that such a violent path was unnecessary—perhaps even counterproductive—in a country such as Chile with strong and stable democratic structures.

As could be expected after spending most of his adult life in politics, Allende was a strict constitutionalist. He openly proclaimed that he was a Marxist, but he also made a distinction between socialism and communism. He declared that socialists would not imitate the Soviet Union. Instead, Chileans would search for their own path toward absolute independence. He contrasted a socialist emphasis on searching for appropriate policies to address national issues with the communists' internationalism that followed dictates from Moscow.

DOCUMENT: POPULAR UNITY GOVERNMENT, "BASIC PROGRAM," 1970

The Popular Unity coalition drafted a detailed platform for the 1970 presidential elections in which it analyzed the main problems facing Chile and the type of socialist transformation it envisioned for the country. The North American Congress on Latin America (NACLA) translated the entire program into English and published it in the March 1971 issue of its newsletter. Following is an extract from the proposed program.

The revolutionary transformation the country needs can only be carried out if the Chilean people take power into their hands and exercise it effectively. Through a long struggle process the Chilean people have conquered certain liberties and democratic guarantees whose continuity call for the maintenance of an attitude of alertness and combativeness without truce. However, power itself is foreign to the people.

The popular and revolutionary forces have not united to struggle for the simple substitution of one president of the republic for another, nor to replace one party for another in the government, but to carry out the profound changes the national situation demands based on the transfer of power from the old dominant groups to the workers, the peasants and the progressive sectors of the middle classes of the city and the countryside.

The popular triumph will open the way to the most democratic political regime in the country's history.

Concerning political structure the popular government has a double task:

1. to preserve and make more effective and profound the democratic rights and the conquests of the workers; and
2. to transform the present institutions so as to install a new state where workers and the people will have the real exercise of power.

The popular government will guarantee the exercise of democratic rights and will respect the individual and social guarantees of all the people. Freedom of conscience, speech, press and assembly, the inviolability of the home and the rights of unions and their organization will rule effectively without the limiting conditions presently established by the dominant classes.

For this to be effective the labor and social organizations of workers, employees, peasants, *pobladores* [residents], housewives, students, professionals, intellectuals, craftsmen, small and middle-size businessmen, and other sectors of workers will be called upon to intervene at their respective places in the decisions of the organs of power. For example, in the welfare and social security institutions we will establish the administration by the depositors themselves, thus assuring them democratic elections and the secret vote for their directive councils. Concerning enterprises of the public sector, their directive councils and their production committees will have the direct participation of workers' and employees' representatives.

In organizations concerned with housing, operating within their jurisdiction and at their own level, the Neighbors' Councils and other organizations of slum dwellers will have the use of mechanisms to inspect their operations and intervene in the many aspects of their functioning. These are only a few examples of the new conception of government which we propose—one in which the people truly participate in the state apparatus.

At the same time the popular government guarantees workers the right of employment and strike and to all the people the right of education and culture with complete respect for all religious ideas and beliefs and guarantees of the exercise of worship.

All democratic rights and guarantees will be extended through the delivery to social organizations of the real means to exercise them and the creation of the mechanisms that permit them to act at the different levels of the state apparatus.

The popular government will base its force and authority essentially on the support the organized people give it. This is our idea of a strong government as opposed to that promoted by the oligarchy and imperialism which identify authority with the coercion exercised against the people.

The popular government will be many-partied. It will include all the revolutionary parties, movements and groups. Thus it will be a genuinely democratic, representative and cohesive executive.

The popular government will respect the rights of opposition that is exercised within legal bounds.

The popular government will begin immediately a genuine administrative decentralization as well as democratic, efficient planning which will eliminate bureaucratic centralism and replace it with the coordination of all state organisms.

Municipal structures will be modernized and will be granted the necessary authority in agreement with the coordination plans of the whole state. There will be a tendency to transform these structures into local organisms of the new political organization.

They will receive adequate financing and authority for the purpose of caring for, in working with the Neighbors' Councils and in coordination with them, the problems of local interests of the communities and their inhabitants. Provincial Assemblies should also enter into operation with this same idea.

The police force should be reorganized so that it cannot again be employed as a repressive organization against the people and so that on the other hand it fulfills the objective of defending the people from antisocial actions. Police procedures will be humanized so as to guarantee effectively the complete respect of dignity and the physical well-being of the person. The prison system, which constitutes one of the worst defects of the present system, must be completely transformed for the purpose of the regeneration and recuperation of those who have committed crimes.

Source: Popular Unity, "Popular Unity Government: Basic Program," *NACLA Newsletter* 5, no. 1 (March 1971): 9–10.

POPULAR UNITY

In the 1970 presidential election, Chile's entire political spectrum shifted significantly leftward. Allende once again ran as a leftist candidate, this time at the head of a Unidad Popular (UP, Popular Unity) coalition. This leftist alliance grouped socialists, communists, the left wing of the Christian Democrats, some dissident radicals, and Christian socialists. Frei was constitutionally barred from running for a second term, so the Christian Democrats ran Radomiro Tomic with a platform that included some policy proposals that were to the left of Allende. Hard-line conservatives broke from the coalition that they had formed with the centrists in the 1964 election and ran Jorge Alessandri—the winner of the 1958 election—as the National Party candidate. Chilean politics had settled into hard thirds, with the population divided between those who supported conservatives, those who identified with the center even as its policy proposals had drifted leftward, and those on the left.

The Mapuche, one of the largest and most vocal Indigenous groups in South America, has a long history of petitioning for their rights. Logically, they sought out collaboration with the broader left to advance their interests. In the 1964 election, Allende had signed a pact with several Mapuche organizations in which he pledged to respect their culture and religion and to introduce policies that would benefit their communities in exchange for their support for his presidential campaign. That agreement opened up political space for the Mapuche to advance their own agenda, particularly with regard to access to land. In turn, Allende campaigned together with Indigenous supporters in their communities. When he won election six years later, he did not forget his promises. Mapuche organizations drafted proposed legislation that Allende brought to congress in May 1971, and it was finally enacted over a year later despite right-wing opposition (see the document included with this chapter). The Indigenous Law officially recognized the country's ethnic diversity and created institutions that fostered the promotion of the social, educational, and cultural development of Indigenous peoples in the country. The legislation was an important achievement and represented a shift to a more democratic, more inclusive view of Chilean citizenship that made Indigenous peoples key participants in UP's political project. It was a significant achievement of the first government to take the needs and concerns of Indigenous peoples seriously.

During the campaign, the UP coalition published a program that outlined its views on the social and economic situation in Chile and proposed a course of action to improve it (see the document included with this chapter). It noted that due to Chile's dependence on imperialist nations and global capitalism together with the development of an export economy, the Chilean people did not benefit from their great wealth of natural resources. The program pointed to the nature of a class struggle in which workers and peasants suffered from social and economic stagnation and widespread poverty while bourgeois groups refused to address fundamental socioeconomic problems. It concluded that these problems were the result of class privileges that the wealthy would never give up voluntarily.

UP advocated replacing the capitalistic and export-oriented economy with a centralized and democratically controlled one. It sought to shift production from luxury items for the wealthy to mass-produced goods for the working class, to free Chile from dominance by foreign capital, to diversify exports, and to combat inflation. UP called for measures to end unemployment, legislation to ensure a minimum subsistence wage for workers, the elimination of wage discrimination based on sex or age, and an end to high salaries for government employees.

Two main points of the UP economic policy were the nationalization of foreign capital and national monopolies and an acceleration of the agrarian reform program begun under the Frei administration. Among the sectors of the economy to be nationalized were natural resources (copper, iron, and nitrate mines), banks, foreign trade, strategic industrial monopolies, and infrastructure (electricity, railroads, air and sea transportation, communications, and petroleum). The agrarian reform program already in place would be expanded to benefit small-scale farmers and rural workers. The plan was to transform the economy into one that would serve the entire population, not just those with the most wealth and privilege.

DOCUMENT: INSTITUTE OF INDIGENOUS DEVELOPMENT, "INDIGENOUS LAW," 1972

While not perfect, the Indigenous Law that the Popular Unity government passed in 1972 reflected an attempt to respond to Mapuche concerns. Excerpted below is the first part of the law that defines who is Indigenous, an inherently complicated proposition, and what lands should be considered as belonging to Indigenous communities. The lengthy legislation then proceeds in quite some detail (not included here) as to how to administer Indigenous affairs. Although the law embodies paternalistic attitudes to a certain degree, it does highlight the government's desire to advance Indigenous issues.

Indigenous Law 17.729

Establishes norms for Indigenous peoples and Indigenous lands. Transforms the Directorate of Indigenous Affairs into the Institute of Indigenous Development. Establishes judicial, administrative, and educational development provisions on the matter and modifies or repeals indicated legal texts.

Whereas the Honorable National Congress has given its approval to the following bill:

TITLE ONE
OF THE INDIGENOUS PEOPLES AND OF INDIGENOUS LANDS
Paragraph One
Definitions and disposition of Indigenous lands.

Article 1. A person shall be considered an Indigenous person, for all legal purposes, if [the person] meets any of the following conditions:

1. Invokes a right that emanates directly and immediately from a gratuitous or free title of ownership granted in accordance with the laws of December 4, 1866, August 4, 1874, and January 20, 1883; Law No. 4,169, of September 8, 1927; Law No. 4,802, of February 11, 1930; Decree No. 4,111, of July 9, 1931; Law No. 14,511, of January 3, 1961, and other legal provisions that modify or complement them;
2. Invokes a right declared by a judgment issued in a trial for the division of an Indigenous community with title conferred in accordance with the legal provisions mentioned in the preceding item, unless such right has been acquired by an onerous title prior or subsequent to the division, and
3. Lives in any part of the national territory, is part of a group that habitually expresses itself in an aboriginal language, and is distinguished from the generality of the inhabitants of the Republic by the conservation of systems of life, norms of coexistence, customs, forms of work or religion that come from the autochthonous ethnic groups of the country.

The status as Indigenous will be accorded through a certificate from the Institute of Indigenous Development. If the latter denies the certificate, the interested party may go before the respective judge who will resolve the issue briefly and summarily, after a report from the Institute.

However, anyone who has an interest therein may in court challenge an Indigenous status that another person invokes, even if [the individual] has a certificate from the Institute, and the Court shall decide with input from the Institute.

Article 2. The following shall be considered as Indigenous lands, for all legal purposes:

1. Those granted on behalf of the Republic, in accordance with the laws of December 4, 1866, August 4, 1874, and January 20, 1883;
2. Those granted by gratuitous title of ownership pursuant to Articles 4 and 14 of Law No. 4,169; Articles 13, 29 and 30 of Law No. 4,802; Articles 70 and 74, both inclusive of Decree No. 4,111, which established the definitive text of Law No. 4,802; Articles 82, 83 and 84 of Law No. 14,511 and other legal provisions that modify or complement them.

Article 3. For all legal purposes, the legal possession of the status as father, mother, husband, wife, or child shall be considered sufficient to constitute the same rights in favor of Indigenous peoples that, according to common laws, emanate from legitimate filiation and civil marriage.

The testimonial information of relatives or neighbors and the report of the Institute of Indigenous Development will suffice to accredit the legal possession of said civil status, without prejudice to the measures for a better resolution that the Court decrees.

The appropriate judge will decide on the legal possession of the civil status and, in case of declaring it accredited with the evidentiary means indicated in the previous paragraph, will order extension of the corresponding entries or rectify the existing ones, as the case may be, for which they will send an official letter to the respective Civil Registry Officer.

It will be understood that half of the assets belong to the husband and the other half to the wife, or to all of them in equal shares, when there are several, unless it is shown that they have been contributed by only one of the spouses.

Source: Instituto de Desarrollo Indígena, *No. 17.729, ley de indígenas* (Chile: Instituto de Desarrollo Indígena, Ministerio de Agricultura, 1972), 1–4 (translation by author).

CHILEAN ROAD TO SOCIALISM

In what became known as the "Chilean Road to Socialism," leftists gained political power in 1970 through the election of Allende to the presidency. On September 4, 1970, Allende eked out a victory in a three-way race with a narrow plurality of 36.6 percent of the vote. The right-wing opposition immediately attempted to thwart Allende's ascension to power. In previous elections, when one candidate did not win an outright majority, the congress as a matter of course certified the top vote getter as president. Allende had followed that custom in the 1958 election when he supported Alessandri's confirmation, even though Alessandri had also only won a narrow plurality of the vote. Elsewhere in the Americas where there were similar electoral systems, other candidates had taken office with an even smaller plurality of the vote. Understood in this broader context, certifying Allende's election would be to follow existing and accepted institutional conventions.

This time, however, Alessandri sought to cut a deal with the Christian Democrats to violate the constitutional pattern of a peaceful transfer of power to prevent Allende's assumption of power. If they would support his candidacy, he would promptly resign and call new elections. Since Frei would no longer be the incumbent, he could thereby dodge the constitutional restriction on immediate reelection. Frei had sufficiently high popularity ratings that he could probably win another term. The Christian Democrats refused to conspire in this scheme, but they did extract guarantees from Allende that he would not restrict political liberties or form a popular militia.

The right-wing opposition made one final attempt to stop Allende's assumption of power. The army's commander-in-chief General René Schneider was a strong constitutionalist and opposed a military coup to prevent Allende's inauguration. The CIA supported right-wing military officers in a plan to kidnap the general and thereby open a path to a coup. The plotters botched the kidnap attempt and killed Schneider in the process. The incident provoked outrage and led people to rally behind Allende. Two days later, on October 24, the Chilean congress certified Allende's victory, and he took office on November 3, 1970. For the first time in history, a Marxist had gained the presidency through a democratic process.

Allende, however, had only gained access to one office, which was far short of taking political power. Without a majority vote in the presidential election, he lacked a clear political mandate for his socialist program. He also faced an antagonistic congress in the hands of centrists and conservatives as well as hostility from the Chilean ruling class that controlled media outlets and the means of production. Political divisions within the UP coalition also hindered the viability of Allende's socialist program. Nevertheless, he pushed forward with plans for a fundamental transformation of society.

When Allende took office in November 1970, he immediately dedicated attention to improving living conditions for the poor and the working class. He raised the minimum wage by 35 percent. His policies resulted in a rise in worker income, an increase in consumer buying power, a sharp drop in unemployment, and a fall in inflation rates. Food production increased, industrial manufacturing rose, and the gross national product (GNP) tripled. The government implemented programs for the provision of free medical care and supplies, including milk for children, pregnant women, and nursing mothers. The programs had positive outcomes, such as an 11 percent decrease in infant mortality rates. UP achieved its short-term goals, and support for the government increased.

Allende pledged to undertake all of these reforms through existing institutional frameworks. He promised to respect democratic structures and individual liberties. In a move away from personalistic forms of governance, Allende ended the practice of placing presidential portraits in government offices. He emphasized that UP's political project was much larger than one man. The Chilean constitution allowed for a single, six-year term of office as president with no possibility of reelection. Allende gave no indication that he would attempt to violate that provision, and by all indications he would step aside at the end of his term and hand power to whomever won the next election.

Nationalization

By 1970, more than one hundred U.S.-based multinational corporations had investments in Chile. A significant part of the Chilean economy was built on copper production, and foreign companies (like Kennecott and Anaconda) owned most of the mines. The UP government quickly implemented a program that extended partial government control over key sectors of the economy. On December 21, 1970, only a month after taking office, Allende called for the nationalization of the foreign-owned copper industry that comprised three-quarters of the country's exports. The proposal was not that controversial and enjoyed broad popular support. Not only had Frei started partial ownership through his "Chileanization" of the industry, but in the 1970 electoral campaign, the Christian Democratic candidate Tomic had also called for full nationalization.

On July 17, 1971, the Allende government, with the unanimous support of congress, nationalized the large copper mines. Based on United Nations principles, Chile compensated the corporations for the book value of the mines minus excessive profits. Allende announced that because of excessive profits that the multinational corporations had taken from Chile over the previous fifteen years, they would receive no compensation. He compared the expropriation to Abraham Lincoln freeing en-slaved peoples in the United States. Lincoln refused to pay the planters both because they had more than recovered their initial investment and because of the immoral-ity of owning another human being. Similarly, the mining companies had earned far more than a fair profit, and Allende argued that the mines rightfully belonged to Chileans. Despite congressional support, opponents in both the legislature and judiciary created political roadblocks for UP's nationalization efforts. In particular, an oppositional congress refused to provide funding for Allende's socialization pro-grams. As a result, Allende was forced to use laws passed during the Frei and previous administrations to move ahead with his programs.

Allende's government also nationalized the coal and steel industries and bought control of most banks and communications industries. The policies frequently targeted foreign firms, in particular International Telephone and Telegraph (ITT) and Ford. Workers pushed Allende's hand in an attempt to force him to move more quickly on the expropriations. They occupied management offices and refused to leave until an expropriation took place. By the end of 1971, the government had taken over more than 150 industries, including 12 of the 20 largest companies in the country. The nationalization programs affected both domestic and foreign corpora-tions. Usually the previous owners were compensated, but sometimes (as in the case of the copper mines) an agreement was difficult to reach.

UP's expropriation campaign concentrated on large corporations. It refrained from attacking small- and medium-sized businesses because it hoped to gain their support for economic changes, although that backing was not always forthcoming. This led to an inherent contradiction, as smaller industries employed 80 percent of the workers, precisely those whom UP sought to help with their policies. They worked in worse conditions and for less pay than did those in the larger corpora-tions that were being expropriated. Because the UP program did not affect the smaller industries, the vast majority of workers realized little gain from the eco-nomic reforms.

Workers put off by the slow pace of the nationalization program began pushing the UP government to adopt more aggressive policies. On April 25, 1971, workers took over the Yarur textile plant and demanded that it be expropriated. When Allende finally agreed, workers occupied eight other plants with similar demands. This led to workers seizing additional small industries that the moderate wing of UP did not want nationalized. Slowly the government began to lose control of the situation, as popular demands outpaced the policies that the leaders were willing to implement. At the same time, the nationalizations gave the U.S. government an excuse to cut off aid to Chile and increase economic aggression against the country.

Agrarian Reform

The UP government accelerated the pace of the agrarian reform process begun in 1967 under Frei's administration. In Chile, agriculture was a less important source of employment and export commodities than in many other Latin American countries. As a result, less resistance to agrarian reform meant that the government could immediately move ahead with plans with a massive, rapid, and radical program to destroy the archaic hacienda system. Allende distributed more land in one year than Frei had done in six. By mid-1972, all farms over eighty hectares had been expropriated. UP chose to proceed with existing legislation—even though it was not completely consistent with the government's preferred policies—out of a concern that expropriations be legal and that time not be wasted in passing new legislation. Any reforms approved through proper legal channels would be harder to challenge, which improved the potential to achieve permanent structural changes.

In order to increase agricultural production, abandoned and underused state land would be cultivated. Expropriated land would be organized into cooperatives and land titles given to the peasants. A problem that the government faced was that agrarian reform requires more than a redistribution of land. Farmers also need credit and access to supplies and equipment. The expropriation was to include the assets, capital, credit, and technical assistance necessary for the peasants to farm the land. The land reform happened so fast, however, that often the government could not provide these services, which limited the effectiveness of the entire program.

While the government proceeded in a legal and constitutional manner with its agrarian reforms, leftist elements in the UP coalition pushed for more aggressive policies. They argued that adherence to existing laws and institutions only served to retard the transition to socialism and protected capitalists and landowners at a cost to poor farmers. Meanwhile, peasants impatient with the slow pace of reform occupied land, including land on small estates not subject to expropriation. Allende condemned these land seizures and the negative influence that they had on rallying the support of the middle class to the cause of the UP government. Some landowners hired armed guards to fight back against the occupations, and others left the country.

Leftist Opposition

UP policies led to significant social and economic gains, which raised expectations for an even greater number of fundamental transformations of society. Allende had strained relations with those to his left because he did not move fast enough with his reforms. Workers demanded higher wages, and peasants illegally occupied land in an attempt to force the government's hand. Left-wing factions pushed for accelerated nationalization of the private sector, price controls, and wage increases. Disagreements within the coalition over the pace and direction that the government should take increased after the short-term gains realized in 1971 gave way in 1972 to rising inflation, shortages, and a lack of foreign exchange. The antagonistic congress refused to increase taxes, which compelled the government to borrow funds to pay for its massive public works projects that helped stimulate the economy. This economic policy increased inflation, which alienated the middle class. Radicals complained that the economic problems were a result of governmental inaction, and their criticisms weakened the government.

Leftist guerrillas who were skeptical about the viability of a peaceful road to socialism founded the Movimiento de Izquierda Revolucionaria (MIR, Revolutionary Left Movement) in 1965. The MIR pressed Allende on the issue of representative democracy, particularly in the face of an entrenched right-wing opposition. They argued that UP's commitment to constitutional changes was bound to fail. From their perspective, a military confrontation was an inevitable result of a class struggle. They urged the president to suspend the constitution, close congress, arm the people, and move directly to a communist government. Others feared that resorting to armed struggle would only lead to a bloody civil war with needless death and the destruction of the gains that the UP government was making.

The moderate wing of the UP coalition—including the communist party—pressed for slower, more evolutionary and less destabilizing change. They opposed the immediate dismantling of the capitalistic economy and the expropriation of small industries. The moderates accused the "ultra-leftists" of playing into the hands of the right-wing opposition and needlessly stoking paranoia and fears. In order to move ahead with their economic programs, UP needed the cooperation of the middle class. According to the moderates, leftist actions alienated popular support by provoking clashes with small entrepreneurs and instigating seizures of factories and farms that had no significant economic importance. The moderates believed that compromises and alliances were important to confront reactionary forces that opposed the UP program. For the MIR and other leftists, these hesitations only hindered and delayed the much-needed radical transformation of society.

Even with disagreements over the proper pace of changes, electoral support for the left continued to grow after Allende's election in 1970. In the April 1971 municipal contest that many viewed as a **referendum** on the Allende administration, the UP coalition gained almost half of the vote in the country. In the March 1973 midterm congressional elections, the UP coalition registered an unprecedented 10 percent rise from its vote in the previous presidential contest. Supporters hoped that the left would win half the seats in congress, which would have allowed it to pass legislation over the opposition of its opponents, but it fell short of that goal. Conservatives, meanwhile, also failed to gain the two-thirds majority that they would need to impeach Allende. The political polarization of the country intensified.

Conservative Opposition

UP faced formidable right-wing opposition to the implementation of its program. The coalition did not control congress. The oligarchy, military, multinational corporations, and most of the media that represented old ruling-class interests were deeply antagonistic to its programs. An educational reform program that took schools away from church control further pushed reactionary sections of the Catholic Church into opposition to the Allende government. Foes organized right-wing paramilitary groups such as Patria y Libertad (Homeland and Liberty) that engaged in terrorist attacks against the government. The opposition to socialist policies designed to benefit the working class could appear to be overwhelming.

Much has been made of Allende's gender gap, with women customarily perceived as voting more conservatively than men. The left typically organized around class issues, whereas conservatives effectively mobilized women along traditional gender lines. Wealthy women led the opposition to Allende's policies because of how they curtailed privileged access to consumer goods in preference for broad availability of basic commodities to working-class families. Women from the ruling class effectively played into old-fashioned gender stereotypes to challenge the male honor of the military leadership. They organized demonstrations at the houses of army commanders, encouraging them to take action against the socialist government and effeminizing them when they failed to do so. They threw chicken feed at the soldiers, implying the soldiers were hens afraid to act. Women engaged in marches with empty pots in a display of their discontent. Shortages hit women, whose gender-defined role was to feed their families, particularly hard. These difficulties led working-class and peasant women to join these protests as well.

Although real wages remained high and unemployment did not increase, in 1972 inflation became rampant. Consumer products became scarce. The middle class moved against the UP government as the economic situation worsened. In October 1972, truckers went on strike in opposition to plans to nationalize their industry. What was essentially an employer's strike caused shortages, which increased discontent with government policies—precisely the intent of the work stoppage. Right-wing groups instigated further disruptions as part of a broader plan to sabotage the economy. Even some working-class and peasant groups that had become disaffected with the slow pace of change joined in the attempt to shut down the economy.

BIOGRAPHY: BEATRIZ ALLENDE, 1942–1977

Beatriz Allende was the revolutionary daughter of Chile's socialist president Salvador Allende and one of his closest advisers and collaborators. Even though she fell significantly to his left politically, she willingly and openly supported and embraced his electoral campaigns. She served as a key networking link with elements of the Chilean and international left, including providing support for a guerrilla insurgency in neighboring Bolivia after Che Guevara's death in 1967. Although Allende's contributions are largely unknown and overshadowed by her much more famous father, her life affords rich insights into revolutionary movements in Latin America.

Beatriz Allende
Source: Biblioteca Virtual Salvador Allende Gossens

Beatriz Allende was the second of Salvador Allende's three daughters. She grew up in a relatively privileged setting in the capital city of Santiago. She trailed her father into the socialist party and participated actively in its youth section. She followed him into medicine as well, selecting the field as a way to promote development. The younger Allende studied at the University of Concepción and subsequently worked in public health as a pediatrician. Reflecting common gendered notions, Salvador Allende wanted a male heir. In a sense, Beatriz became the son he never had.

While Salvador Allende was convinced that a revolutionary transformation of society could occur through constitutional means, Beatriz Allende became convinced that these changes would only materialize through a guerrilla insurgency. For that reason, she was closely aligned with MIR, which sought to emulate the armed path that the Cuban Revolution had laid out. In her travels as a student activist, Allende met Che Guevara, listened to Fidel Castro's speeches, and even stayed at the house of Raúl Castro and Vilma Espín. While in Cuba, Allende met and eventually married a Cuban diplomat named Luis Fernández de Oña who worked with an office that extended assistance to revolutionary movements across the hemisphere. Together they created critical linkages between Cuba, Salvador Allende, and the broader Chilean left.

When Salvador Allende won election as president in 1970, Beatriz left her medical career and her affiliation with the MIR behind to join his administration as a private secretary, adviser, and close confidant. She did not have a leading public face in his government, but she did play a key role behind the scenes in drafting and influencing policy decisions. With her previous history and political involvement, Beatriz Allende provided critical informal networks between her father's administration and those on the revolutionary left both in Chile and transnationally.

During the military coup on September 11, 1973, Beatriz Allende stayed with her father in the presidential palace despite being pregnant. She left only when the president ordered all women and children to evacuate, reflecting both a dominant sexist attitude—that they were to be protected and shielded rather than embraced as active participants in historical processes—as well as a desire to safeguard his daughter. After the coup, Allende went into exile with other members of her family. In Cuba, she worked tirelessly to mobilize a global movement in solidarity with Chileans resisting the Pinochet dictatorship. Facing what seemed to be an insurmountable fascist challenge to socialism and democracy in her home country, she took her own life on October 11, 1977.

Allende's life reflects both the restrictions of a male-dominated Latin American left and how revolutionaries sought to challenge deeply embedded systems of power. While revolutionary leaders were almost universally men and their roles have been reinforced and reified in the retelling of these histories, women, as Allende's involvement makes readily apparent, also made key though often unacknowledged contributions to revolutionary movements. She understood that having to decide between motherhood and political militancy was a false choice. As a woman, she faced structural constraints but also realized opportunities to advance a revolutionary struggle. Approaching the Chilean road to socialism through her life and experiences, as Tanya Harmer does in *Beatriz Allende: A Revolutionary Life in Cold War Latin America*, breaks through these stereotypes and provides a perspective of Latin American revolutions from the bottom and to the left.

COUP

On September 11, 1973, army general Augusto Pinochet led a military coup that overthrew Salvador Allende and the UP government. The coup came on the day that Allende planned to announce a plebiscite to resolve the constitutional crisis that the country faced. Instead, Allende attempted to defend the presidential palace with a small group of his closest supporters as the Chilean air force relentlessly bombed the building. In his last radio broadcast, Allende stated that history was on the side of the workers and that they would determine the future of the country. He declared that he would repay the loyalty of his supporters with his life. The coup plotters made it obvious that if he surrendered, they would not let him go peacefully into exile but instead would torture and humiliate him. The president decided rather to take his own life with a Kalashnikov assault rifle that Fidel Castro had given to him.

The coup itself did not surprise many. A failed June 1973 attempt had made it readily apparent that the military and its right-wing supporters were moving in that direction. In retrospect, the June revolt appeared to be a test run so that plotters could determine who would join them in a subsequent and more serious putsch. What surprised most was the level of physical brutality and the institutional reach of the September coup, and how quickly seemingly entrenched democratic structures crumbled. Many expected that the removal of Allende would lead to new elections and a quick transfer of power, presumably to the Christian Democrats. Instead, the military dismantled the country's sacred democratic institutions and remained in power for seventeen years.

The coup highlighted the extreme polarization of Chilean society. Many conservatives, traditionally allied with the Catholic Church and wealthy landowners, openly embraced a military government in order to save Chile from communism. Industrialists saw a coup as the only way to maintain a capitalistic system that assured continuance of their economic power and class privileges. The centrist Christian Democrats initially welcomed the coup as an opportunistic opening that would allow them to return to power, but they eventually joined a progressive opposition to the military's dismantling of democratic structures. Allende still enjoyed a bedrock of support on the left. On the third anniversary of his September 4, 1970, election, only a week before the coup that removed him from office, Allende's supporters marched in front of the presidential palace in the largest demonstration in Chile's history to publicize their defense of their embattled leader. Allende did not fall for a want of ardent backers.

As with Arbenz in Guatemala, some militants pressed Allende to arm his supporters in order to remain in power. It was naïve, they argued, to attempt a deep transformation of society without expecting and planning for a conservative reaction such as what happened in the coup. In retrospect, many scholars believe that the overwhelming strength of the Chilean military would easily have crushed the pro-Allende forces. A more likely outcome than a leftist victory would have been a bloodbath. The other alternative would have been to follow the Cuban model and preemptively dismantle the existing military structures completely, perhaps including the execution of key leaders who would have been capable of organizing an opposition in exile. Allende, however, was a strong constitutionalist and was unwilling to violate the sacrosanct nature of existing institutions or violate the human rights of his opponents. Those compromises and trade-offs highlight the limitations of attempting to implement a revolution within the confines of an established order.

General Augusto Pinochet

Before joining the coup, Pinochet had been known as a supporter of Chile's constitutional system. Allende had named him as head of the army only three weeks earlier, under the perception that he was a reliable ally. Pinochet's defection to the side of the conspirators removed the last barrier to the coup moving forward. His betrayal surprised Allende. Scholars have subsequently debated whether Pinochet had always been a closet fascist or whether the temptation to amass great fame, fortune, and political power was too great of an opportunity for him to ignore.

Pinochet replaced General Carlos Prats, who had resigned as commander-in-chief on August 22 when the pressure of the wives of other military leaders calling for a coup had become overpowering. Similar to his predecessor Schneider, who had been killed in a botched coup attempt just before Allende's inauguration, Prats was also a strong constitutionalist. Prats went into exile in Argentina after the coup, where Pinochet's secret police assassinated him a year later. Being a respected part of the military hierarchy was not enough to save either Schneider or Prats.

On taking power, Pinochet set out to destroy, not reform, the entire existing political system. The military regime dissolved congress, suspended the constitution, declared political parties illegal, and outlawed labor unions and strikes. The junta quickly reversed Allende's progressive reforms, including undoing his government's agrarian reform program and abrogating measures in the 1972 Indigenous Law that provided for the defense of Indigenous communal lands. Initially, the plan was to share command among four junta members: Pinochet together with the heads of the air force, navy, and police (known as the carabineros). Pinochet soon sidelined the other three officers and concentrated all power in his own hands. In 1980, Pinochet promulgated a new constitution that ensured his personal and perpetual control over the government. The military named itself the guardian of the state. Former presidents and other top officials were given lifetime seats in the new senate, which guaranteed that conservatives would maintain control over political structures regardless of the outcome of any future electoral contests. The coup represented a staggering blow to the political democracy, liberal freedoms, and social reforms that Allende had championed.

The military government engaged in extensive human rights abuses. They executed over three thousand Chileans and imprisoned and tortured many more, most famously in the national stadium. The regime abolished individual liberties, established curfews, and set strict limits on the media. It took over the universities and, in the process, violated the established tradition of university autonomy. In the weeks after the coup, a "caravan of death" toured the country to arrest leftists and labor activists and execute them. The military used Nazi experts to set up concentration camps and carry out international assassinations. A March 1978 amnesty law assured that military officials would be protected from punishment for their political crimes. Together with other military juntas in South America, the regime established Operation Condor as a transnational network of secret police forces to eliminate opponents who had sought refuge in neighboring countries. Many times, the military dictatorships made the assassinations appear as if they were accidents in order to hide culpability. The level of brutality in Chile was no worse than what other military governments committed, but what was stunning was that these abuses took place in a country that saw itself as a beacon of democracy and one that enjoyed stable institutions. This type of coup was not supposed to happen in Chile.

As deadly as any of the military government's political policies was the implementation of a neoliberal shock treatment that economist Milton Friedman had designed at the University of Chicago. Chile became a laboratory for the application of free-market experiments by economists whom Friedman had trained. These so-called Chicago Boys implemented an unfettered capitalistic economy without having to bother with any of the checks that a functioning democratic system would create as barriers to their implementation. Among the policies were drastic cuts in government spending as well as privatization of social security, healthcare, and education, all of which hurt poor peasants and workers. Hundreds of businesses and industries were privatized and sold to cronies of the military government or multinational corporations at low prices. Land that Allende had expropriated for rural workers was returned to their previous owners or sold to a new wealthy ruling class that emerged as a direct result of the neoliberal policies.

Friedman's policies created a superficial and short-lived "economic miracle," but it came at the cost of significant harm to the poor and marginalized. For workers, wages declined and social services disappeared. Foreign capitalists gained more control over the country's economy. The rich became richer and the poor poorer, leading to one of the most inequitable economies in the world. These economic policies that favored an upward redistribution of wealth could not have been implemented without the support of a military dictatorship.

In October 1988, Pinochet held a plebiscite to ask whether he should remain in power for another eight years. Surrounded by supporters, he was convinced that he would easily win the vote. Instead, he lost by a margin of 55 percent to 43 percent. After promising to follow the will of the people, he could not easily back down from his vow to respect the results. In this environment, the military allowed a December 1989 electoral contest to move forward. Patricio Aylwin Azocar, from the Christian Democratic Party, won the election and took office on March 11, 1990. Although Pinochet relinquished the presidency, he remained in power as head of the military and with a seat as senator for life. He could still easily control political decisions through those positions. Although a civilian was formally the president, the military set government policy.

On October 16, 1998, police arrested Pinochet in a London hospital, where he was recovering from back surgery. Spain had requested his **extradition** on behalf of two Spanish judges who were investigating crimes that military leaders in Argentina and Chile had committed. They accused Pinochet of engaging in acts of genocide, torture, terrorism, and other crimes against Spanish citizens in Chile. Because of the 1978 amnesty law, he could not be charged for those crimes in Chile. The Spanish judges claimed that the widespread and systematic human rights violations in Chile during the military government amounted to crimes against humanity, and such crimes were subject to universal jurisdiction. Chilean officials fought against the extradition request and launched the extraordinary defense that executions and torture are official functions of government and thereby immune from prosecution. Prosecutors countered with the charge that Pinochet was not exempt for atrocities committed during the unfolding of the coup on September 11, 1973, before formally proclaiming himself as head of state that evening. This charge sent the military generals scrambling to document when exactly they had killed each of their opponents, to prove the deaths had taken place after they had formally taken power. Pinochet's supporters claimed that his actions were justified because he had dispelled a communist threat and brought financial and political stability to Chile. Conservatives championed a cause of national sovereignty and denounced the Spanish judges as a European attempt to recolonize the Americas.

After being held under house arrest for almost two years in London, prosecutors allowed Pinochet to return to Chile on humanitarian grounds. The veil of invincibility, however, had been broken. Half a year later, Chilean courts stripped Pinochet of his immunity and charged him with human rights abuses. The courts declared that kidnapping was an ongoing crime, and in cases where a dead body could not be delivered, the 1978 amnesty did not apply. In July 2001, however, the courts ruled that the former dictator was unable to stand trial because of an onset of dementia. On December 10, 2006, Pinochet died at the age of ninety-one without having had to answer for his crimes.

United States

Unlike the Central American and Caribbean countries of Guatemala and Cuba that lay well within the U.S. geographic sphere of influence, Chile was much more distant and therefore should have presented less of a challenge to U.S. hegemonic dominance. In addition, Allende's socialist policies had sufficiently alienated his domestic conservative opponents that they would have moved against him whether or not the United States existed as an imperial force in the region. Regardless, rather than encouraging a continuance of Chile's constitutional system, the United States adopted policies that contributed to an undermining of Chile's democratic institutions.

Throughout the 1960s, the CIA had interfered in Chile's internal affairs to prevent Allende's election. Mailings, leaflets, and media advertisements in the 1970 election warned of the end of religion and family life if Allende were to win. The propaganda predicted a total economic collapse with a socialist victory and spread rumors of communist firing squads. The CIA also encouraged the international media to write stories critical of Allende.

When Allende won the election, Henry Kissinger, Richard Nixon's presidential assistant for National Security Affairs, declared that he saw no reason "to stand by and watch a country go communist due to the irresponsibility of its own people." He warned that a Marxist government was unacceptable, even though Allende was a strong constitutionalist and had served for decades in the government without violating institutional norms. Kissinger announced that the United States would not be bound by pieces of paper cast into a ballot box in a faraway country. Nixon pledged to smash Allende.

The Nixon administration pursued a two-track strategy to block Allende from office. The first track was to bribe congress to vote against confirming Allende as president after the close presidential election. That tactic collapsed when the Christian Democrats refused to cooperate with what in essence would have been a constitutional coup. The second track included plans for a military coup, including the removal of generals such as Schneider and Prats who supported Chile's constitutional order.

Shortly after Allende's election, Viron Vaky, Kissinger's top aide on Latin America, argued in a secret memo that attempts to prevent the socialist from taking office were a violation of U.S. policy tenets and moral principles. He questioned whether Allende posed a serious threat to U.S. security interests and whether his election would alter a global balance of power (see the document included with this chapter). Nevertheless, Washington policy makers viewed the election of an avowed Marxist as a definite psychological setback for U.S. hegemonic control over Latin America and an advance for socialism. As such, it would need to be stopped.

One of the Pinochet administration's most infamous attacks against his opponents occurred in the United States. In September 1976, Pinochet's operatives planted a car bomb in Washington, D.C., that killed former Allende ambassador Orlando Letelier and his associate Ronni Moffitt. Letelier was an effective lobbyist against U.S. aid to Pinochet and for that reason needed to be removed. Until September 11, 2001, those murders entailed the most egregious terrorist attack in the country's capital. In response, Secretary of State Henry Kissinger indicated that human rights would not be a priority for the current Gerald Ford administration. Instead, he expressed sympathy for Pinochet's political program. Subsequent president Jimmy Carter tried to press human rights issues upon taking office in 1977, but when Ronald Reagan was elected four years later, he reversed that policy, to Pinochet's relief. Following in the footsteps of his Republican predecessors, in the 1990s president Bill Clinton cited national security concerns in his refusal to release documents that would have revealed Pinochet's role in the attack on Letelier. Only in 2015 did the U.S. government finally declassify documents that definitively proved Pinochet's culpability in the attack.

DOCUMENT: VIRON P. VAKY, "CHILE—40 COMMITTEE MEETING, MONDAY—SEPTEMBER 14," 1970

The following memorandum is remarkable for its open acknowledgment that it was not in the interest of the United States to intervene in Chile's internal affairs to prevent Salvador Allende's election. Viron Vaky was a career foreign service official who was previously acting assistant secretary of state for inter-American affairs and wrote this memo as a member of the National Security Council operations staff for Latin America. Henry Kissinger was the presidential assistant for national security affairs.

Washington, September 14, 1970.
Memorandum for Dr. Kissinger

Attached [not included here] is the CIA paper prepared as the basic document to be considered. You should read it carefully, especially Section I, pp 2–8, outlining the significant new developments that have occurred. This memo summarizes the CIA paper, provides analytical comment and my conclusions.

I. Summary of the Paper

    A. The setting the paper describes includes these major elements:

        1. Military action is impossible; the military is incapable and unwilling to seize power. We have no capability to motivate or instigate a coup.

        2. Because of significant changes in circumstances, a political plan which [Eduardo] Frei has contrived has some chance of success. It is still a very long shot, but it is the only possibility.

        3. The plan involves an effort to corral enough PDC [Christian Democratic Party], Radical votes to elect [Jorge] Alessandri; he would then resign; a new election would be required; Frei would be eligible this time and would run; presumably he would be elected. The process is constitutional and legal, if unusual and untraditional.

        4. The unqualified support and effort of Frei is central to this plan because moving the majority of the PDC congressional bloc to Alessandri is the essence of the maneuver. The attraction to the PDC is another six years of political power. Frei has taken the necessary preliminary steps to position the PDC and himself for such an effort.

        5. The U.S. cannot operate this plan; it must be Chilean and Frei's. Our support and stimulus may be critical, and resources may become important. But in essence we would be backstopping a Chilean effort.

        6. [US ambassador to Chile Edward M.] Korry has in fact already encouraged and pushed this plan, if he did not participate in its creation. He has already committed us to at least moral support and encouragement. Therefore, the issue is not whether we go or do not go; but whether we continue this encouragement and do any more, or draw back.

    B. The possible courses of action to support and stimulate the Frei re-election gambit are described as:

        1. Authorize the Ambassador to encourage the gambit through whatever resources are available to him locally, but on the most discreet basis to minimize exposure of USG [U.S. government]'s role.

        2. Authorize the Ambassador to assure Frei directly that the USG strongly supports and encourages his efforts. This might include an oral message from President Nixon to be used if appropriate.

3. Parallel Ambassador's efforts with outside support to influence Frei—stimulate foreign political figures whom Frei respects to encourage him.
4. Work through European Christian Democratic parties to bolster Frei's leadership and encourage the PDC leaders to contest Allende.
5. Encourage the Radical Party, through established assets, to abandon Allende in favor of Alessandri.
6. Generally keep information lines into the military and close communication to be prepared for any future eventuality.
    The risks of exposure are appreciable, and rise the broader our involvement and contacts.

C. The paper asks the Committee to address the following questions:

1. Should the Ambassador be authorized to continue to encourage and support the Frei plan but with as little risk of exposure as possible? If so, should he be provided with a confidential message of support from President Nixon to Frei to use at the appropriate time?
2. Should his efforts be complemented through outside diplomatic and covert activities designed to encourage Frei? Should a propaganda campaign be conducted outside Chile in support of the Frei gambit?
3. Should an effort be made to swing Radical votes to Alessandri? Should the German Democratic Socialist Party which has close ties be encouraged to weigh in with the Radical Party in this sense?
4. Should we expand and intensify military contacts to be assured of requisite intelligence and stand-by channels of influence?

II. Analysis

The description of events and the proposals must be examined through the following questions:
—What are the chances of success?
—What element would USG involvement provide that would not otherwise be there and what difference would it make?
—What are the consequences of success, and the consequences of failure?
—What are the dangers to the US in getting involved?
—Why should we run these risks and incur these costs at all? Is it really necessary?

Without long narrative, I think a fair analysis would have to say:

5. Chances of Success. Frei says one in twenty; Korry says one in five. No one really knows with much precision, but it is clear that the chances of success are considerably less than even.
6. What does USG involvement add? Probably a great deal in terms of moral support and encouragement. Now that we have already begun this, to quit would almost surely kill the effort. It may not be able to continue without our support. There is less evidence that any material resources would be needed, but some money may be.
7. The consequences of success. It is vital to understand that it is not just a question of defeating Allende and that's it. This sets in motion a number of serious problems:

If Allende is defeated in the run-off, he and his supporters are most likely to go to the streets. Widespread violence and even insurrection is a possibility. He is unlikely to simply meekly run in a new election.

If there is a new election, we would want to make sure Frei wins; hence we would be drawn into further action to support his election.

If Frei is elected, his would be an unstable government facing serious dissension. Such a situation would probably require massive US economic and military assistance support.

8. The consequences of failure. If the gambit fails it will discredit the parties and the democratic institutions. It will give the Communists the excuse to push Allende quickly into a radical course. The restraints that would have been available to slow down or modify his actions would be gone. Failure would in short guarantee a fate that may not have been inevitable.

9. Dangers to the US. The biggest danger is exposure of US involvement. This would wreck our credibility, solidify anti-US sentiment in Chile in a permanent way, create an adverse reaction in the rest of Latin America and the world and perhaps domestically. Exposure of US involvement with an effort that failed would be disastrous; it would be this Administration's Bay of Pigs.

A second major danger is that while we might begin with a limited plan of encouragement, this is a slippery slope; we may very well find ourselves irresistibly sucked into rising degrees of involvement at rising risks to "protect the investment" and find ourselves having slipped into a disastrous situation.

10. Why the need for USG involvement. This is the crux of the issue. Do the dangers and risks of an Allende government coming to power outweigh the dangers and risks of the probable chain of events we would set in motion by our involvement?

What we propose is patently a violation of our own principles and policy tenets. Moralism aside, this has practical operational consequences. Are they rhetoric or do they have meaning? If these principles have any meaning, we normally depart from them only to meet the gravest threat to us, e.g., to our survival.

Is Allende a mortal threat to the US? It is hard to argue this. Is he a serious problem that would cost us a great deal? Certainly. Is it inevitable that he will consolidate his power? He has a very good chance; but it is far from inevitable or that if he does that he will be a success. Does an Allende government start a South American dominoes? Unlikely; the impact of a Marxist state in the rest of Latin America is containable.

III. Conclusions

I conclude that:

1. Any covert effort to stimulate a military take-over is a non-starter. There is no practical possibility at this point.
2. We should keep our lines open and broadened into the military. An opportunity may open up later; but for the moment we should gather information and establish standby channels.
3. Korry has already started us on a political track. We cannot backtrack without killing the Frei plan.
4. The Frei plan has some chance, and it is the only chance.
5. Our support can be important to its success.

6. It is possible to backstop it at this point with a minimum involvement and with acceptable risks.

7. But there are limits to what we can do acceptably. It is not a question of just adding more effort and money. Our capacity to succeed is simply not a function of how much effort we put in, and the greater our involvement the sharper the danger of exposure.

8. We should therefore enter into this in the knowledge that the calculus can change to make it wiser to cut out rather than just progressively be sucked into massive and disastrous involvement to "protect the investment."

9. We should also understand that this is not a limited operation. If it succeeds it opens up still more serious problems as outlined above. We are almost sure to be called upon for continued support of one kind or another for years, (See II 3 above) and success of the plan will almost surely trigger violence in Chile.

10. I would recommend the following:
    a. Authorize the Ambassador to continue to encourage Frei to use resources at his command, but with the utmost discretion and tact and with absolute minimum USG involvement. (I would *not* authorize a personal message from President Nixon; we should protect the President.)
    b. Organize efforts from the "outside," i.e.
       —encourage European Christian Democrats to funnel support, encouragement and ideas; perhaps even funds.
       —encourage other leaders to do so.
       —develop an outside propaganda campaign as Frei suggested.
    c. Develop an internal propaganda campaign to stir fear of a Communist takeover, and expose Communist machinations.
    d. Use our separate assets to work on the Radical Party; try to get the German Social Democrat Party to do the same.
    e. Ask for weekly reports and establish some mechanism to monitor this carefully.

Source: U.S. Department of State, *Foreign Relations of the United States, 1969–1976, Volume XXI, Chile, 1969–1973*, edited by James McElveen and James Siekmeier (Washington, D.C.: U.S. Government Printing Office, 2014), 236–240, Document 86, https://history.state.gov/historicaldocuments/frus1969 -76v21/d86. A scan of the original memo is also available in the National Security Archive Electronic Briefing Book No. 437, at https://nsarchive2.gwu.edu/NSAEBB /NSAEBB437.

ASSESSMENT

Although Chile and Cuba socialized their economies through different means (electoral versus armed), they followed similar economic programs. Both sought to increase the income of people on the lower rungs of the economic ladder. Both pushed for agrarian reform and nationalization programs. Neither had to deal with an economy destroyed by protracted guerrilla warfare, a situation somewhat unusual for new socialist governments. And both faced enormous opposition, both domestic and from the U.S. government. The Cuban Revolution, however, survived, while the Chilean path to socialism went down in flames. Cuban moderates opposed Castro's rapid pace of change and consolidation of political power, but the physical elimination of his opponents ensured his survival. One potential lesson is that it is impossible to implement a socialist agenda if the revolutionaries do not take the necessary steps to maintain themselves in power.

UP's shortcomings together with right-wing opposition in Chile and hostility from the United States contributed to the government's demise. While Allende's conservative opponents cheered the military for saving Chile from communism, others contended that the coup precipitated a dictatorship much worse than what could have possibly emerged from an Allende government. Rather than confronting a threat to democracy, the decision to launch a coup against Allende was the result of a paranoid fear of communism and a belief in a moral imperative to stop it wherever it emerged, not to mention that socialist policies directly challenged imperial economic interests. A successful socialist government would present a psychological challenge to U.S. hegemony in the region. It was necessary to make an experiment in socialism appear to be such a failure that no one would ever dare repeat it.

Some scholars have interpreted the Chilean coup as a political, and not a military, defeat for UP. From this perspective, the Allende government fell because it employed the rhetoric of a socialist revolution without having the authority to implement such policies. It failed to gain the support of the middle-class and working-class women who had nothing to lose and much to gain from an attack on economic monopolies and foreign corporations. If Allende had moved faster in transforming society, he may have been more able to satisfy those rising expectations and hence maintain the UP government in place.

Allende was a strict constitutionalist, and he carefully abided by the legal process to implement UP's program. Similar to the removal of Arbenz in Guatemala, his overthrow led some supporters to question whether socialism could only be implemented through armed struggle. Socialism requires a class struggle that presents a direct challenge to the capitalistic mode of production and as such is not an economic policy for the timid. Chile demonstrated the limits of moving in that direction within the constraints of existing institutional orders that would allow conservative opponents to defeat a socialist government and reverse the social gains it achieved. Some contend that a socialization program must be implemented quickly—before the opposition has an opportunity to mobilize against it—or it must be given up altogether.

Allende killed himself in the presidential palace with a machine gun that Fidel Castro had given him. Several weeks after the coup, Castro justified the gift. He declared, "If every worker and every farmer had a rifle in their hands, there would never have been a fascist coup." The removal of a strong constitutionalist such as Allende raised in the minds of many socialist revolutionaries the question that, if those were the parameters, what other choice existed but to follow Cuba's example and close all channels to external subversion and extend democracy only to those who were willing to abide by the rules that the socialist government established. Peaceful paths to revolutionary change no longer appeared as viable as they had only a few years earlier.

SUMMARY

Chile's experiment with a peaceful and constitutional path to socialism raises the question of whether it is possible to make profound revolutionary changes in society without resorting to violence. The Marxist Salvador Allende won election to the presidency in 1970 after serving in congress for twenty-five years. Although he supported Fidel Castro and the Cuban Revolution, Allende contended that Chile had strong democratic institutions and hence no need for armed struggle. Initially, his UP government made significant progress in transforming the country's economic structures, but those policies alienated both conservative opponents in Chile and U.S.-based corporations with significant investments in the country. On September 11, 1973, General Augusto Pinochet led a brutal military coup that not only overthrew Allende's government but also dismantled the country's treasured democratic institutions. It took seventeen years for the country to return to civilian rule, but even then, the military continued to hold dominance over the country. Chile's path to socialism exemplifies the difficulties that Latin American revolutionaries face in implementing radical changes in their societies.

DISCUSSION QUESTIONS

Did Allende do too much or too little to address Chile's socioeconomic problems?
Was it a mistake for Allende to be such a strict constitutionalist?
Would Allende's government have succeeded had he silenced his opponents?
Why did Allende kill himself? Was doing so a strategic mistake?
In retrospect, what could or should Allende have done differently to prevent his government from being overthrown?

FURTHER READING

The UP government in Chile generated a massive literature, with one joke stating that a thousand books have been published on the topic, one for each day that Allende was in office. The literature is divided into those that examine Allende's government and those that center on Pinochet's coup and its aftermath.

Burbach, Roger. *The Pinochet Affair: State Terrorism and Global Justice.* London: Zed Books, 2003. A damning critique of the Pinochet dictatorship.

De Vylder, Stefan. *Allende's Chile: The Political Economy of the Rise and Fall of the Unidad Popular.* Cambridge: Cambridge University Press, 1976. A compelling study of the Allende government's economic policies.

Dinges, John. *The Condor Years: How Pinochet and His Allies Brought Terrorism to Three Continents.* New York: New Press, 2004. A critical examination of terror networks in South America under military dictatorships.

Figueroa Clark, Victor. *Salvador Allende: Revolutionary Democrat.* London: Pluto Press, 2013. A short biography of Chile's Marxist leader.

Harmer, Tanya. *Beatriz Allende: A Revolutionary Life in Cold War Latin America.* Chapel Hill: University of North Carolina Press, 2020. A very compelling and well-written biography of Salvador Allende's daughter.

Hauser, Thomas. *Missing.* New York: Avon Books, 1982. A journalistic account of the execution of the U.S. citizen Charles Horman, who was caught in the Pinochet coup. Made into a movie by Costa-Gavras.

Kornbluh, Peter. *The Pinochet File: A Declassified Dossier on Atrocity and Accountability.* New York: New Press, 2003. Declassified documents on the U.S. government's role in undermining the Allende presidency.

Loveman, Brian. *Chile: The Legacy of Hispanic Capitalism.* New York: Oxford University Press, 1979. A historical overview of Chile by a leading historian.

McPherson, Alan L. *Ghosts of Sheridan Circle: How a Washington Assassination Brought Pinochet's Terror State to Justice.* Chapel Hill: University of North Carolina Press, 2019. Explores the assassination of Pinochet's leading opponent, the former Chilean ambassador to the United States Orlando Letelier, along with his colleague, Ronni Moffitt, at Sheridan Circle, in the heart of Washington, D.C.

Power, Margaret. *Right-Wing Women in Chile: Feminine Power and the Struggle against Allende, 1964–1973.* University Park: Pennsylvania State University Press, 2002. An impressive examination of women's opposition to Allende.

Stern, Steve J. *Battling for Hearts and Minds: Memory Struggles in Pinochet's Chile, 1973–1988.* Durham, NC: Duke University Press, 2006. The second of a three-volume "memory box of Pinochet's Chile" that starts with the Pinochet coup.

Winn, Peter. *Weavers of Revolution: The Yarur Workers and Chile's Road to Socialism.* New York: Oxford University Press, 1986. A remarkable study of worker mobilizations during the Allende years.

FILMS

The Battle of Chile: The Struggle of an Unarmed People. 1975. A documentary on the fate of Allende's UP government filmed throughout Chile from February to September 1973.

Death and the Maiden. 1995. Fictional story based on a play by noted author Ariel Dorfman of a former prisoner who meets her torturer after the fall of the Pinochet dictatorship.

The House of the Spirits. 1993. Based on Isabel Allende's eponymous novel, the film examines political, social, and economic changes in Chile leading to the September 11 coup.

The Last Stand of Salvador Allende: September 11th, 1973; A Documentary. 1998. A remarkable documentary of the final hours of Salvador Allende.

Machuca. 2004. Portrays the 1973 coup from a child's perspective.

Missing. 1982. True story of the execution of Charles Horman after the 1973 military coup in Chile, based on the eponymous book by Thomas Hauser.

National Stadium. 2001. A documentary about the National Stadium that was used as an improvised detention center in the weeks following the 1973 coup.

Salvador Allende. 2004. A documentary on the Chilean president.

Nicaragua

7

Sandinistas in Nicaragua, 1979–1990

KEY DATES

1856–1860	U.S. **filibusterer** William Walker occupies Nicaragua
1893–1909	Presidency of José Santos Zelaya
1911–1933	U.S. Marines occupation of Nicaragua
1927–1933	Augusto César Sandino fights the U.S. Marines to a standstill
1936–1956	Rule of Anastasio Somoza García ("Tacho")
1956–1967	Rule of Luis Somoza Debayle
1961	Founding of the Sandinista National Liberation Front (FSLN)
1967–1979	Rule of Anastasio Somoza Debayle ("Tachito")
December 23, 1972	Managua earthquake
December 27, 1974	Sandinistas crash Somoza's Christmas party
November 8, 1976	Carlos Fonseca killed
January 10, 1978	*La Prensa* publisher Pedro Joaquín Chamorro assassinated
August 22, 1978	Sandinistas seize national palace
June 20, 1979	ABC journalist William Stewart murdered
July 19, 1979	Sandinistas gain power
March 9, 1981	U.S. President Ronald Reagan authorizes right-wing paramilitary force (the "contras") to overthrow the Sandinistas
November 4, 1984	Sandinistas win first free elections since 1928
June 27, 1986	International Court of Justice rules against United States for terrorist attacks on Nicaragua

January 9, 1987	Nicaragua ratifies new constitution that provides **autonomy** to Atlantic coast
February 25, 1990	Sandinistas lose elections to Violeta Barrios de Chamorro
January 10, 2007	FSLN leader Daniel Ortega reelected president
2018	Protests against social security reforms call for Ortega's resignation

On July 19, 1979, a group of guerrillas entered the capital city of Managua, Nicaragua, having overthrown the Somoza family dynasty that had run the country as their personal fiefdom for nearly half a century. The Frente Sandinista de Liberación Nacional (FSLN, Sandinista National Liberation Front) took control twenty years after Fidel Castro led his guerrilla army to power in Cuba. The Sandinistas provide only the second example of a successful armed revolutionary struggle in Latin America. They failed, however, to make changes in societal structures as deep or as permanent as their counterparts had done in Cuba.

With Che Guevara's defeat in Bolivia in 1967 and the election of Marxist Salvador Allende to the presidency in Chile in 1970, leftist sentiments swung away from searching for revolutionary changes through guerrilla struggles and toward using constitutional and institutional means to transform economic and political structures. For a brief interval, an armed path to social transformation was largely taken off the table. The defeat of Chile's electoral path to socialism with Augusto Pinochet's coup in 1973 ushered in a period of military rule throughout Latin America. With the disappearance of functioning institutional structures, the possibilities for an electoral avenue to revolutionary changes appeared to evaporate. Many leftists now argued that it was naïve to assume that a radical political program could be implemented without the physical elimination of their class enemies. These activists favored returning to armed struggle as the preferred path to power. Only the Sandinistas in Nicaragua realized success with this strategy, while others (discussed in chapter 8) met with failure.

From an orthodox Marxist perspective, Nicaragua was an unlikely candidate for a socialist revolution. Nicaragua was a poor, backward country without the highly developed industrial economy that Marx assumed would be necessary before a more equitable distribution of resources could be undertaken. Nor did it have a strong working-class base on which to build a proletarian revolution. Other countries were more likely candidates for a social revolution. Although Cuba was largely a rural society, a long tradition of communist and labor party organization contributed to the success of its revolution. In addition, the nature of labor in the sugarcane fields had the effect of creating a proletarian consciousness among the workers. In Chile, Salvador Allende built on a long history of working-class militancy to win election as president. Although relegated to a dependent position in a global capitalist economy, both countries were in the process of industrialization. Nicaragua simply had not developed the basic objective economic conditions deemed necessary for a socialist revolution.

The Sandinistas broke from an orthodox Marxist emphasis on the need for an urban proletariat to provide vanguard leadership for a revolutionary struggle. They rejected the notion that the peasants were a reactionary force that could not be relied on for the development of a revolutionary movement. The success of the Cuban Revolution strongly influenced the Sandinistas, particularly in terms of believing that a dedicated cadre could create the necessary conditions for an insurrection. They learned from Ernesto Che Guevara that a revolutionary consciousness could be formed in Nicaragua's peasant population. The Sandinistas looked back to the heroic struggle of General Augusto César Sandino (1895–1934) against the U.S. Marine Corps as an example and inspiration for their revolutionary struggle. Facing seemingly insurmountable odds and in the most unlikely of situations, the revolutionaries found success.

CONQUESTS

Nicaragua has relatively few natural resources, which made it a less desirable destination for Spanish conquistadors than either Mexico or Peru with their rich gold and silver mines. Agricultural production dominated, beginning with cacao during the Spanish colonial period, German coffee production during the nineteenth century, bananas in the twentieth century, and cattle and cotton more recently. Even so, Nicaragua's rough terrain meant that only 10 percent of the land was arable, about a third of what could be cultivated in neighboring El Salvador or the United States. By the middle of the twentieth century, a very small political and economic ruling class controlled this limited agricultural production and held the masses in an oppressed and dispossessed state.

The Spanish conquest of Nicaragua began in 1523 from both Panama to the south and Guatemala to the north. Although Nicaragua was not home to the highly stratified Indigenous empires that the Spanish encountered in Mexico and Peru, it did have a sizable Indigenous population. Nevertheless, because the conquistadors could not tap into preexisting tribute systems, extracting labor from the natives was difficult. Although the Spaniards quickly established a foothold on the Pacific coast, they never controlled the Caribbean (known locally as the Atlantic) side of the country. Indigenous uprisings repelled Spanish advances into their territory. In 1612, the Spanish embarked on a serious campaign to conquer the interior of Nicaragua, an effort that finally succeeded 150 years later, not through military might but thanks to the religious zeal of Franciscan missionaries. In 1743, over two hundred years after the beginning of the Spanish conquest, a series of fourteen Indigenous revolts challenged Spanish rule. An Indigenous delegation walked from northern Nicaragua to the colonial center of power in Guatemala in 1817 to lodge a complaint with the Spanish officials about the low salaries and bad working conditions under which they suffered. Their action marked one of the first labor protests in Nicaragua.

In the seventeenth century, British buccaneers occupied the eastern Atlantic coast and imported enslaved peoples from Africa to grow sugarcane. The British eventually gained control over the Nicaraguan coast as a protectorate. In the nineteenth century, Moravian missionaries brought their Protestant religion to the area. Subsequently, Nicaragua became divided into a western Pacific Spanish and Catholic coast, and an eastern Atlantic seaboard that was English speaking, Protestant, and of African and native descent.

Nicaragua gained strategic significance during the 1849 California gold rush when Cornelius Vanderbilt developed the country as a transshipment point for prospectors traveling west. Since the sixteenth century, some had dreamed of a transcontinental canal across Central America to connect the Atlantic and Pacific oceans. Vanderbilt had secured rights to construct such a waterway, but one had yet to be built.

In 1856, the U.S. adventurer and filibusterer William Walker landed in Nicaragua and took over the country as president. Liberals had invited Walker to help them defeat their conservative archrivals. As president, he reestablished slavery, implemented a vagrancy law that forced peasants to work, and made English the official language. Walker's abusive policies led Nicaraguans to run him out of the country. He attempted to regain the presidency twice more before a Honduran firing squad executed him in 1860. Although private capital financed his campaign, Nicaraguans subsequently remembered Walker as representing the first U.S. attempt to dominate their country.

The fiasco of Walker's administration led to a discrediting of the liberals, and as a result the conservatives dominated Nicaraguan politics for the next thirty years. In 1893, the liberals returned to power with José Santos Zelaya, who as president implemented modernizing policies. He favored foreign capital investment but opposed extensive U.S. control. Zelaya was also a nationalist who attempted to extend Nicaraguan sovereignty over the British-controlled Atlantic coast. Conservative leader Emiliano Chamorro launched seventeen revolts against Zelaya before the United States finally intervened in 1909 to help remove the liberal leader from office. Two years later, the conservative president Adolfo Díaz invited the U.S. Marines back to prevent Zelaya from returning to power. From 1911 to 1933, the marines occupied Nicaragua to protect a minority conservative government against liberal insurrection and civil war.

In 1927, the United States sent a special mission to pacify liberal resistance, which resulted in a peace settlement. Rather than having the ruling conservatives run the 1928 elections that inevitably would lead to their victory, the United States supervised the country's first relatively fraud-free vote. The opposition liberals had the support of about two-thirds of the country's electorate and hence won the election. With this agreement, most liberal insurgents laid down their arms. One nationalist general, Augusto César Sandino, refused to give up his fight and continued his guerrilla struggle from his base in the Nicaraguan mountains. By 1932, the U.S. government saw the futility of its ongoing occupation and began to withdraw the marines.

Somozas

The United States trained a nonpartisan national guard to replace the Nicaraguan army and the occupying marines. They placed Anastasio Somoza García (1896–1956, known as "Tacho") in control of the police force. Somoza had trained in business schools in the United States, and U.S. officials liked him because he spoke English and understood their motivations. The marines completed their withdrawal in 1933, and in 1934 Sandino came down from the mountains having achieved his goal of expelling the foreign intruders. Sandino, however, did not recognize that Somoza presented as large of a threat to his agenda of social reforms as did the U.S. military. Somoza, on the other hand, realized that Sandino was the only person in Nicaragua with sufficient popular support to challenge his grasp on power. Somoza invited Sandino to a state dinner and then had him ambushed and killed when he left the national palace in order to eliminate his competition.

Somoza became president in 1936, and subsequently manipulated laws and the constitution to keep himself in power, sometimes by ruling through puppet presidents. Even though he implemented right-wing policies, much like Porfirio Díaz in Mexico, Somoza used the liberal party machinery to maintain control over the country. As a result, his most diehard opposition came from the competing conservative party whose members wanted to return to power, rather than from the political left that desired radical changes.

At first Somoza enjoyed some popular support, but then he became more brutal and established his personal empire as a family dynasty. Somoza soon was the wealthiest man in Nicaragua, and his family owned almost everything of significance. His foreign policy was entirely submissive to U.S. dictates, including declaring war on the Axis powers in the Second World War and implementing an anticommunist agenda during the Cold War. The Somozas allowed the U.S. military to use Nicaragua as a base for attacks on Jacobo Arbenz's government in Guatemala in 1954 and for the 1961 Bay of Pigs invasion of Cuba. Franklin D. Roosevelt allegedly quipped, "Somoza may be a son of a bitch, but he's our son of a bitch." U.S. government officials were willing to work with authoritarian leaders if it served their imperial interests.

In 1956, the poet Rigoberto López Pérez assassinated Somoza while the latter was drinking coffee in a sidewalk cafe in León. The death of the dictator did not lead to the hoped-for transformation of society but rather the ascension of his son, Luis Somoza Debayle (1922–1967), to the presidency. The second Somoza had also trained in the United States—in agricultural economics at the University of California, Berkeley. He ruled in a reformist environment, including inviting the Alliance for Progress into the country to help develop and modernize the economy. In 1957, his conservative opponents boycotted what would obviously be fraudulent elections. In order to create a fiction of democratic pluralism, Somoza created a Conservative Nationalist party to compete in their stead.

In 1967, at the age of forty-four, the second Somoza died of a massive heart attack. Power subsequently passed to his younger brother Anastasio Somoza Debayle

(1925–1980, known as "Tachito"). Widening income disparities between the rich and the poor and an unequal distribution of land under his rule contributed to discontent and unrest among the workers and peasants. This final Somoza was so militaristic, greedy, and brutal in his quest for more power and wealth that even some of his own ruling-class supporters turned against him and joined in the popular movement that eventually ousted him. As political repression and massacres increased, he faced growing international pressure due to his blatant human rights violations. Nevertheless, he continued to enjoy close relations with the U.S. government because of his strongly reliable anticommunist position.

Nicaraguan Socialist Party (PSN)

Except for Sandino's struggle against the U.S. Marines in the 1920s and 1930s, Nicaragua remained largely isolated from the labor and political organizational efforts undertaken in much of the rest of Latin America. Leftists did not organize the first communist party in Nicaragua until 1944, about twenty years later than their counterparts in most of the rest of the hemisphere. As in Cuba, the Nicaraguan communist party called itself socialist, the Partido Socialista Nicaragüense (PSN, Nicaraguan Socialist Party), in order to present itself as less of a threat to the established international capitalist order. Like other Latin American communist parties of this era, the PSN was a pro-Soviet party that followed the rigid ideology and united front strategy of the Communist International. It was formed during the Second World War under the influence of Earl Browder, the secretary-general of the Communist Party of the United States of America (CPUSA). With Germany threatening the very existence of the Soviet Union, Browder argued that the historic antagonism and contradiction between the bourgeoisie and the working class had disappeared. Members of each country's communist party should unite behind their government and join the war effort to defeat the rise of fascism in Europe. In Nicaragua, the PSN followed the same strategy and for several years worked openly with the Somoza regime, similar to how communists had collaborated with Batista in Cuba. This strategy also benefited the Somoza government, which had temporarily adopted a populist stance in order to undercut the strength of leftist labor leaders.

The PSN's base was in the country's small urban proletariat and remained largely removed from rural organizing efforts. The PSN believed that due to the underdeveloped precapitalist economy, the Nicaraguan masses lacked the potential to develop a class consciousness. From their perspective, Nicaragua did not meet the proper objective conditions for a revolutionary struggle. Instead, the PSN worked for the development of capitalism as a necessary precondition before attempting to move on to a socialist mode of production. In 1948, with the onset of the Cold War, Somoza García outlawed the PSN and imprisoned or exiled its members, or drove them underground. As in Cuba, this party became ineffective in its opposition to a brutal and oppressive dictatorship.

SANDINISTA NATIONAL LIBERATION FRONT

The success of the Cuban Revolution in 1959 convinced several members of the PSN that they, too, could organize a guerrilla movement to topple the Somoza dynasty and replace it with a socialist government. Several minor initial attempts in 1959 failed. Nevertheless, young activists believed they could foment a revolutionary consciousness among the Nicaraguan people. Having lost patience with the conservative and passive nature of the PSN, Carlos Fonseca Amador (1936–1976), Tomás Borge Martínez (1930–2012), and others formed the clandestine FSLN in 1961. For eighteen years, the Sandinistas carried on their efforts at political organization among the Nicaraguan peasant and urban masses before finally claiming victory.

These early Sandinistas condemned the PSN for its policies of class collaboration, support for the bourgeoisie, and acting as an accomplice to U.S. imperialism during the Second World War. The PSN, for its part, denounced the FSLN's efforts as utopian and premature adventurism, much as Cuban communists had criticized Fidel Castro's 26th of July Movement. The PSN opted to wait for the proper economic conditions for a social revolution as it continued slowly to organize the proletariat into a working-class movement. Nevertheless, it was out of this situation that a noncommunist guerrilla movement organized a successful armed socialist revolution in Central America.

BIOGRAPHY: CARLOS FONSECA AMADOR, 1936–1976

Carlos Fonseca Amador was largely responsible for shaping Sandinista ideology in the 1960s. Fonseca brought to the FSLN a Marxist-Leninist analysis of Nicaraguan society that he had learned from the PSN. Fonseca, however, used this analysis to challenge the assumptions of the old-line communist party. Similar to José Carlos Mariátegui in Peru, Fonseca emphasized the importance of a creative and flexible approach to revolutionary theory and stressed that a strategy must be specifically adapted to the concrete circumstances of a country rather than dictated by ideologues in distant Moscow.

Mural of Carlos Fonseca (left) together with Che Guevara (in back) and Augusto César Sandino (right) at the Centro Cultural Batahola Norte, Managua
Source: Photo by Marc Becker

Fonseca began his career as a political activist while a high school student in the 1950s in Matagalpa in northern Nicaragua. He was arrested many times during the course of his life for his political activities. Like Che Guevara, the 1954 military coup against Jacobo Arbenz's government in Guatemala woke his revolutionary consciousness. Fonseca believed that the struggle in Nicaragua was not to change a government but to overthrow an entire system. Together with his classmate Tomás Borge, Fonseca formed a student activist group that established contacts with local labor unions. Fonseca earned a reputation as an outstanding student and an avid reader. Through his studies and during a brief tenure as a librarian in Managua, he came in contact with a wide variety of European and Latin American writers who influenced the development of his Marxist ideas. Fonseca graduated at the top of his high school class in 1955 after writing a thesis on Karl Marx's classic work on political economy, *Capital*.

Fonseca and Borge studied law at the National Autonomous University in León, where their political activism quickly became more important than their studies. Both joined the PSN in 1955 and together organized a communist party cell and a Marxist study group at the university. In 1957, Fonseca visited the Soviet Union for a youth congress and was imprisoned on his return to Nicaragua. The members of the university study group became increasingly militant in their belief that they could create a socialist revolution rather than wait for the development of proper economic conditions. The PSN, they contended, was too orthodox, dogmatic, and unrevolutionary in its policies to lead this struggle. Fonseca visited Cuba in July 1959 and returned convinced that a socialist revolution was possible in a backward country. Influenced by the success of the Cuban Revolution, Fonseca left the communist party in 1959 and joined a guerrilla group that invaded Nicaragua with the intent to overthrow the Somoza dynasty.

The models for guerrilla warfare that Guevara worked out in Cuba strongly influenced Fonseca. He also studied other internationalist philosophies, but ultimately, he believed that the FSLN must root its struggle in Nicaragua's own national realities. To this end, Fonseca resurrected the image of General Augusto César Sandino as a national hero and promoted the social and political aspects of his thought. Somoza had ferociously attacked Sandino and largely had succeeded in erasing him from the memory of the Nicaraguan people. At the same time, the PSN criticized Sandino as a petit bourgeois nationalist without a coherent political or economic program and condemned his alleged lack of a proper class analysis of Nicaraguan society. Fonseca, however, looked to him as a symbol of his struggle much as Castro had used José Martí to gain support for the 26th of July Movement in Cuba. Originally the Nicaraguan guerrillas had planned to form a National Liberation Front (FLN), and it was Fonseca who added "Sandinista" to the name. He adopted Sandino's slogan that only the workers and peasants would go all the way to victory.

As the FSLN's leading intellectual, Fonseca stressed the importance of popular education. Borge later recounted the story of training a group of peasants in the use of weapons, and when Fonseca arrived, he instructed the guerrillas to teach the peasants to read as well. Fonseca's mandate "and also teach them to read" became the slogan of the 1980 literacy crusade that characterized the early years of the revolution. Education was not to remain the sole dominion of the ruling class but a tool to empower the peasant and working-class masses. Fonseca's emphasis on the political education of the peasantry along with his flexible approach to revolutionary theory and his ability to learn from his mistakes contributed to a situation in which the Sandinistas ultimately triumphed in their social revolution.

DOCUMENT: "THE HISTORIC PROGRAM OF THE FSLN," 1969

The Sandinistas presented the manifesto excerpted below to the Nicaraguan people in 1969 as a statement of their political, economic, and social demands. It is striking for the broad range of issues that it engages, including the rights of women and Indigenous peoples and a respect for religious beliefs.

The Sandinista National Liberation Front (FSLN) has emerged from the needs of the Nicaraguan people to build a "vanguard organization" capable of taking political power through a direct struggle against its enemies and of establishing a social system to wipe out the exploitation and poverty that our people have previously suffered.

The FSLN is a political-military organization whose strategic goal is the seizure of political power through the destruction of the military and bureaucratic apparatus of the dictatorship and the establishment of a revolutionary government based on an alliance of workers and peasants and the cooperation of all patriotic anti-imperialist and antioligarchic forces in the country.

The people of Nicaragua suffer under the subjugation of a reactionary and fascist clique that Yankee imperialism imposed in 1932 when Anastasio Somoza García was named commander in chief of the so-called National Guard (GN).

The Somoza clique has reduced Nicaragua to a neocolonial status exploited by the Yankee monopolies and oligarchic groups in the country.

The current regime is politically unpopular and illegal. Recognition and support from the United States is irrefutable evidence of foreign interference in Nicaraguan affairs.

The FSLN has analyzed the national reality seriously and with great responsibility and has resolved to confront the dictatorship with weapons in hand. We have concluded that the triumph of the Sandinista Revolution and the overthrow of the regime that is an enemy of the people will emerge as a result of the development of a hard-fought and prolonged popular war.

Whatever maneuvers and resources Yankee imperialism deploys, the Somoza dictatorship is doomed to complete failure in the face of the rapid advance and development of the Sandinista National Liberation Front's popular forces.

Given this historical juncture the FSLN has developed this political program to strengthen and develop our organization, to encourage and stimulate the people of Nicaragua to march forward, determined to fight to overthrow the dictatorship, and to resist the intervention of Yankee imperialism in order to forge a free, prosperous, and revolutionary homeland.

I. A Revolutionary Government

The Sandinista Revolution will establish a revolutionary government to liquidate the reactionary structure that arose from rigged elections and military coups. Popular power will forge a Nicaragua that is free of exploitation, oppression, and backwardness, a free, progressive, and independent homeland.

The revolutionary government shall adopt the following political measures:

A.   It will create a revolutionary power structure that will allow for the full participation of all people, on both the national and local level.

B.   It will guarantee all citizens the full exercise of all individual freedoms and respect for human rights.

C.   It will guarantee freedom of thought, leading primarily to the vigorous dissemination of popular and patriotic rights.

D.   It will guarantee the freedom for labor organizing in the city and the countryside, and freedom to organize peasant, youth, student, women's, cultural, sporting, and other groups.

E.   It will guarantee the right of Nicaraguan immigrants and exiles to return home.

F.   It will guarantee the right to asylum for citizens of other countries who are persecuted for participation in the revolutionary struggle.

G.   It will severely punish the gangsters who are guilty of persecuting, informing on, abusing, torturing, or murdering revolutionaries and the people.

H.   It will strip political rights from individuals who occupy high political posts as a result of rigged elections and military coups.

The revolutionary government will issue the following economic measures:

A.   It will expropriate large estates, factories, businesses, buildings, transportation, and other property that the Somoza family usurped and accumulated through the misappropriation and waste of the wealth of the nation.

B.   It will expropriate large estates, factories, businesses, transportation, and other property that politicians, military officers, and all kinds of accomplices usurped through the current regime's administrative corruption.

C.   It will nationalize the assets of all foreign companies engaged in the exploitation of mineral, forestry, maritime, and other resources.

D.   It will establish workers' control over the administration of companies and other expropriated and nationalized property.

E.   It will centralize the public transit system.

F.   It will nationalize the banking system, which will be placed at the exclusive service of the country's economic development.

G.   It will establish an independent currency.

H.   It will refuse to honor loans that the Yankee monopolies or other powers imposed on the country.

I.   It will establish trade relations with all countries, whatever their system of government, to benefit the country's economic development.

J.   It will establish an appropriate tax policy, which will be applied with strict justice.

K.   It will prohibit usury for both Nicaraguans and foreigners.

L.   It will protect small- and medium-sized owners (producers, merchants) while restricting the excesses that lead to the exploitation of the workers.

M.   It will establish state control over foreign trade in order to diversify it and make it independent.

N.   It will rigorously restrict the importation of luxury goods.

O.   It will plan the national economy, putting an end to the anarchy characteristic of the capitalist system of production. An important part of this planning will focus on the industrialization and electrification of the country.

VI. Reincorporation of the Atlantic Coast

The Sandinista Popular Revolution will implement a special plan for the Atlantic coast, which has been abandoned in total neglect, in order to incorporate it into the nation's life.

    A.   It will end the unjust exploitation the Atlantic coast has suffered throughout history from foreign monopolies, especially Yankee imperialism.

    B.   It will prepare suitable lands in the area for the development of agriculture and livestock.

    C.   It will establish favorable conditions for the development of fisheries and forestry.

    D.   It will encourage the flowering of the region's local cultural values that flow from the specific aspects of its historic tradition.

    E.   It will wipe out the odious discrimination that the Indigenous Miskito, Sumu, Zambos, and Blacks in that region have faced.

VII. Emancipation of Women

The Sandinista Revolution will abolish the odious discrimination that women have suffered in comparison to men, and establish economic, political, and cultural equality between women and men.

    A.   It will pay special attention to mothers and children.

    B.   It will eliminate prostitution and other social vices, which will raise women's dignity.

    C.   It will end the system of servitude that women suffer that is reflected in the tragedy of abandoned working mothers.

    D.   Revolutionary institutions will establish equal protection for children born out of wedlock.

    E.   It will establish day-care centers for the care and attention of the children of working women.

    F.   It will establish a two-month maternity leave before and after childbirth for working women.

    G.   It will raise women's political, cultural, and vocational levels through their participation in the revolutionary process.

VIII. Respect for Religious Beliefs

The Popular Sandinista Revolution will guarantee the freedom to profess any religion.

    A.   It will respect the right of citizens to profess and practice any religious belief.

    B.   It will support the work of priests and other religious figures who defend the working people.

XI. Solidarity among Peoples

The Popular Sandinista Revolution will put an end to the use of national territory as a base for Yankee aggression against other sister nations and implement militant solidarity with fraternal peoples fighting for their liberation.

    A.   It will actively support the struggle of the peoples of Asia, Africa, and Latin America against old and new colonialism and against the common enemy: Yankee imperialism.

    B.   It will support the struggle of Black people and all the people of the United States for genuine democracy and equal rights.

    C.   It will support the struggle of all peoples against the installation of Yankee military bases in foreign countries.

XIII. Veneration of Our Martyrs

The Popular Sandinista Revolution will maintain eternal gratitude and veneration of our homeland's martyrs and will continue their shining example of heroism and selflessness.

    A.   It will educate new generations in eternal gratitude and reverence for those who have fallen in the struggle to make Nicaragua a free homeland.

    B.   It will establish a secondary school to educate the children of our people's martyrs.

    C.   It will inculcate in all people the imperishable example of our martyrs, defending the revolutionary ideal: Ever onward to victory!!!

Source: Frente Sandinista de Liberación Nacional, *Programa histórico del FSLN* (Managua, Nicaragua: Departmento de Propaganda y Educación Política del FSLN, 1984) (translation by author).

Che Guevara was directly involved with the formation of the FSLN. He helped train and arm the Nicaraguan guerrillas, and at one point he considered personally joining the Sandinista struggle in Nicaragua. Guevara's **foco** theory that a small insurrectionary guerrilla army could spark a broad revolution defined the Nicaraguans' military strategy during the first phase of guerrilla operations from 1962 to 1967. In 1967, the Sandinistas organized a rural guerrilla foco at the remote village of Pancasán, where about forty militants worked with the local peasants. The Sandinistas accidentally ran into the police, who killed all but fifteen of the guerrillas, including key FSLN founders. The national guard responded ferociously to the guerrilla presence, interrogating, threatening, and killing hundreds of suspected Sandinistas. The repression almost wiped out the entire FSLN organization. Rebuilding the movement would be a long, slow, hard process.

As with other guerrilla movements, women played an important part in the Sandinista movement but were largely relegated to traditional support roles. Gladys Báez (1942–) was one of the first women to join as a combatant and was the only woman present at Pancasán. Báez had a long political trajectory, including being active in the PSN and studying in the Soviet Union before joining the Sandinistas. Some leaders, such as Fonseca, wanted more women to join, but others objected, and some even left complaining that the presence of women was a disruption and would slow their movements down. When Báez refused to drop out of the guerrilla force, male chauvinistic attitudes forced others to stay in despite the difficult challenges they faced. If a woman was not going to quit, their egos would not allow them to abandon the struggle either. Notwithstanding sexist attitudes, women's participation grew. By the 1970s, most Sandinista guerrilla bands included some peasant women. Women also suffered repression at the hands of the Somoza regime. Báez was arrested, tortured, and almost killed for her work with the Sandinistas.

Historic Program of the FSLN

As part of reconstructing its popular forces, the FSLN outlined its revolutionary aims and ideology in its 1969 "Historic Program of the FSLN" (see the document included with this chapter). Fonseca drafted this thirteen-point program that combined nationalist, democratic, and anticapitalist demands. The manifesto called for a revolutionary government that would distribute land to the peasants, enact far-reaching labor legislation, grant equal rights to women, end discrimination against African-descent and Indigenous peoples, respect religious freedom, and carry out a revolution in education and culture. The program called for the nationalization of the property that the Somoza family and its cronies owned, natural resources that foreigners controlled, large landholdings, and the banking system. Many of these demands were similar to those from the Mexican Revolution and illustrated the persistent influence of that earlier event on the Latin American left.

The FSLN positioned itself as the vanguard of a worker-peasant alliance and called on people to join in a "patriotic anti-imperialist and antioligarchic" struggle. The Sandinista Front professed its commitment to an agrarian reform that would benefit the peasant masses. In addition, the Sandinistas declared their strong support for international solidarity, including encouragement for the peoples of Asia, Africa, and Latin America in their struggles against U.S. imperialism. Much like Mariátegui before them, the FSLN leaders combined anti-imperialist nationalist sentiments with the idea of an international class struggle. Their 1969 declaration, nevertheless, stopped short of calling for socialism, and they made no such proclamation after seizing power. The Sandinistas were not fighting for an abstract social or Marxist revolution but one firmly grounded in their own historical reality and experience.

The Sandinistas condemned Somoza's neglect and exploitation of the Atlantic coast and vowed to terminate the racial discrimination that Indigenous and Afro-Nicaraguans faced. The Sandinistas enjoyed a high degree of support from the Indigenous neighborhoods of Monimbó in Masaya and Subtiava in León. The Sandinistas drew on their actions and those of Indigenous peoples in Matagalpa as part of a long history of resistance to colonial domination. During years of political organizing in the Nicaraguan mountains, the Sandinistas came in daily contact with mestizo peasants and members of the Miskito, Sumu, and Rama peoples. While in exile in Chile in the early 1970s, Jaime Wheelock Román, who later served as minister of agriculture in the revolutionary government, wrote a treatise titled "Indigenous Roots of the Anti-Colonial Struggle in Nicaragua." He criticized historians for identifying with Spanish colonialists and ignoring the legacy of Indigenous resistance. The Sandinistas gained support because they fought for the rights of marginalized peoples.

The Fall of Somoza

At 12:29 a.m. on Saturday, December 23, 1972, a massive magnitude 6.2 earthquake destroyed central Managua. The earthquake left six thousand people dead, twenty thousand injured, and over a quarter million homeless. As is often the case, the earthquake was as much a political as a natural disaster, and with a better functioning government, the damage would not have been so extensive. Only two buildings, the Intercontinental Hotel and the Bank of America, had been built properly to code and survived the quake. In its aftermath, Somoza bought up land on the outskirts of the city and sold it at inflated speculative prices to the homeless who were afraid to return to the city center. He redirected donated aid to his own warehouses and sold it to the displaced. The Red Cross furnished blood for victims, but Nicaragua lacked a sufficiently functioning medical system to use the blood before it expired, so Somoza resold it on the international market. When he realized the profit he could make on the sale of blood, he set up centers to collect plasma from Nicaraguans and sold that as well. When the corruption reached the level of vampires, the population began to turn against him. The earthquake and subsequent reconstruction efforts laid bare the unscrupulous nature of Somoza's regime and contributed to a resurgence of the FSLN.

Building on the momentum gained from the 1972 earthquake, the Sandinistas engaged in ever more daring actions. Two years later, they earned widespread notoriety and support when on December 27, 1974, they crashed Somoza's Christmas party and took forty guests hostage. Reflecting slowly changing gender relations, three women were part of the thirteen-member squad who carried out the action. The Sandinistas missed Somoza and the U.S. ambassador who had just left the party—although perhaps that was intentional, because their capture might have triggered an undesirable U.S. intervention. The Sandinistas gained freedom for fourteen political prisoners, including future president Daniel Ortega (1945–), a ransom of $1 million, passage to Cuba, and the publication of a communiqué on the radio and in the printed press. The boldness of the action earned the Sandinistas widespread renown. While successful, the action resulted in an increase in repression, as Somoza lashed out at the perpetrators.

In 1975 and 1976, the FSLN broke into three factions, or "tendencies." The *proletarios* (proletarians) followed an orthodox Marxist line that favored concentrating political work among the urban poor. They advocated for the formation of a working-class vanguard party to lead a class struggle against the bourgeoisie. Jaime Wheelock Román, the intellectual who had studied economics in Chile during Salvador Allende's government in the early 1970s, led this wing. In contrast, a second tendency, the *guerra popular prolongada* (GPP, prolonged people's war), emphasized a Maoist strategy of concentrating military forces in the countryside rather than in the city. Those proponents dedicated their efforts to the political and military organization of poor peasants. FSLN founder and future minister of the interior Tomás

Borge led this faction. The third tendency, known simply as the *terceristas* (third way) or insurrectionists, favored a flexible ideology and broad alliances, and eventually became the dominant force in the FSLN.

The terceristas combined elements of the proletarians' class consciousness with the GPP's rural-based military strategy. They argued that the subjective conditions existed in Nicaragua for a popular insurrection. Rather than organizing on the basis of a working-class struggle, they brought Social Democrats, the progressive bourgeoisie, and radical Christians into a unified Sandinista-led movement against the Somoza dictatorship. It was the pragmatic flexibility and ideological plurality of the terceristas that galvanized Sandinista leadership over a popular insurrection and defined a nationalistic direction for the Nicaraguan Revolution. Daniel Ortega emerged as the leader of this faction that deviated significantly from orthodox Marxist theory in their analysis of Nicaragua's historical situation as they developed strategies appropriate to their local reality. Partisans of the other tendencies later blamed the Sandinistas' shortcomings on the lack of a clear ideology that emerged out of this current.

The death of Fonseca in combat on November 8, 1976, was a serious blow to the Sandinistas. The FSLN founder and chief intellectual was the leader most capable of bridging the movement's strategic and ideological divides, but he was less effective as a guerrilla fighter. In 1978, Fidel Castro urged the reunification of these three tendencies, a task that would have been much easier had Fonseca still been alive. Castro argued that the best support he could give the Sandinistas was to do nothing, in order to emphasize the local origins of their struggle. He emphasized that Cuba's assistance would be mostly ideological, moral, and political but not military. From his own success in Cuba, Castro understood that a guerrilla struggle needed to rely on the backing of the local population. In March 1979, the three FSLN factions finally managed to reunite their forces. Three members, all men, from each tendency formed a national directorate that set a unified strategy and policy for the movement.

On January 10, 1978, Pedro Joaquín Chamorro (1924–1978), the publisher of Nicaragua's largest newspaper *La Prensa* and one of Somoza's most outspoken foes, was killed. Although not directly implicated in Chamorro's assassination, Somoza had the most to gain from his death. Chamorro came from a leading conservative family, and his murder galvanized the anti-Somoza business opposition to the dictatorship. Chamorro's death sparked outrage that led to strikes and demonstrations. While most of the reaction was unorganized, the Sandinistas took advantage of the unrest to stockpile arms and organize the urban and rural poor.

Building on this growing antagonism, on August 22, 1978, the Sandinistas seized the national palace in a daring assault. Their raid captured 1,500 people, including 49 deputies, close friends of Somoza, and even Somoza's son. Terceristas Edén Pastora (1936–2020), known as "Comandante Cero" ("Commander Zero"), and Dora María Téllez (1955–) gained widespread fame for their flawless design and execution of the attack. As in 1974, Somoza once again capitulated to the Sandinistas' demands. The guerrillas gained the release of 59 political prisoners, including FSLN founder Tomás Borge; cash; the publication of a communiqué; and passage out of the country, this time to Panama. The audacity of the Sandinista action captured the public's imagination. Thousands of cheering supporters lined the streets as the Sandinistas traveled to the airport for their flight. The successful operation illustrated the guerrillas' ability to penetrate the inner reaches of the government and the extent of their widespread support. The dictator's days were numbered.

In September 1978, the Sandinistas launched a military offensive and a general strike against the Somoza regime. Their actions sparked mass insurrections in cities across the country. In June and July 1979, the FSLN followed with a final offensive during which they captured and controlled key areas of the country. In the final months of the Sandinista insurrection, Somoza launched vicious attacks against the Sandinistas' civilian base, including the aerial bombardment of poor neighborhoods that left them completely destroyed. In the process, the dictatorship killed fifty thousand people and wounded twice as many. The casualty rate in proportion to the total population was higher than that during the 1860s civil war in the United States.

The end of U.S. support for Somoza's regime came with the June 20, 1979, murder of ABC journalist William Stewart. At first Somoza blamed the killing on the Sandinistas and used the death to paint his opponents as cold-blooded assassins. Unbeknown to Somoza, the television crew had filmed the national guard gunning down Stewart during a traffic stop. ABC broadcast the footage on the evening news, which shifted international sentiments against the regime. After the murders of tens of thousands of Nicaraguans, the death of one U.S. citizen forced President Jimmy Carter to cut off military aid. Without the backing of his most loyal ally, Somoza could not hold on to power. Carter called for *Somocismo sin Somoza* (the continuance of a conservative, pro-U.S. government led by wealthy individuals but without the extreme excesses of the Somoza dictatorship), but he could not control the subsequent direction of events.

Somoza left Nicaragua for Miami on July 17, 1979, taking much of the national treasury with him. The Carter administration refused him residency because he had violated an agreement with the U.S. ambassador in Managua not to manipulate his succession in power. Instead, the former strongman settled in Paraguay, where he found a sympathetic environment under the protection of the conservative Alfredo Stroessner dictatorship. Fourteen months later, guerrilla commandos from Argentina and Chile with support from leftists in Uruguay and Paraguay assassinated Somoza in Asunción. The leftists had grown weary of watching dictators destroy their countries and then live out the rest of their lives in comfortable exile, and they were determined not to let that happen to the former Nicaraguan tyrant.

Sandinista Policies

On July 19, 1979, the Sandinistas rolled into Managua and ushered in the second successful armed socialist revolution in Latin America. With Somoza gone, a broad range of the dictator's opponents formed a Junta of National Reconstruction that initially took power. It included wealthy conservative business leaders who had been squeezed out of positions of political power, economic domination, and social prestige. They had more reason to despise the Somoza dictatorship than did the Sandinistas, who attacked the former leader from the left and from below. The pluralistic and ideologically incoherent junta soon gave way to control by the nine-person, all-male FSLN national directorate. The nine were Daniel Ortega, his brother Humberto Ortega, and Víctor Tirado for the terceristas; Jaime Wheelock, Carlos Núñez, and Luis Carrión for the proletarios; and Tomás Borge, Henry Ruiz, and Bayardo Arce for the GPP. The tercerista leader Daniel Ortega was the coordinator of the ruling junta and remained the leader of the Sandinistas during their eleven years in power.

Once in power, the Sandinistas implemented the goals of a mixed economy, a plural political system, and a nonaligned foreign policy. They implemented social programs that emphasized a provision of housing, education, and assistance for rural peasants. The government expropriated and nationalized Somoza's property, redistributed land to rural communities, and created new revolutionary institutions. Unlike in Cuba, the Sandinistas did not engage in revolutionary trials or the execution of their former torturers in Somoza's national guard. They vowed to lead a humane revolution.

GENDERED DIVISIONS

During the insurgency, women made up a third of the Sandinista force. Feminists looked to the FSLN as their best opportunity to gain full equality. In 1977, they organized the Asociación de Mujeres ante la Problemática Nacional (AMPRONAC, Association of Women Concerned about the National Crisis) with the slogan "No revolution without women's emancipation; no emancipation without revolution." They were committed both to the overthrow of the Somoza regime and achievement of women's equality and were responsible for bringing many women into the struggle. Their demands included equal pay and elimination of prostitution.

After the triumph of the revolution, the new government responded to women's demands with executive orders and new social policies and laws that improved the working conditions for women. One of the Sandinistas' first actions was to mandate equal pay for equal work and to ban media portrayals of women as sex objects.

Agrarian reform legislation in 1980 explicitly recognized women as beneficiaries regardless of their marital status. Rural women workers also received the right to control their own income. Other legislation required both men and women to share in the care and raising of their children whether or not they were married. A massive literacy campaign that dramatically increased the number of people who could read and write particularly benefited rural women who were the ones least likely to possess those skills. Broader health and education programs also improved the lives of women.

In the midst of these revolutionary changes, the AMPRONAC renamed itself as the Asociación de Mujeres Nicaragüenses Luisa Amanda Espinoza (AMNLAE, Luisa Amanda Espinoza Association of Nicaraguan Women). Espinoza was a twenty-two-year-old Sandinista leader who died in battle in 1970, the first woman martyr in the guerrilla struggle. As with the Barzolas in Bolivia and the FMC in Cuba, critics charged that the AMNLAE was not a feminist organization that aimed for the full emancipation of women but instead was designed to support the Sandinista government.

As U.S. president Ronald Reagan's terrorist attacks on the country intensified, proposals designed to advance women's interests were placed on the back burner in favor of support for a military draft to defend the revolution. Detractors accused the AMNLAE leadership of paternalistically deciding what was best for Nicaragua rather than representing the class interests of poor and working women. Advocates argued that the best way to gain the emancipation of women was through their integration into the tasks, activities, and goals of the revolutionary process. Even with these limitations, many observers recognized the AMNLAE as a successful organization.

Even though women had participated actively in the Sandinista insurrection, most notably with the leadership of Dora María Téllez in the August 1978 attack on the national palace, they were largely excluded from positions of power in the new Sandinista government. Téllez served as minister of health, the highest-ranking woman in the new government. Others took similarly significant roles, such as Doris María Tijerino (1943–), who served as head of police. But women never reached the proportion of leadership commensurate to their numbers in society or even to their positions in the insurgent guerrilla force. The feminist poet Gioconda Belli (1948–) criticized the Sandinista male leadership in her memoir *The Country under My Skin* for expecting women to play the roles of mother and helpmate rather than assuming a role equal to men in building a new country.

One of the most famous images from the revolution was Orlando Valenzuela's *Miliciana de Waswalito* (*Militia Woman of Waswalito*). The photograph showed Blanca López Hernández (1963–) as a smiling young Indigenous mother breastfeeding her baby Antonio with a Kalashnikov assault rifle slung over her shoulder. The image was intended to illustrate that a patriotic mother should engage in a civil defense patrol to defend her community from contra attacks. The image, however, could also be read as embracing women's contributions only as long as they also fulfilled a domestic role. Sexist attitudes remained deeply embedded in society.

BIOGRAPHY: DORA MARÍA TÉLLEZ, 1955–

Dora María Téllez is best known for her role in 1978 in an operation that captured the Nicaraguan congress while it was in session at the national palace in Managua. She went on to serve as health minister in the subsequent Sandinista government. Since the Sandinista electoral defeat in 1990, Téllez moved into a position of strident opposition to Daniel Ortega.

Téllez was born into a comfortable petit bourgeois family and attended a Catholic school. She began working with the Sandinistas while still a high school student but became much more active in 1974 after entering the Universidad Nacional Autónoma de Nicaragua (UNAN, National Autonomous University of Nicaragua) in León to study medicine. By 1976, the repression had become so great that she was forced to go underground. During that time, she conducted educational work in the mountains.

Dora María Téllez
Source: Wikimedia Commons/Jorge Mejía Peralta

Téllez rose in the FSLN to become a *comandante*, the highest rank in the insurgent force, with the *tercerista* or insurrectionary wing of the Sandinistas. It was in this position that at age twenty-two, as "Commander Two," she was third in command of the operation that seized the National Assembly on August 22, 1978 (Edén Pastora was the leader). She played a central role in negotiating the release of key Sandinista political prisoners, payment of a million-dollar ransom, and the broadcast of a communiqué with the Sandinistas' political agenda. Once in exile in Panama, she became the public voice that spoke to the media about how they had managed to carry out the attack. That successful operation underscored the weakness of the Somoza regime and launched the popular insurrection that led to the fall of Somoza on July 19, 1979.

As minister of health in the Sandinista government from 1979 to 1990, Téllez gained praise for the exceptional progress in the healthcare system in Nicaragua. She was also a strong advocate for women's rights, including reproductive rights, as well as rights for gays and lesbians.

In addition to rising through the ranks of the Sandinista guerrilla army and the subsequent government, Téllez also assumed leadership positions in the Sandinista political party. She headed the party in Managua and served in the legislative assembly. Téllez was positioned to win a seat on the FSLN's national directorate at its first congress in 1991 after its electoral defeat. She would have been the first woman on the directorate, which during the Sandinistas' eleven years in power was comprised of nine men. Party leadership, however, forwarded a slate of candidates for approval rather than having delegates select members individually. That maneuver prevented Téllez's election, which otherwise may have occurred because of the support she enjoyed among rank-and-file members of the party. Instead, Téllez began writing about the history of Nicaragua, which gained her an appointment in 2004 as a visiting professor at the Harvard Divinity School. The U.S. government, however, refused her a visa, contending that under the Patriot Act, her raid on the National Palace in 1978 was a terrorist action.

In 1995, Téllez, along with other prominent militants who had become very critical of Ortega's leadership of the FSLN, left to found the Movimiento Renovador Sandinista (MRS, Sandinista Renovation Movement). In January 2021, they renamed their party Unamos after it was stripped of its legal status. In June 2021, the Nicaraguan government arrested Téllez along with other opposition figures under charges of accepting funds from the U.S. government to intervene in the upcoming November 2021 presidential elections. She had moved from being one of the Sandinistas' principal leaders to one of its most high-profile opponents.

DOCUMENT: ALICIA GORDON, CHRISTA BERGER, AND PILAR LACERNA, "NICARAGUA: WE ARE MILLIONS," 1980

This essay charts the contributions women made to the Sandinista insurrection and summarizes how the movement attempted to incorporate their concerns and demands into the new revolutionary government.

The Nicaraguan Sandinista Revolution that culminated in July 1979 is the product of a long trajectory of struggles and confrontations in which the people demonstrated their decision to declare their independence from both internal dictatorships and imperialism.

Nicaraguan women joined the struggle for national independence at the beginning of the century. Their participation is manifested in different ways: from supporting their children, husbands, and companions to the decision to take up arms directly in the insurrection against tyranny, as in the case of Blanca Arauz, María Altamirano, and Concha Alday, who fought with General Sandino in 1927.

Women's groups began to form in Nicaragua in the 1960s under the influence of movements in Europe and the United States. Student groups were also organized, reflecting the beginning of political awareness and in which women had broad participation. We highlight the Patriotic Alliance of Nicaraguan Women formed by Gladys Báez, who like many others would later join the FSLN.

Doris Tijerino, FSLN militant (and head of the Foreign Relations Committee), states in her book *"Somos millones . . .": La vida de Doris María, combatiente nicaragüense* [published in English as *Inside the Nicaraguan Revolution*] that solidarity and the struggle for the freedom of political prisoners were the first tasks that women had to assume. She recalls, for example, May 30, 1968, when the Revolutionary Student Front held an event on the occasion of Mother's Day, in honor of the mothers of the martyrs of the Sandinista Front.

Again in 1973, the mothers, together with some students, took over a church in Managua—Santa Faz—and organized popular rallies around the place, explaining why their children were imprisoned and the reasons for the struggle of the Sandinista Front.

In general terms, the organized and revolutionary participation of women was closely linked to the student movement. It can be hypothesized that the increased awareness of women is a response to the growing participation of their children and the government's harsh repression of the Nicaraguan youth. The solidarity movement intensified in the last months of the Somoza regime, especially through denunciations of the massacres of young people when it was taken for granted that the young population belonged to the Sandinista Front.

In the aforementioned book by Doris Tijerino, a short chronology of the struggles of Nicaraguan women appears:

August 1958: Hospital strike. Wives and mothers of military men initiate a radio campaign in support of six aviation soldiers condemned for political events.

May–June 1970: Hunger strike of mothers and students for the freedom of political prisoners.

April 1971: Hunger strike by prisoners, supported by their mothers and other relatives, against the brutal treatment they receive.

January 1972: Hunger strike by prisoners, supported by mothers and other relatives.

July 1973: Circulation of a letter that mothers of Sandinista prisoners signed demanding freedom for their children. Included among the prisoners are young people imprisoned since 1967.

Women's organizations and movements

Women's groups in the country traditionally became puppet movements of Somoza, led by female representatives of the bourgeoisie and petit bourgeoisie who were far removed from the demands and problems of the women of the people.

In 1965, a Civic Association of Nicaraguan Women Citizens was organized, a group that the AID (Agency for International Development, of the U.S. State Department) sponsored and that implemented some campaigns for citizens' rights. Soon the bourgeoisie and Somoza's supporters took over the association and transformed it into the women's wing of their liberal party.

For its part, the Socialist Party of Nicaragua (the name in this country of the Communist Party) promoted the formation of the Union of Democratic Women (of the Workers' Central), which played an important role in the struggle for women's rights. Other groups such as the Popular Action Movement, the Vanguard Women's Union, etc. were also formed.

In 1977, the Asociación de Mujeres ante la Problemática Nacional (AMPRONAC, Association of Women Concerned about the National Crisis) was born with a very clear idea: not to be a gringo-style feminist movement. The Association began by calling itself the Commission for the Denouncement of Human Rights, which it effectively did in its first public appearance by denouncing murders and torture and demanding the withdrawal of the so-called Black Code, which imposed prior censorship on the media. But by September 29, 1977, the movement was legalized and registered under the name of the AMPRONAC, comprised of eighty women. Its program defined its objectives around two axes: the defense of human rights and the participation of women in national life.

The AMPRONAC was broad, democratic, and popular. Broad, because any woman could participate in the organization. Democratic, because decisions were always made by majority vote. Popular, because of its base of support in poor and marginalized communities.

At its beginnings, the AMPRONAC appeared as a multiclass organization that was especially noted as a bastion of the anti-Somoza struggle. In its ranks were women from the bourgeoisie and the popular classes who were united around one fact: having understood that feminist demands had no place in the Somoza regime.

The rise of the class struggle itself soon broke with this unity and posed the need for more precise definitions and greater radicalization. The AMPRONAC took sides and supported the armed movement. In fact, the women's organization, which emerged as a broad mass movement, had from its beginnings certain cadres who received their political orientation from the FSLN. However, one of its characteristics, which differentiated it from other groups, was the continuity of its democratic structure and the preponderant role of the grassroots in the orientation of the work and the nature of its political decisions. Perhaps this fact was decisive in its transformation. As it advanced in its insertion into political life, the bourgeois components of the organization were purged. Despite being opponents of Somoza, they distanced themselves when they could not lead the AMPRONAC in line with their own interests.

The AMPRONAC came to constitute what could be considered a Women's Mass Front, with 1,500 members. Its priority was the fall of Somoza, a sine qua non condition from which to demand women's rights.

In July 1978 the Movimiento Pueblo Unido (MPU, United People's Movement) was created (the first popular bloc). Among the founding organizations and members of the MPU were the Organización de Mujeres Demócratas de Nicaragua (OMDN, Organization of Democratic Women of Nicaragua) and the Comité de Madres y Familiares de Reos Políticos (Committee of Mothers and Relatives of Political Prisoners). By September of the same year, the AMPRONAC began working with the MPU, after an extensive discussion with the grassroots to decide its incorporation but without losing the autonomy of their organization.

Within the MPU, women carried out important tasks, especially in infrastructure. They participated in the formation of block committees or, in a very relevant way, in the creation of first- aid kits, clandestine clinics, food storage, and first-aid courses. They also addressed other issues, in combination with the MPU, such as harassment, street graffiti, establishment of safe houses, mail drops, and political and military training schools. All these tasks were carried out on a national scale, since the AMPRONAC had already expanded to the different departments and cities of the interior: León, Chinandega, Masaya, Estelí, and Matagalpa, among others. Even its commitment to the so-called September insurrection unleashed direct repression on the organization, which created the need for semiclandestine and clandestine actions.

After the September insurrection, AMPRONAC began a stage of restructuring its committees, especially after the bombings in Estelí, Matagalpa, and Masaya. This restructuring consisted of going, as if following an umbilical cord, from woman to woman to locate them after the great exodus that had occurred to the valleys and small towns and even the countryside, considering the need to return to the city since their presence there was essential in the organization of support and resistance against the dictatorship.

The political situation that Nicaragua experienced over the last few years definitively altered the programs that the AMPRONAC had established for the short, medium, and long term. In the short term, it was a question of fighting against the Somoza dictatorship, which we achieved. In the medium and long terms, women's demands were raised: women's rights, socialization of domestic work, day-care centers, educational development, and a program of equal pay for equal work. Many of these demands were, however, taken up programmatically by the Sandinista Front.

In fact, the FSLN, whose ranks women joined and fought in conditions of absolute equality, supported the following programmatic measures with respect to women:

FSLN. Proletarian Tendency: Point 7 of its program states: "Promotion of the full participation of women in the political, economic and cultural life of the Nation. Guarantee equal rights and opportunities."

FSLN. GPP: Communiqué No. 4 of the GPP, titled "The march toward victory does not stop," says, "The emancipation of women through economic, political, and cultural equality between women and men should ban prostitution, put an end to the plight of abandoned working mothers, and stop discrimination against children born out of wedlock. Special attention should be given to both mothers and children, thereby avoiding the elimination of women from the productive process" (May 1, 1980).

FSLN. Insurrectional Tendency: "Women have occupied a prominent place in the revolutionary and popular struggle. Since the years of the Yankee intervention, Concepción Alday, María Altamirano, the Villatorio sisters, and Blanca Arauz have stood up. . . . The presence of women in the anti-Somoza and popular struggle has also been expressed in the militant solidarity of the mothers of political prisoners; in the determined cooperation of the laundry and domestic workers, and in comrades who have been involved in combative actions, such as the Sandinista comrade María Castillo, who fell in the heat of guerrilla combat. The FSLN, which on September [December] 27, 1974 took over the residence of José María Castillo, and similarly with the ambush of Kusbawas and El Licupo, highlights Sandinista recognition of all Nicaraguan women who today are organized in unions and broad associations that give greater impetus to the struggle against tyranny. At the same time, we call on the wives, sisters, daughters of soldiers, noncommissioned officers, and officers of the National Guard to demand that their relatives stop getting blood on their hands and go to fight alongside the people" ("Operation: Death to Somocismo. Carlos Fonseca Amador," *Novedades* [Managua], August 28, 1978).

These measures and communiqués assure that the government of National Reconstruction will carry forward the demands of women, which in Latin America constitutes a struggle for the incorporation of women into production.

All the programs being developed in Nicaragua today support the emancipation of women. Another task will be that of their own liberation, a battle that Nicaraguan women will have to undertake starting with their own process of emancipation. Since the triumph of the Revolution, women have come together in the Association of Nicaraguan Women Luisa Amanda Espinoza (AMNLAE), how AMPRONAC was officially renamed in September 1979, in memory of the first FSLN fighter who fell in the struggle. This organization is open to women of all political tendencies and has as its objectives the advancement and consolidation of the revolutionary process and the struggle for women's rights.

Source: Alicia Gordon, Christa Berger, and Pilar Lacerna, "Nicaragua: Somos millones . . . ," *Fem* 4, no. 13 (March–April 1980): 39–41 (translation by author).

LIBERATION THEOLOGY

Nicaragua is a land of poets, and this reality helped emphasize the subjective and emotional aspects of the Sandinistas' revolutionary struggle. Poetry forms a large part of Nicaragua's national identity, and the Sandinistas effectively made use of that literary form in practical ways, such as to instruct the population in the art of making armaments. During the insurrection, sermons from radical priests proved to be more inspirational than dry economic treatises in mobilizing the masses to action. The Sandinistas became one of the first leftist revolutions to accept openly the role and contribution of religious workers in the process of social change. Rather than seeing religion as a form of alienation and false consciousness as orthodox Marxists tended to do, the Sandinistas believed that religion could be used to heighten people's revolutionary awareness.

Traditionally, the Catholic Church, together with the military and wealthy landowners, had been an ally of the conservative oligarchy. Changes in Catholic theology in the 1960s, including the Second Vatican Council's modernization of the church's archaic practices, challenged those alliances. At a 1968 conference at Medellín, Colombia, Latin American bishops declared their "preferential option for the poor." Progressive elements in the church called for religious participation in leftist social movements. Many revolutionaries deemphasized liberal anticlerical views in favor of an acceptance of the positive contributions religious actors could make to revolutionary processes. This structural shift in alliances led to the rise of a political and revolutionary popular church and what came to be known as liberation theology. These developments fostered an environment that welcomed religious people into radical political movements in Nicaragua.

Liberation theology employed Marxist analytical tools of class struggle to reflect critically on societal problems. The Peruvian theologian Gustavo Gutiérrez articulated the central tenets of this approach in his 1971 book *A Theology of Liberation*. The emergence of that theology represented a historic turning point in the attitude of the Catholic Church toward popular movements for social justice. Traditional Christian theology, which emerged from ruling-class articulations, endeavored to dictate orders to poor and marginalized workers and peasants. Liberation theologians sought to reverse that relationship, to give hope to the aspirations of the oppressed, and to lead people to realize that they must take a conscious responsibility for their own destiny. Rather than presenting an escapist religion, liberation theology contributed to political empowerment and structural alterations. An important element of liberation theology was the concept of praxis, the combination of theory and practice in a revolutionary situation. For example, catechists would read the biblical story of the Jewish exodus from slavery in Egypt and discuss how it applied to their situation in fighting the Somoza dictatorship. Liberation theology's praxis led far away from the domain of religion and theology into the realm of politics, economics, and history, with a goal of addressing societal injustices.

The influence of liberation theology left an unmistakable impression on Nicaragua and Sandinista ideology. Unlike their counterparts in Cuba, the Nicaraguans openly embraced religious leaders who joined their ranks. Several factors account for the different attitudes toward religion in Nicaragua and Cuba. The Catholic Church in Cuba was not the strong institution that it was in Nicaragua. In Cuba, it did not reach much beyond the small number of urban professionals and was thus divorced from the reality of the majority of the population. With notable exceptions such as Frank País, who was a Baptist Sunday-school teacher, few combatants in Castro's 26th of July Movement were religious. Nicaragua, on the other hand, had a strong Catholic tradition, and many devout believers joined the FSLN in the campaign to overthrow the Somoza dictatorship. Unlike in Cuba, there was no contradiction in Nicaragua between religious involvement and participation in the Sandinista Revolution. Sandinista party militants who had fused religion and politics visited Cuba, and their presence encouraged the Cuban government to reorient official thinking and party policy toward religion. A direct result of that influence was the aperture of new spaces in Cuba for the involvement of religious actors in the construction of a new society. The Nicaraguan experience contributed to a new openness among the left to people of faith across the hemisphere.

Through the initiative and efforts of Catholic priests and local religious organizations known as Christian Base Communities that were committed to social justice, the struggles of Christians and the Sandinistas were combined into one unified fight against Somoza. During the insurrection, elements of Nicaragua's progressive popular church worked openly with the Sandinista movement, and the Sandinistas willingly accepted their contributions toward the building of a new society. Radical trends in Catholic theology influenced priests who organized social action based on a class analysis of society. Gaspar García Laviana (1941–1978) was one such priest who had become frustrated at the failure of peaceful paths to address long-standing problems of poverty and equality. García Laviana joined the Sandinistas and rose to the position of commander in the FSLN's southern front before he was killed in December 1978. Similarly, Father Uriel Molina (1932–) organized Christian Base Communities to mobilize grassroots support in poor neighborhoods in Managua in favor of the FSLN guerrillas. His church became a sanctuary for activists and a revolutionary armory, with its walls decorated with murals of armed struggle.

Other priests, such as Ernesto Cardenal (1925–2020), Fernando Cardenal (1934–2016), and Miguel d'Escoto (1933–2017), also joined forces with the FSLN and took positions in the Sandinista government after the triumph of the 1979 revolution. Trappist father Ernesto Cardenal emerged out of a religious community at Solentiname in Lake Nicaragua in the 1960s to lead the religious opposition to the Somoza dictatorship. His theological reflections contributed to an increased awareness of the economic injustices in Nicaragua and the need for political action to change that reality. A trip to Cuba in 1970 convinced Cardenal that no contradiction existed between Marxism and Christianity. He became an avowed Marxist revolutionary, and he presented the most articulate fusion of Catholic theology and the theory of

Marxist class struggle in Nicaragua. Cardenal considered primitive Christian communalism to be a precursor of Marxism, and he believed that Christianity expressed, in religious terms, the same class struggle that Marx articulated in scientific terms. This struggle extended itself to a battle between the reactionary Christianity of the Somoza dictatorship and the revolutionary Christianity of the proletariat and the popular church. The goal of the Sandinista struggle was the establishment of the biblical kingdom of heaven on earth that would lead to a society without exploitation or domination and a fraternity of love among people.

Miguel d'Escoto was a Maryknoll priest who assumed the position of minister of foreign relations in the Sandinistas' new revolutionary government. Mahatma Gandhi and Martin Luther King Jr.'s nonviolent protests deeply influenced his policies. He echoed their actions by engaging in a hunger strike and leading people on a peace walk in opposition to U.S. attacks on the country. Ernesto Cardenal served as minister of culture in the government. His brother Fernando, a Jesuit priest, was minister of education.

Catholics were not the only Christians who joined forces with the FSLN. A growing radicalism among small Protestant sects also contributed to the development of the revolutionary process in Nicaragua. Most significant was the Comité Evangélico Pro-Ayuda a los Damnificados (CEPAD, Evangelical Committee for Aid to the Earthquake Victims) that was formed in the aftermath of the 1972 earthquake. Under the leadership of the Baptist minister Gustavo Parajón (1935–2011), CEPAD developed community organizations that established contacts with revolutionary movements. Rather than forming a reactionary force, the Sandinistas believed that a religious faith could aid in the fomenting of a revolutionary consciousness and in the development of a new society. In response, religious believers assumed a larger role in Nicaragua's revolutionary struggle than anywhere else in Latin America.

ELECTIONS

In November 1984, strategically scheduled to parallel balloting in the United States, Nicaragua held its first relatively free election since 1928. The FSLN had moved the planned poll up from 1985 in order to gain international recognition and legitimacy for its revolutionary government. One of the reasons for doing so was the October 1983 U.S. invasion of the small Caribbean island of Grenada. A military coup had deposed the popular revolutionary Maurice Bishop, and the invasion took place under the questionable pretext of rescuing U.S. medical students. Many understood that invasion as putting the Sandinistas on notice that the United States would invade Nicaragua next.

The decision to hold elections was not without controversy. Sandinista leader Tomás Borge ridiculed the idea. He proclaimed, "El pueblo ya votó," meaning the people already voted for the type of government they desired through the direct demonstration of a display of arms without the possibility of fraudulent elections corrupting the process. Given Nicaragua's long experience with rigged electoral systems, his concern was not without merit. Nevertheless, the Sandinistas won the multiparty, Western-style elections in a landslide, with 67 percent of the vote. International observers reported that the vote accurately reflected the popular will of the Nicaraguan people.

Despite broad recognition of the outcome, Reagan called the elections a "sham" and a "farce" and refused to acknowledge the outcome. The only elections that the U.S. government would recognize were the ones that they could control and win. They would never allow the Sandinistas to gain legitimacy as the democratic representatives of the Nicaraguan people.

In 1987, Nicaraguans ratified a new constitution that codified the transformations that they sought to make in the country. The most notable provision of the new document was autonomy for the Atlantic coast. Since 1984, the Sandinistas had engaged in conversations with Indigenous peoples to listen to their demands. Together they formed an autonomy commission and devised a plan to preserve Indigenous languages and cultural expressions. Despite initial tensions resulting from the vast cultural divides between the Pacific and the Atlantic sides of the country, the Sandinistas made significant strides in working out agreements that respected the country's cultural and ethnic diversity. The constitution provided people on the Atlantic coast with more control over their economic, social, and political affairs, including jurisdiction over communal lands and natural resources and provisions for political representation.

DOCUMENT: "DRAFT LAW ON AUTONOMY PROPOSED BY THE GOVERNMENT OF NICARAGUA," 1985

The Sandinista government worked to achieve a compromise between desires for a revolutionary transformation of the country and respect for the rights of local communities. The following is a proposal put forward that reflects the government's understanding of the unique history and needs of Indigenous communities. The second half of the document (not included here) provides specific details on the functioning of regional autonomous governments and their relationship with the central government in the capital city of Managua.

General Considerations and Historical Antecedents

1. In order to understand the situation of the Indigenous peoples and communities of the Atlantic Coast of Nicaragua one has to work from the following assumptions:
    a. The heritage of a national dependent state.
    b. The existence of a historically oppressed Indigenous peoples and communities.

c. A revolutionary project that recognizes the right of self-determination of the Nicaraguan people in the face of imperialism, and the establishment of relations of equity, fraternal collaboration, and real equality for the entirety of the nation.

2. On the base of the socio-economic regime of exploitation of all the workers, and colonial and neocolonial domination in association with the local dominant classes, a dependent Nicaraguan nation was set up that did not give equality of participation to the Indigenous peoples and communities of the Atlantic Coast.

3. As the product of a historical development, the Indigenous peoples and communities of the Atlantic Coast have specific characteristics of language, culture, forms of organization, and economic relations that differentiate them from the rest of the Nicaraguan people. The bourgeois government did not recognize any rights, nor give real participation to the Indigenous peoples and communities of the Atlantic Coast in the socio-economic and political life of the country. The exploitation of natural and human resources was handed over to the rapacious trans-national corporations which deepened their isolation in respect to the rest of the nation.

4. The historic demands of the Indigenous peoples and communities of the Atlantic Coast form part of the struggle of the popular Sandinista Revolution for the affirmation of its popular and anti-imperialist character, and the broadening of democratic liberties.

5. The Autonomy Commission knows well that the ethnic question is not susceptible to magic solutions. Only inside the bounds of the Popular Sandinista Revolution are the conditions for its solution being created.

6. In Latin America the ethnic question has been dealt with from different positions, the Autonomy commission considers the exercise of the rights of autonomy within a specified region, in the context of the nation, as the most suitable for our historical reality.

Historical Considerations

1. The contradictions of colonial and imperialist domination in the country, as well as the practice of anti-popular and oppressive governments, shaped a Nicaraguan nation based on the regional separation and the ethnic division between the Pacific and the Atlantic Coast, under a single system of exploitation of all the workers. This is the historical root of the ethnic problem that the Popular Sandinista Revolution inherited.

2. At the base of this regional separation one encounters the incapacity of the dominant classes to create a single national economy that encompasses the Atlantic Coast, defends national sovereignty in the face of colonial and imperial interests, and allows equal civic participation to the Indigenous peoples and communities of the Atlantic Coast. From this foundation grew localist and ethnocentric expressions that, from the profound nature of the historical colonial process, explains the relations of lack of confidence and prejudice between the populations of the Atlantic and Pacific.

3. The particular history of each one of the Indigenous peoples and communities of the Atlantic Coat, as well as their social relations, relations of production, power structure, language, religion and symbols, in the context of the colonial and anti-imperialist struggles, have shaped a group of Indigenous people and communities with their own identities, and differences with the rest of the nation.

4. Facing a historical process that shaped a national state organized in the Pacific region based on the Catholic Spanish speaking Mestizo population, the Indigenous peoples and communities of the Atlantic Cost raised demands for their necessities, and demanded settlement of particular grievances.
5. In this manner, the Indigenous peoples and communities of the Atlantic Coast, along with the rest of the exploited and oppressed of the country, with the triumph of the revolution expressed demands to improve their condition of life, and moreover, demands related to the use and development of their languages, defense of their traditional forms of social organization, security in the possession of their land, and participation in the making of decision that affect them.
6. The triumph of the revolution permitted the growth and reactivation of militant organizations of the Indigenous peoples and communities of the Atlantic Coast that could count on the backing of the FSLN and the JGRN (Government of National Reconstruction). However, taking advantage of historical contradictions, as well as limitations and errors of the revolution, imperialism manipulated the ethnic questions against the revolution, diverting the legitimate demands of the Indigenous peoples and communities of the Atlantic Coast toward destabilizing objectives. In this way, the ethnic question in Nicaragua acquired a military dimension that now makes the solution more complicated.
7. The Indigenous peoples and communities of the Atlantic Coast that presently inhabit the Atlantic Coast are as follows: approximately 80,000 Miskitos (including those that are in Honduras); 30,000 Creoles; 8,000 Sumos; 1,500 Garifonas; and approximately 800 Ramas; 120,000 Mestizos who are the same as the majority community of the Pacific coast also live in the region.

Principles and Objectives of the Regional Autonomy

1. Nicaragua is a single and indivisible nation and the sovereignty of the revolutionary state extends to all of the national territory.
2. Nicaragua is a multi-ethnic country where every kind of discrimination, racism, separatism, ethnocentrism, localism and hegemonies should be fought against, with the end in mind of successfully advancing harmony, cooperation, and fraternity among the people. The Indigenous peoples and communities of the Atlantic Coast are an indivisible part of the Nicaraguan people.
3. The Popular Sandinista Revolution, upon conquering national independence for all the Nicaraguan people, and liquidating the power of the sell-out bourgeoisies, has created, for the first time in history, the conditions to guarantee the participation of the Indigenous people and communities of the Atlantic Coast in the construction of a new society, in full equality with the rest of the Nicaraguan people.
4. The unity of the Nicaraguan people around their revolutionary objectives with diversity of language, culture or religion, is an unrenounceable proposition of the revolution.
5. Defense of the sovereignty of the country and of the territorial integrity of the nation is the supreme duty of each and every Nicaraguan citizen. The exercising of the rights of autonomy will contribute to the strengthening of national unity, and will intensify the participation of the Indigenous people and communities of the Atlantic Coast in the tasks of defending the sovereignty of the country.
6. The Popular Sandinista Revolution recognizes that the Indigenous peoples and communities of the Atlantic Cost have every right to preserve and develop their

own cultural practices; their historic and religious patrimony; the right of free use and development of their languages; the right to receive education in their mother tongue and in the Spanish language; the right to organize their social and productive activities according to their values and traditions. The cultural and historic traditions of the Indigenous peoples and communities of the Atlantic Coast form part of the national culture and enrich it.

7. The rights of autonomy of the Indigenous peoples and communities of the Atlantic Coast will be exercised in the geographic area that they have traditionally occupied. This right is recognized and guaranteed by the revolutionary government.

8. The Popular Sandinista Revolution recognizes that the preservation of the ethnic identity of the Indigenous peoples and communities of the Atlantic Coast requires its own material base. The Indigenous peoples and communities of the Atlantic Coast have the right of collective or individual proprietorship over the lands they have traditionally occupied, at the same time the procedures of transmission and use of property established by their customs should be respected. These rights will be guaranteed effectively and legally by the corresponding authorities.

9. The Indigenous peoples and communities of the Atlantic Coast have the right to the use of the lands, forest, and waters—surface, subterranean, and coastal, in the area where they live.

10. The strategy of taking advantage of the natural resources of the region ought to benefit the economic and social development of the people of the Atlantic Coast and benefit the equilibrium of the national economy. Exploitation of these resources will bring about reinvestment in the region. The nature of the reinvestment will be determined by the authorities of the Indigenous peoples and communities of the Atlantic Coast. Planning and rational use will also be in their hands.

11. All the Indigenous peoples and communities of the Atlantic Coast will have equal rights independently of their numbers or level of development.

12. The rights of autonomy of the Indigenous peoples and communities of the Atlantic Coast do not lessen or diminish the rights and obligations they have as Nicaraguan citizens.

13. Regional autonomy, national unity, and the revolution, support each other in an economic strategy in favor of popular interests, in an internal market that makes regional equality possible, as well as an external commerce compatible with national economic independence. Historical reality and the ethnic makeup of the Atlantic Coast demand the establishment of a regime of autonomy that exercises all these rights and administers all the affairs of local and regional interest, without prejudice against those rights which are the prerogative of the central government.

We are certain that the autonomy proposal responds to the necessities and demands of the Indigenous peoples of the Atlantic Coast and contributes to deepening the democratic character of the revolution, to the reunification of the Nicaraguan family, as well as achieving peace and unity of the nation.

Source: "Draft Law on Autonomy Proposed by the Government of Nicaragua," Managua, Nicaragua, July 1985.

CONTRA WAR

On March 9, 1981, Reagan signed a secret authorization for the Central Intelligence Agency (CIA) to organize a paramilitary force to overthrow the Sandinista government. Together with the Argentine military, the CIA regrouped Somoza's former national guard and helped arm and train them into a counterrevolutionary force (called the *contras*). Reagan delegated John Negroponte, the U.S. ambassador to Honduras, to run this secret war. The paramilitary force conducted hit-and-run attacks on Nicaragua from Honduras, while the United States positioned warships off the Pacific coast and mined the country's harbors. Rather than direct attacks against military targets, the Reagan administration engaged in a strategy of so-called low-intensity warfare that struck soft targets, such as teachers and healthcare providers, who were less likely to fight back than men with guns. The contras committed atrocities that included murders, torture, kidnapping, and psychological campaigns against the civilian population. In 1985, the United States implemented a trade embargo against the country. Nicaraguan commerce with the United States fell from a third of its imports and exports to nothing. The goal was to produce an internal economic collapse that would drag the country down, halt agrarian and social reforms, and hopefully turn the population against the revolution.

The anticommunist pope John Paul II visited Nicaragua in April 1983. The very religious population warmly welcomed his visit, but political tensions immediately rose to the surface. A deep divide quickly emerged between a popular church that embraced the tenets of liberation theology and the traditional Catholic hierarchy that retained its conservative alliances. On the tarmac upon his arrival at Managua's airport, the pope condemned priests who served in the government even as they requested his blessing. He excommunicated those who refused to resign their posts. The pope denied a mother's request to say a prayer for her sons fallen in combat in the contra war. In a huge outdoor mass, the people chanted that they wanted peace, while the pope ordered them to be silent. He attacked the popular church and grassroots movements that supported the leftist Sandinistas and instead joined the church hierarchy in openly allying with the contras.

In response to the ongoing U.S. military and paramilitary attacks, Nicaragua took its adversary to the International Court of Justice. On June 27, 1986, the court ruled that the U.S. intervention in Nicaragua was an "unlawful use of force" and ordered the United States to desist and pay $17 billion in reparations. Reagan contemptuously dismissed the judgment, declared that the United States would not be bound by the decision, and proceeded to escalate attacks against the country's civilian population. In response, Nicaragua asked the United Nations Security Council to pass a resolution calling on governments to observe international law, but the United States vetoed it. Nicaragua then took a similar resolution to the United Nations General Assembly where it passed almost unanimously, with only U.S. and Israeli opposition. Not only had the International Court of Justice and the United Nations found the

United States guilty of engaging in terrorist actions against Nicaragua, but Reagan was now also in violation of international law.

On October 5, 1986, the Nicaraguans shot down a U.S. military supply aircraft. Sandinista soldiers captured a crew member, Eugene Hasenfus, who acknowledged that the CIA had employed him. This led to the unraveling of the Iran-Contra scandal that implicated Oliver North and other high-ranking officials in the Reagan administration for having secretly sold weapons to Iran and using the profits to supply and train the contras, in violation of a series of laws. In 1989, North was convicted of three felonies, although the convictions were later overturned on appeal because he had admitted to the crimes while testifying under immunity in a congressional hearing.

The United States feared the independent example that the Sandinistas had created in Nicaragua and did not want their model of sovereign development to spread to other Central American countries. Removing the Sandinistas became a linchpin of Reagan's foreign policy. This was the case even though Nicaragua was one of the smallest and poorest countries in the Americas. It had few exports and lacked the economic significance of Guatemala, Cuba, or Chile, where the United States had previously intervened against progressive governments. The war, nonetheless, devastated Nicaragua, killing fifty thousand people, making twice as many homeless, destroying entire communities, and leaving the economy in shambles.

Numerous international solidarity groups came to the defense of the Nicaraguan people. More than one hundred thousand U.S. citizens traveled to Nicaragua to support the Sandinistas or to oppose the contra war. Some came as aid workers bringing educational or technical skills, and others traveled to assist with coffee harvests. Many solidarity groups were religiously based. Witness for Peace was built on the premise that the presence of unarmed U.S. citizens would deter contra attacks. This strategy evolved almost by accident when, in 1983, a religious fact-finding delegation to the border town of Jalapa discovered that contra attacks ceased while international observers were present. The influential Pledge of Resistance vowed to engage in massive public resistance if the United States invaded Nicaragua. The religious magazine *Sojourners* declared on the front page of its August 1984 issue that Reagan was lying about the political changes in Nicaragua. Those who traveled to Nicaragua returned with a very different image of the country than what he had presented. Instead of a repressive regime, they witnessed a government dedicated to the expansion of healthcare and educational opportunities. These grassroots campaigns were successful in preventing overt U.S. military intervention in the country. Even so, economic sanctions and the contra war were slowly destroying the country.

DOCUMENT: CENTRAL INTELLIGENCE AGENCY, "THE FREEDOM FIGHTER'S MANUAL," 1983

As part of the U.S. government's propaganda war against the revolutionary San-dinista government, the CIA produced and distributed a sixteen-page cartoon-format brochure for how to carry out sabotage (figure 7.3). The handbook began with small acts such as coming in late to work or calling in sick and escalated through stealing food, destroying equipment, and preparing Molotov cocktails to firebomb police stations. Notable is the CIA's attempt to subvert revolutionary and nationalist language against the Sandinistas. Excerpted below is the introduction to the manual and one of the pages. The entire document is available on the In-ternet Archive at https://archive.org/details/freedomfightersm00unit. A year later, the CIA published a second, longer manual called Psychological Operations in Guerrilla Warfare. *It became known as "the murder manual" because it advocated the assassination of public officials and the killing of one of the opposition's own members to create a martyr for the cause.*

Practical guide to liberating Nicaragua from oppression and misery by paralyzing the military-industrial complex of the traitorous Marxist state without having to use special tools and with minimal risk for the combatant.

Nicaraguan patriot: to sabotage the Marxist tyranny is to vindicate Sandino's mem-ory. Long live free Nicaragua!

What the free Nicaraguan can do in order to tie down the Marxist tyranny

All Nicaraguans who love their country and cherish liberty—men, women, young and old people, farmers and workers alike—surely ask themselves what they can do with the means at their disposal, in order to participate in the final battle against the usurpers of the authentic Sandinista revolution for which the people of Nicaragua have fought and shed their blood for so many years. Some might think that today's armed struggle requires military supplies and economic resources only available to states or terrorist bands armed by Moscow. There is an essential economic infrastructure that any government needs to function, which can easily be disabled and even paralyzed without the use of armaments or costly and advanced equipment, with the small in-vestment of resources and time.

The following pages present a series of useful sabotage techniques, the majority of which can be done with simple household tools such as scissors, empty bottles, screwdrivers, matches, etc. These measures are extremely safe and without risk for those who use them, as they do not require equipment, skill or specialized activities that can draw attention to the doer.

One combatant can perform many of them, without having to turn to collabora-tors or having to make a detailed plan beforehand. These are acts that can be done practically in an improvised way every time an occasion presents itself. Our sacred cause needs to have more men and women join its ranks in order to perform these sabotage tasks. However, necessary caution should be taken, and only when the task requires it, should another person or persons participate in or have knowledge of a given act. As mentioned above, the techniques found in this manual correspond to the stage of individual sabotage, or at the most cellular—with cells of no more than two individuals—of the clandestine struggle.

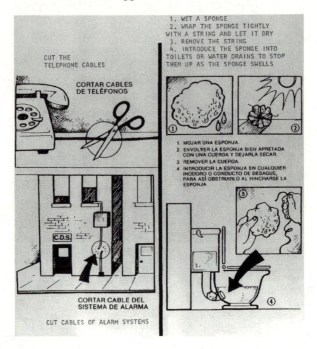

Figure 7.3. *Source*: Central Intelligence Agency, *The Freedom Fighter's Manual* (New York: Grove Press, 1985), https://archive.org/details/freedomfightersm00unit.

1990 ELECTIONS

One lasting legacy of the Sandinistas was the implementation for the first time of a functioning electoral system. The types of fraud that the Somoza dynasty had previously deployed to provide a veneer of democracy to maintain themselves in office would no longer be possible. As the Sandinistas had done in 1984, the revolutionaries once again moved up the date of the 1990 elections to stave off attacks from the United States and gain stronger international legitimacy. The Sandinistas were confident that they would win the vote, as preelection polls had indicated. In a shock to the entire country, the pro-U.S. candidate Violeta Barrios de Chamorro (1929–), the widow of *La Prensa* publisher Pedro Joaquín Chamorro, won instead.

Rather than celebrating the electoral defeat of the Sandinistas, the country seemed to go into shock and mourning. Many people apparently had voted against the Sandinistas not because they wanted the conservative Chamorro to win but because they simply wished that the Sandinistas would be more responsive to popular demands. Furthermore, they wanted the contra war to end. Mothers in particular pressed for an end of the military draft of their sons. Chamorro, dressed entirely in white, played into these sentiments. She campaigned as the pure and good "mother of the Nicaraguans" who extolled traditional conservative notions of women's maternal and domestic roles in society. Ortega, in contrast, presented himself as a "strutting rooster," the young, virile, strong man who would provide people with their material needs and defend them from external attacks.

In the 1990 election, the United States had offered Nicaraguans two options: vote for the Sandinistas and face continued economic warfare against the country or vote for Chamorro and receive extensive aid packages. The United States provided more funding for Chamorro's campaign than Somoza had paid in bribes during his fraudulent elections to justify maintaining himself in power. In the end, the Nicaraguan people cried uncle and hoped a change of government would end the merciless attacks. After Chamorro's election, the U.S. government quickly lost interest in Nicaragua, and the promise of aid never materialized.

In the leadup to the election, the George H. W. Bush administration charged that the election would be fraudulent, and no matter what, they would not accept the results. When Chamorro unexpectedly won, the U.S. State Department was forced to engage in policy backflips, as officials now claimed that these were the cleanest elections ever in Nicaragua's history and that the outcome reflected the democratic will of the Nicaraguan people. Despite charges from the U.S. government that the Sandinistas had set up a dictatorship and would never give up their rule willingly, they readily conceded defeat and facilitated the first peaceful transfer of power in the country's history. The blatant hypocrisy in U.S. policy only proved to underscore the reality that charges of fraud simply mean that someone does not like an outcome, and that the only free and fair elections are the ones that we win—even if those elections happened to take place in another sovereign country.

ASSESSMENT

A decade of U.S.-sponsored contra terror and related economic warfare derailed many of the progressive aspects of the Sandinista Revolution. Economic hardships proved to be more crucial for determining the 1990 electoral defeat than did the revolutionary fervor and idealism of the Sandinistas. Rather than subjective factors fomenting a political consciousness, economic factors pulled Nicaraguan society away from its revolutionary idealism, seemingly demonstrating a lack of a revolutionary class consciousness. In retrospect, some intellectuals believe that the fall of Somoza had come too easily and quickly—that through a longer and more difficult struggle, the general public would have gained a higher level of political awareness that would have helped them withstand the inevitable imperialist attacks that came after victory.

The Sandinistas did not institutionalize their revolution to the extent that the Cubans had done. Unlike Castro's declaration in April 1961, the Sandinista leadership never defined the Nicaraguan Revolution to be socialist. Despite Ronald Reagan's overheated Cold War denunciations of Nicaragua as a communist dictatorship, it is not even clear whether their leader Ortega was a Marxist. Developments in Nicaragua proffer a caution against a purely subjective interpretation of a revolutionary process. Economic factors played a large role in the evolution of social and political events. The defeat of the Sandinista government also indicated that a revolutionary movement could not be a purely (or even chiefly) centralized, statist affair that responded to the interests of charismatic male leaders. The lasting revolutionary changes in Nicaragua were those that popular, mass-based organizations launched. A revolutionary process is not simply a matter of gaining control of a government but rather a question of transforming the political consciousness of the people.

The 1990 electoral defeat of the Sandinistas raised the question of whether opening the country to liberal reforms was a mistake and had led to their defeat. Was it possible to implement socialism through peaceful and democratic means? Was the only viable alternative to follow the Cuban path of closing the country to all opponents of the revolutionary project and only permit the participation of those willing to play by the established rules? Again, if a revolutionary government does not maintain itself in power, it cannot implement the policies that its supporters so desperately desire.

Daniel Ortega ran unsuccessfully again in 1996 and 2001 for the presidency. Finally, in 2007, a much changed and more moderate Ortega regained the presidency. Those to his left complained that he had compromised Sandinista ideals in order to win the election. His family had become wealthy through investments in TV and radio stations, shopping malls, supermarkets, real estate, and other enterprises. Ortega came to an accommodation with the conservative Catholic Church hierarchy and the pro-business Consejo Superior de la Empresa Privada (COSEP, Superior Council for Private Enterprise) that had allied with the U.S. government and the contras against his leftist government in the 1980s. His support for reactionary policies that included one of the world's most draconian antiabortion measures led to a falling-out with feminists and other social movement activists who otherwise would have provided a bedrock of support for his government. Feminists also reacted negatively to revelations that he had repeatedly raped his stepdaughter, Zoilamérica Narváez. As with the MNR in Bolivia, when the Sandinistas returned to power years later, they were not nearly as revolutionary as they had been during their first time in office. Their actions raise the question of whether it is important for the left to gain and hold on to power at all costs.

In 2009, the Supreme Court lifted a ban on consecutive reelection, which allowed Ortega to remain in office. In 2017, he ran with his wife Rosario Murillo (1951–)

as his vice-presidential candidate, contributing to charges that he had established a family dynasty not unlike the previous Somozas had done. The following year, the Ortega administration faced its strongest challenge since the 1980s contra war, as the economy began to stagnate. Massive and sustained protests began as an objection to social security reforms that would have increased taxes and decreased benefits, but they soon spread to other issues, including a call for Ortega's resignation. Much of the organized opposition came from conservatives who half a century earlier had opportunistically allied with the Sandinistas to remove the liberal Somozas from power. Even so, Ortega still enjoyed a strong base of grassroots support from those who had benefited from the Sandinistas' redistributive policies and would be harmed by the neoliberal policies that the right would implement were they to retake control.

SUMMARY

The Sandinistas provide only the second example of an armed guerrilla uprising successfully overthrowing a previously entrenched government and introducing profound and transformative changes. Although the guerrillas fought against the government for eighteen years, their triumph in 1979 came surprisingly quickly as Somoza's former supporters turned against the regime. The Sandinistas soon marginalized their conservative allies from a ruling coalition and took the new government in a leftist direction. Initially Sandinistas achieved significant gains as they expropriated Somoza's property and redistributed resources to marginalized urban workers and rural peasants. They provided land, housing, and education to those who previously did not have access to such social services.

The Ronald Reagan administration quickly moved against the leftist Sandinistas and made their removal a linchpin of its foreign policy agenda. Despite international condemnation, Reagan created and trained a counterrevolutionary paramilitary force that terrorized the civilian population. Years of civil war that ravaged the country followed. The Sandinistas turned to elections to gain international legitimacy for their revolution, but instead the ballot became a mechanism for their conservative opponents to turn them out of power. Ironically, one of the most significant achievements of the Sandinista Revolution—the establishment of a functioning democratic system—led to their undoing. After losing a series of elections, a much-changed Sandinista political party returned Daniel Ortega to the presidency in 2007. This time, they were determined to stay.

DISCUSSION QUESTIONS

Was the Sandinista struggle for socialism or for national liberation?
Was Nicaragua prepared for a socialist revolution?
What were the successful policies and actions of the Sandinista government?

Was it a mistake for the Sandinistas to hold elections?

Why did the Ronald Reagan administration see the Sandinistas as such a threat? Were they a threat?

Did religion play a positive or negative role in the Nicaraguan Revolution?

In retrospect, what could the Sandinistas have done differently to maintain themselves in power?

What kind of organization and leadership is necessary to build a revolutionary movement?

FURTHER READING

The Sandinista Revolution led to a cottage industry of publications on Nicaragua, many with red and black covers—the colors of the Sandinista flag. Many of these books from the 1980s are still valuable as historical studies of the revolution.

Alegria, Claribel, and Darwin Flakoll. *Death of Somoza*. Willimantic, CT: Curbstone, 1996. A compelling journalistic account of the execution of Somoza in Paraguay.

Belli, Gioconda. *The Country under My Skin: A Memoir of Love and War*. New York: Knopf, 2002. An autobiography of a Sandinista militant that critiques the revolution's shortcomings.

Booth, John A. *The End and the Beginning: The Nicaraguan Revolution*. 2nd ed. Boulder, CO: Westview, 1985. The standard survey of the Sandinista Revolution.

Cabezas, Omar. *Fire from the Mountain: The Making of a Sandinista*. New York: Crown, 1985. The most famous autobiography of a Sandinista leader.

Hale, Charles R. *Resistance and Contradiction: Miskitu Indians and the Nicaraguan State, 1894–1987*. Stanford, CA: Stanford University Press, 1994. An anthropological examination of Indigenous peoples on the Atlantic coast.

Hodges, Donald C. *Intellectual Foundations of the Nicaraguan Revolution*. Austin: University of Texas Press, 1986. A probing examination of the underlying ideology of the Sandinista Revolution.

La Botz, Dan. *What Went Wrong? The Nicaraguan Revolution: A Marxist Analysis*. Boston: Brill, 2016. Lengthy, detailed, and very critical analysis of the shortcomings of the Sandinista Revolution that placed power in the hands of individual leaders rather than the working class.

Nolan, David. *The Ideology of the Sandinistas and the Nicaraguan Revolution*. Coral Gables, FL: University of Miami, 1984. An important examination of the different ideological currents within Sandinismo.

Peace, Roger C. *A Call to Conscience: The Anti-Contra War Campaign*. Amherst: University of Massachusetts Press, 2012. A survey of opposition to U.S. intervention in Nicaragua.

Randall, Margaret. *Sandino's Daughters: Testimonies of Nicaraguan Women in Struggle*. Rev. ed. New Brunswick, NJ: Rutgers University Press, 1995. Compelling interviews with women that effectively tell a larger story of the Sandinista Revolution.

Rueda, Claudia P. *Students of Revolution: Youth, Protest, and Coalition Building in Somoza-Era Nicaragua*. Austin: University of Texas Press, 2019. University student opposition to the Somoza dynasty.

Walker, Thomas W., ed. *Nicaragua in Revolution.* New York: Praeger, 1982. An impressive collection of essays outlining the initial changes in Nicaragua after the revolution, edited by a preeminent political scientist.

Zimmermann, Matilde. *Sandinista: Carlos Fonseca and the Nicaraguan Revolution.* Durham, NC: Duke University Press, 2001. An outstanding biography of the most important Sandinista ideologue.

FILMS

Latino. 1985. A Chicano Green Beret begins to question the morality of the secret war he is fighting in the Nicaraguan forests.

Pictures from a Revolution. 2007. Photojournalist Susan Meiselas revisits people she photographed during the Sandinistas' insurgency in the 1970s.

Under Fire. 1983. A fictional portrayal of a photojournalist who helps the Sandinistas overthrow Somoza.

8

Guerrilla Warfare

KEY DATES

1959	Hugo Blanco begins to organize peasants in La Convención Valley in Peru
1960	Che Guevara publishes *Guerrilla Warfare*
1962	In Peru, Luis de la Puente Uceda founds the MIR and Héctor Béjar founds the ELN
1963	Police capture and imprison Hugo Blanco
1964	Founding of the ELN in Colombia
1965	Failure of Luis de la Puente Uceda's foco in Peru
1966	Founding of the FARC in Colombia
1967	Founding of the EPL in Colombia
October 8, 1967	Capture of Che Guevara in Bolivia; he was executed the following day
March 24, 1980	Assassination of Salvadoran archbishop Monsignor Óscar Romero
May 17, 1980	Shining Path launches the armed phase of its "People's War," in Peru
January 1981	FMLN general offensive in El Salvador
1984	Founding of the MRTA in Peru
November 1989	FMLN final offensive in El Salvador
1992	El Salvador peace accord; Peruvian police capture Shining Path leader Abimael Guzmán
2009	Election of FMLN presidential candidate Mauricio Funes in El Salvador
2016	FARC signs peace accords with Colombian government

2019   FMLN loses presidential elections in El Salvador
September 11, 2021   Shining Path leader Abimael Guzmán dies

ACRONYMS

AMES	Asociación de Mujeres de El Salvador (Association of Women of El Salvador)
AMPES	Asociación de Mujeres Progresistas de El Salvador (Association of Progressive Women of El Salvador)
APRA	Alianza Popular Revolucionaria Americana (American Popular Revolutionary Alliance)
CGSB	Coordinadora Guerrillera Simón Bolívar (Simón Bolívar Guerrilla Coordinating Board)
ELN	Ejército de Liberación Nacional (National Liberation Army)
EPL	Ejército Popular de Liberación (Popular Liberation Army)
ERP	Ejército Revolucionario del Pueblo (People's Revolutionary Army)
FARC	Fuerzas Armadas Revolucionarias de Colombia (Revolutionary Armed Forces of Colombia)
FARN	Fuerzas Armadas de la Resistencia Nacional (National Resistance Armed Forces)
FDR	Frente Democrático Revolucionario (Revolutionary Democratic Front)
FMLN	Frente Farabundo Martí para la Liberación Nacional (Farabundo Martí National Liberation Front)
FPL	Fuerzas Populares de Liberación (Popular Liberation Forces)
MAQL	Movimiento Armado Quintín Lame (Quintín Lame Armed Movement)
MIR	Movimiento de Izquierda Revolucionaria (Revolutionary Left Movement)
MLN–T	Movimiento de Liberación Nacional–Tupamaros (National Liberation Movement–Tupamaros)
M-19	Movimiento 19 de Abril (19th of April Movement)
MRTA	Movimiento Revolucionario Tupac Amaru (Tupac Amaru Revolutionary Movement)
PCC	Partido Comunista de Colombia (Communist Party of Colombia)
PCS	Partido Comunista de El Salvador (Communist Party of El Salvador)
PRTC	Partido Revolucionario de los Trabajadores Centroamericanos (Revolutionary Party of the Central American Workers)
UP	Union Patriótica (Patriotic Union)
URNG	Unidad Revolucionaria Nacional Guatemalteca (National Revolutionary Guatemalan Unity)

Guerrilla warfare in and of itself is not a revolution; it is simply a form of combat. Rather than a reliance on large-scale military units as is common in conventional battles, guerrillas depend on small numbers of mobile fighters who live off the land with the support of a local population. The word "guerrilla" comes from the Spanish word for "little war," indicating the irregular nature of the tactics. With only a few combatants, the style of guerrilla warfare can provide a powerful response to a much larger and established military force. This strategy is part of a much longer tradition that predates the emergence of socialist revolutions in the twentieth century. Although guerrilla wars are rarely successful, they can cause their opponents significant problems and bring governments to a standstill.

This chapter begins with an examination of the influence that the Cuban Revolution, and in particular the theoretical contributions that Che Guevara had on guerrilla struggles in the 1960s. It then examines armed movements in Colombia, El Salvador, and Peru that extended into the 1980s and beyond. These three countries experienced the largest and most powerful of these various guerrilla insurgencies, but these revolutionaries failed to take power even though they faced similar conditions to their counterparts in Cuba and Nicaragua. Multiple factors explain that outcome and highlight just how exceptional of an event a successful guerrilla uprising truly is.

1960s

The success of Fidel Castro's 26th of July Movement in Cuba challenged the assumptions of orthodox Marxism and gave hope and inspiration to a new generation of revolutionaries. The triumph of an armed struggle in Cuba led to the flourishing of guerrilla movements throughout the hemisphere. In 1960, Che Guevara published *Guerrilla Warfare* as a manual to guide revolutionaries on how to overthrow a dictatorship and implement a new and more just social order (see the document included with this chapter). Guevara analyzed the Cuban Revolution in order to extract general laws and develop a theory of guerrilla warfare. First, he argued that the Cuban Revolution demonstrated that people could organize themselves as a small guerrilla army and overthrow a large, powerful, established regime. Second, popular movements do not have to wait for the proper economic conditions before organizing a revolutionary war; the insurrectionary guerrilla force can create them. Third, Guevara believed that in Latin America, revolutionary struggles should be based in a rural, peasant population.

BIOGRAPHY: CHE GUEVARA, 1928–1967

Che Guevara
Source: Wikimedia Commons/Alberto Korda

The Guatemalan Spring attracted many leftists and dissidents from across Latin America who were inspired by the ideals and policies of the Jacobo Arbenz administration, particularly in the way it compared to the repressive and exclusionary policies of their own governments. One of those who arrived in Guatemala in 1954 was a young Argentine doctor named Ernesto Guevara de la Serna.

Guevara was born in 1928 to a liberal-left, middle-class family that embraced anticlerical ideas and supported the Republicans in the Spanish Civil War. His mother, Celia de la Serna, had a particularly important influence on the formation of his social conscience. Throughout his life, Guevara suffered from severe asthma attacks, but nevertheless he pushed himself and excelled as an athlete. In 1948, he entered the University of Buenos Aires to study medicine. Before finishing his studies, Guevara joined his friend Alberto Granado on a motorcycle trip that took them across Latin America. Although the motorcycle only made it as far as Chile, the two vagabonds continued on foot, by hitchhiking, and by boat to Peru, Colombia, and Venezuela. For Guevara, it was a consciousness-raising experience that ultimately changed the direction his life would take. The trip converted Guevara into a pan–Latin Americanist. He believed that the region had a shared destiny and that national borders only served to divide people in their struggles for a more just and egalitarian social order.

After finishing his medical studies in 1953, Guevara set out on another trip through Latin America that matured his revolutionary political ideology. In Bolivia, he observed the mobilization of workers and the implementation of agrarian reform following a popular 1952 revolution. In Guatemala, he worked with Jacobo Arbenz's revolutionary government. Guevara lived through the military coup that overthrew the Arbenz administration, and that experience converted Guevara into a dedicated fighter against U.S. imperialism. It also convinced him that it was necessary to destroy the political and military forces of the old system and to arm the masses to protect a revolution from counterrevolutionary forces. Guevara firmly believed that Arbenz would have survived the coup if he had relied on the peasants and workers to defend the revolutionary experiment.

After the Guatemalan coup, Guevara hid in the Argentine embassy before escaping to Mexico, where he began a serious study of Marxism. While in Guatemala, he had met a Peruvian exile named Hilda Gadea, who introduced him to the thought of socialist José Carlos Mariátegui and other leftist ideologies. Now in Mexico, Gadea presented Guevara to a Cuban exile named Fidel Castro, who was planning to return to his native Cuba to ignite a revolution. In 1956, Guevara joined Castro and eighty other guerrillas to launch an armed struggle against the Fulgencio Batista dictatorship. Castro had invited Guevara, the only non-Cuban in the group, to join as a medic. The Cubans gave Guevara the moniker "Che," a Guaraní expression commonly used in Argentina that can be roughly translated as "hey, you." Guevara subsequently became best known by this name.

Shortly after landing in Cuba, the small guerrilla force ran into a military ambush that wiped out about half the group. Forced to choose between a first-aid kit and a box of bullets, Guevara took the ammunition. That decision represented his conversion from a medical doctor to a guerrilla fighter. Guevara fought with the Cubans for two years in the Sierra Maestra mountains, eventually rising to the rank of rebel army commander. He became the third most important leader after Fidel and his brother Raúl Castro.

After the January 1959 triumph of the revolution, Guevara became a Cuban citizen and legally adopted "Che" as part of his name. Drawing on lessons from Guatemala, Guevara advocated the complete destruction of the former regime, which included the execution of its members so that they could not launch a counterattack against the revolution. Guevara also engaged in social engineering projects. He advocated the creation of a "new socialist man" who would be motivated to support the revolution through moral rather than material incentives.

Guevara assumed a series of positions in the new revolutionary Cuban government, including working in the agrarian reform institution, as head of the National Bank, and as minister of industry. Guevara, however, was better suited to the life of a vagabond or guerrilla fighter and soon became restless as a bureaucrat. He traveled internationally as an ambassador for Cuba and vocally denounced U.S. imperialism. He advocated the creation of "two, three, or many Vietnams" to strike a deadly blow against imperialism.

In 1965, Guevara renounced his governmental positions and Cuban citizenship and left the island to continue his revolutionary adventures. He first traveled to Africa to join a guerrilla struggle in the Congo, but that proved to be a frustrating experience. In 1966, Guevara arrived in Bolivia to launch a new continental Latin American revolution. Unlike in Cuba, Guevara's guerrillas, who called themselves the Ejército de Liberación Nacional (ELN, National Liberation Army), had difficulties gaining the support of the rural population. The agrarian reform program that had so impressed Guevara on his first trip almost fifteen years earlier had satisfied a peasant hunger for land, and they were not much interested in another revolution. While training his troops, Guevara prematurely encountered the Bolivian military before he was fully prepared for combat, which put him on the run. On October 8, 1967, an antiguerrilla military unit trained by U.S. Army Special Forces captured Guevara and his few remaining guerrilla fighters. Fearing the potential publicity of a political show trial and possible release or escape, Bolivian dictator René Barrientos ordered his execution. The military publicly displayed his body to prove his death. To many, his corpse looked like a sacrificed Christ, which contributed to an image of Che as a martyr and prophet.

Some critics condemn Guevara for mechanically applying his lessons and theories of guerrilla warfare from Cuba to the Bolivian situation when they were not a good fit and that this ultimately led to his failure and death. Elsewhere in Latin America, revolutionaries attempted to implement his theory that a guerrilla force could create the objective conditions necessary for a guerrilla war, and they similarly met with disaster. Others have criticized Guevara for overemphasizing the role of armed struggle in a revolutionary movement and have pointed out that although a relatively small guerrilla force overthrew Batista in Cuba, this came only after years of leftist political agitations and rising worker expectations. Guevara has also come under criticism for his gendered notions, including leaving his children with their mothers (one with Gadea in Mexico, whom he then divorced and went on to have four more children with a second wife, Aleida March, in Cuba) so he could go off to fight his battles.

Although a dedicated communist revolutionary, Guevara was highly critical of bureaucratic Soviet communism for having lost its revolutionary fervor. Following in the footsteps of earlier Latin American Marxist thinkers such as Mariátegui, Guevara contended that subjective conditions, including the role of human consciousness, were more important for creating a revolutionary situation than an objective economic situation was. Rather than waiting for a highly developed capitalist economy to collapse due to its internal contradictions, he believed that a dedicated cadre must engage in the political education of the masses.

Guevara's efforts to launch a continent-wide revolution to overthrow capitalism and usher in a socialist utopia ultimately failed. Nevertheless, many young idealists admired Guevara for his selfless dedication to a struggle against oppression and for social justice. Decades after his death, Che Guevara continues to be championed as a revolutionary hero in the struggle for social justice and against oppression, exploitation, and marginalization. Although often reduced to a chic icon on T-shirts, his life represents a selfless dedication to the concerns of the underclass, a struggle to encourage people to place the needs of the broader society above their own personal wishes and desires, and a willingness to make extensive personal sacrifices to achieve a more just and equitable social order.

DOCUMENT: CHE GUEVARA, *GUERRILLA WARFARE*, 1960

Che Guevara published Guerrilla Warfare *in 1960 as a manual to guide revolutionaries in other countries on how to launch their own revolutions. In the first several pages, Guevara outlines the general principles he extracted from the Cuban Revolution that he thought applicable to other situations.*

The armed victory of the Cuban people over the Batista dictatorship was not only the triumph of heroism as reported by the newspapers of the world; it also forced a change in the old dogmas concerning the conduct of the popular masses of Latin America. It showed plainly the capacity of the people to free themselves by means of guerrilla warfare from a government that oppresses them.

We consider that the Cuban Revolution contributed three fundamental lessons to the conduct of revolutionary movements in America. They are:

(1) Popular forces can win a war against the army.
(2) It is not necessary to wait until all conditions for making revolution exist; the insurrection can create them.

(3) In underdeveloped America the countryside is the basic area for armed fighting.

Of these three propositions the first two contradict the defeatist attitude of revolutionaries or pseudo-revolutionaries who remain inactive and take refuge in the pretext that against a professional army nothing can be done, who sit down to wait until in some mechanical way all necessary objective and subjective conditions are given without working to accelerate them. As these problems were formerly a subject of discussion in Cuba, until facts settled the question, they are probably still much discussed in America.

Naturally, it is not to be thought that all conditions for revolution are going to be created through the impulse given to them by guerrilla activity. It must always be kept in mind that there is a necessary minimum without which the establishment and consolidation of the first center is not practicable. People must see clearly the futility of maintaining the fight for social goals within the framework of civil debate. When the forces of oppression come to maintain themselves in power against established law, peace is considered already broken.

In these conditions popular discontent expresses itself in more active forms. An attitude of resistance finally crystallizes in an outbreak of fighting, provoked initially by the conduct of the authorities.

Where a government has come into power through some form of popular vote, fraudulent or not, and maintains at least an appearance of constitutional legality, the guerrilla outbreak cannot be promoted, since the possibilities of peaceful struggle have not yet been exhausted.

The third proposition is a fundamental of strategy. It ought to be noted by those who maintain dogmatically that the struggle of the masses is centered in city movements, entirely forgetting the immense participation of the country people in the life of all the underdeveloped parts of America. Of course the struggles of the city masses of organized workers should not be underrated; but their real possibilities of engaging in armed struggle must be carefully analyzed where the guarantees which customarily adorn our constitutions are suspended or ignored. In these conditions the illegal workers' movements face enormous dangers. They must function secretly without arms. The situation in the open country is not so difficult. There, in places beyond the reach of the repressive forces, the armed guerrillas can support the inhabitants.

We will later make a careful analysis of these three conclusions that stand out in the Cuban revolutionary experience. We emphasize them now at the beginning of this work as our fundamental contribution.

Guerrilla warfare, the basis of the struggle of a people to redeem itself, has diverse characteristics, different facets, even though the essential will for liberation remains the same. It is obvious—and writers on the theme have said it many times—that war responds to a certain series of scientific laws; whoever ignores them will go down to defeat. Guerrilla warfare as a phase of war must be ruled by all of these; but besides, because of its special aspects, a series of corollary laws must also be recognized in order to carry it forward. Though geographical and social conditions in each country determine the mode and particular forms that guerrilla warfare will take, there are general laws that hold for all fighting of this type.

Our task at the moment is to find the basic principles of this kind of fighting and the rules to be followed by peoples seeking liberation; to develop theory from facts; to generalize and give structure to our experience for the profit of others.

Source: Che Guevara, *Guerrilla Warfare* (Lincoln: University of Nebraska Press, 1998), 7–9.

The most controversial aspect of *Guerrilla Warfare* was Guevara's belief that a guerrilla force could create the objective conditions necessary for a revolutionary war. Previous theorists had argued that certain political and economic conditions were necessary for a successful struggle. In what became known as his *foco* theory of guerrilla warfare, Guevara argued that the Cuban Revolution demonstrated that a small insurrectionary army (the foco) operating in the countryside could spark a revolution that would then spread to the cities. Only a few guerrillas in each country were necessary to begin a process that would transform Latin America. This caused him to emphasize the importance of a proper geographic setting for an armed struggle. A forested environment that provided good cover for the guerrillas was more important than the ideological preparation of a large civilian base of support.

Almost every Latin American country experienced a guerrilla insurgency in the 1960s. These mobilizations typically referred to themselves as "political-military organizations," emphasizing that armed action was simply a means to a political end. Scholars have broken these movements into a series of "waves." The first began with Castro's successful campaign in Cuba in 1959 and closed with the death of Guevara in Bolivia in 1967. Rural-based, foco-style movements characterized this phase. Guevara's death introduced a second wave where, in a rapidly urbanizing Latin America, the center of guerrilla struggles shifted to cities with an accompanying rejection of the foco theory of guerrilla warfare. From the 1970s onward, a third wave of political-military organizations emerged in Central America and the Andes. These included the Sandinistas in Nicaragua, the subject of the previous chapter, as well as groups in Colombia, El Salvador, and Peru that are examined in this chapter.

Initial attempts to lead foco-type insurrections in 1959 and 1960 against Batista-style dictatorships in Paraguay (Alfredo Stroessner), Nicaragua (Luis Somoza), the Dominican Republic (Rafael Trujillo), and Haiti (François Duvalier, also known as Papa Doc) quickly met with defeat. Many of these were not leftist in inspiration, but more akin to coup attempts to oust a personalist dictator as had happened in Cuba. In fact, one of the early movements in Nicaragua did not intend to implement a socialist government but rather was led by conservatives who sought to displace the liberal Somoza regime.

Most other insurrections that followed were more in line with how we come to think of guerrillas in the 1960s: broad-based movements in pursuit of a radical, socialist transformation of society. A series of guerrilla attempts in Peru initially realized some success but also showed the shortcomings of the foco theory. Hugo Blanco (1934–) was a Trotskyist and a charismatic peasant organizer in La Convención Valley north of Cuzco. He significantly expanded peasant activism under the slogan "land or death" that combined Zapata's "land and liberty" with Castro's "homeland or death." An attempt to lead an armed insurrection failed because Blanco was more of a peasant organizer than guerrilla fighter.

Luis de la Puente Uceda (1926–1965) was the main leader of a second attempt to launch a guerrilla insurrection in Peru. The son of a landowner and lawyer, de la Puente had begun his political career with the Alianza Popular Revolucionaria

Americana (APRA, American Popular Revolutionary Alliance) but was expelled in 1959 when he complained that the party had drifted too far to the right. Influenced by the success of the Cuban Revolution, in 1962, he founded the Movimiento de Izquierda Revolucionaria (MIR, Revolutionary Left Movement) as an extension of the work he had begun in the APRA. Although the proper conditions did not exist for a revolution, under the influence of Guevara's ideas, de la Puente believed that his guerrilla foco could create them. In 1965, the military and police wiped out de la Puente's group, essentially ending the guerrilla threat that the MIR represented. His group had failed because of divisions on the left, poor site selection, and a misreading of the political situation. Blanco's movement had organized peasants in desperate need of guerrilla support. They had seized land but had no guns to defend it. In contrast, de la Puente's guerrillas failed because of a lack of support from an organized peasantry. They had guns but no peasants to defend.

Héctor Béjar (1935–) led a third attempt also in 1962 that was motivated by the triumph of the Cuban Revolution. Not incidentally, it called itself the Ejército de Liberación Nacional (ELN, National Liberation Army), the same name that other Castro-inspired groups selected. Similar to the MIR, it also believed that it could create the necessary conditions for a successful revolution. Its first attempt in 1963 failed when the Peruvian military detected and decimated an advance group in Puerto Maldonado that was trying to enter the country from neighboring Bolivia. Subsequent attempts similarly failed due to ideological, organizational, and personalist fragmentation as well as a lack of organic connections with rural communities. The defeat of these three guerrilla attempts ended guerrilla activity in Peru for fifteen years, until the Shining Path emerged in 1980.

The failure of the Peruvian focos foreshadowed the defeat and execution of Guevara in neighboring Bolivia. Guevara had left Cuba to continue revolutionary struggles elsewhere, first in the Congo in 1965, where he faced defeat, and then in Bolivia, where he was executed in 1967. Guevara hoped his Bolivian foco would trigger a hemispheric revolution, but he seemed to ignore key aspects of his own theory. Critics condemned Guevara for mechanically applying his lessons from Cuba and theories of guerrilla warfare to the Bolivian situation where they did not fit well. These critics contend that Guevara was unable to learn lessons, including from his failure in Congo. Furthermore, many have criticized Guevara for overemphasizing the role of armed struggle in a revolutionary movement. He ignored the fact that a relatively small guerrilla force overthrew Batista in Cuba only after years of leftist political agitations and rising worker expectations. In fact, some argued that he fundamentally misinterpreted why the Cuban Revolution succeeded and as a result misunderstood the lessons of that victory. Nevertheless, Guevara became a renowned martyr for his selfless dedication to a revolutionary struggle. In death, he became a more powerful symbol than he had been in life.

Guevara's death led to a shift from rural- to urban-based guerrilla movements. Abraham Guillén (1913–1993), an exiled veteran of the Spanish Civil War who lived in Uruguay and Argentina, published *Strategy of the Urban Guerrilla* in 1966.

Guillén argued that with demographic shifts to urban areas, it was no longer viable to launch guerrilla warfare from the countryside. He believed that Guevara's foco theory was a recipe for disaster and would only lead to a mounting death toll. The Brazilian revolutionary Carlos Marighella (1911–1969) followed in 1969 with the *Minimanual of the Urban Guerrilla*, which includes advice on how to overthrow a military regime. As with Guevara's earlier *Guerrilla Warfare*, these handbooks became important guides for a new generation of urban guerrillas. After a long history of political activism, including participating in the kidnapping of the U.S. ambassador Charles Burke Elbrick in September 1969, the Brazilian police ambushed and killed Marighella in São Paulo in November 1969, shortly after he wrote his *Minimanual*.

Urban guerrilla movements were largely rooted in student and intellectual populations. One of the most significant was the Movimiento de Liberación Nacional–Tupamaros (MLN–T, National Liberation Movement–Tupamaros) in Uruguay that took its name from the colonial rebel Tupac Amaru. They engaged in spectacular robberies and kidnappings, and distributed food in poor neighborhoods, which gained them an image as Robin Hood–style fighters. Critics blamed the Tupamaros' practice of kidnappings and assassinations for inciting police repression that resulted in a military dictatorship in 1973. After the return to constitutional rule in 1985, the Tupamaros resumed life as a peaceful political party. The former Tupamaro political prisoner José "Pepe" Mujica won election as president of Uruguay with the leftist coalition Frente Amplio (Broad Front) in 2010. Mujica gained renown for maintaining an austere lifestyle rather than leveraging his political success for personal material gain. His trajectory demonstrates that less important than the specific path to power—whether organized as a social movement, engaging in an armed struggle, or running for elected office—was the end goal of working for a transformation of society. Activists would willingly accept whatever strategy was most appropriate given the current conditions.

DOCUMENT: CENTRAL INTELLIGENCE AGENCY (CIA), "THE LATIN AMERICAN GUERRILLA TODAY," 1971

U.S. government officials carefully monitored revolutionary developments in Latin America. In this excerpt from a lengthy intelligence report, the CIA summarizes a shift in guerrilla operations from rural to urban areas. The agency then proceeds to a country-by-country examination of guerrilla movements with a particular emphasis on the urban arena. In retrospect, what is notable is that it considers the FARC in Colombia to be less of a concern than many other groups are. A critical reader can question some of the language choices, including "terrorist" to describe revolutionary activities. The CIA has declassified this document two times on its Freedom of Information Act (FOIA) website, and a comparison of the different redactions reveals a certain amount of randomness and capriciousness in what information the agency still considers to be too sensitive to release.

For more than ten years Fidel Castro has been encouraging and aiding Latin American revolutionaries to take to the backlands and mountains of their own countries to imitate his guerrilla campaign and victory. Today, however, there are fewer than 1,000 rural guerrillas holding out in only a few countries. They are weak, of declining importance, and do not pose serious threats to the governments. Guerrilla insurgency in the hinterlands became increasingly anachronistic and irrelevant in many Latin American countries in the decade of the 1960s as societies urbanized and modernized at accelerated rates.

As rural guerrilla fortunes have faded, however, a new breed of revolutionary has appeared in the cities. In Uruguay, Argentina, Brazil, and Guatemala urban guerrillas have engaged in spectacular acts of terrorism and violence. Six foreign ambassadors have been kidnaped during the last three years, of whom two were murdered. About a dozen other diplomats and a large number of government officials also have been kidnaped. Robberies of banks and arms depots, airline hijackings, arson, sabotage, and killings of police and security officials have reached unprecedented proportions in several countries. Terrorism is likely to increase in at least a half-dozen Latin American countries this year and could challenge the governments of Uruguay and Guatemala.

THE RURAL GUERRILLA AFTER A DECADE

Prominent students of the Cuban revolution believe that Castro never intended to wage a rural guerrilla war when he landed in Cuba from Mexico in 1956, but that he hoped to join in a quick urban putsch. His experience during the preceding ten years as a student radical, adventurer, and violent revolutionary was acquired in the cities. Even after Castro was forced into the sierra after his expedition foundered, he continued to rely heavily on urban support groups. His radio appeals were beamed mainly to middle-class, nationalist audiences, and in April 1958 he helped organize an abortive national strike in the towns and cities.

Castro's small guerrilla band won some skirmishes with regular military forces, but ultimately the Batista regime collapsed because Castro captured the imagination of an oppressed, disenchanted middle class through highly effective public relations. Once in power, however, Castro quickly alienated urban groups through his radical appeals to peasants and workers. The regime exaggerated and glorified the accomplishments of Castro and his guerrilla colleagues, and created a rural, agrarian mystique for the revolution.

In the months following Castro's victory, exiles and revolutionaries from a number of Latin American countries unsuccessfully attempted to initiate guerrilla struggles in their own countries. By 1960 Castro and Che Guevara were giving support to such revolutionaries on a large scale. Misinterpreting their own experiences, they recommended that rural guerrilla methods be employed and gave little consideration to urban tactics. Large numbers of Latin American youths traveled to Cuba for training in rural guerrilla techniques, and Guevara's guerrilla handbook was widely distributed and used throughout the hemisphere. In fact, the Cuban leaders and their revolutionary disciples were so confident of these methods that from 1959 through 1965 almost every country in Latin America skirmished with revolutionaries inspired or supported by Havana. A few of these efforts endured, but by mid-decade most of the remaining guerrilla bands were of declining importance.

These efforts failed principally because the Cuban leaders themselves refused to understand the true dynamics of how they came to power and because they imposed an unworkable strategy on their followers. As rapidly as new guerrilla efforts were conceived, however, security and counterinsurgent forces in many Latin American countries were expanded and became more effective. The rural guerrillas also failed because of ineptness and disputes over leadership, tactics, and ideology. Generally, they were poorly trained and equipped despite Cuban efforts, and, desiring quick results, were unprepared psychologically for protracted conflict. Rural guerrillas have been unable in virtually every instance to attract significant middle-class support, mainly because their programs and campaigns have been directed at rural groups.

In 1966 and 1967 Cuba attempted to revitalize waning guerrilla fortunes in the hemisphere through an intensified, reckless commitment to continental rural guerrilla war. The Latin American Solidarity Organization was founded as a hemispheric revolutionary front. It held its first conclave the summer of 1967. In the meantime, Che Guevara with 16 other Cubans was spear-heading a new guerrilla effort in Bolivia. Cuban advisers were also operating with guerrillas in Guatemala and Venezuela, and possibly in Colombia. Castro insisted more stridently than ever that meaningful change could result only from violent struggle in the countryside. The French Marxist, Regis Debray, earlier had published a treatise expanding the point, asserting that guerrilla action must be an exclusively rural phenomenon without significant aid from the cities. His *Revolution Within the Revolution* became the new Cuban manifesto on guerrilla war.

Cuba's efforts to "export" the revolution reached their zenith during this period. Guevara's summary defeat in Bolivia in October 1967 and the concurrent failures of guerrillas elsewhere demonstrated more clearly than before the bankruptcy of Havana's approach. Young revolutionaries throughout Latin America began to reappraise Cuba's strategy. Castro unintentionally contributed to an acceleration of this reevaluation by publishing Guevara's field diary. Che's poignant memoire of ineptitude, hopeless meanderings in dense jungles, and flight from encircling Bolivian troops has undoubtedly convinced many young revolutionaries that other tactics can lead more quickly to dramatic results. It is ironic that Che's detailed account of his own defeat is likely to endure as a more permanent legacy than his guerrilla handbook or speeches.

Carlos Marighella, the Brazilian author of the *Minimanual of the Urban Guerrilla* has replaced both Guevara and Debray as the primary theoretician of violent revolution in the hemisphere. Debray, who was recently released from a Bolivian prison after serving more than three years of a 30-year term for his part in the Guevara fiasco, admitted on 30 December that he had under-estimated the importance of urban terrorism. He now claims to be rethinking his entire treatise on guerrilla tactics, and has endorsed urban terrorism.

Guevara's precipitate failure also led to a reappraisal of tactics in Cuba. During 1968 and the first half of 1969, Havana appeared to be withdrawing from revolutionary liaisons in Latin America. Cuban support to revolutionaries in Venezuela and Colombia terminated, and guerrillas in other countries were told to acquire their own funds and arms. Castro, however, was reluctant to amend his rural guerrilla strategy and was loath to share the spotlight as foremost revolutionary in the hemisphere with Marighella. Nevertheless, during the second half of 1969 there were signs of a gradual—if grudging—Cuban acceptance of urban methods as urban terrorists accelerated their activities in a number of Latin American cities. In November 1969 Marighella was killed, and two months later Castro came out in support of his line by publishing the *Minimanual*.

Since then, Havana has been more flexible and cautious about endorsing revolutionary groups. Both urban and rural tactics now are supported, and in view of events in Chile [the election of Salvador Allende], the nonviolent path to power is also publicly accepted—at least there. Underlying the pragmatism of this approach, however, is the same enduring commitment to rural guerrilla methods that has characterized the Cuban revolution since the early 1960s. Cuban leaders continue to predict that in most countries rural insurgency will be decisive in the long run and that urban tactics should be employed to create favorable conditions for rural conflict. Marighella himself was making plans to initiate rural guerrilla warfare in Goias State prior to his death.

Today, Guatemala may be the only country receiving material support from Cuba for guerrilla operations. A few Cuban advisers are in the Guatemalan countryside, and Cuban funds have been provided. In other countries, Havana appears to be giving little more than training and propaganda support to revolutionaries. Cuban intelligence agents have been active in Chile since Allende's inauguration, and it is possible that Cuba could increase its contacts with South American terrorists under Chilean cover. In the long run, however, rural guerrilla methods increasingly will be replaced with activities in the cities.

Source: Central Intelligence Agency (CIA), "The Latin American Guerrilla Today," January 22, 1971, CIA Electronic Reading Room, https://www.cia.gov/reading room/document/cia-rdp85t00875r001500030003-6 and https://www.cia.gov/read ingroom/document/0000637157.

GENDERED DIVISIONS

As with the broader history of warfare, male chauvinism and toxic masculinity were commonly present in guerrilla struggles. Most leaders of revolutionary movements, both before, during, and after the rare victory, were men who too often relegated their women comrades to secondary support roles. This has led to an assumption that socialist revolutionaries were primarily interested in class struggle and economic inequality with only a minor, perhaps passing, concern for gender equality and racial discrimination. As this chapter demonstrates, however, the reality was rather more complex. The most enlightened revolutionaries understood that race, class, and gender really deal with different phenomena and must be engaged on different levels and that a true revolutionary transformation of society required engagement with all forms of oppression.

Women have always played a significant role in warfare, but with this new wave of guerrilla movements, they transitioned from support networks that sustained male fighters to armed combatants themselves. The gendered division of labor in guerrilla camps always reflected a certain amount of sexism, but women participants also understood that they aroused less suspicion than men did in carrying out clandestine operations. Women could more easily and safely ferry weapons and messages than men and exploit their femininity to infiltrate the opposition. Haydée Tamara Bunke Bider (1937–1967) was an Argentine-born communist from the German Democratic Republic who joined Guevara's guerrilla army in Bolivia. Under the **nom de guerre** Tania, she effectively penetrated the upper echelons of the Bolivian government, becoming very close to president René Barrientos. When her cover was blown, she joined Guevara as a guerrilla fighter until she was killed in a military ambush.

Tania was the only woman in Guevara's insurgent force and as such became the most famous female guerrilla.

By the 1980s, women regularly constituted about a third of many guerrilla armies and played roles equal to men. Several factors contributed to their increased involvement. In part, their participation reflected economic and social changes, including population shifts from rural to urban areas and an increase in the number of women in the labor force. These factors helped break traditional gender roles that previously limited women to the domestic sphere. A change in guerrilla tactics from small foco groups to mass political mobilizations also necessitated broader popular participation. Inevitably, women were swept up in these movements along with others in their communities.

Women had to fight hard to be accepted in guerrilla movements. One Colombian guerrilla declared that women "had to shoot to be heard," and women came to be respected only after they proved themselves in combat. Comandanta Ramona was one of the chief leaders of the neo-Zapatista guerrillas in Mexico in the 1990s. As a reflection of her importance, she headed their delegation in peace talks with the Mexican government. It was a long struggle, however, and women were never represented in positions of leadership proportional to their numbers in the guerrilla ranks, much less to their portion of society. Feminists commonly complained that guerrilla movements failed to develop a serious women's agenda and that gender issues were always subordinate to a class struggle. Sexism was something that would be addressed in the new society after the war was won, but even then, issues of survival always seemed to take precedence over gender equality.

COLOMBIA

The Fuerzas Armadas Revolucionarias de Colombia (FARC, Revolutionary Armed Forces of Colombia) was Latin America's oldest, largest, and longest-running guerrilla movement. For half a century, the FARC fought a long and bloody war against the Colombian government. Some combatants spent their entire adult lives within the guerrilla force. As the war dragged on, it increasingly relied on the drug trade to fund its struggle. In the face of high levels of U.S. support for the Colombian government, the guerrillas stood little chance of a military victory. Although at different times the FARC managed to control significant swaths of territory, its popularity declined. The FARC provides a cautionary tale of the negative consequences of engaging in a guerrilla struggle without end.

The FARC's origins lie in the 1950s when a monopoly on power between the conservatives and liberals resulted in the social, economic, and political exclusion of other organized political movements. On April 9, 1948, an assassin killed Colombian liberal leader and presidential candidate Jorge Eliécer Gaitán. His death triggered a massive protest colloquially known as the *bogotazo* that left thousands dead and injured and much of downtown Bogotá destroyed. That social explosion

Colombia

introduced a decade of violence (called "La Violencia") between liberals and conservatives for control of the countryside that left at least two hundred thousand people dead. That period of bloodletting ended with a power-sharing agreement between the two parties that shut out other political parties, particularly those on the left. The exclusionary nature of Colombian society created the objective conditions for a civil conflict.

With the end of the civil war, one of the guerrilla fighters, Pedro Antonio Marín, under the nom de guerre Manuel Tirofijo ("Sureshot") Marulanda, retreated to the community of Marquetalia, Tolima, with his supporters. Their goal was to create a society that would meet the needs and concerns of Colombia's rural population. Marulanda formed a self-defense group to protect their agrarian interests, which prompted the government to fear a Cuban-style guerrilla movement in what it dubbed the independent Republic of Marquetalia. In 1964, the Colombian army attacked the community. Marulanda escaped to the mountains along with forty-seven other guerrilla fighters. Survivors of that battle met with members of other communities and formed the Southern Bloc guerrilla group that called for land reform. Two years later, the Southern Bloc reestablished itself as the FARC. It became the military wing of the Partido Comunista de Colombia (PCC, Communist Party of Colombia) as it shifted to offensive tactics. In 1982, the FARC changed its name to the FARC-EP or Ejército del Pueblo ("People's Army"), although in common parlance it was always known simply as the FARC.

The FARC kidnapped politicians and wealthy individuals for ransom to pay for the costs of its guerrilla camps and the social services it provided to communities under its control. In the 1970s, the FARC began to tax drug traffickers. The new revenue stream allowed the guerrilla group to grow rapidly, even as the association with the drug trade began to erode the FARC's reputation as a political movement. Some recruits joined the insurgents for financial rather than ideological reasons, particularly when the FARC paid soldiers higher wages than the Colombian military. Wealthy landowners formed paramilitary groups with names such as Muerte a Secuestradores (MAS, Death to Kidnappers) and the Autodefensas Unidas de Colombia (AUC, United Self-Defense Forces of Colombia) in alliance with the Colombian military to fight back against the guerrillas. The conflict gained the characteristics of a civil war, although one in which combatants targeted the civilian supporters of their opponents rather than armed groups that had weapons with which to fight back.

In the 1980s, the FARC entered into peace talks with the Colombian government under president Belisario Betancur. In 1984, the two parties reached an agreement for a bilateral ceasefire that lasted for three years. As part of the agreement, the FARC together with the PCC founded a political party called the Union Patriótica (UP, Patriotic Union). The UP initially experienced much success and realized a strong showing in the 1986 elections. Right-wing paramilitary groups, drug cartels, and the Colombian military, however, killed thousands of its members and leaders, causing the party to disappear as an important political force.

The FARC grew in size to eighteen thousand soldiers. Almost half of its members were women, and they trained and fought alongside men and rose to positions of leadership. The FARC also gained high-profile foreign recruits, including the Dutch woman Tanja Nijmeijer (Alexandra Nariño), who climbed through the ranks to become an assistant to a senior commander. Having children within a mobile guerrilla force was very complicated, and in fact was forbidden in the FARC. Some have condemned the FARC for forcing pregnant women to undergo abortions and to work as sex slaves for guerrilla commanders. Human rights groups have also criticized the FARC for recruiting those under eighteen as child soldiers.

In 1997, the U.S. State Department added the FARC to its list of Foreign Terrorist Organizations. In 2000, U.S. president Bill Clinton initiated a $9 billion military aid program called Plan Colombia to combat the guerrillas and the drug trade. In

2002, the conservative politician Álvaro Uribe won the presidency and launched an aggressive campaign against the guerrillas. The military successes of his defense minister Juan Manuel Santos slowly led to its decline as a significant threat. The Colombian military gained access to U.S. technology that allowed it to smuggle tracking devices into FARC camps in order to target leaders for assassination. That development significantly undermined the FARC's ability to operate as a clandestine force. Enhanced surveillance techniques may have made traditional notions of guerrilla warfare a thing of the past.

In 2010, Uribe's defense minister Santos won the presidency and restarted the peace process with the FARC. Government and guerrilla negotiators gathered in Havana, Cuba, for discussions that stretched out for years. In 2016, the belligerents finally signed a five-point peace accord and agreed to a ceasefire. The agreement committed the Colombian government to investment in rural development and would allow the FARC to transform itself into a legal political party. In order to give the accord a higher degree of legitimacy, Santos brought it to a public referendum. Santos's predecessor Uribe campaigned fiercely against the referendum, which contributed to its defeat at the polls. The government and guerrillas returned to the negotiating table and quickly hammered out a revised agreement that was more acceptable to the broader public. Santos, meanwhile, won the Nobel Peace Prize for his efforts to bring the long conflict to an end.

As part of the peace agreement, the FARC established a political party it called the Fuerza Alternativa Revolucionaria del Común (Common Alternative Revolutionary Force), deliberately chosen to retain the same FARC acronym. The new party pledged to continue its fight against poverty and corruption and for agrarian reform. The peace accords automatically assured the FARC of ten seats in congress for the next decade, but the party performed very poorly in the electoral arena. A major problem was that after more than half a century of war, the name "FARC" had very negative connotations in many people's minds. In an attempt to address that problem, in 2021 the party renamed itself as simply Comunes (Commons). Meanwhile, in 2018, the right-wing politician Iván Duque won the presidency and returned the government to Uribe's hardline stance against the FARC. In 2019, a dissident FARC faction declared that the Colombian government had not complied with the peace agreement and announced its return to armed struggle. Right-wing paramilitary groups and state security forces had killed hundreds of demobilized guerrillas as the repression increased. It appeared highly unlikely that the peace initiative would be more successful than previous attempts were, and it seemed improbable that it could solve underlying structural issues that occasioned the exclusionary nature of Colombian society.

Other Guerrilla Movements

Several other guerrilla groups emerged alongside the FARC in Colombia. In 1964, students, Catholic radicals, and left-wing intellectuals formed the Ejército de Liberación Nacional (ELN, National Liberation Army), modeled after Guevara's guerrilla struggles. Its most famous member was the priest Camilo Torres Restrepo (1929–1966), a well-known, well-liked university professor who was attracted to liberation theology's radical ideas. Although Torres came from a privileged background, he was openly critical of social and economic inequality in Colombia. In 1965, he joined the ELN as a simple soldier rather than a commander, and he participated in common tasks such as kitchen and guard duty. Torres's first action in combat was an ambush of a military patrol that killed four soldiers. The army mounted a counterattack and killed Torres along with five of his comrades. The military buried the dead guerrillas in an unmarked grave. The former priest subsequently became highly regarded as an ELN martyr and, as with Che Guevara, a symbol of those who set aside their status to struggle for the rights of the oppressed and marginalized.

The ELN never grew as large as the FARC and mobilized about seven thousand fighters at the height of its operations. To fund itself, the ELN kidnapped wealthy Colombians and extorted funds from oil corporations and other businesses in what it called "war taxes." Along with the FARC, the United States listed the ELN as a Foreign Terrorist Organization. Occasionally the FARC and ELN attempted to collaborate, but just as often they competed for the allegiance of communities under their control. The ELN also entered into preliminary peace talks with the Santos administration, although they did not advance as quickly as those conducted with the FARC. Duque suspended the talks after his election in 2018 and demanded extradition of ten ELN leaders who were in Cuba for the negotiations. With the outbreak of the coronavirus pandemic in 2020, the ELN declared a unilateral ceasefire. At the same time, the Colombian military stepped up its attacks on the guerrilla force, placing it on its back foot. It appeared highly unlikely that the ELN would become a significant political force any time soon.

A Maoist offshoot of the PCC formed the Ejército Popular de Liberación (EPL, Popular Liberation Army) in 1967. It never gained the size or presence of the other guerrilla groups. The EPL demobilized in 1991 and formed the political party Esperanza, Paz y Libertad (Hope, Peace, and Freedom). As with the other groups, the EPL failed to gain significant traction as an electoral force.

The Movimiento 19 de Abril (M-19, 19th of April Movement) was a more moderate Colombian guerrilla movement than either the FARC or ELN was. It formed in the aftermath of the allegedly fraudulent April 19, 1970, presidential elections from which it took its name. That loss convinced the founders of the M-19 that it was impossible to gain power through the ballot box. The M-19 drew much of its support from radical students and urban movements. It employed a leftist populist and anti-imperialist discourse but, unlike many other guerrilla groups, not one that was explicitly Marxist.

The M-19 became renowned and gained popular support for its spectacular and highly symbolic urban guerrilla actions. In 1974, members stole one of independence leader Simón Bolívar's swords from a museum, and in 1980 they took fourteen ambassadors hostage in a raid on a Dominican Republic embassy cocktail party. In 1985, they held hundreds of lawyers and judges captive in a siege of the Palace of Justice. This plan, however, backfired when the Colombian army attacked the building and set it ablaze. In the process, the military killed the M-19 commandos and many of their hostages, including eleven supreme court justices. Government forces arrested and tortured many of the M-19 leaders and combatants, with some still missing and presumably dead. Those reversals led to the decline of the group, and it entered into peace negotiations. The demobilized guerrillas formed a political party but faced the same problem as the UP as drug cartels and right-wing death squads killed many of its members.

In 1984, Indigenous activists formed the Movimiento Armado Quintín Lame (MAQL, Quintín Lame Armed Movement) in Cauca, a part of Colombia with a large native population that suffers from unequal land distribution. The group was named after Manuel Quintín Lame Chantre (1880–1967), a leader from the early twentieth century who defended Indigenous rights. The MAQL fought to protect Indigenous communities from landowner and military attacks. It negotiated a demobilization agreement with the Colombian government in 1990, which included their participation in a constituent assembly the following year. As a political force, the MAQL achieved major concessions and the incorporation of Indigenous rights into the 1991 constitution.

In 1987, these five guerrilla groups (FARC, ELN, EPL, M-19, and MAQL) formed an umbrella organization known as the Coordinadora Guerrillera Simón Bolívar (CGSB, Simón Bolívar Guerrilla Coordinating Board). Similar to the M-19's theft of Bolívar's sword, the CGSB's use of the independence hero's name appealed to nationalist sentiments in an attempt to legitimize the guerrilla movement. Competing political ideologies and interests meant that the diverse guerrilla groups failed to merge their organizations as had happened in the Central American countries of Nicaragua, El Salvador, and Guatemala. A lack of unity in the face of a common enemy contributed to the failure of their revolutionary agenda.

Despite repeated attempts, Colombia has never had a strong electoral left. As can be seen with the UP and other initiatives, that was not for a lack of trying. Gustavo Petro (1960–) was one of the most successful. In the 1980s, he was a member of the M-19. When the guerrilla group demobilized, Petro won election to congress. In 2006, he won the second-largest vote in the country as part of the Polo Democrático Alternativo (PDA, Alternative Democratic Pole). In 2011, he was elected mayor of the capital city of Bogotá and performed very well in subsequent presidential contests, including reaching the second round in 2018. As of this writing, his growing popularity has positioned him as a frontrunner in the 2022 elections. Colombia is one of few Latin American countries that has never had a left-wing government, but that might change if Petro proves successful in his bid for the top office.

EL SALVADOR

In 1980, El Salvador appeared to be following Nicaragua on a path toward the triumph of an armed guerrilla uprising. A small oligarchy known as "the fourteen families" controlled most of the land, the entire banking system, and most of the country's industry. In contrast to their wealth, the majority of the country's inhabitants lived in deep poverty. This ruling class engaged in extreme political repression in order to retain their class privileges. The violence and injustice resulted in a civil war that stretched for twelve long years, from 1980 to 1992. After a bloody fight, however, the guerrillas were unable to take power through armed means. Instead, the process of struggle contributed to the creation of a very strong and highly politicized civil society.

Similar to Nicaragua, revolutionary movements in El Salvador had a strong base in liberation theology and grassroots, Christian-based communities. These religious communities engaged poor people in rural areas and urban barrios with a combined study of the Bible and an analysis of economic and social problems. Catholic priests emphasized social justice and the rights of the poor and oppressed. With rising social unrest, government and military officials organized death squads that terrorized the civilian population in order to maintain their class privileges. Repression of these communities led to further politicization and radicalization. Rutilio Grande (1928–1977), a Jesuit who worked in the community of Aguilares, was one of the first killed as the repressive violence increased dramatically in the late 1970s. In March 1977, a death squad murdered him, along with a teenager and a seventy-two-year-old peasant, while Grande was on his way to say mass.

El Salvador

The death of Rutilio Grande deeply influenced the recently appointed archbishop Monsignor Óscar Romero (1917–1980). The archbishop became increasingly vocal in his denunciations of human rights violations and in his calls for social justice. He appealed to President Jimmy Carter to suspend U.S. funding of the Salvadoran government because that aid was only being used to repress the civilian population. Instead, the United States continued to prop up the regime with more than $1 million of military spending a day. With repression on the rise, Romero slowly moved toward support of armed struggle as the only remaining viable option. When asked if he feared for his life, Romero declared, "If I am killed, I shall rise again in the struggle of the Salvadoran people." On March 24, 1980, under instructions from army major Roberto D'Aubuisson, a death squad assassinated Romero while he was celebrating mass. Given the traditional conservative alliance between wealthy landholders, military leaders, and the church's hierarchy, those in the oligarchy came to see Romero as a traitor to his class. At the same time, his martyrdom provided a powerful catalyst for popular struggles.

After Romero's death and with government-sanctioned violence on the rise, all peaceful paths to political changes seemed to be exhausted. In response, many members of civil society joined guerrilla armies. They built on a longer pattern of popular struggles. In 1970, communist party leader Salvador Cayetano Carpio, together with the educational union leader Mélida Anaya Montes and university professors Clara Elizabeth Ramírez and Felipe Peña Mendoza, founded the Fuerzas Populares de Liberación (FPL, Popular Liberation Forces) as a political-military organization. A second group, the Ejército Revolucionario del Pueblo (ERP, People's Revolutionary Army), emerged several years later and drew its support from disaffected youths. Under the leadership of Joaquín Villalobos, the ERP emphasized military action over political work. When internal disputes within the ERP resulted in the assassination of leading ideologue Roque Dalton in 1975, a breakaway faction formed the Fuerzas Armadas de la Resistencia Nacional (FARN, National Resistance Armed Forces). The FARN assumed a more moderate social democratic position than the previous two groups and was willing to collaborate with reformist elements in their opposition to the Salvadoran oligarchy.

Previously the Partido Comunista de El Salvador (PCS, Communist Party of El Salvador) had assumed an orthodox communist position of favoring peaceful political organizing over armed struggle, but in 1980 they agreed to join the FPL, ERP, FARN, and the Partido Revolucionario de los Trabajadores Centroamericanos (PRTC, Revolutionary Party of the Central American Workers) in coordinated military activities. The five leftist groups represented different ideologies and constituencies but came together in a unified Frente Farabundo Martí para la Liberación Nacional (FMLN, Farabundo Martí National Liberation Front). Much like the FSLN's namesake was the Nicaraguan patriot Augusto César Sandino, the FMLN took its name from the communist leader who had directed the failed 1932 uprising. The FMLN coordinated its activities with a broad opposition coalition called the Frente Democrático Revolucionario (FDR, Revolutionary Democratic Front). Under the leadership of Guillermo Ungo and Rubén Zamora, the FDR developed a political platform together with the FMLN that called for social and economic reforms to benefit the poor, a mixed economy, and a nonaligned foreign policy. They stopped short, however, of calling for socialism.

In January 1981, the FMLN launched a general offensive that tried but failed to overthrow the government. In response, the military increased its ferocious attacks on civilian communities. It pursued a policy of draining the ocean of civilians in order to exterminate the guerrilla "fish." In one attack, the elite U.S.-trained counter-insurgency Atlacatl Battalion killed almost one thousand civilians in the village of El Mozote. The massacres and intense levels of repression forced many people in rural communities into exile in refugee camps across the border in neighboring Honduras.

Many, including women, who sensed they had no good alternatives, joined the FMLN in large numbers. About 40 percent of the FMLN members were women, including 30 percent of the combatants and 20 percent of the military leaders. The first significant women's organization was the Asociación de Mujeres Progresistas de El Salvador (AMPES, Association of Progressive Women of El Salvador) that members of the PCS had founded in 1975. Other organizations followed, each associated with a leftist political party or movement. The largest and most noteworthy was the Asociación de Mujeres de El Salvador (AMES, Association of Women of El Salvador). Members of the FPL founded the AMES in 1978, and by 1985, it had grown to ten thousand members (see the document included with this chapter). These women's associations did not begin as explicitly feminist organizations, nor did they initially seek to advance gender-specific demands. Rather, they sought to build a broader, anti-oligarchic, anti-imperialist struggle. As was too often the case, addressing issues of racial discrimination and gendered oppression was something that male leaders relegated as something to be addressed after the triumph of the revolution. Even so, these organizations integrated women into the revolutionary struggle and in the process advanced women's equality as they broke down traditional sexual divisions of labor. Participating in the revolutionary process empowered women, facilitated the emergence of a feminist consciousness, and strengthened an incipient feminist movement.

Years of bloody warfare stretched across the 1980s and caused the deaths of tens of thousands of civilians. Government repression of those suspected of leftist sympathies destroyed existing organizational structures. During this entire time, the Salvadoran government continued to hold legislative and presidential elections that provided the regime with a veneer of legitimacy. Despite mass popular support for the FMLN, the guerrillas were never able to make the label of dictatorship stick to their opponents. That failure to define the narrative is part of the reason they were unable to overthrow the government militarily.

In November 1989, the FMLN launched a massive "final offensive" in another attempt to take power. As in 1981, this uprising also failed, and the military again took advantage of the battles to engage in a new wave of repression. Most notably, soldiers shot six Jesuit priests (Ignacio Ellacuría, Ignacio Martín-Baró, Amando

López Quintana, Juan Ramón Moreno Pardo, Joaquín López y López, and Segundo Montes Mozo) at the Central American University, together with their housekeeper Elba Ramos and her sixteen-year-old daughter Celina Ramos. The military considered the priests to be the FMLN's intellectual leaders. At first the military blamed the guerrillas for the murders, but evidence quickly emerged that once again the Atlacatl Battalion was the culprit. For decades afterward, religious activists commemorated the anniversary of that massacre with protests at the gates of Fort Benning, Georgia, where the U.S. Army trained military leaders from Latin America in torture techniques at its School of the Americas (SOA).

By 1992, after twelve years of war, with seventy-five thousand dead, and with right-wing death squads having "disappeared" an unknown number more, it became apparent that the FMLN could not win militarily. Nor could the Salvadoran government defeat the insurgents, even with endless U.S. aid. Out of this stalemate emerged a peace accord that brought the fighting to an end. But even in these negotiations, racial and gender issues were largely ignored. The FMLN transitioned from a guerrilla army to a political party and continued its struggle for social justice in the electoral realm. In 2009, the FMLN finally realized success with the election of the journalist Mauricio Funes (1959–) as president, defeating the right-wing Alianza Republicana Nacionalista (ARENA, Nationalist Republican Alliance) that had held power for the previous twenty years. While Funes had not previously been a militant activist in the FMLN, in 2014 his vice president and longtime leader of the FPL Salvador Sánchez Cerén (1944–) won the election. Even with the FMLN in office, gang warfare ravaged the country and resulted in homicide rates higher than those during the height of the civil war in the 1980s. Perhaps the FMLN's most significant legacy, however, was creating a highly politicized and aware civil society that continued to struggle against neoliberal economic policies and social exclusion through peaceful means.

After almost three decades in the electoral arena, the FMLN as a political force began to unravel and lost much of the presence it had gained as a guerrilla insurgency. In 2019, the populist business owner Nayib Bukele (1981–) won the presidential election as the candidate of the right-wing Gran Alianza por la Unidad Nacional (GANA, Grand Alliance for National Unity) party, easily defeating both Hugo Martínez of the FMLN to his left and Carlos Calleja of the ARENA to his right. Bukele was the first candidate to win the presidency since the end of the civil war who did not come from either of those two parties. His party also won a resounding majority in the legislature, gaining fifty-five of eighty-four seats and leaving the ARENA with fourteen deputies and the FMLN with only four. In office, Bukele governed in an authoritarian manner, which included removing judges he did not like and sending soldiers into congress to force passage of legislation in what opponents denounced as a self-coup. Even so, his autocratic response to problems of endemic gang violence gained him widespread support, and his popularity ratings soared to in excess of 80 percent.

Bukele had previously won election as mayor of Nuevo Cuscatlán in 2012 and of San Salvador in 2015 as part of the FMLN. As a millennial born after the start of the war, he was a fresh, young face that appeared to represent the future of the FMLN and of the country. In 2017, however, the FMLN expelled Bukele with accusations of promoting internal division within the party, including criticizing the current president Sánchez Cerén. Bukele responded that the FMLN had become corrupt and highlighted many problems with the party. Among these were charges of money laundering and illicit enrichment leveled against former president Funes, who had sought political asylum in Nicaragua rather than face the charges in El Salvador. Those accusations and Bukele's defection led to significant losses for the FMLN in both the 2018 local and legislative elections and the 2019 presidential race. For many former supporters, the FMLN had become just another political party incapable of solving the country's problems rather than a revolutionary force that would lead to a fundamental transformation of society. As a founding generation passed from the scene, an open question remained as to whether what was once one of the most powerful revolutionary movements in Latin America would be able to reinvent itself to face the challenges of the twenty-first century.

A common revolutionary slogan in the 1980s was "Nicaragua won, El Salvador is winning, and Guatemala will win." Popular movements in Guatemala, however, faced a much more genocidal war than those in the other Central American republics. As in Nicaragua and El Salvador, rural mobilizations strengthened in Guatemala in response to exclusionary political and economic conditions and with the encouragement of religious workers, progressive political parties, and labor unions. In 1982, a coalition of four guerrilla forces joined together as the Unidad Revolucionaria Nacional Guatemalteca (URNG, National Revolutionary Guatemalan Unity). Similar to the FMLN, the URNG did not call for socialism but for an end to government repression, equality for the Maya, agrarian reform, and social and economic policies that would meet basic human needs. The Guatemalan guerrillas attempted to replicate the success of the Sandinistas in Nicaragua and of the war the FMLN appeared to be winning in El Salvador. The URNG, however, never gained the strength of those other two groups. The Guatemalan military launched a counterinsurgency campaign that killed as many as a quarter million civilians. With their backs against a wall, in 1996, the guerrillas were forced to accept a peace agreement. The accords brought Central America's deadliest and longest-running civil war to a close, although it left exclusionary structures more entrenched than anywhere else in the region.

DOCUMENT: THE ASSOCIATION OF SALVADORAN WOMEN, "PARTICIPATION OF LATIN AMERICAN WOMEN IN SOCIAL AND POLITICAL ORGANIZATIONS," 1981

Revolutionary women in Latin America situated their struggle within a broader context of economic and political issues. What follows is the introduction to a longer paper that a representative of the AMES (the Association of Salvadoran

Women) presented at the First Latin American Research Seminar on Women, in San Jose, Costa Rica, in November 1981. The essay clearly articulates how the AMES understood the interaction between gendered oppression and class relationships as they theorized about the oppression of women under capitalism. The overthrow of capitalism was necessary but not enough to gain the full emancipation of women. The translation is by Bobbye Ortiz, and the entire document is available on the Monthly Review *website at* https://doi.org/10.14452/MR-034-02 -1982-06_2.

Traditionally the mode of development of the Latin American economies has been structured around the production of raw materials and oriented toward satisfying the demands of the foreign market and the interests of the bourgeoisie. Concomitant with this was high concentration of income, large foreign debt, inflation, and military dictatorship. Permanent economic, political, and social crisis is therefore characteristic of the great majority of the countries of the continent; and in its wake, poverty, super-exploitation, and repression.

Latin American women, who face double oppression, have not been exempt from this dramatic reality. Although the principal source of our subjection is capitalism, even before its advent feudal society had already assigned a subordinate role to women. The oppression of women is a suffocating cultural heritage, and, as Simone de Beauvoir has pointed out, "One is not born, but rather learns to be, a woman." We Latin American women have undoubtedly been learning: learning *not* to be accomplices of the myth of Cinderella, who waited for Prince Charming to free her from misery and convert her into the happy mother of numerous little princes; learning to take to the streets to fight for the elimination of poverty; learning to be active protagonists in the forging of our social destiny.

To be a member of the working class is not the same as being a member of the upper class; to be a North American or a European is not the same as being a Chilean or a Salvadoran. We are all, to some degree, exploited and we all carry the burden of our patriarchal heritage, but unquestionably our class interests transcend those of gender. What has a Domitila, a working-class woman of the Bolivian mines, to do with the wife of Abdul Gutiérrez, the bloody colonel of the Christian Democratic military junta of El Salvador? For women of the low-income sectors, joining the labor force is linked with a survival strategy similar to that of men of the same class and obeying the same necessities. However, for the women of the middle and higher strata, incorporation into production is determined by the number and age of their children, by their level of education, by the gap between the family wage and their consumer expectations.

There are also differences arising from the degree of development of a region, or from the pattern of urban and rural zones. Our struggle as Latin American women is different from that of women in developed countries. Like us, the latter play a fundamental role as reproducers of labor power and ideology, but *our* problematic arises fundamentally from the economic, political, and cultural exploitation of our people. Our struggle is, thus, not only for immediate demands; nor is it an individual one or against men. We seek the liberation of our countries from imperialism, dictatorship, and the local bourgeoisie—although we work simultaneously around the question of the specific condition of women and our oppression within the capitalist and patriarchal system.

While in the developed countries there is a struggle for contraception and abortion, in Latin America we must also fight against forced sterilization and certain birth-control projects which some governments have agreed to under pressure from the United States. For us women, it is not a question of demanding collective services such as day-care centers or laundries, but rather of demanding general community services such as water, light, housing, and health care.

For Latin American women "the double day" has another dimension which converts "wages for housework" into a remote goal; our short-term goals are related to employment and job opportunities, to the exploitation of the principal wage-earner, and the impossibility of survival with starvation wages. It makes no sense to struggle against the consumerism of one part of society if we are faced with poverty and the impossibility of consuming by the other part, which constitutes the majority of the people.

In sum we are fighting for a thoroughgoing change which will include women in the production process, which will free both women and men from exploitation and poverty. At the same time the search for solutions to the specific problems of women must not be neglected.

Source: The Association of Salvadoran Women, "Participation of Latin American Women in Social and Political Organizations: Reflections of Salvadoran Women," *Monthly Review* 34, no. 2 (June 1982): 11–13.

PERU

A Maoist wing of the Partido Comunista del Perú (PCP, Communist Party of Peru) known in common parlance as Sendero Luminoso (Shining Path) was the strongest and most violent of guerrilla movements in Latin America in the 1980s. The Shining Path emerged in the context of a military government that brought a series of failed guerrilla experiments in the 1960s to an end. In 1968, General Juan Velasco Alvarado (1910–1977) overthrew Fernando Belaunde's elected civilian government. At first the military coup appeared to be just another change in the occupant of the presidential palace, one who would leave existing social structures intact. Velasco quickly clarified that this was not his intent. He announced a plan to pursue a third path of national development that would be neither capitalist nor socialist in nature. Velasco's Revolutionary Government of the Armed Forces pursued a top-down approach that emphasized a radical program of nationalization of the means of production, promotion of worker participation in the ownership and management of industries, and an agrarian reform plan named after Tupac Amaru. After twelve years of military rule, the pace of Velasco's reforms slowed and even reversed. A 1978 constituent assembly extended citizenship rights for the first time to nonliterate Indigenous peoples, and a 1980 election returned Belaunde to office. Shining Path militants, however, were not interested in peaceful paths to power.

The Shining Path surfaced as one of a series of factions that emerged after the Sino-Soviet split in 1963, beginning with Patria Roja (PR, Red Homeland) and followed by Bandera Roja (BR, Red Flag). In 1970, Abimael Guzmán (1934–2021), a philosophy professor at the University of Huamanga in the highland city of Ayacucho, created yet another schism. He announced his intent to push forward "por el sendero luminoso de José Carlos Mariátegui," by the shining path of José Carlos Mariátegui, the founder of Latin American Marxist theory. Observers began to call Guzmán's group the Shining Path in order to distinguish it from other factions of the party, although militants did not identify as such—from their perspective they

Peru

were simply members of the one true PCP. Under the nom de guerre of Presidente Gonzalo, Guzmán presented his movement as the beacon of world revolution. He developed his own "Gonzalo thought" that positioned himself as the "fourth sword" of Marxism, after Marx, Lenin, and Mao.

Rather than joining leftist coalitions that participated in massive national strikes that pushed Peru toward a civilian government, the Shining Path decided at a 1979 Central Committee meeting to prepare for armed struggle. In 1980, as the rest of the country went to the polls to elect a new president, the Shining Path launched its "People's War" with symbolic actions such as hanging dogs from lampposts and blowing up electrical towers. The dogs represented the notion of the "running dogs of capitalism," meaning people who served the interests of exploitative capitalists. They gained popular support through their emphasis on popular justice and moral behavior, including holding "people's trials" that often ended in the execution of abusive property owners, police officers, and other unpopular figures. Much of their support came from rural students and schoolteachers, who found their social mobility blocked by racial prejudice and economic stagnation. At the height of its activities, the Shining Path had ten thousand to twelve thousand people under arms and could draw on the collaboration of a civilian base perhaps ten times that size.

The Shining Path had a special appeal to women, and many of its members and almost half of its party leaders were women. Often these women were more militant than their male counterparts. Stereotypes of cruel and savage Indigenous women who cannot be reasoned with—unlike their more rational (and moderate) husbands—and who pressed their more timid spouses into engaging in bloodbaths date back at least to the role that Micaela Bastidas played in the 1780–1781 Tupac Amaru revolt. These negative images, designed to denigrate women's involvement, obscure more than they reveal about their motivations and contributions. The party provided women with a protected space in which they knew they would not face humiliation or discrimination for being poor, Indigenous, and female. In exchange, they fought for a better world for future generations.

Even though women constituted a significant segment of the movement, the Shining Path imposed a top-down leadership style with a man of European descent—Abimael Guzmán—indisputably at the apex of the party. An authoritarian approach eliminated the divisive ideological and personal tendencies that had torn earlier guerrilla movements apart. A vertical hierarchy and carefully designed autonomous cell structure allowed for efficient actions and tight security that proved very difficult for the government to penetrate. The capture of one militant could only provide officials with very limited information, not intelligence that would lead to the apprehension of the movement's leaders and the unraveling of the organization. These strengths, however, were also its weaknesses. The Shining Path's rigid nature and failure to empower people at a grassroots level alienated potential supporters and ultimately limited its effectiveness.

Initially, the Shining Path gained sympathy both within Peru and internationally because of its idealism and advocacy for the rights of marginalized and impoverished rural communities. The Shining Path pursued a Maoist strategy of prolonged popular war that included laying siege to the cities from the countryside, eventually bringing its war to poor shantytowns on Lima's periphery. As the guerrilla army grew larger, its brutal tactics and dogmatic philosophy became more apparent. It committed what others would see as serious tactical mistakes, which included imposing control over agricultural harvests and commerce and placing young people—including women—in control over communities where, in a patriarchal society, male elders traditionally had assumed leadership roles. Militants executed violators of social norms rather than using lesser and what others might see as more appropriate punishments. The movement accepted no opposition to its policies and often treated other leftists more harshly than it did members of the oligarchy. It accused those engaged in social reforms of sustaining a fundamentally unjust system rather than discarding it in favor of something new and better.

One of the Shining Path's most noted victims was María Elena Moyano, an Afro-Peruvian community leader in Villa El Salvador on the outskirts of the capital city of Lima. She had organized community soup kitchens and was head of the neighborhood Vaso de Leche (Glass of Milk) program that offered breakfast to impoverished children. Moyano provided strong and independent leadership, and she called for an end to both Shining Path's violence and government repression. In 1992, the guerrillas blew up her body with dynamite in front of her family, not so much to eliminate a competitor as to intimidate and instill fear in those who might challenge the Shining Path's dominance.

The war killed an estimated seventy thousand people, most of them civilians, with a disproportionate number of Quechua-speaking rural and Indigenous victims. What was unusual was that the Shining Path was responsible for a large share of the deaths, while in most guerrilla wars, the military and right-wing paramilitary death squads committed the lion's share of the murders. According to a government-sponsored Truth and Reconciliation Commission report at the end of the war, Shining Path forces were responsible for 46 percent of the deaths, government forces 30 percent, and village self-defense militia or vigilante groups the rest. The war also displaced a quarter million peasants and resulted in $24 billion in property damage. It appeared that, militarily, the Shining Path could not take power and that the government was incapable of destroying the movement. Nevertheless, given the Shining Path's ruthless dedication to the pursuit of its ultimate goal, whether it took one generation or one hundred years, victory seemed eventually inevitable.

On September 12, 1992, the government captured Abimael Guzmán. The tightly centralized control over the party that had made the Shining Path so powerful now proved to be its undoing. Anonymous military tribunals with 97 percent conviction rates and other judicial abuses not only helped collapse the Shining Path's support structures but also resulted in the imprisonment of many innocent people. From jail, Guzmán called for an end to the armed struggle and negotiated a peace agreement with the government. The deadly violence had accomplished little, and Peru seemed no closer to a socialist revolution than before the war started. Latin America's most deadly guerrilla war had come to an end, but the underlying conditions of poverty and exclusion that had originally led to the insurgency remained unresolved.

After almost thirty years in prison, Guzmán died on September 11, 2021, from an infection at the age of eighty-six. A controversy emerged over what to do with his remains. His widow, the Shining Path leader Elena Iparraguirre, whom he had married while in prison, asked to cremate the body and keep the ashes. Authorities denied her request and instead disposed of his ashes in an undisclosed location. They wanted to avoid a grave site that could become a pilgrimage site for supporters. Even in death, Guzmán still instilled fear in his opponents.

A smaller Peruvian guerrilla group was the Movimiento Revolucionario Tupac Amaru (MRTA, Tupac Amaru Revolutionary Movement), that similarly fought to establish a socialist government in Peru. In 1995, the police arrested U.S. citizen Lori Berenson, accused her of collaborating with the MRTA, and sentenced her to twenty years in prison. In the MRTA's most famous action, in December 1996, fourteen guerrillas stormed the Japanese ambassador's residence in Lima. They held seventy-two people hostage for more than four months. In April 1997, the military attacked the residence, killing one of the hostages and all of the guerrillas. It was later revealed that the soldiers had summarily executed several of the guerrillas after they had surrendered. The government captured many of its other leaders, and the MRTA lost its strength. Although the MRTA followed a very different ideological and strategic path than the Shining Path did, it was no more successful in achieving its ultimate objectives.

BIOGRAPHY: AUGUSTA LA TORRE (COMRADE NORAH), 1946–1988

The Shining Path was best known for its founder and leader Abimael Guzmán, but it is also credited with providing significant political space to women. In fact, the numbers two and three in the organization's hierarchy were Augusta La Torre, who operated under her nom de guerre Comrade Norah, and her close friend and collaborator Elena Iparraguirre (Comrade Míriam) (1947–).

La Torre was born in the Huanta Valley in the Peruvian highlands to a prominent, landowning family who had a long history of involvement in radical politics. In fact, her father, Carlos La Torre, was a member of the local communist party. La Torre joined the PCP in 1962 when she was seventeen years old. In the early 1960s, the family relocated to the city of Ayacucho where Guzmán, who was a professor of philosophy at the local University of Huamanga, was a frequent houseguest. Two years later the two were married. In 1965, they traveled together to China to receive both theoretical and practical training on how to lead a revolution. Their relationship was as much political as it was personal.

While Guzmán was an intellectual, La Torre was much more of a militant leader and political organizer, and she urged him to put his theories into practice. La

Torre had the advantage of speaking Quechua and having intimate knowledge of the Andean landscape. She possessed the personality and charisma to mix freely with Andean peasants and the skills to mobilize them to action. La Torre personally led some of the first armed guerrilla assaults. If it were not for La Torre and her friend Iparraguirre, it is unlikely that the Shining Path faction of the PCP would have moved to armed struggle or engaged in such violence.

La Torre was a strong feminist who led women's groups in the communist party. The most significant was the Centro Femenino Popular (Popular Women's Center) that La Torre and Guzmán founded in Ayacucho in 1965. Both La Torre and Iparraguirre disdained liberal bourgeois feminism. Instead, they brought a Marxist class analysis to the role of women in society. It was largely thanks to La Torre and Iparraguirre's efforts that the Shining Path attracted so many women, both as leaders and to the rank and file. Almost half of the leaders at a party congress in 1988 were women whom La Torre and Iparraguirre had recruited. The large number of women in the movement together with its male leader led detractors to portray the guerrilla group as a sex cult. In reality, Guzmán took women's ideas seriously and claimed they made better guerrillas then men.

La Torre died, apparently by suicide, in 1988, though lurid speculations and conspiracy theories as to the exact circumstances of her death have run wild. The tabloid press published stories of a murderous love triangle involving Guzmán, La Torre, and Iparraguirre, although no evidence exists of such, and those with direct knowledge of the events have denied the rumors. After La Torre's death, Iparraguirre became the second-in-command of the Shining Path and later married Guzmán. She was arrested in Lima in 1992 and, along with Guzmán, sentenced to life imprisonment.

Abimael Guzmán at wake for Augusta La Torre, 1988
Source: Wikimedia Commons/Public Domain

As with Micaela Bastidas two centuries earlier, some opponents portrayed La Torre as a cruel communist mastermind who urged her more reserved husband to perpetrate a bloodbath. In contrast, some portray women like La Torre as victims led astray by powerful husbands. Neither narrative acknowledges the women's agency and active role in determining the outcome of historical events. When examined from the perspective of women leaders and participants, we gain a more complete and more accurate understanding of revolutionary movements.

DOCUMENT: POPULAR WOMEN'S MOVEMENT, "MARXISM, MARIÁTEGUI AND THE WOMEN'S MOVEMENT," 1975

A common but mistaken assumption is that Marxists are economic reductionists who are not interested in gender and racism. In reality, as the following excerpts from the Shining Path demonstrate, revolutionaries were fully engaged with these themes, but they appear differently when examined through a Marxist lens of class struggle. For this reason, the document proceeds to denounce liberal bourgeois feminism that only serves to divide a popular movement. It closes with a call to follow the path of Mariátegui to correct these problems. The Shining Path published its material under collective authorship (in this case the Movimiento Femenino Popular, the Popular Women's Movement), but the Peruvian researcher and feminist Catalina Adrianzen, who directed the party's work among women in Ayacucho, drafted this pamphlet together with Augusta La Torre and Elena Iparraguirre. Adrianzen was arrested in 1982, tortured, and exiled to Sweden. The entire document and the English translation from which this extract is taken is available on the Marxists Internet Archive at https://www.marxists.org/espanol /adrianzen/mmmf and https://www.marxists.org/subject/women/authors/adrian zen/1974.htm.

I. The Woman Question and Marxism

The woman question is an important question for the popular struggle and its importance is greater today because actions are intensifying which tend to mobilize women; a necessary and fruitful mobilization from the working-class viewpoint and in the service of the masses of the people, but which promoted by and for the benefit of the exploiting classes, acts as an element which divides and fetters the people's struggle.

In this new period of politicization of the masses of women in which we now evolve, with its base in a greater economic participation by women in the country, it is indispensable to pay serious attention to the woman question as regards study and research, political incorporation and consistent organizing work. A task which demands keeping in mind Mariátegui's thesis which teaches that: "WOMEN, LIKE MEN, ARE REACTIONARIES, CENTRISTS OR REVOLUTIONARIES, THEY CANNOT THEREFORE ALL FIGHT THE SAME BATTLE SIDE BY SIDE. IN TODAY'S HUMAN PANORAMA CLASS DIFFERENTIATES THE INDIVIDUAL MORE THAN SEX." That way, from the beginning, the need to understand the woman question scientifically doubtlessly demands that we start from the Marxist concept of the working class. . . .

3. Marxism and the emancipation of women

Marxism, the ideology of the working class, conceives the human being as a set of social relations that change as a function of the social process. Thus, Marxism is absolutely opposed to the thesis of "human nature" as an eternal, immutable reality outside the frame of social conditions; this thesis belongs to idealism and reaction. The Marxist position also implies the overcoming of mechanical materialism (of the old materialists, before Marx and Engels) who were incapable of understanding the historical social character of the human being as a transformer of reality, so irrationally it had to rely on metaphysical or spiritual conditions, such as the case of Feuerbach.

Just as Marxism considers the human being as a concrete reality historically generated by society, it does not accept the thesis of "feminine nature"—which is but a complement of the so-called "human nature" and therefore a reiteration that woman has an eternal and unchanging nature—either; aggravated, as we saw, because what idealism and reaction understand by "feminine nature" is a "deficient and inferior nature" compared to man.

For Marxism, women, as much as men, are but a set of social relations, historically adapted and changing as a function of the changes of society in its development process. Woman then is a social product, and her transformation demands the transformation of society.

When Marxism focuses on the woman question, therefore, it does so from a materialist and dialectical viewpoint, from a scientific conception which indeed allows a complete understanding. In the study, research and understanding of women and their condition, Marxism treats the woman question with respect to property, family and State, since throughout history the condition and historical place of women is intimately linked to those three factors.

An extraordinary example of concrete analysis of the woman question, from this viewpoint, is seen in *Origin of the Family, Private Property and the State*, by F. Engels, who, pointing to the substitution of mother right by father right as the start of the submission of women, wrote:

"Thus, the riches, as they went on increasing, on one hand provided man with a more important position than woman in the family, and on the other planted in him the idea of taking advantage of this importance to modify the established order of inheritance for the benefit of his children. . . . That revolution—one of the most profound humanity has known—had no need to touch even one of the living members of the gens. All its members could go on being what they had been up to then. It merely sufficed to say that in the future the descendants of the male line would remain in the gens, but those of the female line would leave it, going to the gens of their father. That way maternal affiliation and inheritance by mother right were abolished, replaced by masculine affiliation and inheritance by father right. We know nothing of how this revolution took place in the cultured peoples, since it took place in prehistoric times. . . . *The overthrowing of mother right was* THE GREAT HISTORIC DEFEAT OF THE FEMALE SEX THROUGHOUT THE WORLD. *Man also grabbed the reigns of the house; woman saw herself degraded, turned into a servant, into the slave of man's lasciviousness, in a mere instrument of reproduction.*" (Our emphasis.)

This paragraph by Engels sets the fundamental thesis of Marxism about the woman question: the condition of women is sustained in property relations, in the form of ownership exercised over the means of production and in the productive relations arising from them. This thesis of Marxism is extremely important because it establishes that the oppression attached to the female condition has as its roots the formation, appearance and development of the right to ownership over the means of production, and therefore that its emancipation is linked to the destruction of said right. It is indispensable, in order to have a Marxist understanding of the woman question, to start from this great thesis, and more than ever today when supposed revolutionaries and even self-proclaimed Marxists pretend to have feminine oppression arising not from the formation and appearance of private property but from the simple division of labor as a function of sex which had attributed less important chores to women than those of men, reducing her to the sphere of the home. This proposal, despite all the propaganda and efforts to present it as revolutionary, is but the substitution for the Marxist position on the emancipation of women, with bourgeois proposals which in essence are but variations of the supposed immutable "feminine nature."

Source: Movimiento Femenino Popular, *El marxismo, Mariátegui y el movimiento femenino*, 2d ed. (Lima: Editorial Pedagógica Asencios, 1975), 11, 18–21.

SUMMARY

The Cuban Revolution was a watershed event in twentieth-century Latin America, and for leftists it came to be seen as a normative manner by which to transform society. Examining the efforts of other revolutionaries who attempted but failed to emulate the Cuban example provides instructive counterexamples. Although revolutionaries found Che Guevara's foco theory of guerrilla warfare very compelling in the early 1960s, by the 1970s it had become largely discredited. Activists looked elsewhere for models on which to base their transformation of society.

Achieving change through a guerrilla struggle is a very difficult undertaking, as revolutionaries in Colombia, El Salvador, and Peru discovered. In each case, activists launched powerful insurgencies, but in each case their efforts devolved into lengthy and bloody civil wars. Profound ideological and strategic disagreements divided revolutionaries in Colombia and Peru, while their counterparts in El Salvador were more successful in unifying around a shared agenda. Peace agreements had a limited effect on solving underlying problems of exclusionary social structures. Most successful was El Salvador, where the guerrilla struggle resulted in a civilian population with a high level of political consciousness. Even that country, however, was plagued with gang warfare that killed more people than had died in combat during the 1980s. Achieving permanent and sustainable revolutionary transformations remained an elusive goal.

DISCUSSION QUESTIONS

What leads people to turn to violence to solve political problems?
To what extent is guerrilla warfare an inherently male undertaking?

Was the FARC's pursuit of state power through violent means for half a century an example of admirable determination or an abject failure?

Could the FMLN have won the presidency in El Salvador without engaging in a twelve-year-long civil war?

Why was the Shining Path more violent than other guerrilla groups?

FURTHER READING

The literature on guerrilla movements is extensive. Included here is a highly selective list largely focusing on ethnographic treatments of the 1980s guerrilla movements discussed in this chapter. Not included are theoretical works on guerrilla warfare and those that discuss an earlier wave of movements in the 1960s.

Anderson, Jon Lee. *Che Guevara: A Revolutionary Life*. New York: Grove Press, 1997. A comprehensive biography of the famous guerrilla leader.

Brittain, James J. *Revolutionary Social Change in Colombia: The Origin and Direction of the FARC-EP*. London: Pluto Press, 2010. A sympathetic overview of the Colombian guerrilla insurgency.

Danner, Mark. *The Massacre at El Mozote: A Parable of the Cold War*. New York: Vintage Books, 1994. Examination of a brutal 1981 massacre of a village by an elite Salvadoran military force.

Degregori, Carlos Iván. *How Difficult It Is to Be God: Shining Path's Politics of War in Peru, 1980–1999*. Madison: University of Wisconsin Press, 2012. Collection of essays from a leading Peruvian critic of the Shining Path.

Gavilán Sánchez, Lurgio. *When Rains Became Floods: A Child Soldier's Story*. Durham, NC: Duke University Press, 2015. A rare autobiography from a Shining Path soldier who later joined the Peruvian military and then studied to be an anthropologist.

Gorriti Ellenbogen, Gustavo. *The Shining Path: A History of the Millenarian War in Peru*. Chapel Hill: University of North Carolina Press, 1999. Journalistic account of the founding and early years of the Shining Path guerrilla insurgency.

Henríquez Consalvi, Carlos. *Broadcasting the Civil War in El Salvador: A Memoir of Guerrilla Radio*. Austin: University of Texas Press, 2010. Description from a journalist as to how he maintained a radio station for the guerrillas in El Salvador during the war.

Herrera Calderón, Fernando. *Twentieth Century Guerrilla Movements in Latin America: A Primary Source History*. New York: Routledge, 2021. Translated documents from a range of guerrilla groups, mostly from the 1960s through the 1980s.

Kampwirth, Karen. *Women and Guerrilla Movements: Nicaragua, El Salvador, Chiapas, Cuba*. University Park: Pennsylvania State University Press, 2002. Interviews with women in guerrilla movements.

Kruijt, Dirk, Eduardo Rey Tristán, and Alberto Martín Álvarez, eds. *Latin American Guerrilla Movements: Origins, Evolution, Outcomes*. New York: Routledge/Taylor & Francis Group, 2020. Collection of studies of guerrilla movements in different countries in Latin America from the late 1950s to the present by both expert academics and those personally involved in revolutionary activism.

La Serna, Miguel. *With Masses and Arms: Peru's Tupac Amaru Revolutionary Movement*. Chapel Hill: University of North Carolina Press, 2020. History of the smaller of two guerrilla movements in Peru in the 1980s.

Leech, Garry M. *The FARC: The Longest Insurgency*. Halifax, Canada: Fernwood, 2011. Journalistic overview of guerrilla insurgency in Colombia.

Marchesi, Aldo. *Latin America's Radical Left: Rebellion and Cold War in the Global 1960s*. Cambridge: Cambridge University Press, 2019. Transnational study of the militant left during the 1960s and 1970s, with a particular emphasis on Argentina, Chile, and Uruguay and some discussion of Brazil and Bolivia.

May, Rachel A., Alejandro Schneider, and Roberto González Arana. *Caribbean Revolutions: Cold War Armed Movements*. Cambridge: Cambridge University Press, 2018. A basic introduction to guerrilla movements in Guatemala, El Salvador, Nicaragua, Colombia, and Puerto Rico.

Starn, Orin, and Miguel La Serna. *The Shining Path: Love, Madness, and Revolution in the Andes*. New York: W. W. Norton & Company, 2019. Written for a popular audience from a perspective that is very critical of the Shining Path.

Stern, Steve J., ed. *Shining and Other Paths: War and Society in Peru, 1980–1995*. Durham, NC: Duke University Press, 1998. Edited collection of critical scholarship on the Shining Path.

Todd, Molly. *Beyond Displacement: Campesinos, Refugees, and Collective Action in the Salvadoran Civil War*. Madison: University of Wisconsin Press, 2010. Sympathetic study of human impact of the civil war in El Salvador.

————. *Long Journey to Justice: El Salvador, the United States, and Struggles against Empire*. Madison: University of Wisconsin Press, 2021. Fascinating study of transnational solidarity organizations.

Vásquez Perdomo, María Eugenia. *My Life as a Colombian Revolutionary: Reflections of a Former Guerrillera*. Philadelphia: Temple University Press, 2005. Autobiography of an M-19 guerrilla.

FILMS

Courage. 1998. Based on the life of community leader María Elena Moyano, whom the Shining Path executed in February 1992.

The Dancer Upstairs. 2002. Fictional portrayal of the capture of Shining Path leader Abimael Guzmán from the police perspective.

"Fire in the Mind." 1993. Part 9 of a ten-part PBS documentary, *Americas*, examining revolutions in El Salvador and Peru.

La Boca del Lobo. 1988. A study of a bloody encounter between the Peruvian Army and the Maoist Shining Path in Chuspi, a small, isolated village in the Andes.

Maria's Story: A Portrait of Love and Survival in El Salvador's Civil War. 1990. Documentary based on the life of Salvadoran guerrilla leader María Serrano.

1932 Scars of Memory. 2002. Documentary on 1932 peasant uprising in El Salvador that the military brutally repressed.

Plan Colombia: Cashing In on the Drug-War Failure. 2003. Documentary of U.S. involvement in the Colombian conflict.

Proof of Life. 2000. Fictional portrayal of a U.S. aid worker kidnapped by the FARC guerrillas in Colombia.

Romero. 1990. Moving depiction of assassination of Archbishop Óscar Romero in El Salvador.

Salvador. 1985. An Oliver Stone movie about the civil war in El Salvador through the eyes of a U.S. journalist.

Tupamaros. 1996. José "Pepe" Mujica and others of the Tupamaros recount their involvement in an urban guerrilla group and its transition to a legal political party.

Venezuela

9

Venezuela's Bolivarian Revolution, 1999–

KEY DATES

January 23, 1958	Popular uprising removes Colonel Marcos Pérez Jiménez from power
1958	Pact of Punto Fijo establishes power-sharing agreement between Democratic Action (AD) and the Independent Political Electoral Organization Committee (COPEI), the two main political parties
1976	President Carlos Andrés Pérez nationalizes the petroleum industry
1982	Hugo Chávez forms the Bolivarian Revolutionary Movement 200 (MBR-200)
February 27, 1989	Massive street protests known as the *caracazo,* against structural adjustment measures, occur
February 4, 1992	Chávez leads a military-civilian coup d'état against Carlos Andrés Pérez
1997	Chávez founds the Fifth Republic Movement (MVR)
December 6, 1998	Chávez elected president
December 15, 1999	Voters approve new constitution
July 30, 2000	Chávez reelected under new constitution
April 11, 2002	Failed coup against Chávez
December 2002	Employer strike at state oil company, Venezuela Petroleum (PDVSA)
August 15, 2004	Chávez handily wins recall referendum
January 30, 2005	Chávez declares the socialist nature of the Bolivarian Revolution

December 3, 2006	Chávez wins third term and forms the United Socialist Party of Venezuela (PSUV)
October 7, 2012	Chávez wins fourth term as president
March 5, 2013	Chávez dies and power passes to Nicolás Maduro
April 14, 2013	Maduro wins a special election to replace Chávez
March 9, 2015	President Barack Obama declares that Venezuela presents an unusual and extraordinary threat to the United States
January 23, 2019	United States names Juan Guaidó interim president of Venezuela
April 30, 2019	Guaidó attempts a military uprising that fails
May 3, 2020	In Operation Gideon, U.S.-backed mercenaries fail in their attempt to kidnap Maduro
September 2020	Arrest of CIA operative Matthew John Heath in Venezuela

By the end of the twentieth century, extreme socioeconomic polarization characterized Venezuelan society. Eighty percent of the population, overwhelmingly those of African and Indigenous descent, lived in poverty despite the fact that the country had one of the largest petroleum reserves in the world. Wealth and power were concentrated in the hands of the other 20 percent of the population, who were primarily of European heritage and worked in professional jobs related to the petroleum industry. It was in this context that Hugo Chávez (1954–2013) won election as president in 1998 on the promise of implementing policies that would shift resources toward the most disadvantaged sectors of society. In the process, Chávez introduced a new wave of revolutionary fervor that swept across Latin America.

Chávez's reforms in Venezuela engaged many of the same debates concerning revolutionary policies that flowed across Latin America throughout the twentieth century. After a failed 1992 coup, Chávez rejected armed struggle and turned toward electoral politics to gain power. After a 2002 coup temporarily removed him from office, a massive grassroots mobilization returned him to the presidency. Rather than contradictory or ironic, these competing strategies—armed struggle, electoral politics, and the general strike—indicate the presence of different and not necessarily opposing paths in a common struggle. Revolutionaries simply used the tactic that was the most appropriate at any given moment to achieve the desired goal of a fundamental transformation of society.

As with previous revolutionaries, Chávez was a charismatic leader who provided the inspiration that drove his movement. Similar to how Fidel Castro appealed to José Martí and Carlos Fonseca to Augusto César Sandino, Chávez embraced Latin American independence leader Simón Bolívar (1783–1830) as his symbolic nationalist hero. Even though Venezuela is primarily an urban country, Chávez emphasized the importance of, and drew support from, rural peasant and Indigenous peoples. His social programs brought education and healthcare to the working class and significantly raised their standard of living. Chávez not only learned the lessons of a century of revolutionary movements but also embodied a synthesis of their struggles and gains.

Chávez's social and economic policies to benefit the poor and marginalized, along with his fervent anti-imperialist rhetoric, led to strong opposition from both the U.S. government and a wealthy but now politically displaced domestic ruling class. Unlike Salvador Allende in Chile, Chávez weathered an April 11, 2002, right-wing coup attempt and consolidated his hold on power. Even so, Chávez and his successor Nicolás Maduro (1962–) faced unrelenting opposition, including sanctions that destroyed the economy and attacks intended to roll back revolutionary gains and restore the previous ruling class to power. Che Guevara contended that conservative reactions were an inevitable consequence of a class struggle and an indication that a true revolution was underway because otherwise a right-wing opposition would have no need to defend its economic interests. As Frederick Douglass noted, those in power never give up their privileges willingly. "Those who profess to favor freedom and yet deprecate agitation are men who want crops without plowing up the ground," he declared. The challenges that the Bolivarian Revolution in Venezuela encountered underscored the complex difficulties of attempting a fundamental transformation of society, particularly through peaceful and institutional means.

PETROLEUM ECONOMY

Christopher Columbus made his first landfall in South America in 1498 in what today is the country of Venezuela. Located in the northeastern part of the continent, its rich resources allowed disparate local populations to thrive based on hunting, gathering, and agricultural production. Venezuela's Indigenous communities lived in an environment of plenty and therefore never needed to create the large centralized empires of the high Andes or Mexico's central valley to provide for a population that placed pressure on the land's carrying capacity. Unable to tap into preexisting tribute systems, the Spanish made slow progress in colonizing the region and turned instead to Catholic missions to "civilize" the native population. Indigenous leaders such as Guaicaipuro (1530–1568) led resistance to European encroachments onto their lands. Because they faced difficulties in extracting labor from the local population, the Spanish colonizers brought people from Africa they had enslaved to work on their plantations.

In 1821, Bolívar led Venezuela to independence from Spain with the vision of unifying all of Latin America against foreign domination. Bolívar's dream failed, and Latin America fragmented into separate republics. Meanwhile, the descendants of the European colonizers continued to subjugate Indigenous and African descent peoples. The nineteenth-century peasant leader Ezequiel Zamora advocated a far-reaching land reform program to address their oppression but failed to dislodge the landowning aristocracy.

At the beginning of the twentieth century, the government of Juan Vicente Gómez (1908–1935) discovered oil in Venezuela and subsequently sought to develop the petroleum industry. Peasants flooded to urban areas to join in the oil boom, but most of the wealth flowed to trained professionals who worked in the oil industry or for foreign companies. Over time, the abandonment of agriculture led to a highly distorted economy. Landownership became extremely unbalanced, with 5 percent of the population owning three-quarters of the agricultural land. Much of that land was poorly used, forcing the country to import most of its food.

Rómulo Betancourt (1908–1981) came to power in 1945 in a military coup. He founded the Acción Democrática (AD, Democratic Action) party to lead the country on a path of nationalist, bourgeois development. Conservative military officers under the leadership of Colonel Marcos Pérez Jiménez (1914–2001) overthrew Betancourt in a coup in 1948. On January 23, 1958, a popular uprising removed Pérez Jiménez from power. The AD and a Social Christian party known as the Comité de Organización Política Electoral Independiente (COPEI, Independent Political Electoral Organization Committee) entered into a power-sharing agreement called the Pact of Punto Fijo. These two parties governed in favor of privileged groups and excluded the vast majority from participation in politics. Because of this pact—and unlike in most of Latin America—after Pérez Jiménez's removal in 1958, Venezuela did not return to military rule.

In 1960, about two-thirds of Venezuela's six million people lived in the countryside and worked in the agriculture sector. About 60 percent of those agricultural laborers toiled on large plantations, leaving them poor, landless, and unable to support themselves. U.S. development programs such as the Alliance for Progress favored capital-intensive, industrialized agricultural production that did little to provide peasants with education, training, or access to land. Rather than improving Venezuela's ability to feed itself, these schemes only deepened the country's economic dependence on foreign powers.

A second oil boom, in the 1970s, turned Venezuela, a cofounder of the Organization of the Petroleum Exporting Countries (OPEC), into one of the world's largest petroleum producers. The wealth, however, was not equally shared across society and instead increased economic and social inequity. The government ignored rural areas and dedicated its attention to urban and industrial sectors. In response, peasants continued to flood into urban areas in search of jobs and economic prosperity. With few other options, these internal migrants settled into "misery belts" that surrounded Venezuela's cities. Unemployment, a lack of utilities that included water and electricity, and high crime rates plagued these slums. At the end of the twentieth century, 87 percent of the country's twenty-five million people lived in cities. Not only did government policies leave the countryside underdeveloped but they also increased problems in urban areas.

A legacy of this history of unequal development was that most of the country's resources, population, and wealth were concentrated in large cities. The cities were overpopulated and the countryside was underpopulated, thus limiting Venezuela's potential for economic development and ability to feed itself. While Venezuela was one of the world's largest oil exporters, it imported about 70 percent of its food, even though it had plenty of rich agricultural land. It had the smallest agricultural sector in all of Latin America (6 percent of its gross domestic product [GDP]) and remained the only country in the region that was a net importer of agricultural products. In this distorted economy, the wealthy gained the most value from oil production while displaced peasants lacked work and went hungry because they no longer had land on which to practice subsistence agriculture.

In a commonly repeated trope, pundits now reflect back on this period as a time when Venezuela was the richest country in Latin America. That is true only in the sense that if Jeff Bezos or Elon Musk wandered into a college classroom, that class would suddenly be the richest one in the history of the world. Such an observation tells us nothing of how great wealth and resources are distributed or who benefits from that system.

1992 COUP

Hugo Chávez first burst onto the public scene in Venezuela after a failed February 4, 1992, military-civilian coup d'état against the elected government of Carlos Andrés Pérez (1922–2010). In 1976, during a previous term as president, Pérez had nationalized the oil industry. When he returned to office in 1989, Pérez implemented draconian International Monetary Fund (IMF) structural adjustment measures that curtailed social spending and removed price controls on consumer goods. These neoliberal policies designed to halt inflation disproportionately hurt poor people. An increase in bus fares and bread prices triggered massive street protests in the capital city of Caracas on February 27, 1989, known as the *caracazo*. Security forces killed hundreds of protesters in an attempt to put down the unrest.

Although Chávez did not play a role in those demonstrations, they set the stage for his eventual rise to power. The caracazo convinced him, along with a growing number of his fellow military officials, that Venezuela's political system was fundamentally corrupt. He blamed the Pact of Punto Fijo for excluding the vast majority of Venezuelans from participating in the political system. He believed that the military could force an end to the pact, which led to his coup attempt. After the power grab fell apart, Chávez made a brief appearance on national television to call on other rebels to lay down their arms to prevent unnecessary further bloodshed. His statement that they had failed "por ahora," or "for the moment," indicated that he would continue the struggle through other means. Taking a stand against corruption and the exclusionary rule of privileged groups made him a hero for Venezuela's impoverished masses who had not benefited from the country's petroleum-fueled economic growth.

Due to popular pressure, Chávez received a presidential pardon after spending only two years in prison. He continued his political struggle and in 1997 organized the Movimiento Quinta República (MVR, Fifth Republic Movement) to call for a refounding of the country based on progressive principles designed to benefit the country's excluded majority. Now, rather than engaging in military coups, the former military official entered the electoral realm.

BIOGRAPHY: HUGO RAFAEL CHÁVEZ FRÍAS, 1954–2013

Hugo Chávez with Latin American Indigenous and peasant leaders in October 2003
Source: Photo by Marc Becker

Venezuelan president Hugo Chávez was a contentious and polarizing figure. He was a charismatic and personalistic leader who appealed to those who felt as if they never before had had anyone in power who understood them, but his political ideology and working-class status alienated him from the traditional power brokers. To his opponents, Chávez's nationalist and populist rhetoric was seen as authoritarian demagoguery that harmed Venezuela's economic growth and threatened its political stability. For the poor, Indigenous, and Afro-Venezuelan underclass who formed his base of support, Chávez represented their best hope for remaking the world so that it responded to their needs.

Chávez was born on July 28, 1954, the child of provincial schoolteachers. He was a career military officer, one of the few avenues for social advancement available to common people in Latin America. In the military, Chávez had access to positions of power that otherwise would have been denied him because of his class and race background. Eventually he rose to the rank of lieutenant colonel. Chávez gained a political consciousness in the military barracks as he witnessed economic exploitation and racial discrimination. He was part of a tradition of military socialists in Latin America that dates to the 1930s and permeated working-class sectors of the military. Rather than operating in its traditional role as a ruling-class tool of oppression of marginalized communities, these low-ranking officers used the military as a mechanism to bring economic development to marginalized areas, even as they did so in a centralized and hierarchical fashion rather than empowering the grassroots to solve their own problems. In 1982, with both military and civilian co-conspirators, Chávez formed the Movimiento Bolivariano Revolucionaro 200 (MBR-200, Bolivarian Revolutionary Movement 200), so named for the bicentennial of the birth of Venezuelan independence hero Simón Bolívar the following year, to challenge the existing political system and open the way for social change.

Chávez always remained an outsider to the wealthy and powerful, European-oriented world of the capital city of Caracas. Unlike previous leaders in Venezuela and throughout Latin America who gravitated toward Europe and the United States, Chávez was proud of his Indigenous and African heritage. He claimed that one of his grandmothers was a Pumé Indian and that a great-grandfather was an agrarian revolutionary. During his 1998 presidential campaign, he signed a "historic commitment" to rule on behalf of the country's half a million Indigenous peoples. He kept that promise, and doing so earned him the undying support of that sector of the population. At the same time, those policies gained him the animosity of the traditional power brokers who bristled at the thought of an Indigenous or African Venezuela.

Chávez spoke directly to the country's population in a weekly, live call-in program, *Aló Presidente* (Hello, President). He broke from a centralized vision of the country and proclaimed his desire to rule on behalf of all Venezuelans. He traveled to rural communities and invited people to join him on TV. He proposed programs to bring government benefits to previously overlooked regions and sectors of the country. All of those factors made Chávez an extremely polarizing figure.

DOCUMENT: HUGO CHÁVEZ, WORLD SOCIAL FORUM, 2005

In a speech to the 2005 World Social Forum in Porto Alegre, Brazil, Hugo Chávez declares for the first time the socialist nature of the Bolivarian Revolution. Notably, he does not claim that the Bolivarian Revolution has all of the solutions but rather that social transformations are a matter of experimenting and learning from mistakes. He also underscores the inherent international context in which revolutions emerge.

Ignacio Ramonet, in his introduction, mentioned that I am a new kind of leader. I accept this, especially coming from a bright mind such as Ignacio's, but many old leaders inspire me.

Some very old like for example Jesus Christ, one of the greatest revolutionaries, anti-imperialist fighters in the history of the world, the true Christ, the Redemptor of the Poor.

Simón Bolívar, a guy who crisscrossed these lands, filling people with hope, and helping them become liberated.

Or that Argentine doctor, who crisscrossed our continent on a motorcycle, arriving in Central America to witness the gringo invasion of Guatemala in 1954, one of so many abuses that North American imperialism perpetrated on this continent.

Or that old guy with a beard, Fidel Castro, Abreu Lima, Artigas, San Martín, O'Higgins, Emiliano Zapata, Pancho Villa, Sandino, Morazán, Tupac Amaru, from all those old guys one draws inspiration.

Old guys that took up a commitment and now, from my heart, I understand them, because we have taken up a strong commitment. They have all returned.

One of these old guys, he was being ripped into pieces, pulled by horses from each arm and leg. Empires have always been brutal, there are no good or bad empires, they are all aberrant, brutal, perverse, no matter what they wear or how they speak. When he felt he was about to die, he shouted, "I die today but some day I'll return and I'll be millions." Atahualpa has returned and he is millions, Tupac Amaru has returned and he is millions, Bolívar has returned and he is millions, Sucre, Zapata, and here we are, they have returned with us. In this filled up Gigantinho Stadium.

I'm here because the World Social Forum is the most important political event in the world. I'm here because, with my comrades from the Venezuelan delegation, we have come to learn. In Venezuela what we are honestly doing is a test run and as every test run it needs to be monitored and improved; it is an experiment open to all the wonderful experiences happening in the world.

The World Social Forum, in these five years, has become a solid platform for debate, discussions, a solid, wide, varied, rich platform where the greater part of the excluded, those without a voice in the corridors of power, come here to express themselves and to raise their protests, here they come to sing, to say who they are, what they want, they come to recite their poems, their songs, their hope of finding consensus.

I don't feel like a president, being president is a mere circumstance. I'm fulfilling a role as many fulfill a role in any team. I'm only fulfilling a role, but I'm a peasant, I'm a soldier, I'm a man committed to this project of an alternative world that is better and possible, necessary to save the Earth. I am one more militant of the revolutionary cause.

I have been a Maoist since I entered military school, I read Che Guevara, I read Bolívar and his speeches and letters, becoming a Bolivarian Maoist, a mixture of all that. Mao says that it is imperative, for every revolutionary, to determine very clearly who are your friends and who are your enemies. In Latin America this is particularly important. I'm convinced that only through the path of revolution we will be able to come out of this historical conundrum in which we have been stuck for many centuries.

Today we also have the Missions, for example Barrio Adentro. It is a national crusade involving everybody, civilians, soldiers, old, young, communities, the national and local governments, grassroots community organizations, helped by Revolutionary Cuba. Today there are almost 25 thousand Cuban doctors and dentists living among the poorest, plus Venezuelan male and female nurses. The budget to pay the medicine, for which the people pay not one cent, to pay the doctors and the transportation systems, the communication systems, ambulatory center building, the equipment, all that, the majority of all these is paid for with income from the oil industry, money that before left the country. In 2004, the mission Barrio Adentro took care of 50 million patients, completely with free medicine.

Another example of the Venezuelan revolution, those kids are in the Bolivarian University, which is a year old. The majority of these kids were waiting for years to enter universities, but couldn't because they were privatized. That's the neoliberal, imperialist plan. The health system was privatized; that cannot be privatized because it's a fundamental human right. Health, education, water, energy, public services—they cannot be given to private capital that denies those rights to the people. That's the road to savagery. Capitalism is savagery.

Every day I'm more convinced, less capitalism and more socialism. I have no doubt that it is necessary to transcend capitalism, but I add, capitalism cannot be transcended from within. Capitalism needs to be transcended via socialism, with equality and justice, that's the path to transcend the capitalist power—true socialism, equality, and justice. I'm also convinced that it's possible to do it in democracy but watch it, what type of democracy not the one Mr. Superman wants to impose.

Although I admire Che Guevara very much, his thesis was not viable. His guerrilla unit, perhaps 100 men in a mountain, that may have been valid in Cuba, but the conditions elsewhere were different, and that's why Che died in Bolivia, a Quixotic figure. History showed that his thesis of one, two, three Vietnams did not work.

Today, the situation does not involve guerrilla cells, that can be surrounded by the Rangers or the Marines in a mountain, as they did to Che Guevara, they were only maybe 50 men against 500, now we are millions, how are they going to surround us. Careful, we might be the ones doing the surrounding . . . not yet, little by little.

Empires sometimes do not get surrounded, they rot from inside, and then they tumble down and get destroyed as the Roman Empire and every empire from Europe in the past centuries. Some day the rottenness that it carries inside will end up destroying the US Empire.

Goliath is not invincible. The empire is not invincible. Three years ago only Fidel and I, in those president's summits, other than us, it was like a neoliberal choir and one felt almost like an infiltrated agent, conspiring. Today almost nobody dares to defend the neoliberal model. So that is one of the weaknesses that undresses the empire. The ideological weaknesses are evident. Even the economic weaknesses are evident. And everything indicates that these weaknesses will increase. It's enough to see the internal repression in the U.S. The so-called PATRIOT Act is nothing more than a repressive law against North American citizens. They speak about freedom of expression, but they violate it every day.

So here we are in Latin America, it is not the same Latin America of even five years ago. I cannot, out of respect for you, comment on the internal situation of any other country. In Venezuela, particularly the first two years, many of my partisans criticized me, asking me to go faster, that we had to be more radical. I did not consider it to be the right moment because processes have stages. Compañeros, there are stages in the processes, there are rhythms that have to do with more than just the internal situation in every country, they have to do with the international situation. And even if some of you make noise, I will say it: I like Lula, I appreciate him, he is a good man, with a big heart, a brother, a compañero, and I'm sure that Lula and the people of Brazil, with Néstor Kirchner and the Argentine people, with Tabaré Vázquez and the Uruguayan people, we will open the path towards the dream of a United Latin America, different, possible.

A big hug, I love you all very much, a big hug to everybody, Many, many thanks.

Source: Hugo Chávez Frías, "Capitalism Is Savagery," *Z Magazine* (November 2006): 44–46, https://zcomm.org.

ELECTIONS

In December 1998, Chávez won Venezuela's presidential election with nearly 60 percent of the vote. The previously dominant political parties, AD and COPEI, had followed neoliberal economic policies that eliminated social spending as well as subsidies for foodstuffs, petroleum, and agriculture. These discredited policies harmed the country's poor and marginal populations. Chávez won largely based on the support of working-class people who had previously been excluded from the country's economic development.

Chávez took office on February 2, 1999, and immediately began to remake Venezuela's political landscape. He implemented policies that expanded social spending and halted privatization plans, although he never took steps away from the country's extreme dependency on petroleum exports. The president's failure to break from a monoculture export economy led some early observers to comment that Chávez's bark was worse than his bite—that his strident anti-neoliberal rhetoric was not reflected in his economic policies. Nevertheless, building on his support among the poor, Chávez proceeded to redraw the country's political structures. He drafted a new constitution to replace the one in force since 1961. The new constitution increased presidential power while at the same time implementing socioeconomic changes—including expanding access to education and healthcare. It strengthened civil rights for women, Indigenous peoples, and others marginalized under the old system. Symbolically, the constitution included gender-inclusive language. It also changed the name of the country from the "Republic of Venezuela" to the "Bolivarian Republic of Venezuela," pointing to an internationalist vision that built on Bolívar's pan–Latin Americanism.

The new constitution so fundamentally rewrote Venezuela's political structures that it required new congressional and presidential elections. Chávez handily won reelection in 2000 with about 60 percent of the vote, a margin of support that he consistently enjoyed. Despite earlier involvement in a military coup, Chávez was content to remake the face of Venezuela through the political process and relished the challenges of electoral campaigns.

International observer missions, including the Carter Center, declared Venezuela's voting system to be one of the most clean, transparent, and accurate in the world. Duplicate procedures to prevent fraud included electronic thumbprint identification machines and paper printouts of each vote. Former U.S. president Jimmy Carter acknowledged that the Venezuelan process was cleaner and more legitimate than the 2000 vote in the United States that awarded the presidency to George W. Bush even though he had lost the popular vote to Al Gore.

SOCIAL POLICIES

If the success of a revolution can be defined in terms of how it responds to the needs of the most marginalized members of society, the Bolivarian Revolution scores quite well. Although its undisputed leader Hugo Chávez emerged out of the ranks of the military and was accustomed to a hierarchical command structure, he strove to use that privilege to create spaces and empower those who had been disadvantaged under previous neoliberal regimes. The result was a profound transformation for women, Indigenous peoples, and others that previous administrations had relegated to the margins of society. The Bolivarian Revolution could not advance without them.

Venezuela has a small but diverse Indigenous population that primarily lives far from the capital city of Caracas on the country's border regions with Guyana, Brazil, and Colombia. They only number about 2 percent of Venezuela's twenty-eight million people and are divided into twenty-eight different groups. The largest is the Wayúu (also known as the Guajíra) with about two hundred thousand members in the state of Zulia on the Colombian border. In 1989, in the context of the caracazo protests, these diverse peoples formed the Consejo Nacional Indio de Venezuela

(CONIVE, Venezuelan National Indian Council) to protect their rights and sovereignty against the government's neoliberal policies. The election of Chávez a decade later provided them with an opportunity to realize significant gains in education, healthcare, and land rights, for which they had been struggling for years.

Many of the demands of Indigenous communities were codified into the 1999 constitution, which leaders from Indigenous communities and organizations helped draft. This included respect and preservation of their languages, cultures, identities, religions, and medicinal practices; recognition of their social, political, and economic organizations; and control over their own educational system. In particular, the constitution deemed land rights to be collective, inalienable, and nontransferable—a critical concession, given that historically Indigenous peoples had lost much of their territorial base through confiscation for nonpayment of debts, many of which surrounding white landholders had often unfairly and illegally imposed.

The constitution granted Indigenous peoples the right to political participation in the government, including representation in the National Assembly. With this provision, three longtime Indigenous activists (Nohelí Pocaterra, José Luis González, and Guillermo Guevara) were elected to congress, and other leaders assumed positions of authority. CONIVE president and future minister of Indigenous affairs Nicia Maldonado, a member of the Yekuana, from the Amazon, warmly welcomed these gains, proclaiming that never before had a previously marginalized population enjoyed such recognition and rights. These advances were the result of decades of Indigenous organization.

Similar to an expansion of Indigenous rights, the Bolivarian Revolution also established key legal and institutional guarantees for women in Venezuela. The government prioritized the active participation of women in political and economic projects, thereby placing the country at the vanguard of global struggles for gender equality. The government opened up spaces and empowered women, particularly those in marginalized and working-class communities, with programs in health, education, nutrition, day care, and other areas.

On taking power in 1999, the new government quickly promulgated legislation to protect the rights of women. A Law on Violence against Women and Families addressed issues of sexual harassment and domestic violence. In terms of agrarian legislation, women were able to qualify as heads of households, which provided them with access to land titles. The new constitution was the first in the world to recognize that women's domestic labors are work and therefore need to be recognized and compensated as such (see the document included with this chapter).

The Bolivarian Revolution encouraged the development of a variety of initiatives to advance women's concerns. One of the most significant was the Instituto Nacional de la Mujer (INAMUJER, National Institute for Women). INAMUJER aimed to fight for equal opportunity and equality before the law for all Venezuelan women. Its proposals included domestic-violence shelters for women and free legal services for women. Chávez was very supportive of those efforts, and the institute was so successful that even those who were otherwise opposed to his government benefited from and supported this project.

Women's political participation in government also increased dramatically; it included providing leadership in the National Assembly, the supreme court, and the National Electoral Council. Although still not equal to their numbers in society, the percentage of seats that women held in congress and in other electoral offices increased dramatically. On a local level, the government established communal councils to empower popular participation in their communities. Women often took the initiative in these neighborhood councils in order to identify and address their most pressing needs. This was part of a process to empower community members to make decisions that would affect them most on a local level.

BIOGRAPHY: NORA CASTAÑEDA, 1942–2015

Nora Castañeda
Source: Agencia Venezolana de Noticias (AVN)

Nora Castañeda was a Venezuelan economist who is best known for her work as president of the Banco de Desarrollo de la Mujer (Banmujer, Women's Development Bank). She headed it from its founding in 2001 until her death in 2015. Banmujer was the first government-backed financial institution of its kind to provide small, low-interest loans to women to assist them in the formation of cooperatives and other economic associations. The goal was to create employment and reduce poverty among women and to empower their participation in the economic and social transformations underway in the country. Women were disproportionately represented among those living in poverty, so the program was key to the creation of a more equal society. Millions of women benefited from the loans, training programs, and counseling services. Castañeda presented the bank as a way to create an economy that served the needs of humans rather than humans being at the service of the economy.

Castañeda was a lifelong political activist. She joined the Socialist League in the 1970s. In the late 1970s, she joined the Sandinista National Liberation Front (FSLN) in Nicaragua in its fight against the Somoza dictatorship. Back in Venezuela in the 1980s, she joining the working-class women's movement. She taught in the school of economics and social sciences at the Central University of Venezuela for more than thirty years. In the 1990s, she became an adviser to and ally of President Hugo Chávez.

Castañeda made significant contributions to the 1999 constituent assembly that drafted a progressive constitution that codified many rights for women. The government had invited people to submit proposals, and the women organized along with other groups to make their voices and concerns known. The result was a recognition of their demands, including equal rights for men and women and the granting of the right to social security to women homemakers. On a symbolic level, Castañeda insisted that the constitution include both male and female pronouns, the first to do so. For that reason, it became known as the nonsexist Magna Carta. Because of this organizational presence, the final document was one of the most progressive charters on gender issues in the Americas.

Castañeda brought a vision that included an analysis of gender, race, and class in her work, and was dedicated to advancing the needs of the most vulnerable and marginalized women in society. Her work with women represented a revolution within a revolution. At the same time, Castañeda acknowledged that it took a revolution to provide an opportunity for women to gain their social and economic recognition.

DOCUMENT: "CONSTITUTION OF THE BOLIVARIAN REPUBLIC OF VENEZUELA," 1999

The 1999 Venezuelan constitution was a very progressive document that codified many rights for the Venezuelan people. The section on social and family rights included here guarantees equal rights for men and women, an achievement that would be realized in the United States were the Equal Rights Amendment (ERA) to be passed. Nora Castañeda called Article 88 the most revolutionary article in the constitution because of how it valued women's work. This section then proceeds to protect the rights of workers, including guaranteeing the eight-hour workday, a minimum wage, and the right to organize unions, collectively bargain, and strike (not printed here).

Chapter V

Social and Family Rights

Article 75: The State shall protect families as a natural association in society, and as the fundamental space for the overall development of persons. Family relationships are based on equality of rights and duties, solidarity, common effort, mutual understanding and reciprocal respect among family members. The State guarantees protection to the mother, father or other person acting as head of a household. Children and adolescents have the right to live, be raised and develop in the bosom of their original family. When this is impossible or contrary to their best interests, they shall have the right to a substitute family, in accordance with law. Adoption has effects similar to those of parenthood, and is established in all cases for the benefit of the adoptee, in accordance with law. International adoption shall be subordinated to domestic adoption.

Article 76: Motherhood and fatherhood are fully protected, whatever the marital status of the mother or father. Couples have the right to decide freely and responsibly how many children they wish to conceive, and are entitled to access to the information and means necessary to guarantee the exercise of this right. The State guarantees overall assistance and protection for motherhood, in general, from the moment of conception, throughout pregnancy, delivery and the puerperal period, and guarantees full family planning services based on ethical and scientific values.

The father and mother have the shared and inescapable obligation of raising, train-ing, educating, maintaining and caring for their children, and the latter have the duty to provide care when the former are unable to do so by themselves. The necessary and proper measures to guarantee the enforceability of the obligation to provide alimony shall be established by law.

Article 77: Marriage, which is based on free consent and absolute equality of rights and obligations of the spouses, is protected. A stable de facto union between a man and a woman which meets the requirements established by law shall have the same effects as marriage.

Article 78: Children and adolescents are full legal persons and shall be protected by specialized courts, organs and legislation, which shall respect, guarantee and de-velop the contents of this Constitution, the law, the Convention on Children's Rights and any other international treaty that may have been executed and ratified by the Republic in this field. The State, families and society shall guarantee full protection as an absolute priority, taking into account their best interest in actions and deci-sions concerning them. The State shall promote their progressive incorporation into active citizenship, and shall create a national guidance system for the overall protec-tion of children and adolescents.

Article 79: Young people have the right and duty to be active participants in the development process. The State, with the joint participation of families and society, shall create opportunities to stimulate their productive transition into adult life, in-cluding in particular training for and access to their first employment, in accordance with law.

Article 80: The State shall guarantee senior citizens the full exercise of their rights and guarantees. The State, with the solidary participation of families and society, is obligated to respect their human dignity, autonomy and to guarantee them full care and social security benefits to improve and guarantee their quality of life. Pension and retirement benefits granted through the social security system shall not be less than the urban minimum salary. Senior citizens shall be guaranteed to have the right to a proper work, if they indicate a desire to work and are capable to.

Article 81: Any person with disability or special needs has the right to the full and autonomous exercise of his or her abilities and to its integration into the family and community. The State, with the solidary participation of families and society, guar-antees them respect for their human dignity, equality of opportunity and satisfac-tory working conditions, and shall promote their training, education and access to employment appropriate to their condition, in accordance with law. It is recognized that deaf persons have the right to express themselves and communicate through the Venezuelan sign language.

Article 82: Every person has the right to adequate, safe and comfortable, hygienic housing, with appropriate essential basic services, including a habitat such as to humanize family, neighborhood and community relations. The progressive meeting of this requirement is the shared responsibility of citizens and the State in all areas. The State shall give priority to families, and shall guarantee them, especially those with meager resources, the possibility of access to social policies and credit for the construction, purchase or enlargement of dwellings.

Article 83: Health is a fundamental social right and the responsibility of the State, which shall guarantee it as part of the right to life. The State shall promote and develop policies oriented toward improving the quality of life, common welfare and access to services. All persons have the right to protection of health, as well as the duty to participate actively in the furtherance and protection of the same, and to comply with such health and hygiene measures as may be established by law, and in accordance with international conventions and treaties signed and ratified by the Republic.

Article 84: In order to guarantee the right to health, the State creates, exercises guidance over and administers a national public health system that crosses sector boundaries, and is decentralized and participatory in nature, integrated with the social security system and governed by the principles of gratuity, universality, completeness, fairness, social integration and solidarity. The public health system gives priority to promoting health and preventing disease, guaranteeing prompt treatment and quality rehabilitation. Public health assets and services are the property of the State and shall not be privatized. The organized community has the right and duty to participate in the making of decisions concerning policy planning, implementation and control at public health institutions.

Article 85: Financing of the public health system is the responsibility of the State, which shall integrate the revenue resources, mandatory Social Security contributions and any other sources of financing provided for by law. The State guarantees a health budget such as to make possible the attainment of health policy objectives. In coordination with universities and research centers, a national professional and technical training policy and a national industry to produce healthcare supplies shall be promoted and developed. The State shall regulate both public and private health care institutions.

Article 86: All persons are entitled to Social Security as a nonprofit public service to guarantee health and protection in contingencies of maternity, fatherhood, illness, invalidity, catastrophic illness, disability, special needs, occupational risks, loss of employment, unemployment, old age, widowhood, loss of parents, housing, burdens deriving from family life, and any other social welfare circumstances. The State has the obligation and responsibility of ensuring the efficacy of this right, creating a universal and complete Social Security system, with joint, unitary, efficient and participatory financing from direct and indirect contributions. The lack of ability to contribute shall not be ground for excluding persons from protection by the system. Social Security financial resources shall not be used for other purposes. The mandatory assessments paid by employees to cover medical and health care services and other Social Security benefits shall be administered only for social purposes, under the guidance of the State. Any net remaining balances of capital allocated to health, education and Social Security shall be accumulated for distribution and contribution to those services. The Social Security system shall be ruled by a special organic law.

Article 87: All persons have the right and duty to work. The State guarantees the adoption of the necessary measures so that every person shall be able to obtain productive work providing him or her with a dignified and decorous living and guarantee him or her the full exercise of this right. It is an objective of the State to promote employment. Measures tending to guarantee the exercise of the labor rights of self-employed persons shall be adopted by law. Freedom to work shall be subject only to such restrictions as may be established by law. Every employer shall guarantee employees adequate safety, hygienic and environmental conditions on the job. The State shall adopt measures and create institutions such as to make it possible to control and promote these conditions.

Article 88: The State guarantees the equality and equitable treatment of men and women in the exercise of the right to work. The state recognizes work at home as an economic activity that creates added value and produces social welfare and wealth. Housewives are entitled to Social Security in accordance with law.

Source: "Constitution of the Bolivarian Republic of Venezuela," https://en.wikisource.org/wiki/Constitution_of_the_Bolivarian_Republic_of_Venezuela.

Missions

Following the consolidation of his power, Chávez proceeded to implement a series of social programs called "missions" designed to attack the endemic poverty that plagued a third of Venezuela's population. The government commonly named these programs after national heroes. One of the most successful was Plan Robinson, a literacy program named for Simón Rodríguez, Bolívar's mentor, who was nicknamed Robinson because of his fascination with the novel *Robinson Crusoe*. This mission employed the Cuban literacy campaign model that eradicated illiteracy from that island in 1961. Venezuela was the eighteenth country to use that program and successfully taught 1.2 million people who did not previously know how to read and write. Plan Ribas, named after independence hero José Félix Ribas, granted diplomas to 5 million high school dropouts. Other missions dispensed subsidized food to poor people, supported women's reproductive and family planning rights, recognized women's work as mothers and caretakers, and formalized social security payments for mothers.

In the first years of Chávez's administration, public spending on healthcare quadrupled. Venezuela led the world in numbers of plastic surgeons and beauty queens but lacked doctors who were willing to engage in general practice, particularly in poor urban and rural areas. In order to address this shortage, Barrio Adentro (Into the Neighborhood) brought Cuban doctors to impoverished communities that never before had received sufficient medical attention. The government also granted scholarships so that more Venezuelans could train to be doctors. The expansion of rural clinics and free emergency care led to a dramatic drop in the infant mortality rate. The Misión Milagro (Miracle Plan) extended this funding to eye care, providing the "miracle" of vision to people who could not previously see.

The new government struggled to address the failures of previous agrarian reform programs. In November 2001, Venezuela enacted a law to foster land and agricultural development. The legislation instituted a cap on the size of landholdings, imposed taxes on properties that were not in production, and distributed land to landless peasants. The main goals of this legislation were to address issues of social injustice and to increase agricultural production. On February 4, 2003, Chávez signed a presidential decree that launched Plan Zamora to speed up the process of agrarian reform. Named after the radical nineteenth-century peasant leader, this plan supported sustainable agricultural development based on a philosophy of a just distribution of land in accordance with values of equality and social justice. Plan Zamora was key to achieving the government's goals of food security, economic self-sufficiency, and ending dependence on imported goods.

Together with these social reforms were ideas of creating a new form of "participatory protagonist democracy" in which people could have a tangible voice in the political process. Mechanisms such as communal planning councils fostered citizen engagement. A goal was to replace a representative democracy that entrenched wealth and power in the hands of the ruling class with grassroots organizations that empowered local communities. Over the years, these structures took different forms, including Bolivarian Circles and Communal Councils.

Populism and Socialism

Chávez was often called a populist, which, in Latin America, has the negative connotations of the authoritarian and corporatist legacy of Getúlio Vargas in Brazil and Juan Perón in Argentina. In what is known as "talk left, walk right," such populists opportunistically appeal to the impoverished masses for support but implement policies designed to secure their hold on power rather than remake state structures with the goal of realizing social justice for the dispossessed. Chávez was sometimes called a "left populist" to indicate that he used rhetoric to appeal to the poor but also implemented concrete policies to shift wealth and power away from the ruling class. Detractors complained that he used skyrocketing petroleum prices to fund social programs to shore up his base, while supporters noted that these were precisely the policies on which he had campaigned. Chávez's potential for success offered much hope to his supporters while at the same time feeding apprehension among his opponents.

Initially Chávez denied that he intended to implement a socialist agenda in Venezuela. Instead, he emphasized a nationalistic "Bolivarian Revolution" that followed in Bolívar's footsteps. As Chávez consolidated power, however, he embraced a socialist discourse. At the World Social Forum in Porto Alegre, Brazil, in January 2005 (see the document included with this chapter), Chávez declared, "Every day I'm more revolutionary. It's the only path we can take to break down hierarchy and imperialism." He pointed to the failures of savage capitalism and argued that capitalism could only be transcended with socialism through democracy. It was his first public statement in favor of socialism. The following year the World Social Forum moved to Caracas, where Chávez presented an even stronger declaration. He proclaimed that the world faces two choices: socialism or death, "because capitalism is destroying life on earth." He consistently utilized religious language, calling Jesus Christ "one of the biggest anti-imperialist and revolutionary leaders in history" who contributed "to the socialist project of the twenty-first century in Latin America." In December 2006, after winning a third term in office, Chávez announced that all of the disparate political parties that had supported his candidacy would now join forces in one Partido Socialista Unido de Venezuela (PSUV, United Socialist Party of Venezuela). The PSUV subsequently became Venezuela's dominant political force.

Opposition

Everything from Chávez's African and Indigenous heritage and his working-class mannerisms and colloquial speech patterns to his social policies and economic priorities alienated him from Venezuela's small ruling-class minority that had long held political power. During his first term in office under the new constitution (2000–2006), Chávez faced three significant challenges and overcame each one. The first and most dramatic was an April 11, 2002, coup that removed Chávez from office for two days, but a wellspring of popular support from marginalized neighborhoods brought him back to power. A December 2002 employer strike in the state oil company Petróleos de Venezuela (PDVSA, Venezuela Petroleum) and other industries significantly damaged the economy but failed to undermine Chávez's popular support. Finally, after failing in these extraconstitutional efforts to remove Chávez, the ruling class turned to a provision in Chávez's own constitution that allowed for the recall of elected officials midway through their terms. Chávez handily won the vote on August 15, 2004, further strengthening his hold on power. These defeats discredited the entire opposition, including both traditional political parties AD and CO-PEI and newer ones such as Primero Justicia. Facing the prospects of a complete rout in the 2005 congressional elections, conservatives withdrew from the campaign and handed Chávez and his leftist allies complete control over the National Assembly.

The actions of a mobilized rural population threatened the privileged position of wealthy landholders who, in alliance with traditional political parties, exercised significant control in rural areas. Paramilitary groups operated with impunity and killed hundreds of peasant leaders. At the same time, low prices for agricultural commodities frustrated peasants' attempts to earn a living. These peasants wanted Chávez to do more and move faster to transform societal inequalities.

Internationally, the U.S. government denounced and undermined Chávez through a variety of avenues. The National Endowment for Democracy (NED) supported and funded opposition groups. Chávez accused the United States of plotting his assassination and stridently condemned U.S. imperialism and neoliberal economic policies. He signed commercial agreements with China, India, and other new markets in an attempt to break Venezuela's dependency on oil exports to the United States. Chávez presented the Alternativa Bolivariana para América Latina (ALBA, Bolivarian Alternative for Latin America) as a substitute to the U.S.-sponsored Free Trade Area of the Americas (FTAA). His demands to put people before profits gained him a good deal of international support as he challenged U.S. hegemonic control over the region.

Death and Legacy

After struggling with cancer for two years, Chávez died on March 5, 2013. Power passed to his vice president and anointed heir, Nicolás Maduro. Even in his death, observers disagreed on whether Chávez was a democrat dedicated to transforming Venezuela to benefit the poor or an archetypical autocrat bent on amassing personal power.

During fourteen years in office, Chávez's policies cut poverty in half and reduced extreme poverty by more than 70 percent. Income inequality fell from one of the highest to the lowest in the region. Unemployment was slashed in half, and the number of people eligible for public pensions tripled. Reversing a twenty-year decline before Chávez's presidency, per capita income grew by more than 2 percent annually, from 2004 to 2014. Investment in social missions improved the quality of life of the country's poor majority, vastly expanding access to healthcare, education, and housing. Chávez's policies also significantly increased citizen participation in politics.

Despite these economic gains, Venezuela faced significant problems at the end of Chávez's life. Homicides quintupled during his time in office, reaching one of the highest murder rates in the world. Corruption, waste, and incompetence among government officials continued to be major problems. The country also faced high inflation rates that undermined the significant increases in wages and social services. Further complicating the economic situation, a slump in oil prices in 2014 dried up a revenue stream that funded government subsidies and social programs. Critics blamed the problems on the economic mismanagement of Chávez's successor Maduro, including his maintenance of multiple foreign-currency exchange rates that encouraged the smuggling of subsidized goods at a cost to the country's poor and marginalized populations. Supporters retorted that opponents were guilty of sabotaging the economy. Government backers condemned repeated U.S. attacks on the country, and pointed to the inherent difficulties of building a socialist economy in a country still dominated by a capitalist mode of production.

JUAN GUAIDÓ

On January 23, 2019, Juan Guaidó (1983–)—a little-known back-bench legislator for the far-right Voluntad Popular (VP, Popular Will) party and current head of the congress—declared himself "interim president" of Venezuela with the vocal support of the U.S. government. He made that claim based on Article 233 of the Venezuelan constitution, even though none of its six conditions applied to the situation that the country faced. President Nicolás Maduro had not died, resigned, or abandoned his position, nor had the supreme court removed him from office, nor had he been recalled by a popular vote. As part of an agreement with a coalition of right-wing parties, Guaidó had only recently assumed the head of the legislative assembly for a year. Not only did that position not put him next in line to the presidency were that position to became vacant—that would be vice president Delcy Rodríguez—but an interim president must call elections within thirty days, and that is something Guaidó did not do.

Luis Almagro, the secretary general of the Organization of American States (OAS), promoted U.S.-backed regime change operations. Following a longer pattern that the OAS had played in Latin America of supporting the coup in Guatemala in 1954 and opposing Cuba after its revolution, Almagro claimed that the elections that had brought Maduro were fraudulent, though he provided no evidence to back up that assertion. Along with the U.S. government, Almagro declared the elected sitting government to be illegitimate and insisted on recognizing Guaidó as president. Both the U.S. government and the OAS continued to do so even after his one-year term as head of the assembly had ended, and then a year later after his constitutionally mandated term in congress expired. Any claims to the presidency that Guaidó might have made, as tenuous as they were, had evaporated, but that made no difference to those who wished to overthrow a left-wing government by any means necessary.

Guaidó was part of a fractured right-wing opposition that had won congressional elections in 2015, and for first time since Chávez had come to power, conservatives controlled the assembly. Nevertheless, the Supreme Tribunal of Justice had found the body to be in judicial contempt because it had sworn in three deputies who were suspended because of voting irregularities in their districts. This created a constitutional logjam that Maduro sought to resolve by calling for elections for a constituent assembly. For the next several years, the two assemblies operated in parallel with each other. Meanwhile, right-wing opposition parties participated in the 2017 gubernatorial elections but boycotted the 2018 presidential election (that Maduro won) and the 2020 legislative elections (that the PSUV carried). Evidently, the opposition boycotted elections it thought it would lose and was only willing to compete in those it hoped to win, even though all of the elections were run in the same way and by the same rules. Once again, the mentality in play was, "The only free and fair elections are the ones we win; otherwise, they are fraudulent." Largely left unstated was the reality that the conservative opposition had become deeply unpopular and no longer was competitive electorally.

Guaidó's claim to the presidency was part of a U.S.-backed maximum-pressure campaign for regime change that empowered an extremist faction of the country's opposition while simultaneously destroying the economy with sanctions. This included coercing the Maduro government in every way possible, including with threats of war, in the hopes of driving ordinary citizens to despair so they or the military would rise up and set up a parallel government ready to step in after a coup. These efforts predated Guaidó's appearance on the public scene. On March 9, 2015, President Barack Obama preposterously declared a national emergency, claiming that Venezuela presented an "unusual and extraordinary threat" to the national security of the United States. Once Donald Trump took the reins of power, he only upped the ante by putting a military option on the table and sanctioning PDVSA. These campaigns to overthrow the Venezuelan government violated international law, including the United Nations charter and other treaties to which the United States is a signatory.

Over the course of the next several years, Guaidó and his U.S. backers continued their campaign to force Maduro from office through extraconstitutional means. On April 30, 2019, Guaidó attempted a military uprising that quickly collapsed when few soldiers joined him. A year later, on May 3, 2020, mercenaries attempted to sneak into the country to kidnap Maduro. Again, the Venezuela military quickly put down the putsch, killing eight people and capturing and imprisoning others in the process. A U.S. citizen named Jordan Goudreau had orchestrated and Guaidó had authorized this Operation Gideon in what was widely derided as the "Bay of Piglets" (see the document included with this chapter). Similar to the U.S.-backed invasion of Cuba almost sixty years earlier, the perpetrators had fundamentally underestimated the willingness of people to rise up against a revolutionary government that ruled in their interests.

In September 2020, the Venezuelan government arrested a former U.S. marine and likely CIA operative, Matthew John Heath, for spying and planning to sabotage oil refineries and electrical services. For this failed attempt to overthrow the government, Heath was charged with terrorism, trafficking illegal weapons, and conspiracy. As with Cuba, it appeared that the attacks on the Bolivarian Revolution would never cease.

Meanwhile, the U.S. government continued with its punishing sanctions that halted the ability of the Venezuelan economy to function. The left-leaning Center for Economic and Policy Research (CEPR) contended that these sanctions fit the definition of collective punishment of the civilian population as outlawed by both the Geneva and Hague international conventions. Estimates ranged as high as one hundred thousand people dead as a result of the sanctions. Experts debated how much the problems in Venezuela were due to the shortcomings of the Maduro administration and what difficulties were a result of economic warfare. Even faced with all of these challenges, Guaidó's popularity fell to around 10 percent, and a deeply divided opposition failed to unify around a strategy to remove Maduro from office. Venezuela was trapped in a deeply polarized situation without any easy exit.

DOCUMENT: "GENERAL SERVICES AGREEMENT BETWEEN THE VENEZUELAN OPPOSITION AND SILVERCORP," 2019

In a desperate attempt to seize power in Venezuela, opposition leader Juan Guaidó signed the following agreement with a paramilitary group in the United States. What is notable about the agreement is both its transactional and business nature. The financial interests at play are stated up front: Silvercorp CEO Jordan Goudreau hopes to be paid when Guaidó gains control over Venezuela's rich petroleum deposits. The document reads as if it were a Terms of Service (TOS) agreement for use of something like a computer app, which on the surface obscures the very serious issues at play. A lengthy attachment (not included here, but available on the Washington Post *website (https://www.washingtonpost.com /context/read-the-attachments-to-the-general-services-agreement-between-the -venezuelan-opposition-and-silvercorp/e67f401f-8730-4f66-af53-6a9549b88f94) dives into much more detail as to the specifics of the planned operation to kidnap Maduro and install Guaidó as president. When it was clear that the operation would fail, Guaidó attempted to back out, while Goudreau insisted on still being paid. Goudreau proceeded with what proved to be a foolhardy endeavor. The original spelling and errors are preserved in this transcription of the document.*

GENERAL SERVICES AGREEMENT
Entered Into This: 16th day of October 2019

This GENERAL SERVICES AGREEMENT (hereinafter "Agreement") is made this 16th day of October, 2019, by and between LA REPUBLICA BOLIVARIANA DE VENEZUELA (hereinafter "Administration") Juan Gerardo Guiado, acting President, and any successor administration(s) or duly elected Venezuelan government(s) and SILVERCORP USA, Inc. (EIN 30-1039889) of Melbourne, Florida (hereinafter "Service Provider").

I. BACKGROUND & CIRCUMSTANCES OF AGREEMENT

The Administration, by the authority set forth in The Resolution of the National Assembly of Venezuela (23 January 2019) considering articles 233, 333, and 350 of the Bolivarian Republic Constitution, engages the Service Provider for the services set forth in this Agreement. The Administration is of the opinion that the Service Provider has the necessary qualifications, experience and abilities to provide services to the Administration. The Service Provider is capable to provide and execute the services, and agreeable to provide services to the Administration on the terms and conditions set out in this Agreement. All Attachments in this agreement are reserved.

II. SERVICES TO PROVIDE

The Administration hereby agrees to engage the Service Provider to provide the Administration with services (hereinafter "Services") consisting of, but not limited to: strategic planning/advising; project leadership; equipment procurement; hiring of personnel; logistics consultation; project execution advisement.

The Services will also include any other tasks that the parties may agree on during the term of the Agreement. The Service Provider hereby agrees to provide those tasks to the Administration during the term of this Agreement. Such Services, and other tasks shall be set forth in Attachments to be mutually agreed to by the parties and by the parties into this Agreement. The attachments are considered part of the General Services Agreement and are legally bound to this agreement. The Parties agree to do everything necessary to ensure that the terms of this Agreement take effect.

III. TERM OF AGREEMENT & FEES

The term of this Agreement (the "Term") will begin on the date this Agreement is executed by the parties and will remain in full force and effect indefinitely until terminated as provided for in this Agreement. Service Provider and Administration agree the minimum duration of this agreement is 495 days. See Attachment A- Timing and Length of Agreement. Except as otherwise provided for in this Agreement, the obligations of the Administration and Service Provider will end upon the termination of this Agreement. Administration agrees to pay Service Provider the minimum amount of money required to fulfill this agreement which is $212,900,000.00 USD over the course of the Term. The amount of money needed to fulfill the first part of Service Provider services is $50,000,000.00 USD. All money will be backed/secured with Venezuelan barrels of oil. All monies in this agreement are in USD. Administration agrees to pay any loan within 1 year. Service Provider will secure a loan for at least first part of services.

IV. CONFIDENTIALITY

The parties enter this Agreement and anticipate that disclosure of certain information by the Administration to the Service Provider will be central to the relationship. The parties desire to maintain the confidentiality of such information. This information (hereinafter referred to as "Confidential Information") may include, but is not limited to any data or information relating to the Administration which would reasonably be considered to be proprietary to the Administration including, government information and records where the release of that Confidential Information could reasonably be expected to cause harm to the Administration or citizens of Venezuela.

The Service Provider agrees that they will not disclose, divulge, reveal, report or use, for any purpose, any Confidential Information which the Service Provider has obtained, except as authorized by the Administration. This obligation will survive indefinitely upon termination of this Agreement. All written and oral information and material disclosed or provided by the Administration to the Service Provider under this Agreement is Confidential Information regardless of whether it was provided before or after the date of this Agreement or how it was provided to the Service Provider. The Service Provider shall take all measures reasonably necessary to protect the Confidential Information received from the Administration, at least as great as the measures it takes to protect its own confidential information. The Service Provider shall further assure that Confidential Information received from the Administration shall be separated from other Service Provider information in order to prevent commingling.

The Service Provider shall use the Confidential Information solely for the purpose of evaluating serviced for the Administration, and performing services for the Administration. In no way shall the Service Provider use the Confidential Information to the detriment of the Administration.

Nothing in this Agreement is intended to grant or imply any rights, by license or otherwise, to the Service Provider under any copyright, trade or intellectual property right. Nor shall this Agreement grant or imply to the Service Provider any rights in the Administration's Confidential Information.

The Service Provider agrees to indemnify the Administration against any and all losses, damages, claims, expenses, and attorneys' fees incurred or suffered by the Administration as result of a breach of confidentiality.

The Service Provider shall return to the Administration any and all records, notes, and other written, printed or other tangible materials in their possession pertaining to the Confidential Information immediately upon request by the Administration. Upon termination of this Agreement, the Service Provider shall promptly: a) deliver to the Administration all tangible documents and materials containing, reflecting, incorporating, or based upon confidential information; b) permanently erase all confidential information from its computer database(s); and, c) certify in writing to the Administration that it has complied with the requirements of this section.

The Service Provider understands and acknowledges that any disclosure or misappropriation of Confidential Information in violation of this Agreement may cause the Administration irreparable harm, the amount of which may be difficult to ascertain, and therefore agrees that the Administration shall have the right to apply to a court of competent jurisdiction for specific performance and/or restraining order.

V. RELATIONSHIP & REPRESENTATIONS OF THE PARTIES

In providing the Services under this Agreement it is expressly agreed that the Service Provider is acting as an independent contractor and not as an employee. The Service Provider and the Administration acknowledge that this Agreement does not create a partnership or joint venture between them, and is exclusively a contract for service. Attachment B Rules of Service Provider Engagement.

VI. NOTICE & DISPUTE RESOLUTION

All notices, requests, demands or other communications required or permitted by the terms of this Agreement will be given in writing and delivered to the Parties of this Agreement.

In the event a dispute arises out of or in connection with this Agreement, the Parties will attempt to resolve the dispute through good-faith consultation. If the dispute is not resolved within a reasonable period then any or all outstanding issues may be submitted to mediation in accordance with any statutory rules of mediation. If mediation is unavailable, or is not successful in resolving the entire dispute, any outstanding issues will be submitted to final and binding arbitration in accordance with the laws of State of Florida of the United States of America. The arbitrator's award will be final, and judgment may be entered upon it by any court having jurisdiction within the State of Florida.

VII. MODIFICATION OF AGREEMENT

Any amendment or modification of this Agreement or additional obligation by either party in connection with this Agreement will only be binding if evidenced in writing signed by each party or an authorized representative of each party.

IX. TIME OF THE ESSENCE

Time is of the essence in this Agreement. No extension or variation of this Agreement will operate as a waiver of any provision, term or condition as set forth in this Agreement.

X. ASSIGNMENT OF OBLIGATIONS

The Service Provider will not voluntarily or by operation of law assign or otherwise transfer its obligations under this Agreement without the prior written consent of the Administration.

XI. CANCELLATION FOR CONVENIENCE

Administration may not at any time and for no reason terminate Service Provider's services and work at Administration's convenience. Service Provider may not terminate services and work at Service Provider's convenience. If Service Provider terminates agreement he forgoes all pay, compensation and expenses. Furthermore, Service Provider must pay back all money that was transferred with the exception of the initial retainer. If Administration terminates agreement, Administration will be responsible for all payments currently owed, all future payments defined in the Term of this agreement and three more months of payments on top of the agreed upon contract duration.

XII. GOVERNING LAW

It is the intention of the Parties to this Agreement that this Agreement and the performance under this Agreement, and all suits and special proceedings under this Agreement be construed in accordance with and governed, to the exclusion of the law of any other forum, by the laws of the State Florida of the United States of America, without regard to the jurisdiction in which any action or special proceeding may be instituted.

XIII. MISCELLANEOUS

a) None of the provisions of this Agreement shall be deemed to have been waived by any act, omission, or acquiescence on the part of the Administration or the Service Provider without a written instrument signed by the parties.

b) Waiver by either Party of a breach, default, delay or omission of any of the provisions of this Agreement by the other Party will not be construed as a waiver of any subsequent breach of the same or other provisions.

c) The Headings in the Agreement are inserted for the convenience of the Parties only and are not to be considered when interpreting this Agreement.

d) This Agreement can be changed at any time by written mutual consent hereto by the parties.

e) This Agreement, along with any attachments, encompasses the entire Agreement, and supersedes any and all previously written or oral understandings and agreements between the parties, respecting the subject matter hereof. The parties hereby acknowledge and represent, by affixing their hands and seals hereto, that said parties have not relied on any representation, assertion, guarantee, warranty, collateral contract or other assurance, except those set out in this Agreement, made by or on behalf of any other party or any other person or entity whatsoever, prior to the execution of this Agreement. The parties hereby waive all rights and remedies, at law or in equity, arising or which may arise as the result of a party's reliance on such representation, assertion, guarantee, warranty, collateral contract or other assurance, provided that nothing herein contained shall be construed as a restriction or limitation of said party's right to remedies associated with the gross negligence, willful misconduct or fraud of any person or party taking place prior to, or contemporaneously with, the execution of this Agreement.

f) The provisions of this agreement are severable. If any provisions of this Agreement shall be held to be invalid or unenforceable for any reason, the remaining provisions shall continue to be valid and enforceable.

THEREFORE, in consideration of the matters described above and of the mutual benefits and obligations set forth in this Agreement, the receipt and sufficiency of which consideration is hereby acknowledged, the Administration and the Services Provider agree to this Agreement and attachments. This Agreement has been signed on the 16th day of October, 2019, in two original copies in both the Spanish and English languages. The English version is superior in legal procedures.

By signing this General Service Agreement, Juan Gerardo Guaido, as president of the Bolivarian Republic of Venezuela, accepts, agrees and approves the terms and conditions described hereafter as well as the attachments of this General Service Agreement. The attachments will be signed by the designated Commissioners Sergio Vergara and Juan Jose Rendón.

IN WITNESS WHEREOF the Parties duly affix their signatures under hand and seal on this 16th day of October, 2019.

SIGNED, SEALED, AND DELIVERED in the presence of or by video conference: LA REPUBLICA BOLIVARIANA DE VENEZUELA (Administration)

By: [signature]
Juan Gerardo Guaido
President of Venezuela

By: [signature]
Sergio Vergara, Comisionado
High Presidential Commissioner for Crisis Management

By: [signature]
Juan Jose Rendon, Comisionado
High Presidential Commissioner General Strategy and Crisis Management
SILVERCORP USA, Inc. (Service Provider)

By: [signature]
Jordan Goudreau,
CEO Silvercorp USA

[signature]
Manuel J. Retureta
Witness

Source: "General Services Agreement between the Venezuelan Opposition and Silvercorp, Oct. 16, 2019," updated May 6, 2020, https://www.washingtonpost.com/context/general-services-agreement-between-the-venezuelan-opposition-and-silvercorp-oct-16-2019/a86baff6-40fa-4116-a9cb-9725c84bf4e0.

SUMMARY

The election of Hugo Chávez as president in 1998 rocked Venezuela's political establishment and set the continent on a leftist political trajectory. His triumph reinforced an idea that dramatic political changes could be made through institutional structures rather than resorting to armed struggle to alter the existing order. While conservative opponents ceaselessly opposed Chávez's government, previously marginalized populations rallied to his cause. Even as both Maduro and Guaidó faced low approval ratings, surveys revealed that even after his death, Chávez was still the country's most popular politician. Despite the significant problems and reversals that it faced, the Bolivarian Revolution appeared to be a truly transformative event.

DISCUSSION QUESTIONS

Is representative or participatory democracy better at governing in the interests of the popular will of the people?

What was it about the Bolivarian Revolution that imperial powers found so threatening? Were these fears justified?

How important was charismatic leadership for the success of the Bolivarian Revolution?

How much did the Bolivarian Revolution change Venezuela? Was this a true revolution?

FURTHER READING

Hugo Chávez's election as president of Venezuela triggered a burst of interest among political scientists and journalists in the Bolivarian Revolution, leading to the publication of a large number of outstanding works on the leftist government.

Angosto-Ferrández, Luis Fernando. *Venezuela Reframed: Bolivarianism, Indigenous Peoples and Socialisms of the Twenty-First Century*. London: Zed Books, 2015. An examination of Indigenous support for the Bolivarian Revolution.

Azzellini, Dario. *Communes and Workers' Control in Venezuela: Building 21st Century Socialism from Below*. Leiden, Netherlands: Brill, 2017. Similar to Ciccariello-Maher, provides a history from below, in which workers, peasants, and the urban poor have led the struggle for twenty-first-century socialism.

Ciccariello-Maher, George. *Building the Commune: Radical Democracy in Venezuela*. London: Verso, 2016. An exploration of Venezuela's efforts to create a participatory democracy.

———. *We Created Chávez: A People's History of the Venezuelan Revolution*. Durham, NC: Duke University Press, 2013. An influential book that convincingly argues that grassroots movements, not vanguard leadership, defined the direction of the Bolivarian Revolution.

Cooper, Amy. *State of Health: Pleasure and Politics in Venezuelan Health Care under Chávez* Oakland: University of California Press, 2019. Fascinating ethnographic exploration of how historically disempowered Venezuelans—poor people, people of color, and women—the vast majority of the country's population, experienced the healthcare system.

Ellner, Steve. *Rethinking Venezuelan Politics: Class, Conflict, and the Chávez Phenomenon*. Boulder, CO: Lynne Rienner, 2008. A careful analysis of the Chávez government from a leading Venezuela scholar.

Gonzalez, Mike. *Hugo Chávez: Socialist for the Twenty-First Century*. London: Pluto Press, 2014. A short and sympathetic biography of the Venezuelan president.

Gott, Richard. *Hugo Chávez and the Bolivarian Revolution*. London: Verso, 2005. A solid journalistic summary of Chávez's rise to power.

Martinez, Carlos, Michael Fox, and JoJo Farrell. *Venezuela Speaks! Voices from the Grassroots*. Oakland, CA: PM Press, 2010. A collection of interviews with social movement activists supportive of the Chávez government.

Ponniah, Thomas, and Jonathan Eastwood, eds. *The Revolution in Venezuela: Social and Political Change under Chávez*. Cambridge, MA: Harvard University David Rockefeller Center for Latin American Studies, 2011. Distinguished authors analyze social change in Venezuela from a broad range of ideological perspectives.

Tinker Salas, Miguel. *Venezuela: What Everyone Needs to Know*. Oxford: Oxford University Press, 2013. An introduction to Venezuela by a preeminent historian.

Wilpert, Greg. *Changing Venezuela by Taking Power: The History and Policies of the Chávez Government*. London: Verso, 2007. A critical appreciation of the strengths and shortcomings of the Chávez administration.

FILMS

Hugo Chavez at the 2005 World Social Forum, Porto Alegre, Brazil. 2005. Venezuelan president
  Hugo Chávez discusses the goals and achievements of his administration.
The Revolution Will Not Be Televised. 2002. A powerfully moving film that describes Chávez's
  removal from office in a coup on April 11, 2002, and his return to power three days later.
Venezuela Bolivariana: People and Struggle of the Fourth World War. 2004. A documentary
  about the Bolivarian Revolution of Venezuela and its links to the worldwide movement
  against capitalist globalization.

10

Socialisms of the Twentieth and Twenty-First Centuries

KEY DATES ("PINK TIDE" GOVERNMENTS)

Hugo Chávez (Venezuela, 1999–2013)
  April 11–13, 2001: Failed military coup
Ricardo Lagos (Chile, 2000–2006)
Jean-Bertrand Aristide (Haiti, 2001–2004)
Luiz Inácio Lula da Silva (Brazil, 2003–2010)
Néstor Kirchner (Argentina, 2003–2007)
Evo Morales (Bolivia, 2005–2019)
  November 10, 2019: Morales resigns under pressure from military (a.k.a. military coup)
Tabaré Vázquez (Uruguay, 2005–2010)
Manuel Zelaya (Honduras, 2006–2009)
  June 28, 2009: Military coup
Michelle Bachelet (Chile, 2006–2010)
Daniel Ortega (Nicaragua, 2007–)
  April 2018–: Sustained calls for Ortega to resign
Rafael Correa (Ecuador, 2007–2017)
  September 30, 2010: Failed police mutiny
Cristina Fernández de Kirchner (Argentina, 2007–2015)
Fernando Lugo (Paraguay, 2008–2012)
  June 22, 2012: Express impeachment
Mauricio Funes (El Salvador, 2009–2014)
José "Pepe" Mujica (Uruguay, 2010–2015)
Dilma Rousseff (Brazil, 2011–2016)
  August 31, 2016: Impeached on politically motivated charges

Nicolás Maduro (Venezuela, 2013–)
  January 23, 2019: Juan Guaidó declares himself interim president
  April 30, 2019: Guaidó leads failed military uprising
  May 3, 2020: Operation Gideon fails to kidnap Maduro
Michelle Bachelet (Chile, 2014–2018)
Salvador Sánchez Cerén (El Salvador, 2014–2019)
Tabaré Vázquez (Uruguay, 2015–2020)
Alberto Fernández (Argentina, 2019–)
Luis Arce (Bolivia, 2020–)
Pedro Castillo (Peru, 2021–)

Hugo Chávez's election as president of Venezuela in 1998 was followed at the dawn of the twenty-first century with the election of Evo Morales in Bolivia and Rafael Correa in Ecuador. Those two leaders pursued a road of implementing progressive policies similar to the one Chávez had paved before them, and all three men enjoyed unprecedented and sustained high approval ratings. Voters elected less radical leftist governments in most other South American countries (particularly Argentina, Brazil, and Chile) as well as in Nicaragua and El Salvador in Central America. Latin America had moved significantly from the 1970s, when the military governed in most of the region. With the return to civilian rule in the 1980s, armed struggle was largely off the table as a path for the left to assume political power. Civilian rule, however, did not mean democracy in the sense of popular governments that implemented policies that benefited the majority of the population. Before Chávez's election, conservative governments held power in all of Latin America with the sole exception of Cuba. They implemented neoliberal economic policies that privatized public resources to the benefit of the ruling class, with a resulting increase in inequality and poverty for workers. In what some have termed the "**pink tide**," by the end of the first decade of the twenty-first century, almost the entire region was under leftist rule.

NEW SOCIAL MOVEMENTS

A resurgence of mass mobilizations against neoliberal economic policies in the decade before Chávez's election opened political space for the election of progressive governments across the hemisphere. With the electoral defeat of the Sandinistas in 1990 and the failure of other guerrilla movements in Latin America, academic and political attention had shifted away from a preference for armed paths to power. Instead, activists formed social movements—sometimes called popular movements because of their roots in marginalized populations—that fought for the realization of civil or social rights. Rather than engaging in electoral campaigns or guerrilla struggles with the goal of gaining direct control over governmental structures to transform society, these movements typically had more limited goals of influencing specific policies. They functioned as part of civil society and were known as nonstate actors.

Sociologists distinguished new social movements (NSMs) from older movements that were rooted in traditional political parties, labor unions, or guerrilla insurgencies that advocated for political and social changes. Researchers interpreted NSMs as responding to immediate and specific crises with concentrated and definitive demands. Examples of NSMs included gender and women's rights organizations, neighborhood associations, human rights promotion, ecological activism, support for political prisoners and the disappeared, and champions for the rights of Indigenous peoples and those of African descent. While the old movements were commonly rooted in a Marxist understanding of class struggle, NSMs embraced identity politics. Leftist scholars challenged this as an artificial divide and noted that neither had the "old" movements entirely ignored issues of gender, race, and ethnicity nor had the "new" ones discarded economic demands. More attention began to be paid to how various expressions—including class relations, ethnicity, and gendered identities—intersected with each other in specific historical contexts.

A key demand of many social movements in the 1990s was to roll back the neoliberal economic policies that many of Latin America's conservative governments had implemented in the 1980s. International lending agencies, such as the International Monetary Fund (IMF), had encouraged countries to privatize state enterprises and reduce subsidies for public programs such as transportation and education. A goal was to halt high rates of inflation and fuel economic growth, but these policies increased socioeconomic inequality and undermined the livelihoods of the most marginalized members of society. Movements that initially formed as apolitical groups to address specific matters soon found themselves engaging with much larger structural concerns. These new movements opened up political spaces, articulated popular demands, and politicized issues (such as gender rights) that had been formerly confined to the private realm. To achieve their objectives, they engaged in similar strategies and tactics of earlier movements such as demonstrations, strikes, and marches in order to wrestle concessions from the government.

Brazil's Movimento dos Trabalhadores Rurais Sem Terra (MST, Landless Workers Movement) was one of Latin America's largest social movements, and it bridged the artificial divide between the demands and strategies of old and new movements. Rural activists formed the MST in the late 1970s to defend the rights and lives of peasants who had been expelled from their lands. The MST engaged in land occupations as a strategy to pressure the government for positive policy changes, including an agrarian reform that included access to land, healthcare, education, dignity, infrastructure, water, housing, and support for the young to stay on the land. The MST helped found the Via Campesina (Spanish for "Peasants' Way") in 1993 as an international movement to raise family farmers' voices in international debates. The Via Campesina opposed corporate-driven agriculture that destroyed the environment and instead defended small-scale, sustainable agriculture as a way to promote social justice and dignity. Activists proposed the concept of food sovereignty as the right of communities to produce healthy food on their own land rather than relying on neoliberal export economies that contributed to poverty and climate crises.

The 1992 quincentennial of Columbus's arrival in the Americas raised the profile of Indigenous struggles. One of the best-organized Indigenous movements was the Confederación de Nacionalidades Indígenas del Ecuador (CONAIE, Confederation of Indigenous Nationalities of Ecuador). Leading up to the quincentennial, CONAIE organized a powerful uprising that paralyzed Ecuador for a week. Activists blocked roads with boulders, rocks, and trees that halted the transportation system, which effectively cut off the food supply to the cities and shut down the country, to force the government to negotiate agrarian reform demands. The movement's most controversial proposal was to revise the constitution to recognize the "plurinational" character of Ecuador. Activists called for the incorporation of the unique contributions of diverse populations into state structures, a proposition that the dominant culture repeatedly rejected as undermining the unity and integrity of the country.

The World Social Forum (WSF) was the largest gathering of civil society and presented the most significant challenge to neoliberal economic policies. The WSF first met in Porto Alegre, Brazil, in 2001, but had its roots in earlier organizing efforts such as the 1992 Earth Summit at Rio de Janeiro, Brazil, and the First International Encounter for Humanity and against Neoliberalism that the Zapatistas organized in Chiapas, Mexico, in 1996. It quickly grew from an assembly of ten thousand people (mostly from Latin America, France, and Italy) who gathered to talk about creating a "globalization from below," to more than one hundred thousand within three years. Under the slogan "Another World Is Possible," the WSF presented a direct challenge to the conservative British prime minister Margaret Thatcher's claim that "there is no alternative" to the ravages of neoliberal capitalism. The forum created an open platform for activists to discuss strategies of resistance to neoliberal globalization and to present constructive alternatives.

The WSF provided an arena for perennial discussions concerning the relationship between social movements and political parties in achieving social change. With an emphasis on civil society, the WSF excluded political parties and armed groups from its discussions. The rise of new left governments in Latin America during the first decade of the twenty-first century pushed many activists to rethink their assumptions about the relationship between social movements and political parties. Although parties could not mobilize massive demonstrations the way social movements did, those movements lacked the governmental authority necessary to implement positive policy proposals. Organized as part of civil society, the WSF was better situated than any other force to open up the political spaces necessary for the election of a new wave of left-wing governments that could then pursue progressive policy decisions. As leftists had understood across the twentieth century, it was not an either/or situation of having to choose between the options of social movements, armed struggle, or electoral politics. Rather, it was a matter of finding the best strategy for that moment.

LATIN AMERICA'S LEFT TURNS

Chávez's Bolivarian Revolution blazed a pathway forward and provided a model for subsequent leftist governments in Latin America. Unlike Cuba half a century earlier, all of them came to power through what were widely recognized as open and free elections. Critics spoke of two lefts: a more moderate trend represented by Néstor Kirchner in Argentina, Luiz Inácio Lula da Silva in Brazil, first Ricardo Lagos and then Michelle Bachelet in Chile, and Tabaré Vázquez and José "Pepe" Mujica in Uruguay; and a "populist" left of Chávez in Venezuela, Evo Morales in Bolivia, and Rafael Correa in Ecuador. The "good" left was willing to work within the confines of existing market economies, while opponents condemned a more radical left for returning to allegedly discredited nationalist, **clientelist**, and statist models of governance. None of the governments approached the radical policies of the twentieth-century revolutions that led to the expropriation of Standard Oil in Mexico, United Fruit Company land in Guatemala, tin mines in Bolivia, sugar mills in Cuba, or copper mines in Chile—hence the reference to a "pink" tide, thereby implying that the governments were not all that "red."

In reality, all of these governments took very different directions. Latin America had not just two but many different lefts. A year after Chávez's victory in 1998, the socialist lawyer Ricardo Lagos won election in Chile, seemingly returning the country to a path that had been interrupted by Augusto Pinochet's military coup in 1973. Lagos played a significant role in a 1988 plebiscite that brought Pinochet's dictatorship to an end. In what appeared to be a repeat of history, the socialist Lagos followed the son of the Christian Democrat Eduardo Frei (also named Eduardo Frei), who preceded Salvador Allende in the 1960s. Six years later, the socialist, medical doctor, and single mother Michelle Bachelet succeeded Lagos in office and returned for a second term four years later. Chilean radicals criticized Lagos and Bachelet for their relatively moderate policies and failures to break from Pinochet's neoliberal economic policies.

Institutional policies implemented during Pinochet's regime, including constitutional provisions that ensured conservative control over the legislature, constrained the pace of changes that socialists could make. This legislative control limited possibilities to reform Pinochet's 1980 constitution that would have allowed for reforms to end neoliberal economic policies that contributed to Chile's continuing high rates of socioeconomic inequality.

After three unsuccessful campaigns for office, labor leader Luiz Inácio Lula da Silva won the presidency in Brazil in 2003 as the candidate for the Partido dos Trabalhadores (PT, Workers' Party). After two terms in office, he passed the mantle to his chief of staff, Dilma Rousseff, a student activist and guerrilla member in the 1960s whom the military government had imprisoned and tortured. As leaders of the world's eighth-largest economy, both presidents followed fairly moderate reform policies that made only modest gains in addressing Brazil's severe socioeconomic inequalities. The MST in particular expressed disappointment that they did not dismantle the country's agroindustrial export economy.

Néstor Kirchner of the left-populist Peronist party also won election in Argentina in 2003. After serving a term in office, his spouse Cristina Fernández de Kirchner succeeded him in 2007. Under their neo-Keynesian state-led development policies, poverty rates dropped by 70 percent and extreme poverty by 80 percent. Unemployment fell from more than 17 percent to less than 7 percent. Their approach alternated between inflammatory populist positions designed to motivate their base and quite orthodox policies that alienated that same base. Their leftist rhetoric also earned them the animosity of the U.S. government. Kirchner's plan to alternate terms in office with his wife was undermined when he died in 2010. His widow Fernández won reelection in 2011 and successfully completed two terms in office.

The physician Tabaré Vázquez led the left to its first presidential victory in 2005 in neighboring Uruguay. As the candidate of the Frente Amplio (Broad Front) leftist coalition, Vázquez introduced middle-of-the-road social democratic policies that introduced considerable improvements in education and working conditions, a significant expansion of the welfare system, and a dramatic reduction in poverty. In 2010, José "Pepe" Mujica, a former guerrilla fighter with the Tupamaros, succeeded Vázquez in office. Mujica gained renown for his austere lifestyle, including giving up many of the perks of the presidential office. He preferred instead to live in his own simple house and drive his old Volkswagen Beetle. In 2015, Vázquez returned for a second term in office.

In contrast to these relatively moderate governments from South America's southern cone, Hugo Chávez in Venezuela gained two strong allies on the radical left in the Andes with the election of Evo Morales in Bolivia in 2005 and Rafael Correa in Ecuador the following year. Both followed Chávez's lead in revising their countries' constitutions in a way that fundamentally remapped political structures. The new constitutions increased presidential power, including allowance for presidential reelection. Opponents charged that the leaders sought to maintain themselves permanently in office while advocates feared that their positive gains would be turned back without strong leadership. All three presidents used the earnings from the export of commodities to fund economic development. They implemented social programs that significantly reduced poverty and inequality. The new constitutions protected the rights of Indigenous and African-descent peoples, and pledged to follow a path of local, sustainable economic development. The three presidents also had complicated relations with the social movements that helped place them in power. Sometimes they tangled more with radicals who tried to push their revolutions in a leftist direction in favor of more thoroughgoing redistributive policies than they did with the members of the discredited traditional oligarchy who wished to return to neoliberal economic structures that privileged a wealthy minority.

Many of the new left governments faced significant threats to their hold on power. In 2006, Manuel Zelaya won election with the liberal party in Honduras. Once in office, he moved significantly to the left and implemented policies to benefit the country's impoverished majority. His proposals threatened the traditional oligarchy that had initially supported his presidency. Three years into his term, the military removed him from office under the questionable charge that he attempted to revise the constitution to allow for presidential reelection. The military coup triggered massive grassroots protests as marginalized communities pressed for the realization of the policy objectives that Zelaya had proposed.

In 2008, the bishop Fernando Lugo, who had been influenced by liberation theology, won election in Paraguay. A lack of support in congress continually frustrated his goal of implementing policies to benefit the poor Paraguayan farmers to whom he had ministered as a priest. In 2012, the legislature engaged in an express impeachment without giving the president time to prepare a defense. His removal took the form of a constitutional coup. In countries with an entrenched and conservative oligarchy, winning the presidency only meant a tenuous hold on one office. Electoral victories remained distant from the goal of actually gaining power and radically modifying political and economic structures. These defeats highlighted the limitations of institutional paths to power that proscribed a complete dismantling of the structures of the old regime.

In 2007, after two failed campaigns, the Sandinista Daniel Ortega returned to office in Nicaragua. He made extensive compromises with the conservative Catholic Church hierarchy, wealthy business interests, and the U.S. government in order to engineer his election. These concessions initially guaranteed him high approval ratings and ensured his continuance as president but came at the cost of significantly limiting his ability to implement progressive policies. Once he was back in the presidency, opponents complained that he was ruling in an authoritarian fashion as he dismantled democratic institutions to guarantee his hold on power.

In El Salvador, the leftist Farabundo Martí National Liberation Front (FMLN), which had fought a bloody guerrilla war in the 1980s, finally won the presidency through electoral means in 2009 with the journalist Mauricio Funes at the head of the ticket. Five years later, the former guerrilla fighter Salvador Sánchez Cerén succeeded him in office. The aftermath of the civil war left violent criminal gangs in place, resulting in higher homicide rates than those at the height of the fighting in the 1980s. Gaining power through existing institutional structures meant that the FMLN had limited means to address the significant problems facing the country, and as a consequence, its level of popular support declined precipitously.

KEY AND PERENNIAL ISSUES

Many of the key issues that faced revolutionaries at the dawn of the twentieth century were still very much present a century later, although they would often be channeled through the specific lens of a current historical context. These included such topics as the nature of leadership and its relationship to a mass movement but also reflected new twists on old topics, including how to confront the limitations of an export-dependent economy.

Charismatic Leadership

Charismatic and strong leaders dominated Latin America's new left governments. If the leaders left office, the projects they headed threatened to fall apart. The presence of such commanding presidents led to doubts as to whether they ruled in the interests of the broader public or followed a nineteenth-century caudillo tradition of all-powerful leaders with their own personal vested concerns. An open question was whether their political projects were designed to maintain one person in power—typically a man—or to transform societal structures. Some supporters willingly traded the limitations of egotistical leadership for the very real social gains they were able to implement. Others feared that reliance on one leader might mean a political project would disintegrate were that person to disappear, and they advocated instead for taking advantage of the new political openings to train new leaders. Few new leaders emerged, however, who were equal to or excelled in the skills of those who had originally initiated the left turn.

Opponents charged that leftist presidents maintained themselves in office through clientelistic programs of strategic handouts designed primarily to solidify their electoral support. Government defenders contended that shifting resources to disadvantaged populations was not an opportunistic move but a fundamental part of an administration's redistributive goals. Conservatives charged that these governments irresponsibly spent resources on social programs rather than saving for a rainy day. Leftist militants cautioned that clientelism and handouts replaced the more difficult task of raising people's political consciousness and empowering them so that they could rule on their own behalf. These radicals advocated prioritizing fundamental structural alterations to address underlying issues of oppression and exploitation and to transform society.

Social Movements and Electoral Politics

Elected leftist governments in the twenty-first century emerged on the back of social movements that had created new political spaces in which they could operate, but they often clashed with those movements that should have been their firmest and most loyal allies. In a sense, these conflicts were part of a long-running feud between anarchists and Marxists over the role of the state in making transformational changes. In contemporary language, the debate was between horizontal and vertical forms of organization: whether trust and power should be placed in the grassroots or whether strong leadership was necessary to advance a political agenda.

This friction provided a contemporary counterpart to the tensions that Allende felt in Chile in the 1970s, when he wanted to make permanent societal changes through institutional structures while those to his left hoped to move much more quickly to a socialist society. Brazil's Landless Workers Movement (MST) initially had high expectations when Lula da Silva won election in 2003 but vocally complained about the president's compromises once he was in office. Political parties cautioned these "ultra-leftists" against making unrealistic demands of their new governments. With conservatives out of power and their neoliberal economic policies largely discredited for having contributed to poverty and inequality, twenty-first-century socialist presidents worried that those to their left presented more of a threat to the stability of their governments than their traditional enemies in the oligarchy. For grassroots social movements, winning a presidential election was simply one more step in a centuries-long struggle against oligarchical domination of their country. Once the opportunity presented itself, they wanted to move in a more radical direction than previously had been possible.

Leftist political parties learned that winning an election is not the same as taking power. The presidency is only one of many political offices, and an antagonistic legislature and judiciary can significantly curtail a president's actions. In Venezuela, it took Hugo Chávez a decade to consolidate control over government structures and move forward with socialist reforms. These are the limitations of working within the confines of a constitutional framework rather than gaining power through an armed struggle that destroyed the ancien régime, as happened in Cuba and Nicaragua.

Although twenty-first-century leftist governments employed radical rhetoric, their policies were more moderate than any of the twentieth-century revolutionary experiments. They rarely spoke of nationalizing industries or changing the mode of production. A common debate in the twentieth century was whether to reform existing systems or replace them with much more radical solutions. In the twenty-first century, socialist governments opted for social evolution rather than violent revolution that might disrupt the smooth functioning of society. Some social movements concluded that the relative moderation and failure to deliver on radical promises represented a continuation rather than a break from previous capitalist policies. These ongoing debates and tensions were not easily resolved.

Neoextractivism

Latin America's new left governments flourished in the midst of a commodity boom. They were able to fund an expansion of social programs with windfall profits from petroleum and mineral extraction. As a result, their economies grew dramatically, and poverty rates plummeted. Chávez and other left-populist governments that followed him claimed that their socioeconomic gains were a direct result of their return to state-centered development projects that previous neoliberal governments had disassembled.

Leftist critics complained that pursuing such policies failed to make a fundamental break with previous export-dependent economies. Environmental and social movement activists criticized the unsustainable nature of these policies, as well as the fact that local communities that bore the brunt of these endeavors rarely shared in their benefits. Protests against mineral extraction spread across the Americas, with both left and right governments arguing that large-scale mining was preferable and less ecologically damaging than the alternative of small-scale artisanal mining.

In one of many examples of the tensions between leftist governments and social movements, Indigenous organizations in Bolivia in 2011 marched to protest government plans to build a highway through the Isiboro-Sécure Indigenous Territory and National Park (TIPNIS) ecological reserve. Evo Morales was an Aymara who leveraged his credentials as a leader of Bolivia's powerful social movements to win election as the country's first president of Indigenous descent. In office, he pressed for construction of the road because it was key to Bolivia's economic development. At first Morales refused to listen to protests that the road would destroy one of the world's most biodiverse regions, but social movements pressured him to change his position. He learned to negotiate policies with rural communities in order to maintain both high approval ratings and impressive economic growth rates.

In 2013, Ecuadorian president Rafael Correa announced his decision to drill for oil in the ecologically sensitive Yasuní National Park in the eastern Amazonian forest. A proposal not to exploit the Ishpingo Tiputini Tambococha, or ITT, oil fields in exchange for international development aid was a signature policy objective of his administration and one of the president's most popular proposals. Although Indigenous and environmental organizations opposed the policy reversal, the plan was consistent with the president's actions since he first took office in 2007. Correa favored resource extraction in an attempt to fund programs to end poverty and fuel economic development, even though it threatened to sacrifice marginalized communities and damage the environment. It was a trade-off he was willing to make, even as it also earned him the animosity of those his policies were designed to benefit the most.

The developmental policies of new left governments highlight how difficult it is to break from the capitalist logic of an export-driven economy. Bolivian vice president Álvaro García Linera in particular championed what he termed Andean-Amazonian capitalism as a method of developing the country. He advocated exporting natural resources and investing that income to lift marginalized people out of poverty. These policies echoed the arguments of orthodox Marxists in the 1950s that Latin America lacked the proper objective conditions to implement socialist programs. Instead, the intermediate goal should be to build capitalism to develop the economy before moving on to the more advanced stage of communism. This was, of course, an argument that Fidel Castro in Cuba and Carlos Fonseca in Nicaragua rejected. Nevertheless, a perennial question was how quickly a leftist government could change society and whether administrations should dedicate their efforts to achieving moderate reforms rather than striving for a much more radical socialist revolution that might destabilize society.

These resource-extraction strategies ran counter to the claims of 1960s dependency theorists that export-oriented economies would underdevelop the Latin American periphery. Most of the value from the export of natural resources accrues to the industrial core that converts the imports into finished products. A failure to end dependent relations on industrialized countries in Europe and North America ran Latin American governments afoul of those who should have been their strongest supporters on the Indigenous and environmental left. Progressive governments and social movements continued a complicated dance in an attempt to achieve a common objective of sustainable development that would benefit all peoples.

After a decade of record-high commodity prices and significant social gains, by 2014 petroleum and mineral prices had dropped and an economic boom came to a halt. During the boom years, some critics questioned how much specific governmental policies had contributed to economic growth and whether such gains would have been realized under any government. As economies stalled and inflation rates rose, voters turned back to the previously discredited conservative politicians who still held to their neoliberal doctrines of privatization and austerity. It appeared as if in good economic times, the general public was willing to turn toward leftist socialists with their promises of redistribution, but during tougher periods they preferred conservative capitalists with their emphasis on economic growth.

Capturing the Narrative

A common complaint leveled against many of Latin America's new left governments was that in their drive to advance social programs, they had sacrificed individual liberties, particularly freedom of the press. Theoretically, one might ask why social and individual rights often convey the impression of being in tension with each other, but in examining historical realities, it does not appear to be much of a mystery. In Guatemala in the 1950s, for example, the CIA broadcast anti-Arbenz propaganda into the country, and those media campaigns undermined the government. In Nicaragua in the 1980s, the opposition press played havoc with the economy simply by falsely reporting an upcoming shortage of a commodity, thereby causing a run on that item and, as a result, artificially creating a supply problem. Other progressive administrations faced similar problems. The conservative aristocracy retained a firm hold on media outlets and exploited them to advance their economic and political interests even when out of office. If a leftist government attempted to forward an alternative narrative, the oligarchy inevitably cried foul and claimed censorship. Fighting disinformation was always a significant problem.

In the twenty-first century, despite impressive social and economic gains, one would be hard-pressed to find positive stories in the international mainstream media about Latin America's new socialist governments. News outlets openly cheered the reversal of political gains for the working class. This antagonism was even true of nominally leftist media outlets, such as London's *Guardian,* that one would typically expect to be sympathetic to these socialist experiments. Most reporters, and many academics as well, enter a country in the company of privileged sectors of society and hence report from that perspective, often remaining largely unaware of the advances that social programs have brought to the working class. Deep racial divides mean that they had little contact with marginalized peoples, who provided a bedrock of support for leftist governments. Even when they did have contact, they had little understanding of, or sympathy for, the perspectives of marginalized peoples. For many governments caught up in a fight to advance a social revolution, the nicety of freedom of the press was a luxury they could ill afford if the opposition refused to play fair.

Despite a common narrative that leftist governments control the press, in most countries, the owners of the mainstream media outlets are members of a conservative oligarchy who are committed to neoliberal economic policies and are deeply antagonistic to the redistributive goals of socialist governments. Given their class position, one could hardly expect them to act otherwise. It is for this reason that left governments created their own media outlets in an attempt to craft their own narrative. In the process, they discounted or ignored any legitimate critique of their policies and turned to propaganda to reinforce public support for their administrations. Resorting to these tactics often was to the leaders' own detriment, as they created an echo chamber in which officials became numb to growing popular discontent. In part, this is what culminated in the Sandinistas' electoral defeat in Nicaragua in 1990 and contributed to the renewed protests they faced in 2018. Outside observers are left confused by competing narratives that talk past each other. An easy solution to this conundrum is not readily apparent in an environment where class opponents of a socialist experiment are dedicated to its overthrow by any means necessary.

Imperialism

At the dawn of the twenty-first century, the heavy imperial hand of the U.S. government continued to be as present in Latin America as it had been throughout the twentieth century. U.S. opposition to leftist governments was rarely expressed through overt military intervention. More common was to work through covert means, as had happened in Guatemala and Cuba, with the domestic opposition as in Chile, or with proxy paramilitary forces as was the case with the contras in Nicaragua. By the twenty-first century, instead of centering policies on a geopolitical conflict with the Soviet Union as during the Cold War, the largest threat to U.S. hegemony was China, which sought the region's resources to fuel its own economic development.

More effective than direct U.S. military intervention in Latin America's internal affairs were neocolonial economic policies in which the value of raw commodities in Latin America accrued to corporations in the United States rather than supporting local development. International lending agencies such as the IMF also made it difficult for governments to fund social programs. On occasion, the U.S. government also followed the policy that it had implemented with the Revolutionary Nationalist Movement (MNR) in Bolivia of attempting to draw what could otherwise be an antagonistic government into its sphere of influence. While not common, such an approach could be the most effective way to moderate what otherwise would have been radical objectives of a leftist government. No longer was it necessary to colonize Latin America directly, as William Walker had done in Nicaragua in the 1850s.

CONSERVATIVE RESTORATION

After a decade of almost hegemonic control of leftist governments in Latin America, previously discredited conservative politicians who favored a return to the capitalist neoliberal policies of privatization and austerity measures appeared to be making a comeback with electoral victories in Argentina and Venezuela in 2015. After twelve years of Kirchner rule in Argentina (2003–2015), the conservative Mauricio Macri won the presidency on an openly neoliberal economic platform that denounced Venezuela, pledged loyalty to the United States, and pursued anti-immigrant policies. Several weeks later, voters flipped control of Venezuela's National Assembly to a stridently anti-Chávez but politically incoherent opposition. In Brazil, the conservative congressional leader Eduardo Cunha led a politically motivated impeachment campaign against president Dilma Rousseff. Her vice president, Michel Temer, assumed office and moved quickly to undo thirteen years of progressive policies. Ecuador's Rafael Correa faced a constitutional ban on his reelection in 2017, and in Bolivia, Evo Morales lost a referendum that would have allowed him to run for reelection in 2019. The international media cheered these developments as the end of Latin America's left turn.

In 2017, Correa's former vice president Lenín Moreno won election in Ecuador with promises to continue his Citizen's Revolution but then took a hard-right turn in government. Pontificating pundits proclaimed, with little basis in factual data, that during a period of economic downturn, leftist presidents preferred to sit out a term of office rather than see their popularity compromised, with plans to return once the economy returned to its previous growth patterns. The pundits also declared, with a certain amount of glee, that the populace had "tired" of the socialist policies of redistribution and voted for a return to "democracy."

Others argued that a resurgent right was part of typical political swings. After two terms of socialist rule in Chile under Lagos and Bachelet (2000–2010), the conservative billionaire Sebastián Piñera won, only to have Bachelet return to office four years later. After her successful first term in office, Bachelet faced very low poll numbers during her second term, and Piñera won the 2017 election. He similarly ended his second term under a dark cloud, with the left well situated to return to the presidency in 2022.

Rather than a political swing, the conservative victory in Argentina in November 2015 can be better understood as a result of the weakness of the nominally leftist candidacy of Daniel Scioli; the failures of his previous administration as governor of the province of Buenos Aires; divisions on the left, with many supporting instead the insurgent candidacy of the more radical Sergio Massa; the personalist nature and campaign style of Macri; and an antagonistic media campaign against the Kirchner governments, not to mention objective conditions of rising inflation that undermined economic growth. In an electoral system, an effective campaign and the personal appeal of a candidate can play a larger role in determining an outcome than a political ideology or specific economic programs. In 2019, Alberto Fernández won the presidency with the former president Cristina Fernández de Kirchner as his running mate, thereby bringing a populist left back to office. Reports of the death of the left were premature.

Similarly in Venezuela, high crime rates, low oil prices, bad government economic policies, corruption, and the fact that Nicolás Maduro was significantly less charismatic than Hugo Chávez all contributed to the left's legislative defeat in December 2015. Leading up to the election, the conservative opposition charged that the voting would be rigged, or that the government would refuse to recognize the results. Similar to the Sandinistas' electoral beating in Nicaragua in 1990, many Venezuelans voted against the government not because they favored a return to capitalism but because they wanted officials to pay more attention to a rapidly declining economic situation. After an almost unbroken seventeen-year stretch of leftist electoral victories (the only loss was a 2007 referendum to reform the constitution), Maduro accepted the defeat with grace. Despite a conservative opposition determined to remove the socialist government by any means necessary, as with the 1980s Sandinista Revolution, one of the most significant triumphs of the Bolivarian Revolution was the entrenchment of a transparent and legitimate electoral system. Repeatedly across the Americas, an allegedly antidemocratic left conceded to the apparent will of the people when it lost an election, whereas conservatives were less likely to do so, as became apparent in the United States when Donald Trump lost the 2020 presidential race and his far-right counterpart Jair Bolsonaro similarly indicated that he would not accept the results were he to lose the 2022 presidential race in Brazil.

On occasion, hard-right candidates were able to win only by barring those to their left from competing in the race. One such example was Ecuador, where the right-wing Guillermo Lasso, a former banker and an adherent of the reactionary Opus Dei sect of the Catholic Church, won in 2021 largely by excluding former president Correa from either the top or the vice-presidential spot on the ticket and even by preventing his replacement, Andrés Arauz, from using his image or voice in campaign advertisements. A more extreme example was Brazil, where what in retrospect were clearly fraudulent and politically motivated corruption charges had led to the imprisonment of the former popular president Luiz Inácio Lula da Silva, thereby precluding him from running for the top office in 2018. This paved the way for Bolsonaro to win the election and impose extremely conservative policies in the country. When Lula was exonerated and his constitutional rights restored, he immediately jumped to the front of the pack in early polls for the 2022 race, making a second Bolsonaro term unlikely.

In Bolivia, Morales first won election in 2005 and had a very successful run in office, winning reelection by wide margins. He began to lose support when he sought to maintain himself in office rather than grooming a successor, but nevertheless, after overturning a bar on continual reelection, he won the 2019 presidential race by a very small margin. The Organization of American States (OAS), which from its founding has played a role of attempting to remove progressive governments from office as it did in Guatemala in 1954 and in Cuba after its revolution, claimed that Morales had won through fraudulent means. A study from the left-leaning Center for Economic and Policy Research (CEPR), however, conclusively demonstrated that no statistically significant evidence of fraud existed that would have altered the outcome of the election.

In the face of violent right-wing protests and under pressure from the military, Morales resigned on November 10, 2019, even though his current term of office had not yet expired and no one had questioned the legitimacy of his presence in that position. Typically, the office would pass to the vice president—in this case his vice president, Álvaro García Linera—but he was also forced out. Next in line was the president of the senate, Adriana Salvatierra, also from the Movement toward Socialism (MAS) party, but the conservative opposition made it clear that no ally of Morales would be acceptable. In this vacuum, a minor conservative senator named Jeanine Áñez, who had won her post with 4 percent of the vote, claimed the role of interim president. She did so at a session of congress that did not have a quorum because the opposition prevented the entrance of MAS delegates. Áñez's presidency lacked constitutional legitimacy but she assumed office anyway with the backing of the U.S. government and the OAS. Her one task in that position should have been to call for new elections, but instead she prolonged her time for almost a full year and took the country in a hard-right direction. When she finally convoked elections almost a year later, Morales's protégé, Luis Arce, resoundingly won the vote, and this time the OAS was forced to recognize the results. Bolivia had returned to the progressive fold.

RETURN OF THE LEFT

If the political center had begun to swing rightward in 2015, by 2021 it was definitely swinging back to the left. The movement started in 2019 with a series of vocal social protests known as the *estallido social* or "social outburst" that had spread across the continent against the neoliberal economic policies of austerity and privatization that right-wing governments had imposed. In October 2019 in Ecuador, the conservative Moreno government faced sustained protests against his attempt to remove long-standing fuel subsidies, as well as against other dramatic IMF-stipulated austerity measures that would have a negative impact on workers. Eleven days of large protests forced Moreno to backtrack on his proposals. This was quickly followed in Chile with a series of massive demonstrations in response to an increase in subway fares, the cost of living, privatization, and inequality. The conservative Piñera administration responded with excessive force, including killing dozens and blinding hundreds more by shooting them in the face with rubber bullets. At the same time, the citizenry overwhelmingly voted in favor of a constitutional assembly to rewrite the 1980 Pinochet-era document and gave the left a supermajority in the body. Pinochet had drafted that constitution to prevent a return to Allende's socialist policies, to inscribe neoliberal capitalism as the mode of production, and to assure continued conservative domination of the country. After forty years, that legacy was finally coming to an end.

In a closely contested election in Peru in 2021, the socialist Pedro Castillo defeated the perennial right-wing candidate Keiko Fujimori, daughter of Alberto Fujimori, the man who had defeated the Shining Path in the 1990s. Fujimori claimed fraud and refused to concede, but—after the debacle in Bolivia—the OAS seemingly had learned its lesson and did not contest the result. The race reflected deep racial, cultural, and geographic divides that ran through Peru and all of the Americas, with Fujimori gaining much of her support in wealthy, urban areas on the coast and Castillo polling strongest in the poorer and more Indigenous interior known as the "other Peru." Castillo had campaigned on a platform of breaking from U.S.-backed drug interdiction and regime change operations, and of economic policies that would shift resources to the poor and marginalized. His administration also unexpectedly brought Héctor Béjar, who had led a failed guerrilla uprising in the 1960s, back to the limelight. The now eighty-five-year-old author and university professor briefly served as minister of foreign affairs in the Castillo administration until he was forced out for his leftist stances.

Most surprising was Colombia. While the country had suffered the long-running Revolutionary Armed Forces of Colombia (FARC) insurgency and had a very strong labor movement, it was generally not known for large social mobilizations. During the entire run of the pink tide, it was a rare outlier that never had enjoyed a progressive government. Together with Honduras in Central America, its conservative governments were the most loyal allies of the United States and often functioned as a proxy to advance that imperial agenda in the region. Nevertheless, its hard-right president Iván Duque had become deeply unpopular. Social leaders and Indigenous activists were being murdered at alarming rates of one every three days. Colombia was the most dangerous place in the Americas to petition for one's rights. Facing this situation, hundreds of thousands of Colombians took to the streets in November 2019 in a massive general strike in protest of Duque's economic policies. In April 2021, immense and sustained protests once again flared up, with the Duque government responding with intense repression that killed dozens of people. These social mobilizations set up a situation in which the front-runner in the 2022 presidential race became the former M-19 guerrilla leader Gustavo Petro. If he were to be successful, Colombia might have its first progressive president in its history.

In reality, various elements determined these political outcomes, and similar issues had influenced the rise and fall of social revolutionary projects during the twentieth century. No single factor explains the emergence of a revolutionary situation or its defeat, but often these historical developments are the result of a complex interplay of many different considerations, including leadership, ideology, and access to resources.

SUMMARY

Contemporary leftist governments confront many of the same issues that revolutionaries faced throughout the twentieth century. This book has explored competing paths that revolutions have taken in Latin America. All of them followed diverse paths and realized varying degrees of success. The 1910 Mexican Revolution introduced a century of profound changes in the hemisphere and highlighted that the movements responded to local concerns and forwarded solutions that emerged out of domestic interests. A pair of midcentury reform movements in Guatemala and Bolivia opened a path to deep societal transformations that were eventually slowed and stopped with military coups. The 1959 Cuban Revolution was the most successful revolution in Latin America and offers a standard by which others are measured. Unfortunately, none of the other twentieth-century movements realized their transformative potential. Salvador Allende's elected socialist government ended in a military coup, whereas the Sandinistas came to power in Nicaragua through an armed uprising, only to be evicted in an election. In contrast, Chávez used these same institutions to collapse the old order in Venezuela and introduce a period of profound and revolutionary changes. He left existing power structures largely intact, however, and those forces continued to challenge the Bolivarian Revolution.

Historians have not reached consensus on which events should be labeled as revolutionary. As this book demonstrates, revolutions need not be violent, and some of the most significant transformations can be achieved through peaceful and institutional means. A barrier to permanent change, however, was the persistence of preexisting power structures that remained intact and threatened the left's hold on power. For a revolution to be successful, wealth and power must be transferred from the ruling class to a previously impoverished and dispossessed group of people. Those revolutions were informed by a socialist ideology that envisioned a more equal and just society without profound class divisions.

In addition to a clear ideology, revolutions relied on a variety of other factors to realize success. Charismatic vanguard leadership that could provide guidance for movements was a key theme that ran throughout Latin America's revolutionary tradition. Despite an assumption that revolutions emerged out of repression and deprivation, in reality they required the mobilization of significant material and human resources. Revolutions succeeded in the midst of the collapse of a previous, discredited political system. They surfaced in a political vacuum as much as they resulted from a successful armed struggle. Armed struggles were only victorious when available legal avenues for change appeared to be closed off.

A variety of issues underlie all of these movements. Participants debated on how quickly they should and could make changes, and on whether a gradual reform of existing structures was preferable to a rapid and potentially destabilizing transformation of society. They questioned whether successful and permanent alterations were better achieved through peaceful and legal means or via violent and extraconstitutional avenues. Revolutionaries disagreed on how broad to build a movement and whether tightly controlled governing structures best ensured success. Ideologues and tacticians also disagreed on which sectors of society were the most revolutionary. They deliberated whether struggles need to be rooted in a working-class consciousness, as Marx envisioned, or whether in Latin America revolutions would emerge in the countryside among agrarian farmers. Warfare has traditionally been gendered male, and revolutionaries struggled with the relegation of women to marginal and domestic roles. Most leaders came from privileged, European-descent sectors of society. Even when they gained a consciousness of the needs of marginalized peoples and critiqued racist structures, that was not the same as a movement emerging from the bottom and the left, as was the case with the Haitian Revolution. Over the course of the twentieth century, the function of the Catholic Church evolved. Whereas religious leaders traditionally allied with wealthy landholding interests, after the Second Vatican Council in the 1960s, a new and popular church associated with the aspirations of poor and marginalized people materialized. Finally, revolutionaries disagreed on whether to mobilize primarily around local issues or to embrace transnational aspects of a movement.

Revolutions are an inherently messy and complicated business and raise intrinsically complicated issues. Transforming unequal, unjust, racist, and sexist societal structures is a difficult undertaking that does not lend itself to simple solutions. Understanding present-day political events helps analyze earlier developments, and studying Latin America's revolutionary history contributes to a fuller appreciation of the current challenges the hemisphere faces.

DISCUSSION QUESTIONS

Did social movements in the 1990s emerge out of the successes or the failures of the 1980s guerrilla wars?

What role do social movements play in defining the policies of leftist governments?

How important are elections to leftist strategies?

Are new left governments a threat to democratic governance?

FURTHER READING

The Bolivarian Revolution in Venezuela introduced a left turn in South America as well as an explosion in literature on new progressive governments. Given the current nature of these events, political scientists have published the bulk of the scholarly work on the subject, and much of it has appeared as essays in edited volumes.

Burbach, Roger, Michael Fox, and Federico Fuentes. *Latin America's Turbulent Transitions: The Future of Twenty-First-Century Socialism.* London: Zed Books, 2013. A broad exploration of Latin America's left turn.

Castañeda, Jorge G., and Marco A. Morales, eds. *Leftovers: Tales of the Latin American Left.* New York: Routledge, 2008. A conservative, quantitative critique that condemns the policies of leftist governments.

Dangl, Benjamin. *Dancing with Dynamite: States and Social Movements in Latin America.* Oakland, CA: AK Press, 2010. A journalistic account of the complicated dynamics between social movements and leftist governments.

Ellner, Steve, ed. *Latin American Extractivism: Dependency, Resource Nationalism, and Resistance in Broad Perspective.* Lanham, MD: Rowman & Littlefield, 2021. Leading scholars critique the environmental and social impacts of contemporary extractive economies in countries with both leftist and conservative governments.

————, ed. *Latin America's Pink Tide: Breakthroughs and Shortcomings.* Lanham, MD: Rowman & Littlefield, 2019. Authors from a variety of disciplinary perspectives examine the successes and failures of pink tide governments.

————, ed. *Latin America's Radical Left: Challenges and Complexities of Political Power in the Twenty-First Century.* Lanham, MD: Rowman & Littlefield, 2014. A collection of essays that explores Latin America's leftward turn.

Levitsky, Steven, and Kenneth M. Roberts, eds. *The Resurgence of the Latin American Left.* Baltimore: Johns Hopkins University Press, 2011. A critique of leftist governments by mainstream political scientists.

Prevost, Gary, Carlos Oliva Campos, and Harry E. Vanden, eds. *Social Movements and Leftist Governments in Latin America: Confrontation or Co-option?* London: Zed Books, 2012. A collection of essays that analyzes the complicated dynamics between social movements and leftist governments.

Ross, Clifton, and Marcy Rein, eds. *Until the Rulers Obey: Voices from Latin American Social Movements.* Oakland, CA: PM Press, 2014. Interviews with social movement activists behind Latin America's leftist turn.

Sader, Emir. *The New Mole: Paths of the Latin American Left.* London: Verso Books, 2011. A thoughtful analysis from a preeminent Brazilian sociologist of the need to support leftist governments.

Stahler-Sholk, Richard, Harry E. Vanden, and Marc Becker, eds. *Rethinking Latin American Social Movements: Radical Action from Below.* Lanham, MD: Rowman & Littlefield, 2014. Provides a horizontalist, social movement perspective on leftist governments.

Webber, Jeffery R., and Barry Carr, eds. *The New Latin American Left: Cracks in the Empire.* Lanham, MD: Rowman & Littlefield, 2013. A collection of essays that explores Latin America's leftward turn.

FILMS

South of the Border. 2010. Director Oliver Stone visits seven presidents in five countries in South America to gain an understanding of the political and social ideas underlying Latin America's left-wing governments.

Strong Roots (Raiz forte). 2000. Documentary on the Brazilian Landless Workers Movement (MST).

Glossary

agrarian reform. Government program of redistributing land from wealthy owners with extensive holdings to those who work the land, as well as provision of credit, technical training, distribution networks, and other resources necessary to work it.

anticlericalism. Opposition to the institutional power of the Catholic Church because of its outsize influence on political and social affairs, with a desire that a secular government replace religious control over education, marriage, and other institutions.

autonomy. Control over local decisions affecting a self-governing territory while it remains part of a larger political unit or country.

bourgeoisie. Capitalist class that owns the means of production and typically embodies materialistic values or conventional attitudes to ensure the preservation of their privileged position in society.

capitalism. An economic theory that favors private ownership of the means of producing economic goods, with an emphasis on profit rather than use.

Christian Democracy. A political philosophy that combines traditional Catholic social teachings with modern democratic ideals, typically conservative on social issues and liberal on economic ones.

científicos. Porfirio Díaz's technocratic advisers trained in positivist "scientific politics" with a goal to modernize Mexico.

class consciousness. Awareness of one's place in a system of social classes, especially as it relates to a class struggle.

clientelism. Gaining political support in exchange for providing goods or services.

communism. An economic and political system that stresses that decisions related to the production of economic goods should reside in the hands of the workers.

Communist (or Third) International, also called the Comintern. An international political party with local branches in different countries; it was founded in Moscow in 1919 to lead a global revolution.

conservative. A reliance on the Catholic Church, the military, and wealthy landholders to maintain a highly stratified society.

coup. From the French term "coup d'état," or blow against the state, the illegal seizure of government through a sudden, violent military action.

death squad. Armed vigilante group that conducts extrajudicial killings or forced disappearances of people for the purposes of political repression.

democracy. Rule of the people, including the idea that people should have equal access to, and a say in, the distribution of the wealth and resources of a country. A representative democracy is where a small group of people is selected to rule on behalf of an entire society, and a participatory democracy is one in which everyone has an equal voice in making decisions.

dependency. The state of one country being controlled by another, often through economic means.

dictatorship. Absolute rule by an authoritarian leader; commonly used in a derogatory sense to delegitimize a political opponent.

ejido. A communally owned and operated farm, with community members individually working specific plots that rotate from year to year to maintain a balance of equal access to better and lesser quality land.

embargo. A ban on trade with another country. The Cuban government calls the U.S. embargo on Cuba a "blockade," which means the sealing off of a place to prevent goods or people from entering or leaving.

expropriation. The act of a government confiscating private property to use it in the public interest.

extradition. Transfer of a suspected or convicted criminal between countries to stand trial or serve a prison sentence.

fascism. An extremely authoritarian, militarist, and nationalist ideology. It relies on a strong leader, is based on a corporate organization of society, and subjugates individual liberties to the interests of the government and business interests.

feminism. Advocacy for equal rights for all. First-wave feminism in the nineteenth century fought for suffrage rights for women, a second wave that began in the 1960s campaigned for legal and social equality, and a third wave that emerged in the 1990s was a reaction against second-wave feminism that treated the interests of women from privileged classes as normative.

filibusterer. A military adventurer who engages in an unauthorized military expedition to foment a change of government in another country.

foco. A theory that emerged out of the Cuban Revolution that a small insurrectionary guerrilla army could spark a broad revolution.

gross national product (GNP). A broad measure of a country's total economic activity.

guerrilla. From the Spanish word for "small war," it refers to an irregular form of fighting against a larger, established military force.

hacienda.   A large, landed estate similar to a plantation. It was commonly owned either by a wealthy individual or the Catholic Church, and it exploited a rural labor force.

imperialism.   The domination of a larger and more powerful country over a smaller and weaker one, typically through economic, diplomatic, or military means.

indigenista.   Representation of Indigenous peoples by non-Indians, typically motivated by paternalistic notions of improving their lives.

Indigenous.   The original inhabitants of an area, often retaining a unique culture that distinguishes them from the rest of society.

junta.   A military or political group that rules a country after taking power by force.

latifundia.   A system of large, landed estates (known as latifundios—fundos—or haciendas) on which impoverished peons work for the benefit of an absentee landowner.

left.   A broad term for those who support communal concerns over individual liberties. The term comes from the 1789 French Revolution, when those favoring the monarchy sat to the president's right in the National Assembly, and supporters of the revolution sat to his left.

Leninism.   Political theory that the organization of a vanguard party is necessary for a socialist revolution, as developed by Vladimir Lenin in the context of the 1917 Bolshevik Revolution.

liberalism.   An ideology that champions individual rights, civil liberties, and private property.

liberation theology.   A Catholic approach to social problems that utilizes Marxist tools of class struggle.

Maoism.   Political theory derived from Mao Tse-tung's peasant-based communist revolution in China.

massacre.   Indiscriminate killing of a large number of people.

national guard.   A militia with police powers that often acquires the characteristics of a formal military force.

nationalization.   Placing private industries under public ownership so that the profits benefit an entire society rather than select individuals.

neoliberalism.   Economic policies of privatization, austerity, deregulation, free trade, and reduction in government spending.

nom de guerre.   A pseudonym under which a person fights.

oligarchy.   A power structure in which a small group of wealthy people command authority over the rest of society.

Pan-Americanism.   Advocacy of political or economic cooperation among people or governments on the American continents.

paramilitary.   An unofficial military force, often organized in parallel with a professional military or recognized government but technically separate to avoid legal sanction.

peasants.   Poor rural farmers, often with negative connotations of being uneducated and ignorant.

pink tide. Wave of left-wing electoral victories in the first decade of the twenty-first century.

plebiscite. A poll of public opinion on an important, frequently constitutional, issue.

popular front. A policy that the Communist International adopted in 1935 to ally with liberal and other leftist political parties in a broad coalition against conservative and fascist forces.

populism. Personalistic rule by a nationalist and charismatic leader.

proletariat. The working class, often wage earners in an industrial society.

referendum. An up or a down vote on a political question.

right. A broad term for those who support private property and individual liberties over communal concerns. The term comes from the 1789 French Revolution, when those favoring the monarchy sat to the president's right in the National Assembly, and supporters of the revolution sat to his left.

Sandinistas. Members of the Frente Sandinista de Liberación Nacional (FSLN, Sandinista National Liberation Front) that took power in 1979 after an eighteen-year guerrilla struggle.

social movement. A group of people organized around a specific issue on a civic rather than political or military basis.

socialism. An economic, social, and political doctrine that advocates for the equal distribution of wealth through the elimination of private property and the exploitative ruling class.

suffrage. The right to vote (also called the franchise) as a condition of citizenship.

syndicate. A group of people organized to promote a common interest, typically related to working conditions and wages.

terrorism. Use of violence and intimidation of a civilian population to achieve a political purpose.

Trotskyism. A radical form of socialism named after the Russian revolutionary Leon Trotsky, who argued in favor of a permanent revolution or an ongoing global revolutionary process.

Index

About the Author

Marc Becker is professor of Latin American history at Truman State University. His research focuses on constructions of race, class, and gender within popular movements in the Andes. He is the author of *The CIA in Ecuador* (2021), *The FBI in Latin America: The Ecuador Files* (2017), *Pachakutik: Indigenous Movements and Electoral Politics in Ecuador* (2011), *Indians and Leftists in the Making of Ecuador's Modern Indigenous Movements* (2008), and *Mariátegui and Latin American Marxist Theory* (1993); the coeditor (with Richard Stahler-Sholk and Harry E. Vanden) of *Rethinking Latin American Social Movements: Radical Action from Below* (2015) and (with Kim Clark) of *Highland Indians and the State in Modern Ecuador* (2007); and editor and translator (with Harry Vanden) of *José Carlos Mariátegui: An Anthology* (2011). Becker has received Fulbright, SSRC-MacArthur, NEH, and other fellowships to support his research. He is a participating editor for *Latin American Perspectives*. Becker has served on the executive committees and has been web editor of the Ecuadorian Studies and Ethnicity, Race, and Indigenous Peoples (ERIP) sections of the Latin American Studies Association (LASA); the Andean and Teaching Materials committees of the Conference on Latin American History (CLAH); the Peace History Society (PHS); and Historians for Peace and Democracy (H-PAD). See http://www.yachana.org.

LATIN AMERICAN PERSPECTIVES IN THE CLASSROOM

Series Editor: Ronald H. Chilcote

Urban Latin America
  edited by Tom Angotti
Rereading Women in Latin America and the Caribbean: The Political Economy of Gender
  edited by Jennifer Abbassi and Sheryl L. Lutjens
Contemporary Latin American Revolutions, 2nd edition
  by Marc Becker
Development in Theory and Practice: Latin American Perspectives
  edited by Ronald H. Chilcote
Latin American Extractivism: Dependency, Resource Nationalism and Resistance in Broad Perspective
  edited by Steve Ellner
Latin America's Pink Tide: Breakthroughs and Shortcomings
  edited by Steve Ellner
Latin America's Radical Left: Challenges and Complexities of Political Power in the Twenty-First Century
  edited by Steve Ellner
Venezuela: Hugo Chávez and the Decline of an "Exceptional Democracy"
  edited by Steve Ellner and Miguel Tinker Salas
Contemporary Latin American Social and Political Thought: An Anthology
  edited by Iván Márquez
Mayan Lives, Mayan Utopias: The Indigenous Peoples of Chiapas and the Zapatista Rebellion
  edited by Jan Rus, Rosalva Aída Hernández, and Shannan L. Mattiace
The United States and Cuba: From Closest Enemies to Distant Friends
  by Francisco López Segrera
Rethinking Latin American Social Movements: Radical Action from Below
  edited by Richard Stahler-Sholk, Harry E. Vanden, and Marc Becker
Memory, Truth, and Justice in Contemporary Latin America
  edited by Roberta Villalón
Latin American Social Movements in the Twenty-First Century: Resistance, Power, and Democracy
  edited by Richard Stahler-Sholk, Harry E. Vanden, and Glen David Kuecker
Transnational Latina/o Communities: Politics, Processes, and Cultures
  edited by Carlos G. Vélez-Ibáñez and Anna Sampaio, with Manolo González-Estay